105
Retirement Planning Textbook

Financial Education — KAPLAN UNIVERSITY — SCHOOL OF PROFESSIONAL AND CONTINUING EDUCATION

At press time, this edition contains the most complete and accurate information currently available. Due to the nature of advanced designation examinations, however, information may have been added recently to the actual test that does not appear in this edition. Please contact the publisher to verify that you have the most current edition.

This publication is designed to provide accurate and authoritative information in regard to the subject matter covered. It is sold with the understanding that the publisher is not engaged in rendering legal, accounting, or other professional services. If legal advice or other expert assistance is required, the services of a competent professional should be sought.

We value your input and suggestions. If you found imperfections in this product, please let us know by reporting it to Updates/Errata at www.schweser.com.

105 RETIREMENT PLANNING TEXTBOOK 2015
©2014 Kaplan, Inc. All rights reserved.

Published by Kaplan Financial Education

Printed in the United States of America.

ISBN: 978-1-4754-2941-1 / 1-4754-2941-X
PPN: 3200-5807

14   15   16   10   09   08   07   06   05   04   03   02   01

Contents

Introduction

INTRODUCTION

In this course, you will consider the following broad concepts:

- Retirement needs analysis

- Types of retirement plans

- Qualified plan tax requirements

- Distributions from retirement plans and IRAs

- Traditional and Roth IRAs

- Tax-advantaged plans and nonqualified plans

- Social Security

- Retirement plan selection for individuals and business

LEARNING OBJECTIVES

Throughout this course you will see many learning objectives (LOs) that emphasize the knowledge and application skills you will gain from this course. These specific statements, based on CFP Board's Principal Topics List, advise you on what you should know and be able to do at the completion of this course.

On the following pages is a list of the CFP® Certification Principal Topics, nine of which are covered in this course. These nine topics are highlighted in the topic list. You will also find a list of the CFP® Certification Job Task Domains. Each question on the CFP® Certification Examination will be associated with one of these domains.

CERTIFIED FINANCIAL PLANNER
BOARD OF STANDARDS, INC.

CFP® Certification Examination
Principal Topics

The following Principal Topics are based on the results of CFP Board's 2009 Job Analysis Study and serve as a curricular framework.

General Principles of Financial Planning

- Financial planning process
- Financial statements
- Cash flow management
- Financing strategies
- Function, purpose, and regulation of financial institutions
- Education planning
- Financial planning for special circumstances
- Economic concepts
- Time value of money concepts and calculations
- Financial services regulations and requirements
- Business law
- Consumer protection laws

Insurance Planning

- Principles of risk and insurance
- Analysis and evaluation of risk exposures
- Health insurance and health care cost management (individual)
- Disability income insurance (individual)
- Long-term care insurance (individual)
- Annuities
- Life insurance (individual)
- Income taxation of life insurance
- Business uses of insurance
- Insurance needs analysis
- Insurance policy and company selection

Investment Planning

- Characteristics, uses and taxation of investment vehicles
- Types of investment risk
- Quantitative investment concepts
- Measures of investment returns
- Asset allocation and portfolio diversification
- Bond and stock valuation concepts
- Portfolio development and analysis
- Investment strategies

Income Tax Planning

- Income tax law fundamentals
- Tax compliance
- Income tax fundamentals and calculations
- Characteristics and income taxation of business entities
- Income taxation of trusts and estates
- Basis
- Tax consequences of the disposition of property
- Alternative minimum tax (AMT)
- Tax reduction/management techniques
- Passive activity and at-risk rules
- Tax implications of special circumstances
- Charitable contributions and deductions

2

Retirement Planning
- Retirement needs analysis
- Social Security (Old Age, Survivor, and Disability Insurance, OASDI)
- Types of retirement plans
- Qualified plan rules and options
- Other tax-advantaged retirement plans
- Regulatory considerations
- Key factors affecting plan selection for businesses
- Investment considerations for retirement plans
- Distribution rules, alternatives, and taxation

Estate Planning
- Characteristics and consequences of property titling
- Methods of property transfer at death
- Estate planning documents
- Gifting strategies
- Gift tax compliance and tax calculation
- Incapacity planning
- Estate tax compliance and tax calculation
- Sources for estate liquidity
- Powers of appointment
- Types, features, and taxation of trusts
- Qualified interest trusts
- Charitable transfers
- Use of life insurance in estate planning
- Marital deduction
- Intra-family and other business transfer techniques
- Deferral and minimization of estate taxes
- Generation-skipping transfer tax (GSTT)
- Fiduciaries
- Income in respect of a decedent (IRD)
- Postmortem estate planning techniques
- Estate planning for non-traditional relationships

Interpersonal Communication
- Client and planner attitudes, values, biases and behavioral characteristics and the impact on financial planning
- Principles of communication and counseling

Professional Conduct and Fiduciary Responsibility
- CFP Board's *Code of Ethics and Professional Responsibility* and *Rules of Conduct*
- CFP Board's *Financial Planning Practice Standards*
- CFP Board's *Disciplinary Rules and Procedures*

CERTIFIED FINANCIAL PLANNER
BOARD OF STANDARDS, INC.

CFP® Certification Examination
Job Task Domains

The following Job Task Domains are based on the results of CFP Board's 2009 Job Analysis Study and will serve as the blueprint for the March 2012 and later administrations of the CFP® Certification Examination. Each exam question will be linked to one of the following domains, in the approximate percentages indicated following the general headings.

Targeted First Test Administration: March 2012

8 Major Domains:

1. Establishing and Defining the Client-Planner Relationship (8%)

2. Gathering Information Necessary to Fulfill the Engagement (9%)

3. Analyzing and Evaluating the Client's Current Financial Status (25%)

4. Developing the Recommendation(s) (25%)

5. Communicating the Recommendation(s) (9%)

6. Implementing the Recommendation(s) (9%)

7. Monitoring the Recommendation(s) (5%)

8. Practicing within Professional and Regulatory Standards (10%)

 CERTIFIED FINANCIAL PLANNER™ | **CFP®**

2

Domain 1 - Establishing and Defining the Client-Planner Relationship (8%)

    A. Identify the client (e.g., individual, family, business, organization)
    B. Discuss financial planning needs and expectations of the client
    C. Discuss the financial planning process with the client
    D. Explain scope of services offered by the CFP® professional and his/her firm
    E. Assess and communicate the CFP® professional's ability to meet the client's needs and expectations
    F. Identify and resolve apparent and potential conflicts of interest in client relationships
    G. Discuss the client's responsibilities and those of the CFP® professional
    H. Define and document the scope of the engagement with the client
    I. Provide client disclosures
        1. Regulatory disclosure
        2. Compensation arrangements and associated potential conflicts of interest

Domain 2 - Gathering Information Necessary to Fulfill the Engagement (9%)
    A. Identify the client's values and attitudes
        1. Explore with the client their personal and financial needs, priorities and goals
        2. Explore the client's time horizon for each goal
        3. Assess the client's level of knowledge and experience with financial matters
        4. Assess the client's risk exposures (e.g., longevity, economic, liability, healthcare)
        5. Assess the client's risk tolerances (e.g., investment, economic, liability, healthcare)
    B. Gather Data
        1. Summary of assets (e.g., cost basis information, beneficiary designations and titling)
        2. Summary of liabilities (e.g., balances, terms, interest rates). Summary of abilities (e.g., balances, terms, interest rates)
        3. Summary of income and expenses
        4. Estate planning documents
        5. Education plan and resources
        6. Retirement plan information
        7. Employee benefits
        8. Government benefits (e.g., Social Security, Medicare)
        9. Special circumstances (e.g., legal documents and agreements, family situations)
        10. Tax documents
        11. Investment statements
        12. Insurance policies and documents (e.g., life, health, disability, liability)
        13. Closely held business documents (e.g., shareholder agreements)
        14. Inheritances, windfalls, and other large lump sums
    C. Recognize need for additional information

Domain 3 - Analyzing and Evaluating the Client's Current Financial Status (25%)
    A. Evaluate and document the strengths and vulnerabilities of the client's current financial situation
        1. Financial status
             A. Statement of financial position/balance sheet
             B. Cash flow statement

3

          C. Budget

          D. Capital needs analysis (e.g., insurance, retirement, major purchases)

    2. Risk management and insurance evaluation

          A. Insurance coverage

          B. Retained risks

          C. Asset protection (e.g., titling, trusts, business form)

          D. Client liquidity (e.g., emergency fund)

    3. Benefits evaluation

          A. Government benefits (e.g., Social Security, Medicare)

          B. Employee benefits

    4. Investment evaluation

          A. Asset allocation

          B. Investment strategies

          C. Investment types

    5. Tax evaluation

          A. Current, deferred and future tax liabilities

          B. Income types

          C. Special situations (e.g., stock options, international tax issues)

    6. Retirement evaluation

          A. Retirement plans and strategies (e.g., pension options, annuitization)

          B. Accumulation planning

          C. Distribution planning

    7. Estate planning evaluation

          A. Estate documents

          B. Estate tax liabilities

          C. Ownership of assets

          D. Beneficiary designations

          E. Gifting strategies

    8. Business ownership

          A. Business form

          B. Employer benefits

          C. Succession planning and exit strategy

          D. Risk management

    9. Education planning evaluation

          A. Sources of financing

          B. Tax considerations

    10. Other considerations

          A. Special circumstances (e.g., divorce, disabilities, family dynamics)

          B. Inheritances, windfalls, and other large lump sums

          C. Charitable planning

          D. Eldercare (e.g., CCRCs, LTC, Nursing Home)

B. Identify and use appropriate tools and techniques to conduct analyses (e.g., financial calculators, financial planning software, simulators, research services)

4

Domain 4 - Developing the Recommendation(s) (25%)
- A. Synthesize findings from analysis of client's financial status
- B. Consider alternatives to meet the client's goals and objectives
    1. Conduct scenario analysis (e.g., changing lifestyle variables)
    2. Conduct sensitivity analysis (e.g., changing assumptions such as inflation rate, rates of return, time horizon)
- C. Consult with other professionals on technical issues outside of planner's expertise
- D. Develop recommendations
    1. Considering client attitudes, values and beliefs
    2. Considering behavioral finance issues (e.g., anchoring, overconfidence, recency)
    3. Consider interrelationships among financial planning recommendations
- E. Document recommendations

Domain 5 - Communicating the Recommendation(s) (9%)
- A. Present financial plan to the client and provide education
    1. Client goals review
    2. Assumptions
    3. Observations and findings
    4. Alternatives
    5. Recommendations
- B. Obtain feedback from the client and revise the recommendations as appropriate
- C. Provide documentation of plan recommendations and any applicable product disclosures to client
- D. Verify client acceptance of recommendations

Domain 6 - Implementing the Recommendation(s) (9%)
- A. Create a prioritized implementation plan with timeline
- B. Assign responsibilities (e.g., CFP® professional, client, other professional(s))
- C. Support the client directly or indirectly with implementation of the recommendation(s)
- D. Coordinate and share information, as authorized, with others
- E. Define monitoring responsibilities with the client (e.g., explain what will be monitored, frequency of monitoring, communication method(s)

Domain 7 - Monitoring the Recommendation(s) (5%)
- A. Discuss and evaluate changes in the client's personal circumstances (e.g., aging issues, change in employment)
- B. Review the performance and progress of the plan with the client
- C. Review and evaluate changes in the legal, tax and economic environments
- D. Make recommendations to accommodate changed circumstances
- E. Review scope of work and redefine engagement as appropriate
- F. Provide client ongoing support (e.g., counseling, education)

5

Domain 8 - Practicing within Professional and Regulatory Standards (10%)
    A. Adhere to CFP Board's *Code of Ethics and Professional Responsibility* and *Rules of Conduct*
    B. Understand CFP Board's *Disciplinary Rules and Procedures*
    C. Work within CFP Board's *Financial Planning Practice Standards*
    D. Manage practice risk (e.g., documentation, monitor client noncompliance with recommendation(s)
    E. Maintain awareness of and comply with regulatory and legal guidelines

CFP® Certification Examination Principal Topics

Retirement Planning

CFP Board Topic	Unit		Kaplan Schweser Learning Objective
44. Retirement Needs Analysis			
A. Assumptions for retirement planning	Unit 10	44.1	Perform a retirement needs analysis taking into account various assumptions such as inflation rate, retirement period, life expectancy, income sources, and other variables.
	Unit 10	44.2	Determine financial needs during the retirement period and calculate future values.
	Unit 10	44.5	Discuss the various assumptions such as inflation rate, retirement period, life expectancy, income sources, and other variables used in retirement needs analysis.
B. Income sources	Unit 7	44.3	Describe the choice of beneficiary considerations as they relate to a qualified plan or IRA.
C. Financial needs	Unit 10	44.1	Perform a retirement needs analysis taking into account various assumptions such as inflation rate, retirement period, life expectancy, income sources, and other variables.
	Unit 10	44.6	Determine financial needs during the retirement period and calculate future value of the projected first-year retirement income need.
	Unit 10	44.9	Determine financial needs during the retirement period and calculate future values when utilizing current retirement assets.
D. Straight-line returns vs. probability analysis	Unit 10	44.2	Determine financial needs during the retirement period and calculate future values.
E. Pure annuity vs. capital preservation	Unit 10	44.2	Determine financial needs during the retirement period and calculate future values.
	Unit 10	44.7	Determine whether to use a serial or a level payment approach to fund a future retirement need.
F. Alternatives to compensate for projected cash-flow shortfalls	Unit 10	44.2	Determine financial needs during the retirement period and calculate future values.
	Unit 10	44.8	Review alternatives when client is unable to meet the retirement savings goal.
G. Work-retirement transitions	Unit 10	44.4	Explain various patterns of work-to-retirement transitions and phased retirement.

45. Social Security (Old Age, Survivor, and Disability Insurance—OASDI)

CFP Board Topic	Unit		Kaplan Schweser Learning Objective
A. Paying into the system	Unit 8	45.1	Explain how the Social Security program is funded.
B. Eligibility and benefit	Unit 8	45.2	Analyze a given situation to determine eligibility of an individual for Social Security benefits and identify types and amounts of benefits that are available under the system.
	Unit 8	45.6	List who is covered and who is excluded from the Old Age, Survivors, and Disability Insurance Program.

Qualified Plan Requirements and Regulatory Plan Considerations

REFER TO

CFP® Certification Principal Topics – Retirement Planning, Types of Retirement Plans

CFP® Certification Principal Topics – Retirement Planning, Qualified Plan Rules and Options

CFP® Certification Principal Topics – Retirement Planning, Regulatory Considerations

Supplemental Readings Section of this 105 Retirement Planning Student Guide

(For specific assignments, refer to class syllabus.)

INTRODUCTION

Qualified plan requirements and regulatory plan considerations are two of the most complicated topics covered throughout this course. Nevertheless, to provide effective client advice, a financial planner should understand how employer-sponsored retirement plans are structured, the benefits they can provide for clients, and the rules governing their tax qualification. Complying with the Tax Code rules regarding plan qualification is critical because, if met, the rules allow the sponsoring employer of a retirement plan to take an immediate deduction for plan contributions made on behalf of an employee.

Sometimes, qualified retirement plans are referred to as Section 401(a) plans after the Internal Revenue Code section of the same number and subsection. There are some 31 technical requirements specified in IRC Section 401(a) with which a retirement plan must comply to be tax qualified. However, because this topic is so highly complex, we will discuss in this unit only a summary of the more important requirements with which a financial planner should be familiar.

LEARNING OBJECTIVES

After completing this unit, you should be able to achieve the following learning objectives:

CFP® Certification Principal Topics – Retirement Planning, Types of Retirement Plans

LO 46.1   Describe major differences between qualified and nonqualified retirement plans.

CFP® Certification Principal Topics – Retirement Planning, Qualified Plan Rules and Options

LO 47.1   Describe the eligibility, coverage, and testing requirements of qualified plans.

LO 47.2   Explain the permitted disparity rules and how retirement plans can be integrated with Social Security.

LO 47.3   Describe the limitations on contributions and benefits in qualified plans.

LO 47.5   Explain the top-heavy requirements and the effects on contributions or benefits.

CFP® Certification Principal Topics – Retirement Planning, Regulatory Considerations

LO 49.1   Explain the key provisions of the Employee Retirement Income Security Act (ERISA).

LO 49.2   Describe how the U.S. Department of Labor (DOL) and the Pension Benefit Guaranty Corporation (PBGC) are involved in retirement plan regulation.

LO 49.3   Describe the fiduciary considerations for qualified plan fiduciaries.

LO 49.4   Explain the prohibited transaction rules.

LO 49.5   Describe the reporting and disclosure requirements for qualified plans.

█ KEY TERMS

1% owner

5% owner

21-and-1 rule

50/40 test

Active participation

Advance determination letter

Annual additions limit

Annual report (Form 5500 series)

Average benefits percentage test

Contributory plan

Controlled group rules

Catch-up contribution

Covered

Covered compensation

Department of Labor (DOL)

Defined benefit plans

Defined contribution plans

Elective deferral limit

Eligibility

Employee Retirement Income Security Act (ERISA)

Excess method

Fiduciary

Highly compensated employee

Individual accrued benefit statement

Integrated plan

Internal Revenue Service (IRS)

Noncontributory plan

Nonqualified plans

Offset method

Party in interest

Pension Benefit Guaranty Corporation (PBGC)

Percentage test

Greater than 5% owner

Permitted disparity rules

Prohibited transaction exemptions (PTEs)

Prohibited transaction rules

Qualified plans

Ratio test

Summary annual report (SAR)

Summary of material modification (SMM)

Summary plan description (SPD)

Top heavy

Vesting

A. REGULATORY PLAN CONSIDERATIONS

LO 49.1   Explain the key provisions of the Employee Retirement Income Security Act (ERISA).

LO 49.2   Describe how the U.S. Department of Labor (DOL) and the Pension Benefit Guaranty Corporation (PBGC) are involved in retirement plan regulation.

Internal Revenue Service

The **Internal Revenue Service (IRS)** carries out the administrative duties of the qualified plan system (and, to a lesser extent, the nonqualified plan system) by:

- supervising the creation of new retirement plans and monitoring and auditing the operation of existing plans;

- interpreting federal legislation, especially with regard to the tax consequences of certain pension plan designs; and

- administering the qualified plan system.

Employee Retirement Income Security Act

The **Employee Retirement Income Security Act** of 1974 **(ERISA)** is a federal law that governs the non-tax aspects of retirement plans and other employee benefits. It is intended to protect the retirement interests of plan participants. ERISA established equitable standards and curtailed potential plan abuse.

Qualified plans must meet ERISA requirements, including the following:

- Coverage

- Participation

- Vesting

- Reporting and disclosure

- Fiduciary requirements

ERISA requires plan sponsors to report and disclose plan information to the Internal Revenue Service, Department of Labor (DOL), Pension Benefit Guaranty Corporation (PBGC), and plan participants. There is some overlap between ERISA and the Internal Revenue Code in the areas of plan participation, vesting, and prohibited transactions.

Department of Labor Regulatory Responsibilities

The **Department of Labor (DOL)** is involved in retirement plans through its Office of Pension and Welfare Benefit Plans. The DOL ensures compliance with ERISA's plan reporting and disclosure rules and oversees compliance with the prohibited transaction rules. As part of this function, it issues **prohibited transaction exemptions (PTEs)**. Prohibited transaction exemptions to the prohibited transaction rules may be limited or unlimited within the parameters of the requested exemption (e.g., for a single transaction or for all transactions within that requested exemption).

The DOL regulates the actions of plan fiduciaries, which include individuals or firms that exercise discretionary authority over plan assets or that provide investment advice for a fee.

Pension Benefit Guaranty Corporation

The **Pension Benefit Guaranty Corporation (PBGC)** was created under ERISA and is responsible for insuring plan participants against loss of benefits from plan termination. Benefit payments by the PBGC are financed by premiums paid by the sponsors of defined benefit plans.

It insures only defined benefit plans, not defined contribution plans. Professional service employers with 25 or fewer active participants are exempt from PBGC insurance requirements.

The PBGC can terminate a defined benefit plan if:

■ minimum funding standards are not met;

■ benefits cannot be paid when due; and

■ the long-run liability of the company to the PBGC is expected to increase unreasonably.

B. QUALIFIED VERSUS NONQUALIFIED PLANS

LO 46.1   Describe major differences between qualified and nonqualified retirement plans.

Retirement Plans

Qualified plans[A]			Nonqualified plans
Defined benefits (DB) plans[D]	Defined contribution (DC) plans	Other tax-advantaged plans	
DB pension plans[B]	DC pension plans[B]	◼ SEP plan	◼ Section 457 plan
◼ Traditional DB pension plan	◼ Money purchase pension plan	◼ SARSEP plan	◼ Deferred compensation plan
◼ Cash balance pension plan	◼ Target benefit pension plan[D]	◼ Traditional IRA	
		◼ Roth IRA	
DB(k) (hybrid plan combining defined benefit pension benefits with Section 401(k) provisions for elective deferrals)		◼ SIMPLE IRA	
		◼ Section 403(b) plan	
	DC profit-sharing plans (PS)[C]		
	◼ Traditional profit-sharing plan		
	◼ Stock bonus plans		
	◼ ESOP (employee stock ownership plan)		
	◼ Section 401(k) plan[E]		
	◼ Thrift plan		
	◼ SIMPLE 401(k) plan		
	◼ Age-based profit-sharing plan[D]		
	◼ New comparability plan[D]		

[A] Distributions from qualified plans may qualify for 10-year forward averaging and other tax advantages; other tax-advantaged plans and nonqualified plans do not qualify

[B] Pension plans promise either benefits or contributions; therefore, annual funding is mandatory

[C] Profit-sharing plans do not require mandatory annual funding

[D] These plans are tested for discrimination on the basis of benefits as opposed to contributions

[E] These plans are tested for discrimination regarding employee elective deferrals and employer-matching contributions

At first look, trying to understand each of the many types of retirement plans available can be quite overwhelming. Studying the various plans reveals there are many repetitive rules and plan similarities. It is sometimes helpful to start with the very big picture in mind. For example, in the summary chart, notice that there are three general categories: qualified plans, tax-advantaged plans, and nonqualified plans. Remembering the category under which a plan operates is a good start. Also notice under the qualified plans category that a qualified plan is either classified as a defined benefit (DB) plan or a defined contribution (DC) plan. Defined benefit plans and defined contribution plans are further classified as either a pension plan or a profit-sharing plan. Defined benefit plans are pension plans whereas a defined contribution plan may either be a pension plan or a profit-sharing plan (most DC plans are profit-sharing plans). A basic understanding of these broad categories is helpful because once the proper classifications are determined, the basic rules and limitations applicable to the classification are repetitive across the various types of plans within the category.

Qualified plans are retirement plans that meet a number of requirements as specified in Internal Revenue Code (IRC) Section 401(a) (and immediately subsequent sections) and ERISA. As such, two government agencies are involved in the regulation of qualified plans: the Internal Revenue Service (interested in the tax aspects of such a plan) and the Department of Labor (interested in the labor law/employee relations aspects). In return for meeting these requirements, the employer-sponsor of the plan is afforded a major tax advantage, namely, the immediate deductibility of all contributions made to the plan. In addition, the employee does not pay income tax on plan contributions or the earnings from the plan contributions as long as a plan distribution does not occur.

A tax-advantaged plan does not meet all of the requirements to be classified as a qualified plan but often operates very similarly to a qualified plan with tax-deferred earnings and perhaps pretax (or tax-deductible) contributions.

Nonqualified plans are benefit arrangements that do not meet the IRC Section 401 requirements for qualified plans. They are used to provide benefits to key employees beyond the qualified plan IRC Section 415 limits. These plans typically are referred to as nonqualified plans or nonqualified deferred compensation (NQDC) plans.

One of the advantages of nonqualified plans is that they do not have to meet the nondiscrimination requirements of qualified plans. Also, the benefits and contributions can exceed IRC Section 415 limits. Nonqualified plans are not subject to the same ERISA requirements as qualified plans. Generally, they are merely a promise by the employer to pay the employee benefits. Benefits must be subject to a substantial risk of forfeiture (i.e., subject to the claims of general creditors); otherwise, there will be constructive receipt and taxable income to the participant. Benefits are not deductible by the employer until paid and are includable in the employee's taxable income at the time of receipt.

A summary of the major differences between qualified and nonqualified retirement plans follows.

Attribute/Characteristic	Qualified Plans	Nonqualified Plans
Discrimination in favor of select employees	No	Yes
Subject to ERISA requirements	Yes	No (either in total or in part)
Tax benefits	Immediate employer deduction and employee deferral of tax on earnings	Postponed employer deduction and possible employee deferral of tax
Funding	By due date of return (includes extensions)	Not required/informal funding possible
Distributions	Taxed as ordinary income; some tax reduction options available	Taxed as ordinary income; may be taxed before actual receipt of funds

C. QUALIFIED PLAN REQUIREMENTS

LO 47.1   Describe the eligibility, coverage, and testing requirements of qualified plans.

LO 47.2   Explain the permitted disparity rules and how retirement plans can be integrated with Social Security.

LO 47.3   Describe the limitations on contributions and benefits in qualified plans.

LO 47.5   Explain the top-heavy requirements and the effects on contributions or benefits.

ERISA and IRC requirements that apply to qualified plans are numerous and complex. As they relate to the CFP® Certification Examination, the following will be covered in respective order:

1.   Eligibility

2.   Coverage, including the nondiscrimination tests and controlled group rules

3.   Limitations on contributions and benefits

4.   Vesting requirements

5.   Top-heavy plans

6.   Integration with Social Security (also known as the permitted disparity rules)

Eligibility for the Plan

Under a qualified plan, any employee who has attained the age of 21 and one year of service must be permitted to enter the plan within six months. For **eligibility** purposes, a year of service means a 12-month period during which the employee has worked at least 1,000 hours. As an alternative to this **21-and-1 rule**, the waiting period to enter the plan may be increased to two years of service. However, if adopting this rule, the employer-sponsor cannot use the normal vesting schedules for employer contributions and, instead, must immediately vest all employer contributions for employees (100% vesting). Also note that the popular Section 401(k) retirement plan cannot use the two-year waiting period alternative.

Once an employee has met the eligibility requirements, entrance to the plan is on the next available entrance date. However, under ERISA, a plan cannot require an employee to wait more than six months to enter into the plan after becoming eligible. Because of this rule, most qualified plans will adopt two entrance dates, usually January 1 and July 1.

Finally, plan eligibility is important because that is when the employer begins to make plan contributions on behalf of the participant. This should be distinguished from plan vesting percentages that accrue from the date of the employee-participant's hiring and not the plan eligibility date.

PRACTICE
QUESTION   *Choose the best answer for the question below.*

1. If a qualified plan has been designed using normal eligibility requirements, which combination of the following would require an employee to be eligible to participate in the plan?

    1. 18 years of age

    2. 21 years of age

    3. Completion of 1 year of service; at least 1,000 hours worked per year

    4. Completion of 3 years of service; average 600 hours per year

    A. 1 and 3
    B. 1 and 4
    C. 2 and 3
    D. 2 and 4

    Answer: C.   The participation requirements for a plan using normal eligibility requirements (non-2-year eligibility standards) are attainment of age 21 by the employee and completion of 1 year of service of at least 1,000 hours annually (the 21-and-1 rule).

Highly Compensated Employee

A **highly compensated employee (HCE)** is an employee who meets one of the following criteria:

- Was a **greater than 5% owner** of the employer at any time during the current year or preceding year

- For the preceding year, had compensation greater than $120,000 (2015) from the employer

If the employer makes an election, only persons in the top 20% of compensation and earning greater than $120,000 in the prior year (2015) are included as highly compensated. This exception is often for large employers and helps the plan pass the coverage or actual deferral percentage (ADP) test for Section 401(k) plans (see next section). Note that the 20% election only removes a participant from the HCE group if the participant qualifies as HCE based on compensation only. The election will not remove a participant from HCE if the participant qualifies as HCE based on being a greater than 5% owner (regardless of compensation).

Nonhighly compensated employees (non-HCE) are those employees who do not fit the criteria stated previously.

In IRS publications, the terms 5% owner and 1% owner are used interchangeably with the terms greater than 5% owner and greater than 1% owner. This is because in the Tax Code, 5% owner and 1% owner are titles, not specific percentages of ownership. An HCE is defined in the Tax Code as an employee who is a 5% owner at any time during the current or preceding year as defined in Section 416(i)(1). Percentage owners are specifically defined in Section 416(i)(1) as:

- **5% owners**—an individual who owns more than a 5% interest in the company; and

- **1% owners**—an individual who owns more than a 1% interest in the company.

For IRS purposes, if an individual owns 2% of the company, the taxpayer is considered a 1% owner and if an individual owns 7% or 90% of a company, the taxpayer is considered a 5% owner. The 1% owners are discussed further in the section of this unit on key employees.

Coverage Under the Plan

As a general rule, the employer-sponsor of the qualified plan must cover at least 70% of the nonhighly compensated employees. This is referred to as the **percentage test**. For purposes of the coverage tests, **covered** means an employee is benefiting under the plan. For the popular 401(k) retirement plan, an employee is considered covered as long as he is eligible to defer part of his compensation; he does not have to actually make contributions. Note that **active participation** for purposes of determining deductibility of IRA contributions differs from being covered under a qualified plan. Specifically, an employee must be contributing to the plan, having employer contributions or forfeitures allocated on his behalf, or accruing a benefit in a defined benefit plan before he is considered an active participant in a qualified plan for IRA purposes.

Plans that do not meet the percentage test must satisfy either:

- the **ratio test**; or

- the **average benefits percentage test**.

Under the ratio test, the percentage of nonhighly compensated employees (non-HCEs) covered by the plan must be at least 70% of the percentage of highly compensated employees (HCEs) who are covered. In formula terms, this may be written as:

$$\text{Ratio test} = \frac{\% \text{ of non-HCEs covered}}{\% \text{ of HCEs covered}} \geq 70\%$$

Under the average benefits percentage test, the average benefits percentage accrued for non-HCEs as a group must be $\geq 70\%$ of the average benefits percentage accrued for the HCEs. In formula terms, this may be written as:

$$\text{Average benefits percentage test} = \frac{\text{average benefits \% non-HCEs}}{\text{average benefits \% HCEs}} \geq 70\%$$

E X A M P L E   An employer employs 200 eligible employees of whom 10 are HCEs. Nine of the 10 HCEs and 120 of the 190 non-HCEs benefit from the plan. The average benefit for the HCEs is 8%, and the average benefit for the non-HCEs is 6%. Therefore, the results of the coverage tests are as follows:

1. Percentage test:

$$\frac{120 \text{ non-HCEs}}{190 \text{ non-HCEs}} = 63\% \text{ of all non-HCEs covered}$$

2. Ratio test:

$$\frac{(120 \div 190) \text{ non-HCEs}}{(9 \div 10) \text{ HCEs}} = \frac{.6316}{.90} = .7018 \text{ (or 70.18\%)}$$

3. Average benefits percentage test:

$$\frac{6\%}{8\%} = 75\%$$

Although this plan fails the percentage test, it passes both the ratio and the average benefits percentage test. However, two consequences are notable here.

- Seventy-one employees are excluded from coverage. Even though they are eligible under the participation test (21-and-1 or 2-year eligibility test), they may belong to an excluded class as determined by the employer. Employers are permitted to design qualified plans that exclude certain classes of employees from coverage, as long as the plan meets one of the coverage tests. For example, an employer may exclude salaried employees, commissioned employees, hourly employees, etc. However, employees may not exclude classes of employees based on age and service because there are already rules (eligibility rules) related to age and service.

- In the example, the average benefit percentages for both non-HCEs and HCEs were given as a stipulated fact. In reality, these percentages are not easy to determine and often require an actuary or professional plan administrator. Therefore, if the percentage test is not satisfied, most employer-sponsors use the ratio test to determine plan compliance under the coverage rules.

A qualified plan may discriminate against HCEs without risking plan disqualification, but it may not discriminate in favor of HCEs. If the employer wishes to discriminate in favor of an HCE (typically an executive or officer of the corporation), it may implement a nonqualified plan.

PRACTICE
QUESTIONS   *Choose the best answer for each of the questions below.*

1. Which of the following employees are HCEs of XYZ Corporation for the year 2015? Assume the top 20% election was made by XYZ Corporation.
   1. Bill, who owns 10% of XYZ and is an employee
   2. Mary, the president of XYZ, whose compensation was $130,000 last year and is in the top 20% of all paid employees
   3. Ralph, an employee salesman, who earned $135,000 last year and was the top paid employee at XYZ this year
   4. Joe, who earned $115,000 last year as XYZ legal counsel and is not in the top 20% of all paid employees

   A. 1 and 2
   B. 1, 2, and 3
   C. 2 and 3
   D. 2, 3, and 4

   Answer: B.   Joe is not an HCE because he did not earn more than $120,000 in the previous year, is not in the top 20% of all paid employees, and does not have any ownership of the corporation.

2. ABC Co. employs 200 eligible employees, 20 of whom are HCEs. Sixteen of the 20 HCEs and 125 of the 180 non-HCEs benefit from the ABC qualified pension plan. The average benefits accrued for the HCEs are 8%. The average benefits accrued for the non-HCEs are 3%. Which one of the following statements is CORRECT with respect to the coverage tests applied to the ABC plan?
   A. The plan meets the ratio test and the average benefits percentage test.
   B. While the plan does not meet the ratio test, it meets the average benefits percentage test.
   C. The plan does not meet the average benefits percentage test, but it meets the ratio test.
   D. The plan does not meet the ratio test or the average benefits percentage test.

   Answer: C.   The ratio test is satisfied because the plan covers 86.8% of the non-HCEs in proportion to the HCEs that are covered:

   $$\text{Ratio test} = \frac{125 \div 180 \text{ non-HCEs}}{16 \div 20 \text{ HCEs}}$$
   $$= \frac{.6944}{.80}$$
   $$= .8681 \text{ (or 86.8\%)}$$

   The average benefits percentage test is not met because that percentage is only 37.5% (3% divided by 8%).

50/40 Test

In addition to meeting one of the three coverage tests identified previously (percentage, ratio, or average benefits percentage test), defined benefit pension plans must meet the **50/40 test**. Specifically, it mandates that all defined benefit pension plans must benefit no fewer than the lesser of:

■ 50 employees; or

■ 40% of all eligible employees.

If the employer has five or fewer employees and maintains a defined benefit pension plan, at least two employees must be covered by the plan.

Controlled Group Rules

Controlled group rules are designed to prevent discrimination against nonhighly compensated employees. Employers that have a significant degree of common ownership are treated as a single employer for purposes of meeting the participation and coverage rules. Types of controlled groups include businesses that are related as either brother-sister or parent-subsidiary corporations (as separately defined in the Tax Code). Other types of related employers are those that employ individuals through any form of affiliated service organization or lease employees from a leasing organization for an inordinately long period of time.

PRACTICE QUESTION

Choose the best answer for the question below.

1. Which one of the following statements correctly describes the purpose of the controlled group rules?
   A. They are intended to prevent discrimination against nonhighly compensated employees through the use of separate entities.
   B. They are intended to prevent discrimination against highly compensated employees through the use of separate entities.
   C. They are intended to promote the use of separate entities.
   D. They are intended to afford an employer/qualified plan sponsor flexibility in plan design.

   Answer: A.   The purpose of the controlled group rules is to prevent discrimination against nonhighly compensated employees through the use of separate entities.

Limitation on Contributions and Benefits

To prevent a qualified plan from being used primarily as a tax shelter for highly compensated employees and executives, the Tax Code imposes a limitation on plan benefits and contributions. For purposes of determining these benefits, employee compensation is capped at a specified amount. For 2015, this cap on **covered compensation** is $265,000 annually. Thus, only the first $265,000 of any participant's compensation may be used to determine contributions for a qualified plan.

The IRC imposes limits on both defined benefit pension plans and defined contribution pension plans and profit-sharing plans, but does so in different methods. The IRC limitation for defined benefit pension plans is applied to the actual benefit the participant will receive at retirement, while the limitation for defined contribution plans is applied to the amount of annual contributions that may be made to the by the employer and participant, which is referred to as the annual additions limit.

With respect to **defined benefit pension plans**, the benefit paid at normal retirement age, as specified in the plan documents (usually age 65 or the Social Security normal retirement age), cannot exceed the lesser of:

- 100% of the participant's compensation averaged over the three highest consecutive years of compensation, with covered compensation considered in the average being limited to $265,000 (2015); or

- $210,000 annually (2015).

Regarding **defined contribution plans**, the **annual additions limit** for a plan sponsored by any one employer (including a related employer) cannot exceed the lesser of:

- 100% of the participant's annual compensation; or

- $53,000 annually (2015).

For this purpose, annual additions include:

- employer contributions;

- employee contributions (both pretax and after-tax contributions); and

- forfeitures allocated to the defined contribution plan on behalf of the employee.

Forfeitures are non-vested amounts returned to the plan when a participant separates from service without being 100% vested.

Note, however, that the annual additions limit does not include catch-up contributions for participant-employees age 50 or older. Also, a taxpayer who has two separate sources of income (for example, works for two unrelated employers) is eligible for two annual additions limits—one for each source of income—or a contribution total of $106,000 for 2015. However, elective deferrals by a participant are aggregated between all plans in applying the annual limit. For example, an employee would not be able to defer $18,000 in a Section 401(k) plan at one employer and an additional $18,000 in a Section 401(k) plan at a second employer in the same year.

The one exception is that elective deferrals into a Section 457 plan are not aggregated with elective deferrals into other plans.

> **E X A M P L E** In 2015, Sherry, who is age 49, works for XYZ Corporation and earns compensation of $270,000. XYZ maintains a defined contribution plan for the benefit of its employees. Therefore, for purposes of the annual additions limit to Sherry's account, XYZ can only consider $265,000 of her compensation in making contributions on her behalf. Further, XYZ can contribute no more than $53,000 (less Sherry's contributions and reallocated forfeitures) to the defined contribution plan on her behalf. Sherry is not eligible for catch-up contributions until next year when she reaches age 50.

Contributory Versus Noncontributory

Qualified retirement plans may be distinguished as either a **contributory plan** (employee makes some contribution) or a **noncontributory plan** (employer pays all). Most pension and profit-sharing plans are noncontributory. The common exceptions are the Section 401(k) plan and the thrift plan (an after-tax savings plan).

The reason most qualified plans are noncontributory is that both employers and employees view them as part of an overall compensation package paid for by the employer.

Deduction Limit

Planners should keep in mind the difference between employer contributions made on behalf of an employee (generally subject to a limit of 100% of employee covered compensation) and employer tax deductions taken for those contributions (generally subject to a limit of 25% of covered employee compensation). The limit on contributions is determined with respect to individual employee covered compensation, whereas the limit on the deduction is determined with reference to the aggregate covered compensation of the company. Thus, it is indeed possible that the employer contribution on behalf of one employee can exceed 25% of his compensation as long as it is balanced out by another employee's percentage contribution so as not to exceed the overall 25%-of-covered-compensation employer deduction limit for contributions to a defined contribution plan.

An employer's maximum annual deduction for contributions to a defined benefit pension plan is limited to an amount determined actuarially under standards in Section 404(a) of the Internal Revenue Code or the amount required to meet minimum funding standards, whichever is greater. The 25%-of-covered-compensation limit does not apply to the funding of a defined benefit pension plan, and the deduction is restricted only to that actuarial amount necessary to fund the employee's promised benefit. As a result, an employer who wants a substantial, immediate tax deduction for plan contributions should consider implementing a defined benefit plan as long as employee demographics also favor such a plan.

Regarding defined contribution, Section 403(b), Section 457, SEP, and SIMPLE plans, the covered compensation amount upon which the 25% limit is based is not reduced by the aggregate amount of employee-elective deferrals being made into the plan.

> **EXAMPLE**   Joe receives $50,000 in compensation and defers $10,000 of his salary under the Section 401(k) profit-sharing plan sponsored by his employer. Margaret, the only other employee, receives $100,000 in compensation and defers $8,000 of her salary. In applying the annual additions limit, the employer is limited to a $40,000 ($50,000 − $10,000) profit-sharing contribution on Joe's behalf and $45,000 ($53,000 − $8,000) on Margaret's behalf. However, the employer may only take an income tax deduction of up to $37,500 (25% of $150,000). In this example, note the application of the maximum annual additions limit illustrates both the lesser of (1) 100% of covered compensation or (2) $53,000. In Joe's case the maximum contribution is limited by 100% of compensation, but in Margaret's case the maximum contribution is limited by the annual additions limit.

PRACTICE QUESTIONS   *Choose the best answer for each of the questions below.*

1. ABC Corporation maintains a profit-sharing plan with Section 401(k) provisions on behalf of its employees. The company matches 100% up to 3% of all contributions made by an employee. Josh, age 40, is an employee of ABC Corporation and is paid $100,000 for 2015. Assuming he defers the maximum elective deferral contribution of $18,000 in 2015 and that ABC allocates no forfeitures to his account for that year, how much can the company contribute as a profit-sharing contribution to Josh's account (exclusive of the mandatory employer-match)?

   A. $3,000
   B. $18,000
   C. $32,000
   D. $33,000

   Answer: C.   The applicable annual additions limitation here is the lesser of 100% of Josh's compensation ($100,000) or $53,000. Therefore, subtract from the $53,000 limit the total of Josh's elective deferrals ($18,000) and the already-contributed company match ($3,000). This leaves an additional profit-sharing contribution of $32,000 ($53,000 − $21,000) that may be made to Josh's account by ABC Corporation.

2. In 2015, DEF Corporation maintains an employee-covered compensation totaling $100,000. The employees of DEF Corporation also make elective deferrals to the company's defined contribution qualified plan of $10,000. What is the total amount that DEF may take as an employer deduction for employer contributions made to its qualified plan in 2015?

   A. $10,000
   B. $25,000
   C. $27,500
   D. $100,000

   Answer: B.   The 25% employer deduction limit is based on gross covered compensation of $100,000. DEF's deduction is $25,000. The employee elective deferrals do not count toward the $25,000 limit; therefore, DEF may contribute and deduct as much as $25,000.

Vesting Requirements

Vesting occurs when an employee's nonforfeitable right to receive a present or future retirement plan benefit is accrued over time per the schedule identified in the employer-sponsored retirement plan.

A **non top-heavy** defined benefit pension plan must vest at least as rapidly as one of the following two schedules.

■ Five-year 100% or cliff vesting: In this schedule, no **vesting** is required before five years of employee service, with 100% vesting then required at the end of five years of service.

■ Three- to seven-year graduated or graded vesting: Using this schedule, the plan must provide vesting that is at least as fast as those listed in the following table.

Years of Service	Vesting Percentages
3	20%
4	40%
5	60%
6	80%
7 or more	100%

(**Note:** If the two-year eligibility rule is used, 100% immediate vesting is required upon the date of employee enrollment.)

The Pension Protection Act of 2006 (PPA) requires that employer contributions made after December 31, 2006, to defined contribution plans must vest at least as rapidly as a three-year cliff vesting schedule, or a two-to-six-year graded vesting schedule illustrated below. A top-heavy defined benefit pension must also use three-year cliff or two-to-six graded vesting. Top-heavy plans are discussed later in this unit.

Years of Service	Vesting Percentages
2	20%
3	40%
4	60%
5	80%
6 or more	100%

■ For vesting purposes, the "years of service" schedule begins with an employee's hire date, not the employee's entrance into the plan. In a plan with the traditional 21-and-1 eligibility requirement, an employee with one year of participation in the plan would normally have two years of service for vesting purposes, and so forth.

■ With a three-year cliff vesting schedule, no vesting is required before three years of service. Upon completion of three years of service, 100% vesting is required.

■ The employer may choose a vesting schedule that is more favorable to the employer but not less favorable than cliff vesting.

■ If a qualified plan provides for employee contributions (on a before-tax or after-tax basis), the portion of the benefit or account balance attributable to those contributions must be 100% vested at all times.

■ When an employee attains normal retirement age, the employee will automatically be 100% vested.

■ In the event that the qualified plan is terminated, the employee-participant immediately becomes 100% vested in all plan contributions and benefits.

PRACTICE
QUESTIONS   *Choose the best answer for each of the questions below.*

1. Which of the following plan contributions must be immediately (100%) vested to the employee-participant?

1. Employer contributions in a terminated qualified plan

2. Employer contributions to a defined benefit plan

3. Employee contributions to a defined contribution plan

4. Employer contributions on behalf of an employee made eligible according to the 21-and-1 rule

A. 1 only

B. 1 and 3

C. 2 only

D. 2 and 4

Answer: B. Employer contributions must be 100% vested immediately in the case of terminated plans and employees required to meet the 2 years of service eligibility requirement. Employee contributions are always 100% vested.

2. Jean has given her CFP® professional, Harry, information about the qualified retirement plan she wants to implement in her closely-held C corporation. She has given him a census of her employees which includes dates of hire, compensation, and position in the company. She told Harry the general staff stays an average of 4 years but her small executive staff is made up of family members and does not turn over. Jean is interested in determining which vesting schedule would be best if she chooses a qualified plan. She wants to minimize the impact her employee turnover has on plan assets, saving the company money on retirement plan costs. What does Harry do next?

A. Harry tells Jean a qualified plan that can have a 5-year cliff vesting schedule is best for her company.

B. Harry analyzes and evaluates the information Jean has given to him before making a recommendation.

C. Harry considers alternatives to the qualified plan Jean has selected and gives her vesting schedule suggestions based on those plans as an alternative.

D. Harry recommends a vesting schedule and waits for feedback from Jean on his recommendation.

Answer: B.   Harry's next step is to analyze and evaluate the information Jean has given him. Choice A is communicating the recommendation. Choice C is developing the recommendations. Choice D is also communicating the recommendation. (Domain 3: Analyzing and evaluating the client's current financial status)

Key Employees

A key employee for purposes of the top-heavy rules is an employee who, at any time during the plan year, is:

■ an officer of the employer having annual compensation from the employer of more than $170,000 (2015);

■ a greater than 5% owner of the employer; or

■ a greater than 1% owner of the employer having annual compensation from the employer of greater than $150,000 (not indexed for inflation).

In addition, for these purposes, no more than 50 employees (or, if lesser, the greater of three or 10% of the employees) will be treated as officers.

Top-Heavy Requirements

A defined benefit plan that provides more than 60% of its aggregate benefits or account balances to key employees is considered **top heavy**. If a defined benefit plan is top heavy, there are two consequences:

■ It must provide accelerated three-year cliff or two-to-six-year graded vesting.

■ It must provide a minimum benefit accrual of 2% times the number of years of service up to 20% for all non-key employees.

Under a top-heavy defined contribution plan, the employer must make a minimum contribution of at least 3% of annual compensation to each non-key employee's account. If the contribution for key employees is less than 3%, the contribution for non-key employees can be equal to the contribution for key employees. For example, the employer can make a 1% contribution for all participants (key employees and non-key employees).

PRACTICE
QUESTION   *Choose the best answer for the question below.*

1.   Ben Scott, age 42, wants to establish a qualified defined contribution plan for his small business. Ben currently earns $115,000 annually. He employs 4 people whose combined salaries are $58,000 annually and ages range from 24 to 30. The average employment period is 3½ years. Which vesting schedule is best suited for Ben's qualified plan?
A.   Three-year cliff vesting
B.   Three-to-seven-year graded vesting
C.   Five-year cliff vesting
D.   Two-to-six-year graded vesting

Answer: D.   Because the plan is a defined contribution plan, Ben must adopt a vesting schedule that is at least as generous as the three-year cliff vesting or two-to-six-year graded vesting for all employer contributions to a defined contribution plan in 2015. Given the average length of employment, the most suitable vesting schedule from Ben's perspective is two-to-six-year graded vesting.

Integration with Social Security (Permitted Disparity Rules)

The formula used to calculate a worker's retirement benefit from Social Security inherently discriminates against workers whose compensation is above the annual Social Security taxable wage base because compensation above the wage base is not considered in the benefit formula. To help remedy this inequality, the law allows most qualified plans and the tax-advantaged SEP to utilize a concept known as Social Security integration, sometimes called permitted disparity rules. An **integrated plan** accounts for the disproportionate benefit accrual and provides for a tiered benefit formula, providing a base benefit for compensation up to an integration level, which is typically the Social Security taxable wage base of $118,500 (2015), and then provides a higher benefit for compensation above the wage base. Total compensation considered in the plan benefit formula is limited to $265,000 (2015).

Integration of Defined Benefit Plans

There are two methods of integrating defined benefit formulas with Social Security: the **excess method** (the more common) and the **offset method**. Under the excess method of integration, the plan defines a level of compensation (referred to as the integration level) and then provides a higher rate of contributions and benefits for compensation above this level. Typically, the integration level chosen is the covered compensation table under the Social Security system. Under the offset method of integration, a formula approximates the existence of Social Security benefits and reduces the plan formula. However, under either method, the maximum permitted disparity between the benefit percentage below and above the covered compensation level is three-fourths of 1% times the employee's years of service, up to 35 years. Thus, the maximum percentage difference is 26.25%.

Integration of Defined Contribution Plans

Defined contribution plans can only be integrated with Social Security using an excess method of integration; the offset method is not permitted. The excess method provides higher contributions above the integration level (usually the Social Security taxable wage base) than below this level. The contribution level below the integration level is called the base percentage, whereas the contribution level above the integration level is referred to as the excess percentage. Under the **permitted disparity rules** applying to integration of defined contribution plans, the maximum allowable excess percentage is the lesser of:

- two times the base percentage; or

- the base percentage plus 5.7%.

> **EXAMPLE** If the base contribution percentage for a defined contribution integrated plan is 5%, the permitted disparity is also 5%, making the excess percentage equal to no more than 10% (5% + 5%) of compensation above the integration level. Alternatively, if the base contribution percentage is 6%, the permitted disparity is 5.7%, resulting in an excess percentage amount of no more than 11.7% (6% + 5.7%).

As noted, the integration level for integrated defined contribution plans is usually equal to the Social Security taxable wage base. This amount is $118,500 for 2015. The integration level may be lower than the Social Security wage base, which allows more income to be considered for the excess contribution percentage. However, if the integration level is lowered, so is the maximum difference between the base percentage and the excess percentage.

Plans prohibited from integration with Social Security include employee stock ownership plans (ESOP), SARSEP, and SIMPLE plans. In addition, employee elective deferrals (e.g., to a Section 401(k) plan) and employer matching contributions cannot be integrated with Social Security.

PRACTICE QUESTION

Choose the best answer for the question below.

1. Apollo Company sponsors a defined contribution plan that provides a base contribution of 12.3% of employee compensation. Assuming the integration level equals the Social Security taxable wage base, what is the maximum excess percentage allowed under the permitted disparity rules?

   A.   5.7%

   B.   12.3%

   C.   18.0%

   D.   25.0%

   Answer: C.   The excess percentage cannot exceed the lesser of 2 times the base percentage (24.6%) or the base percentage plus 5.7%. Therefore, the maximum excess percentage is 18.0% or (12.3% + 5.7%).

D. ESTABLISHING A QUALIFIED PLAN AND REPORTING REQUIREMENTS

LO 49.5   Describe the reporting and disclosure requirements for qualified plans.

An employer-sponsor must legally establish and adopt a qualified plan during the employer's tax year for which the plan will take effect. If the plan will use a tax-exempt trust for funding (the usual case), the trust must also be established by the end of the year of adoption and must be valid under the law of the state in which it is established. Certain small employers are eligible for a tax credit of up to $500 in start-up costs or employee education expenses incurred with the adoption of a qualified plan.

Because of the complexity of qualified plan technical requirements and the tax cost of having the plan potentially disqualified by the IRS, some employers apply to the IRS for a favorable ruling that the plan provisions meet the Tax Code requirements. This ruling is known as an **advance determination letter** and is issued by the District Director of the IRS district in which the employer is located. An alternative to the time and cost of such a letter is for the employer to adopt either a master or prototype plan. These are standardized plans of various types (e.g., a profit-sharing plan) that use standardized language approved by the IRS. A master plan is distinguished from a prototype plan in that a master plan uses only a single financial institution for funding, while a prototype plan usually allows more funding possibilities.

The organizations that can provide plan services include trust companies, commercial banks, investments firms, asset management groups, and insurance companies.

Reporting and Disclosure Requirements

Qualified plans must satisfy the reporting and disclosure requirements specified by the ERISA legislation. Following are the major elements of reporting and disclosure.

- A **summary plan description (SPD)** must be provided automatically to all plan participants within 120 days after the plan is established or 90 days after a new participant enters an existing plan.

- An **annual report (Form 5500 series)** must be filed with the IRS annually by the end of the seventh month after the plan year ends. The Form 5500 is also required to be filed with the Department of Labor. A simplified Form 5500 (the Form 5500 SF) is available for smaller qualified plans. One-participant plans may use Form 5500-EZ. One-participant plans with assets of $250,000 or less are exempt entirely from filing Form 5500-EZ or any other 5500 form (except in the plan's final year).

- A summary annual report (SAR), summarizing the basic information included in the Form 5500 series, must be provided to plan participants each year within nine months of the end of the plan year. Participants also have a right to see the full annual report (Form 5500 series) if they need information about the plan's financial status.

- An **individual accrued benefit statement** must generally be provided to a plan participant within 30 days of the request. In addition, under PPA, defined contribution plans must provide benefit statements at least quarterly to participants who direct their own investments and annually to those who cannot.

- A **summary of material modification (SMM)**, explaining any substantive changes that occurred to the SPD within the past year must be issued as needed.

E. FIDUCIARY CONSIDERATIONS AND PROHIBITED TRANSACTIONS UNDER ERISA

LO 49.3   Describe the fiduciary considerations for qualified plan fiduciaries.

LO 49.4   Explain the prohibited transaction rules.

The Department of Labor regulates the actions of qualified plan fiduciaries, which are generally the plan sponsor, administrator (if different than the plan sponsor), and plan trustee. In addition, ERISA specifies that any investment adviser who renders investment advice for a fee is also a **fiduciary**. As a result, plan service providers (such as mutual fund families) and investment adviser representatives have been reluctant to provide full advice about retirement plan investing for fear of fiduciary liability. The Pension Protection Act (PPA) permits retirement plan service providers and investment adviser representatives to give advice to qualified plan participants and, if warranted, recommend their own funds without violating fiduciary rules. The legislation does this by providing an exemption to the prohibited transaction rules for advice provided under an eligible investment advice arrangement. As defined in the PPA, an eligible investment advice arrangement exists where either:

- the investment adviser's fees are neutral (meaning the fees do not vary on the basis of which investment options are chosen); or

- an unbiased computer model certified by an independent expert to create a recommended portfolio for the client's consideration is used.

Before initially advising clients, the investment adviser must provide written notice (on paper or electronically) including information on past performance and rates of return for each of the plan's investment options and any fees or other compensation to be received by the advisor. Finally, it should be noted that investment advisors for IRAs may only use the neutral fee option and not the computer model option when providing eligible investment advice.

The fiduciary standards of ERISA include a prudence and diversification requirement. Under the prudence standard, the fiduciary is required to act with the care, skill, and prudence of an individual familiar with the circumstances. The diversification requirement does not mandate a specific percentage limit on any one investment (or investment class). Instead, the diversification depends on the facts and circumstances of each plan and plan participant.

Prohibited Transaction Rules

ERISA also prohibits certain transactions between a qualified plan and a party in interest or a fiduciary with respect to the plan. While the term **party in interest** is broader than the term fiduciary, a party in interest does include a fiduciary and an investment adviser providing advice to plan participants. Prohibited transactions include:

- the sale, exchange, or lease of any property between the plan and a party in interest;

- loans between the plan and any party in interest;

- the transfer of any plan assets or use of plan assets for the benefit of a party in interest; and

- the plan's acquisition of employer securities or real property in excess of legal limits.

Loans from the plan to plan participants are also generally prohibited transactions unless such loans meet the requirements of IRC Section 4975(d)(1). These requirements will be discussed in detail later in this course when taxable plan distributions (and the exceptions thereto) are addressed.

If there is a violation of these rules, the penalty imposed is 15% of the amount involved in each transaction from the date of first occurrence until the date of its correction. To correct the transaction, it must be undone to the extent possible so as to place the plan in a position no worse than it would have been had the party in interest acted under the highest fiduciary standards. If the transaction is not corrected, there is an additional penalty tax of 100% of the amount involved, including the potential personal liability of the party in interest if the plan assets are not sufficient to pay the penalty.

PRACTICE QUESTION *Choose the best answer for the question below.*

1. Scott Benjamin is a fiduciary of the XYZ qualified retirement plan. Which governmental entity regulates his actions as a fiduciary?
   A. ERISA
   B. PBGC
   C. DOL
   D. SOS

   Answer: C. The DOL regulates the actions of plan fiduciaries. It also ensures compliance with the ERISA plan reporting and disclosure requirements.

▌105 UNIT 1 POST-STUDY CHECKLIST

☐ Can I describe the major differences between qualified and nonqualified retirement plans?

☐ Can I describe the eligibility, coverage, and testing requirements of qualified plans?

☐ Am I able to explain the permitted disparity rules and how retirement plans can be integrated with Social Security?

☐ Do I know the limitations on contributions and benefits in qualified plans?

☐ Am I able to explain the top-heavy requirements and the effects on contributions or benefits?

☐ Am I able to explain the key provisions of the Employee Retirement Income Security Act (ERISA)?

☐ Can I describe how the U.S. Department of Labor (DOL) and the Pension Benefit Guaranty Corporation (PBGC) are involved in retirement plan regulation?

☐ Do I understand the fiduciary considerations for qualified plan fiduciaries?

☐ Am I able to explain the prohibited transaction rules?

☐ Can I describe the reporting and disclosure requirements for qualified plans?

Am I able to define and understand the application of the following terms to financial planning?

☐ 1% owner (IRS definition)

☐ 5% owner (IRS definition)

☐ 21-and-1 rule

☐ 50/40 test

☐ Active participation

☐ Advance determination letter

☐ Annual additions limit

☐ Annual report (Form 5500 series)

☐ Average benefits percentage test

☐ Contributory plan

☐ Controlled group rules

☐ Catch-up contribution

☐ Covered

☐ Covered compensation

☐ Department of Labor (DOL)

☐ Defined benefit plans

☐ Defined contribution plans

☐ Elective deferral limit

☐ Eligibility

☐ Employee Retirement Income Security Act (ERISA)

☐ Excess method

☐ Fiduciary

☐ Highly compensated employee (HCE)

☐ Individual accrued benefit statement

☐ Integrated plan

☐ Internal Revenue Service (IRS)

☐ Noncontributory plan

☐ Nonqualified plans

☐ Offset method

☐ Party in interest

☐ Pension Benefit Guaranty Corporation (PBGC)

☐ Percentage test

☐ Greater than 5% owner

☐ Permitted disparity rules

☐ Prohibited transaction exemptions (PTEs)

☐ Prohibited transaction rules

☐ Qualified plans

☐ Ratio test

☐ Summary annual report (SAR)

☐ Summary of material modification (SMM)

☐ Summary plan description (SPD)

☐ Top heavy

☐ Vesting

Defined Benefit and Other Pension Plans

REFER TO

CFP® Certification Principal Topics – Retirement Planning, Types of Retirement Plans

Supplemental Readings Section of this 105 Retirement Planning Student Guide

(For specific assignments, refer to class syllabus.)

INTRODUCTION

This is the first of three units on the various types of employer-sponsored retirement plans. This unit addresses the first broad category of qualified plans: those that provide retirement benefits on the basis of defining benefits, also known as defined benefit plans. Sometimes, the word pension is substituted for the traditional form of defined benefit plan and, while that word is technically correct, defined benefit plans are not the only types of pension plans. There are also pension plans that fall under the defined contribution type of qualified plans, notably the money purchase and target benefit forms of pension plans. Nonetheless, pension plans promise either benefits or contributions building toward a benefit. Mandatory annual funding and no in-service withdrawals (except to employees age 62 or older) are a hallmark of these types of plans. Two forms of defined benefit pension plans are the traditional defined benefit pension plan and the cash balance pension plan. Both are tested for discrimination based on benefits rather than contributions.

While money purchase and target benefit pension plans have been declining in popularity since passage of the Economic Growth Tax Relief Reconciliation Act (EGTRRA) legislation in 2001 that increased the contribution limit for profit-sharing plans to equal that of defined contribution pension plans, you will nonetheless need to know the characteristics of these types of plans as well as when it may be appropriate to recommend one of the forms to a small business owner-client.

LEARNING OBJECTIVES

After completing this unit, you should be able to achieve the following learning objectives:

CFP® Certification Principal Topics – Retirement Planning, Types of Retirement Plans

LO 46.2   Explain the differences between the different types of qualified plans including the basic provisions of each plan.

LO 46.4   Describe a money purchase pension plan and its advantages and disadvantages.

LO 46.5   Explain the features of a target benefit pension plan and how it favors older participants.

LO 46.13   Describe the main features of a defined benefit pension plan including its advantages and disadvantages.

LO 46.14   Describe the main features of a cash balance pension plan and how it differs from a traditional defined benefit pension plan.

LO 46.15   Explain a fully insured plan and when it is appropriate to use.

KEY TERMS

Career average method	Interest rate credit
Cash balance pension plan	Money purchase pension plan
DB(k) plan	Pension Protection Act of 2006 (PPA)
Defined benefit pension plan	Section 412(e)(3) plan
Final average method	Section 415
Flat amount formula	Tandem plan
Flat percentage formula	Target benefit pension plan
Forfeitures	Unit benefit formula

▌A. THE TRADITIONAL DEFINED BENEFIT PENSION PLAN

LO 46.2   Explain the differences between the different types of qualified plans including the basic provisions of each plan.

LO 46.13   Describe the main features of a defined benefit pension plan including its advantages and disadvantages.

The traditional **defined benefit pension plan** is an employer-sponsored qualified retirement plan that guarantees a specified benefit level (pension) at the employee-participant's date of retirement. As such, the objective of the plan is to provide an adequate level of retirement income to each employee regardless of age at plan entry. It is typically most suitable for businesses that have two distinguishing features:

■ A predominately older workforce, typically with key executives age 50 or older

■ A stable cash flow because the requirement to make annual contributions to this type of plan is mandatory

There are several advantages and disadvantages of the traditional defined benefit pension plan. Among the advantages are the following.

■ The benefit levels are guaranteed, both by the employer and, to a limited extent, by the Pension Benefit Guaranty Corporation (PBGC), the government agency that insures defined benefit pension plans.

■ For older, highly-paid employees, a defined benefit pension plan generally allows the maximum amount of contributions to be made for their benefit.

■ Defined benefit pension plans may encourage early retirement.

The following are some disadvantages.

■ Because of the actuarial and PBGC costs necessary to administer the plan, defined benefit pension plans tend to be expensive to administer.

■ They are complex, both in operation and design.

■ The employer assumes the risk of poor investment results in the plan.

Under **Section 415** of the Tax Code, there is a limit on the projected annual benefit that the plan can provide to the employee-participant at age 65. For 2015, this maximum benefit is the lesser of:

■ $210,000 of annual compensation; or

■ 100% of the participant's compensation averaged over the participant's highest three consecutive years of earnings.

If plan provisions permit, it is possible for the employee to retire earlier (at age 62) with no reduction in benefits.

Benefit payments by the PBGC are financed through the payment of premiums by defined benefit plan sponsors. This premium consists of both a base premium (based on the number of plan participants per year) and a variable premium. Under the **Pension Protection Act of 2006 (PPA)**, a special reduced premium is effective for employers with 25 or fewer employees. In addition, a defined benefit plan that is maintained by a professional service employer (such as a physician or attorney) with 25 or fewer employees does not have to be covered by the PBGC.

For 2015, the maximum monthly benefit (for those who retire at age 65 in 2015) guaranteed by the PBGC for any type of defined benefit plan for which it assumes financial responsibility is $5,011 per month ($60,132 annually). This amount may be much smaller than the amount otherwise guaranteed to the participant under a fully funded corporate defined benefit plan.

One of the following three formulas is typically used by the defined benefit plan to calculate the amount of a participant's promised benefit.

- **Flat amount formula:** A specified dollar amount is promised to the employee per month for life, beginning at age 65 (or otherwise specified date); the formula does not differentiate among employees with different compensation and does not use an accrued benefit actuarial cost method.

- **Flat percentage formula:** This formula provides a retirement benefit that is a percentage of the employee's average earnings and will usually require a certain amount of minimum years of service before the full percentage benefit is payable.

- **Unit benefit formula:** A percentage of earnings is paid for each year of employee service, usually 1–2%; for example, with a 30-year service career and a 2% per year accrual, the employee would receive a retirement payment equal to 60% (30 × 2) of her preretirement income.

Average earnings under the benefit formulas are calculated by the **career average method** or the **final average method**. Generally, use of the final average method (average earnings over the final three to five years of service) will generate a larger benefit for the employee. Keep in mind (as discussed in Unit 1) that only the first $265,000 of employee compensation may be taken into account when calculating the promised benefit, regardless of the earning method used.

Annual funding of the defined benefit pension plan is mandatory on the part of the employer-sponsor, and contributions may be waived only with the consent of the IRS and DOL. Earnings generated on these contributions, as well as other factors, affect the required funding. For example, plan earnings in excess of projected earnings lower annual funding costs while underperforming plan assets increase annual funding costs. Regardless, in a traditional defined benefit pension plan, the present value amount of funding required (to fund future benefits due) must be determined with the assistance of a licensed actuary. This is in contrast to the defined contribution approach that does not fund a future promised benefit and does not require the services of an actuary.

Defined benefit pension plan forfeitures (unvested amounts in the plan that accrue from departing employees) must be used to reduce the employer contributions for that plan year. When employee turnover increases, the employer contribution can be lowered. The employer contribution, as calculated by the actuary each year, is deductible by the employer. There is no limit on this deduction as it is the amount required by the plan to pay projected benefits. Contrast this with the limits imposed on the employer's deductible contribution to other types of retirement plans covered in this course.

Multiple variables affect the costs of a defined benefit pension plan. Many are related, either inversely or directly, in that a change in one variable effects change in another.

An inverse relationship between variables exists when the increase or decrease in Variable A causes the opposite effect in Variable B. If plan investment returns increase and the plan increases in value, the cost to the employer in the form of a plan contribution for that year decreases. If the investment return decreases, the plan costs increase.

A direct relationship occurs where the increase in Variable A causes an increase in Variable B. If the life expectancies of plan participants increase, the plan costs to the employer also increase.

A summary of the defined benefit variables and impact on the potential costs of the plan follows.

Analysis of Defined Benefit Variables and Impact on Plan Costs

	Direction Compared to Expected	Impact on Plan Costs	Relationship of Variable to Plan Costs
Investment returns	↑ ↓	↓ ↑	Inverse
Turnover of employees	↑ ↓	↓ ↑	Inverse
Mortality	↑ ↓	↓ ↑	Inverse
Life expectancies	↑ ↓	↑ ↓	Direct
Wages	↑ ↓	↑ ↓	Direct
Average age of new employees	↑ ↓	↑ ↓	Direct
Cost-of-living adjustments	↑ ↓	↑ ↓	Direct

DB(k) Plans

A **DB(k) plan** is a hybrid plan designed to address the potential shortfalls in Section 401(k) plans and a decline in the establishment of defined benefit pension plans. A DB(k) plan allows a traditional defined benefit pension plan will be permitted to accept Section 401(k)-type (pretax) employee contributions. A sponsoring employer with no more than 500 employees may offer the DB(k) plan. As a part of this plan, the Section 401(k) component must include an automatic enrollment feature and a fully vested 50% match on the first 4% of compensation deferred by an employee. Additional requirements apply.

Employee advantages of a DB(k) plan include the following:

■ Guaranteed monthly income at retirement

■ Encourages employers without pension plans to establish a plan

■ Combines the security employees get through traditional defined benefit pension plans with individual investment control

■ Allows automatic enrollment provisions which encourage employees to save more than they may have in a traditional Section 401(k) plan

Employer advantages of a DB(k) plan include the following:

■ Exemption from the top-heavy rules

■ Allows small employers to sponsor a defined benefit pension plan with more predictable costs because the Section 401(k) matching contribution is not contingent upon factors such as employee mortality, plan investment returns, and other factors that affect defined benefit pension plan contributions

■ Specifications and defined benefit formula are defined

■ Offers simplified administration and potentially lower costs than having two individual plans

■ Requires only one plan document, one trust, one Form 5500 filing, one Summary Plan Description (SPD), and one set of statements

Businesses that may consider implementing a DB(k) plan include the following:

■ Section 401(k) plan-only sponsors

■ Employers without a defined benefit pension plan

■ Employers without a defined contribution plan

■ Small plan sponsors with both defined benefit and defined contribution plans

Section 401(k) plans will be discussed in Unit 3 of this course.

PRACTICE QUESTIONS

Choose the best answer for each of the questions below.

1. Gwen is 52 years old and just started a new job with ABC Industries. She is concerned about having enough income during her retirement that will begin when she reaches age 65. Gwen recently left XYZ Industries, her former employer, in part because XYZ did not sponsor a traditional defined benefit pension plan. ABC does sponsor such a plan, and Gwen has requested information from you about the plan's general provisions. Which of the following statements regarding defined benefit pension plans is(are) CORRECT?

  1. They allow discretionary employer contributions.
  2. They favor older employee-participants.
  3. They require the services of an actuary on an annual basis.
  4. They are insured by the PBGC.

  A. 1, 2, and 4
  B. 2 only
  C. 2 and 3
  D. 2, 3, and 4

Answer: D. The only incorrect statement is Statement 1. Defined benefit pension plans have mandatory contribution formulas, require the services of an actuary on an annual basis, and require the payment of PBGC insurance premiums. Such plans also tend to favor older participants.

2. Which of the following would increase the employer's annual contribution to a defined benefit pension plan using a unit benefit formula?

  1. Forfeitures are lower than expected.
  2. Salary increases are higher than expected.
  3. Investment returns are less than expected.
  4. Benefits are cost-of-living adjusted as expected.

  A. 4 only
  B. 1 and 2
  C. 2 and 3
  D. 1, 2, and 3

Answer: D.   Defined benefit pension plan contributions would increase due to the circumstances described in Statements 1, 2, and 3. Benefits are expected to be cost-of-living adjusted; this would not increase the employer's annual contributions.

3.   Janet is 59 and a new client for Larry, a CFP® professional. They have just signed the client engagement letter. Janet's financial planning goals include determining where she stands in her retirement planning. She would like to retire a few years earlier than her normal retirement age of 67 but is not certain she has the retirement assets in place to do so. Janet has worked for Sell-Buy, Inc., for 20 years and is a participant in the company's traditional defined benefit pension plan. Her employer's retirement plan offers retirement at age 60. Her salary is $275,000 annually and her salary increases should continue to be as consistent as they have been in the past. Janet is wondering what her projected benefit will be and if it will be enough for her early retirement. What should Larry do next to assist Janet in attaining her retirement planning goal?

   A.   Larry should request all the documents Janet has available on her retirement plan, her income history, all of her other assets and liabilities, income and expenses, and any other documentation she has on any other investments she has that could be available for retirement planning.

   B.   Larry should call the plan administrator and ask what Janet's benefit will be if she retires earlier than her normal retirement age.

   C.   Larry should recommend that Janet continue to work until her normal retirement age to allow time to accrue an increase benefit from her defined benefit pension plan.

   D.   For the next few months, Larry should monitor the performance of Janet's investments and calculate Janet's anticipated retirement plan benefit to see if her goal is achievable.

Answer: A.   Larry is very early in the financial planning process with Janet and in order to help her achieve her goals, he should request all the documentation and information available about Janet's financial situation, including her anticipated retirement plan benefits, before he can start evaluating Janet's situation. Larry is not at the recommendation stage at this time. The plan administrator for Janet's defined benefit pension plan will not be able to give Larry information over the telephone. (Domain 2: Gathering the information necessary to fulfill the engagement)

B. CASH BALANCE PENSION PLAN

LO 46.14   Describe the main features of a cash balance pension plan and how it differs from a traditional defined benefit pension plan.

A **cash balance pension plan** is a type of defined benefit pension plan that includes features of a defined contribution plan. The cash balance pension plan provides for annual employer contributions at a specified rate to a hypothetical individual account. Thus, it stays true to the pooled concept of defined benefit pension plans but credits an **interest rate credit** (known as a guaranteed return). This rate of return may be fixed or tied to some market rate of interest, usually a Treasury security. The employer attempts to minimize the future annual contribution by investing contributed funds in securities with returns exceeding the return guaranteed to employees. Section 415(b) limits the benefits that may be provided under the plan to the lesser of $210,000 (2015) or 100% of the participant's highest consecutive three-year average compensation.

Like traditional defined benefit pension plans, a cash balance plan also has several advantages and disadvantages. Advantages include:

- a certain level of plan benefits are guaranteed by the PBGC; and

- there are significant cost savings for the employer as compared to the traditional defined benefit pension plan.

Among the disadvantages are:

- the employer bears the risk of poor investment performance;

- the retirement benefits may be inadequate for older plan entrants; and

- if the plan is a converted traditional defined benefit pension plan, the lump-sum payout at the employee's retirement date may be considerably less under the cash balance formula.

A cash balance plan is typically most appropriate when the workforce is relatively large and young (younger than 50). The type of employer that would use the cash balance plan is a mid-size or large company that already has a well-funded traditional defined benefit pension plan and is desirous of cost savings with respect to its sponsored retirement plans.

PRACTICE QUESTION

Choose the best answer for the question below.

1. Which one of the following is a feature of a cash balance pension plan?
   A. It allows for investment discretion on the part of each employee-participant.
   B. There is a guaranteed minimum investment rate of return.
   C. It tends to favor older plan entrants.
   D. The plan is not subject to the minimum funding standards that also apply to traditional defined benefit pension plans.

Answer: B.   The employer directs the plan's investments while guaranteeing a minimum rate of return to the employee. Unlike the traditional defined benefit pension plan, the cash balance pension plan favors younger plan entrants. Like the traditional defined benefit pension plan, a cash balance pension plan is subject to the minimum funding standards included in Section 412 of the Internal Revenue Code.

C. FULLY INSURED PENSION PLANS (SECTION 412(E)(3) PLANS)

LO 46.15   Explain a fully insured plan and when it is appropriate to use.

A fully insured pension plan (Section 412(e)(3) Plan) is a type of traditional defined benefit pension plan funded exclusively by cash value life insurance (typically whole life) or annuity contracts. In such a plan, no qualified plan trust exists as is common with other retirement plans. In addition, using insurance as a funding vehicle guarantees the payment of a death benefit to plan beneficiaries, usually a surviving spouse and children.

A defined benefit pension plan that is fully insured is exempt from minimum funding standards, unless there is an outstanding loan against the insurance policy funding the defined benefit pension plan. In addition, such plans are eligible for simplified reporting requirements (Form 5500 series) and are not required to be certified by an enrolled or licensed actuary.

Fully insured funding may be incorporated into a new or existing defined benefit pension plan, although it is most prevalent with a newly designed plan. Benefits from the plan are guaranteed by the insurance company with the employer transferring all investment risk to the third party. Because of the conservative nature of the guaranteed cash values used in the funding formula, fully insured pension plans often allow far greater deductible contributions to be made into the plan. This element was originally one of the attractive features of this type of plan, but in recent years the limited opportunity for growth has made the plans far less common.

A fully insured plan is inappropriate for an employer who cannot commit to regular premium payments. A stable business, rather than one experiencing (or expecting to experience) fluctuating cash flow, is the best prospect for a Section 412(e)(3) plan.

PRACTICE
QUESTION   *Choose the best answer for the question below.*

1. Can a policy loan be outstanding under a fully insured plan funding approach and still be exempt from the minimum funding standards of Section 412 of the Tax Code?
    A. Yes
    B. No

    Answer: B.   If a loan is made from the policy (usually to the businessowner), the plan loses its fully insured status and the minimum funding standards apply.

▌ D. MONEY PURCHASE PENSION PLAN

LO 46.4   Describe a money purchase pension plan and its advantages and disadvantages.

A **money purchase pension plan** is a type of defined contribution pension plan in which an employer makes annual mandatory contributions to each employee's individual account. While the amount of final benefit is not guaranteed or promised, there is an employer promise to contribute to the plan. The formula under the plan requires a contribution of a specified percentage of each employee's annual compensation by the employer. The plan does not require the services of an actuary and, because it uses a defined contribution approach, insurance cannot be purchased by the employer from the PBGC. The maximum annual contribution to the participant's account under the plan is the lesser of 100% of the eligible employee's compensation or $53,000 (for 2015). The maximum covered compensation that may be considered for a participant in the plan is limited to $265,000 (2015). The deduction for employer contributions is limited to 25% of aggregate covered compensation.

Advantages of the plan are:

■   it is relatively straightforward and simple to explain to potential participants; and

■   the account balance generated under the plan may be distributed as a lump sum or an annuity or rolled over to an IRA.

The primary disadvantage of the plan is its lack of contribution flexibility. For example, in the event of declining employer cash flow, plan contributions still must be made. In addition, money purchase pension plans severely limit the ability to use plan contributions to buy employer stock. Generally, the employer securities held by the plan cannot exceed 10% of the FMV of plan assets at the time the employer securities are purchased.

Money purchase pension plans were popular in employer-sponsored retirement planning before the EGTRRA legislation of 2001 that increased the deductible employer contributions permitted in profit-sharing plans to 25%. Still, when an employer wants to install a qualified retirement plan that is relatively simple to administer, has a younger workforce, and can assume the burden of mandatory funding, a money purchase pension plan may be appropriate.

Forfeitures

In any qualified plan, **forfeitures** are created when non-vested or partially vested employees terminate their service with the sponsoring employer. As a result, this unvested portion reverts back to the plan.

In defined benefit pension plans (traditional or cash balance), these forfeitures may only be used to reduce future employer contributions. In other words, there is no mechanism for the remaining employee-participants to benefit from the forfeited balance of their now-departed colleagues.

This is not the case in defined contribution plans, including the money purchase pension plan. In a defined contribution plan, forfeitures may be:

■ used to reduce future employer contributions; or

■ reallocated among the remaining plan participants, increasing their potential individual account balances.

Reallocation of plan forfeitures must be on a nondiscriminatory basis, typically using a pro rata formula based on a participant's covered compensation relative to the other remaining plan participants' covered compensation. Reallocated plan forfeitures are included in the application of the annual additions limit.

PRACTICE QUESTION

Choose the best answer for the question below.

1. ABC Corporation sponsors a money purchase pension plan for its employees. ABC utilizes plan forfeitures to reduce future employer plan contributions. Therefore, which of the following factors must be considered in determining the maximum annual additions limit?
   1. Investment earnings
   2. Forfeitures
   3. Rollover contributions
   4. Employer and employee contributions to all defined contribution plans

   A. 1, 2, and 3
   B. 1 and 3
   C. 2 and 4
   D. 4 only

   Answer: D.   Investment earnings are not a factor in calculating annual additions. In this case, forfeitures will be used to reduce employer contributions and, therefore, will not be a factor in determining the annual additions limit. Rollover contributions do not count against the annual additions limit.

E. TARGET BENEFIT PENSION PLANS

LO 46.5   Explain the features of a target benefit pension plan and how it favors older participants.

A **target benefit pension plan** is a qualified defined contribution pension plan in which employer contributions are made for each participant in an actuarially determined amount to reach a targeted benefit at the plan's specified normal retirement age. In such a plan, the plan designer chooses actuarial assumptions (in the first year of plan operation only) to determine how much must be contributed for participants entering the plan at various ages. Thus, in the first year of plan operation, the services of an actuary are required. Subsequent to that year, however, there are no periodic actuarial valuations and the plan is funded like a money purchase pension plan—that is, using the percentage of compensation approach. In addition, like any other defined contribution plan, there is no guarantee to the employee of the ultimate account balance that is accumulated. Unlike a traditional defined benefit pension plan, annual contributions are not adjusted to guarantee the final benefit.

Target benefit pension plans share the following similarities with defined benefit pension plans:

■ They favor older participants (generally an employee age 50 or older).

■ They (initially) require an actuary.

■ They are a type of pension plan.

■ Mandatory minimum funding standards apply.

Target benefit pension plans share the following similarities with defined contribution plans:

■ The employee bears the risk of plan investment performance.

■ Each employee has a separate (individual) account.

■ PBGC insurance is not available.

■ The final actual dollar benefit is not guaranteed.

Like money purchase pension plans, target benefit pension plans require mandatory annual funding. Accordingly, target benefit pension plans have also been declining in popularity since the EGTRRA of 2001 and the liberalization of the 25% deduction limit for profit-sharing plan contributions. Before 2002, target and money purchase pension plans were paired with profit-sharing plans, called **tandem plans**, to obtain a greater tax deduction at the cost of two plan administration expenses as well as a partial mandatory employer contribution. The typical employer contributions consisted of a mandatory 10% money purchase pension plan contribution and a maximum discretionary 15% contribution to a profit-sharing plan. This is no longer necessary since EGTRRA because deductible contributions to a profit-sharing plan may be as high as 25% of covered compensation on a discretionary basis.

A target benefit pension plan permits a low contribution level for younger, lower-paid employees and an extremely high contribution level for older employees. This is possible by using a permitted concept known as cross-testing to meet qualified plan nondiscrimination rules. Cross-testing will be discussed in greater detail in the next unit in discussing age-weighted profit-sharing plans, which are also cross-tested.

Choose the best answer for the question below.

1. Which statement(s) regarding a target benefit plan is(are) CORRECT?
1. The employee's benefit is not guaranteed by the employer.
2. The plan requires actuarial assumptions.
3. The maximum deductible employer contribution is 25% of covered payroll.
4. The participant's maximum annual addition is the lesser of 100% of compensation or $53,000 (2015).

A. 1 and 4
B. 4 only
C. 2 and 3
D. 1, 2, 3, and 4

Answer: D.   All of these statements are correct. Because target benefit plans prescribe a percentage of compensation for contributions, the features described in Statements 3 and 4 are commonly combined into a contribution limit of the lesser of 25% of compensation or $53,000 (2015).

105 UNIT 2 POST-STUDY CHECKLIST

☐ Do I know how to differentiate between the different types of qualified plans and explain the basic provisions of each plan?

☐ Can I describe a money purchase pension plan and its advantages and disadvantages?

☐ Am I able to explain the features of a target benefit plan and how it favors older participants?

☐ Can I describe the main features of a defined benefit pension plan and identify its advantages and disadvantages?

☐ Can I describe the main features of a cash balance pension plan and how it differs from a traditional defined benefit pension plan?

☐ Am I able to explain a fully insured plan and when it is appropriate to use?

Am I able to define and understand the application of the following terms to financial planning?

☐ Career average method	☐ Interest rate credit
☐ Cash balance pension plan	☐ Money purchase pension plan
☐ DB(k) plan	☐ Pension Protection Act of 2006 (PPA)
☐ Defined benefit pension plan	☐ Section 412(e)(3) plan
☐ Final average method	☐ Section 415
☐ Flat amount formula	☐ Tandem plan
☐ Flat percentage formula	☐ Target benefit pension plan
☐ Forfeitures	☐ Unit benefit formula

3

Profit-Sharing and Other Defined Contribution Plans

REFER TO

CFP® Certification Principal Topics – Retirement Planning, Types of Retirement Plans

CFP® Certification Principal Topics – Retirement Planning, Qualified Plan Rules and Options

CFP® Certification Principal Topics – Retirement Planning, Other Tax-Advantaged Retirement Plans

Supplemental Readings Section of this 105 Retirement Planning Student Guide

(For specific assignments, refer to class syllabus.)

█ INTRODUCTION

As has been discussed, there are types of defined contribution plans (notably money purchase and target benefit pension plans) that fund a pension at the participant's retirement date. However, when most planners speak of a defined contribution type of qualified plan, they are referring to some form of discretionary profit-sharing plan established by the employer for the benefit of its employees. In addition to providing a retirement planning vehicle, a profit-sharing plan can also serve as a performance incentive for employees. For example, if a certain specified net income (profit) for the company is not achieved, a profit-sharing contribution by the employer may not be made.

There are several types of profit-sharing plans, but the most prevalent today is a traditional profit-sharing plan with a Section 401(k) feature. A Section 401(k) plan is an arrangement within a qualified profit-sharing or stock bonus plan that allows an eligible employee to make pre-tax elective deferrals into it. This unit will consider Section 401(k) plans from a variety of perspectives.

Also considered in this unit are cross-tested plans that have become increasingly popular. Such plans are a means of legally discriminating in favor of older, more experienced employees, who are generally highly compensated employees (HCEs).

LEARNING OBJECTIVES

After completing this unit, you should be able to achieve the following learning objectives:

CFP® Certification Principal Topics – Retirement Planning, Types of Retirement Plans

LO 46.2   Explain the differences between the different types of qualified plans including the basic provisions of each plan.

LO 46.3   Describe the main features of a defined contribution plan and the advantages and disadvantages.

LO 46.6   Describe the basic provisions of a traditional profit-sharing plan.

LO 46.7   Describe the general characteristics and types of Section 401(k) plans.

LO 46.8   Describe the characteristics of an age-based profit-sharing plan.

LO 46.9   Explain the features of a stock bonus plan and how it differs from other profit-sharing plans.

LO 46.10   Explain how to structure an employee stock ownership plan (ESOP) and where it is used in business and retirement planning.

LO 46.11   Explain the features of a new comparability plan and how it can satisfy the nondiscrimination rules.

LO 46.12   Describe the characteristics of a thrift plan and when it is appropriate for a business to choose.

CFP® Certification Principal Topics – Retirement Planning, Qualified Plan Rules and Options

LO 47.3   Describe the limitations on contributions and benefits in qualified plans.

CFP® Certification Principal Topics – Retirement Planning, Other Tax-advantaged Retirement Plans

LO 48.7   Identify special rules applicable to a retirement plan for self-employed owners.

KEY TERMS

Actual contribution percentage (ACP) test	Negative election
Actual deferral percentage (ADP) test	Net unrealized appreciation (NUA)
Age-based profit-sharing plan	New comparability plan (NCP)
Automatic Enrollment Notice	Profit-sharing plan
Cash or deferred arrangement (CODA)	Qualified automatic contribution arrangement (QACA)
Cross-tested plan	Qualified Default Investment Notice
Defined contribution plan	Qualified matching contributions
Elective deferral	Qualified nonelective contributions
Employee stock ownership plan (ESOP)	Resources test
Financial needs test	Roth 401(k) plan
Hardship withdrawal	Safe harbor Section 401(k) plan
HR-10 plan	Savings/thrift plan
In-plan Roth rollover	SIMPLE 401(k) plan
In-service distribution	Stock bonus plan
Keogh plan	Substantial and recurring
Leveraged ESOP (LESOP)	Traditional Section 401(k) plan

Note: LOs 46.2 and 46.3 are covered in all sections of this unit and will only be listed in Section A.

A. TRADITIONAL PROFIT-SHARING PLAN

LO 46.2   Explain the differences between the different types of qualified plans including the basic provisions of each plan.

LO 46.3   Describe the main features of a defined contribution plan and the advantages and disadvantages.

LO 46.6   Describe the basic provisions of a traditional profit-sharing plan.

A traditional **profit-sharing plan** is a qualified **defined contribution plan** featuring a flexible, discretionary employer contribution provision. Accordingly, the employer's contribution to the plan each year may be purely discretionary or may be a formula related to a percentage of employer profits. Regardless, as a qualified plan, contributions must still be made in a nondiscriminatory manner so as not to violate the coverage rules discussed in Unit 1. In addition, for a profit-sharing plan to remain qualified, Treasury Regulations require that contributions be made on a **substantial and recurring** basis, usually interpreted to mean that a contribution must be made in three of every five years. Annual contributions to a participant's account are limited to the lesser of 100% of employee compensation or $53,000 (2015) with only the first $265,000 (2015) of employee compensation taken into account. The most common formula for profit-sharing contributions provides for contributions to be allocated to individual participant accounts on a pro rata basis determined by a given participant's covered compensation in relation to the aggregate covered compensation of all participants. The deduction for employer contributions is limited to 25% of aggregate covered compensation.

A major advantage of any profit-sharing plan (including one with a Section 401(k) feature) is the option of **in-service distributions**, or the ability of the participant to access the individual account balance prior to retirement. Most notable among qualifying distributions is a withdrawal from the plan because of financial hardship. A **hardship withdrawal** must meet the following tests.

- **Financial needs test**: the hardship must be due to an immediate and heavy financial need of the participant-employee.

- **Resources test**: the participant must not have other financial sources sufficient to satisfy the need.

In addition to meeting these tests, the money may only be withdrawn for the following reasons:

- Payment of unreimbursed medical expenses or funeral costs

- Purchase of a primary residence

- Payment of higher education expenses for the participant, the participant's spouse, or dependent children

- Payment necessary to prevent foreclosure on the participant's primary residence

Finally, if a hardship withdrawal is approved and made, the distribution is taxable and a 10% early distribution penalty may apply.

When to Use a Profit-Sharing Plan

A traditional profit-sharing plan may be appropriate when:

- an employer's profits, or cash flow, fluctuate from year to year;

- an employer wishes to implement a qualified plan with an incentive feature by which an employee's account balance increases with employer profits;

- the majority of employees are young (under age 50) and have substantial time to accumulate retirement savings; or

- the employees are willing to accept a degree of investment risk in their individual accounts.

PRACTICE
QUESTION   *Choose the best answer for the question below.*

1. Which statement about a traditional profit-sharing plan is NOT correct?
   A. Profit-sharing plans are qualified defined contribution plans.
   B. Profit-sharing plans are suitable for companies that have unstable cash flows.
   C. A company that adopts a profit-sharing plan is required to make contributions each year.
   D. Company profits are not a prerequisite for employer contributions.

Answer: C.   Profit-sharing plans are not required to make annual contributions. As a discretionary plan, profit-sharing plans are suitable for companies that have unstable cash flows. Company profits are not required (that is, the company can make the contribution out of retained earnings if it wishes).

B. AGE-BASED PROFIT-SHARING PLAN

LO 46.8   Describe the characteristics of an age-based profit-sharing plan.

An **age-based profit-sharing plan** is a profit-sharing plan in which allocations to participants are made in proportion to the participant's age-adjusted compensation. It is an example of a **cross-tested plan** where compliance with the nondiscrimination rules is tested in accordance with benefits rather than contributions. Under such a plan, each participant's compensation is weighted by an age factor. The employer contribution is then allocated to create an actuarially equivalent benefit at the normal retirement age under the plan for each participant (typically, when the participant reaches age 65). A participant's compensation is age-adjusted by multiplying the participant's actual compensation by a discount factor based on the participant's age and the interest rate elected by the plan sponsor. As a result, older employees (the businessowner is usually among them) receive the greatest allocation.

An age-based profit-sharing plan is most appropriate when the businessowner is significantly older than most of the employees and wishes to skew the annual contribution on his behalf without violating the nondiscrimination rules. When a profit-sharing plan is age-weighted, however, the businessowner is still limited to a dollar contribution of the lesser of $53,000 (2015) or 100% of compensation with no more than $265,000 (2015) of annual compensation taken into account for plan contribution purposes.

C. NEW COMPARABILITY PLAN

LO 46.11   Explain the features of a new comparability plan and how it can satisfy the nondiscrimination rules.

A **new comparability plan** is a type of cross-tested profit-sharing retirement plan in which the employee-participants are divided into groups or classes. Common group classifications used include job category, age, or years of service. Each group or class typically receives a different level of employer contribution as a percentage of compensation. The plan works particularly well when there is more than one owner of a business, with each owner of a substantially different age, thus precluding the age-based profit-sharing approach. Because the new comparability plan is a form of a cross-tested plan, it may also be tested for nondiscrimination on the basis of benefits rather than contributions, thus permitting considerable flexibility in plan design. The goal of a new comparability plan is often to skew plan contributions in favor of highly compensated, key employees, management and owners.

The new comparability plan will only satisfy nondiscrimination rules if the plan design satisfies one of two minimum gateways.

- Each eligible non-HCE must receive an allocation of at least 5% of compensation.

- If the plan provides an allocation rate of less than 5%, the minimum allocation rate for non-HCEs is one-third of the highest allocation rate under the plan. For instance, if the top allocation rate is 12%, the minimum allocation rate for non-HCEs would be 4% (12% divided by 3).

PRACTICE
QUESTION

Choose the best answer for the question below.

1. Which of the following is an example of a cross-tested plan?
   1. Age-based profit-sharing plan
   2. Traditional profit-sharing plan
   3. New comparability profit-sharing plan
   4. Profit-sharing plan with a Section 401(k) feature

   A. 1 and 2
   B. 1 and 3
   C. 2 and 3
   D. 2 and 4

Answer: B. An age-based profit-sharing plan and a new comparability profit-sharing plan are examples of defined contribution plans that may be tested for nondiscrimination on the basis of benefits—in other words, cross-tested plans.

D. STOCK BONUS PLAN

LO 46.9 Explain the features of a stock bonus plan and how it differs from other profit-sharing plans.

A **stock bonus plan** is a type of profit-sharing plan with one major difference from a traditional profit-sharing plan: the employer contributions and benefits distributed from the plan are generally made in the form of employer stock, not in cash. In a stock bonus plan, the employer contributes either cash or employer securities to the individual participants' accounts in accordance with normal defined contribution rules and limitations. A stock bonus plan is appropriate for an employer with unstable cash flow who does not wish to deplete needed cash and, instead, wishes to make contributions in the form of listed or closely held stock.

A major employee tax advantage of participating in a stock bonus plan is the ability to defer **net unrealized appreciation (NUA)** on employer securities if the distribution of stock is in a lump sum. Under the NUA tax benefit, participant retirees are not taxed on the full FMV of employer stock when it is distributed. Instead, the NUA is taxed as long-term capital gain when the participant or beneficiary subsequently sells the stock. At the time of distribution, the participant recognizes as ordinary income an amount equal to the value of the stock at the time of contribution. This ordinary income recognition establishes a tax basis in the employer stock for the employee-participant that is recovered tax free as a return of basis upon sale of the stock. Any further appreciation of the stock subsequent to the time of the lump-sum distribution is then subject to short-term or long-term capital gain tax treatment, depending on the holding period after the lump-sum distribution. The NUA portion of the lump-sum distribution will always be treated as long-term capital gain, regardless of the holding period after the lump-sum distribution.

There are disadvantages associated with investing so much of a retirement plan's assets in employer stock. A primary disadvantage is the participant now has a largely undiversified, or concentrated, portfolio. Another disadvantage is the dilution of existing ownership that occurs under both a stock bonus and employee stock ownership plan.

Finally, under the Pension Protection Act of 2006 (PPA), for plan years beginning after 2006, employers that sponsor qualified plans in which a portion of the plan accounts is invested in the employer's publicly traded stock must permit participants to immediately divest themselves of the stock and diversify the proceeds into other plan investments. This diversification rule is not applicable to employee stock ownership plans that do not hold employee contributions.

EXAMPLE   Brett received a lump-sum distribution of stock (10,000 shares) from his employer's qualified plan valued at $1 million. The fair market value of the stock contributed over the years was $250,000.

- In this example, $750,000 is treated as net unrealized appreciation (NUA) and is not taxed upon distribution. In the year of the lump-sum distribution, $250,000 will be taxable as ordinary income.

- Because $250,000 was treated as ordinary income at the time of distribution, Brett's adjusted taxable basis in the 10,000 shares equals $250,000. If Brett sells shares of stock, his adjusted taxable basis for tax purposes will equal $25 per share and any gain will be subject to capital gains tax, short or long term, depending on Brett's holding period since the distribution.

E. EMPLOYEE STOCK OWNERSHIP PLAN (ESOP)

LO 46.10   Explain how to structure an employee stock ownership plan (ESOP) and where it is used in business and retirement planning.

An **employee stock ownership plan (ESOP)** is a type of stock bonus plan in which individual participant accounts are invested primarily in employer stock. It has a unique advantage over every other type of qualified plan in that the ESOP may borrow money in the name of the plan without violating the prohibited transaction rules. If the ESOP does borrow money in the plan's name, it is commonly referred to as a **leveraged ESOP (LESOP)** and engages in a series of transactions, diagrammed on the following page.

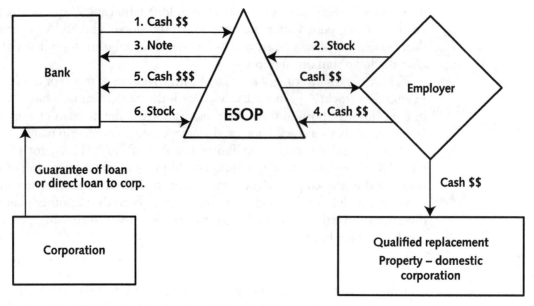

1. The plan trustee secures a bank loan.
2. The plan trustee purchases employer stock with loan proceeds.
3. The stock is pledged as loan collateral.
4. With the cash from the stock sale, the employer makes a contribution to the ESOP.
5. The employer's cash contribution is used to pay off the loan.
6. The bank releases the stock to the ESOP.

Important observations regarding the previous diagram include the following:

- The employer stock is pledged as collateral for the loan secured in the name of the ESOP; thus, an ESOP is only appropriate for an incorporated business (a C or S corporation).

- With the cash from the sale of the stock, the employer makes a cash contribution to the ESOP; thus, in selling the stock to the employees of the business, the employer is now making them owners of the business.

- A market is created for employer stock that helps improve the marketability of the stock for existing shareholders; thus, an ESOP is appropriate for creating a market for stock (particularly for closely held stock).

Like the stock bonus plan, an ESOP provides the tax advantages of NUA for employer stock distributed in a lump sum to employee-shareholders.

An ESOP is a rather complex retirement plan and is most appropriate when:

- the employer wishes to make the employees owners of the business through a tax advantaged means and at a relatively low cost;

- the employer wishes to provide an advantageous vehicle for the company to borrow money for business needs; and

- the owner of the business wants to engage in estate and financial planning that creates a market for the stock (at the expense of having additional shareholders).

As mentioned in Unit 1, an ESOP may not be integrated with Social Security.

Choose the best answer for the question below.

1. ABC Corp. is considering establishing a qualified plan and has the following objectives:

■   Simplicity

■   Ability of the plan to be integrated with Social Security

■   Funding flexibility

■   Ability to invest in company stock in an unrestricted manner

■   Employees can make in-service withdrawals

■   Distributions of the plan retirement benefits in cash if the company so chooses

■   Immediate tax deduction for the value of the stock contributed to the plan

Which one of the following types of qualified plans would meet ABC's objectives?

A.   ESOP
B.   Stock bonus plan
C.   Money purchase pension plan
D.   Cash balance pension plan

Answer: B.   A stock bonus plan for ABC Corp. is the best choice. An ESOP cannot be integrated with Social Security. Money purchase pension plans and cash balance pension plans cannot invest in company stock in an unrestricted manner, nor does it have contribution (funding) flexibility.

F. SECTION 401(K) PLANS

LO 46.7   Describe the general characteristics and types of Section 401(k) plans.

The plural of the Section 401(k) heading is used here because there is more than one type of Section 401(k) plan. There are actually four types of **Section 401(k)** plans. They are the:

■   traditional Section 401(k) plan;

■   safe harbor Section 401(k) plan;

■   SIMPLE 401(k); and

■   Roth 401(k).

Traditional Section 401(k) Plan

A **traditional Section 401(k) plan** is also known as a qualified **cash or deferred arrangement (CODA)**. It is a qualified profit-sharing or stock bonus plan under which plan participants have an option to contribute money to the plan on a pretax basis, known as an **elective deferral**, or receive taxable cash compensation. Although elective deferrals are not subject to income taxation, they are subject to FICA and FUTA taxes. As in all qualified plans, the employee is immediately 100% vested in all elective deferrals and their accrued earnings. Because the participant has the right to receive cash compensation, a Section 401(k) plan is an exception to the constructive receipt rules of income taxation. Amounts contributed to the Section 401(k) plan are not taxable until withdrawn by the participant.

The maximum amount that may be contributed to the Section 401(k) plan by the participant on a pretax basis is specified by law and is indexed for inflation. The maximum elective deferral is $18,000 (2015). Participants at least age 50 by the end of the taxable year can make additional catch-up contributions of $6,000 (2015). As discussed earlier, an employer can make additional contributions to the participant's account in the form of matching contributions or profit-sharing contributions. Employer-matching contributions are typically a dollar-for-dollar match or $0.50 match for each dollar the participant defers, up to a specified limit. Employer deductions for plan contributions cannot exceed 25% of the aggregate covered compensation of plan participants. The annual additions limit of $53,000 (2015) applies to individual participants.

A Section 401(k) plan must not only satisfy the general nondiscrimination tests (percentage coverage, ratio, or average benefits percentage test) but must also satisfy special nondiscrimination tests known as the **actual deferral percentage (ADP) test** and **actual contribution percentage (ACP) test**. Because of these tests, a traditional 401(k) plan can be relatively costly and complex to administer. In the ADP test, the employer must compare the average percentage of eligible HCEs' pretax elective deferrals to the average percentage of the eligible non-HCEs' elective deferrals. Catch-up elective deferrals are not considered in the ADP calculation.

The ACP test follows the same procedure but uses employer matching contributions and employee after-tax contributions in the calculations.

To satisfy the ADP test, a traditional 401(k) plan must meet one of the following two tests:

- The ADP for eligible HCEs must not be more than the ADP of all other eligible employees multiplied by 1.25.

- The ADP for eligible HCEs must not exceed the ADP for other eligible employees by more than 2%, and the ADP for eligible HCEs must not be more than the ADP of all other eligible employees multiplied by 2.

Summary of ADP Rules

If ADP for non-HCE:	Maximum ADP for HCE is:
≤ 2%	2 × ADP of non-HCE
> 2%, but ≤ 8%	2% + ADP of non-HCE
> 8%	1.25 × ADP of non-HCE

PRACTICE
QUESTION

Choose the best answer for the question below.

1. If the ADP for non-HCEs is 3%, what is the maximum ADP for the HCEs?

Answer: The maximum ADP for HCEs is 5% (3% plus 2%).

If the ADP test fails, the employer has two options.

- A corrective distribution can be made that will decrease the ADP of the HCEs, converting pretax dollars of the HCEs to taxable dollars.

- An additional matching or nonelective contribution may be made for the non-HCEs by the employer.

Both employer matching and nonelective contributions made on behalf of non-HCEs are known as **qualified matching contributions** and **qualified nonelective contributions**. These contributions count toward meeting the defined contribution annual additions limit. Corrective distributions have no effect on the non-HCEs.

The ACP test applies to employer matching and employee after-tax contributions (not pretax contributions or elective deferrals). Compliance with the ACP test is only a concern if the employer matches the employee elective deferrals. If the employer does not match employee elective deferrals or does not allow employee after-tax contributions, only the ADP test must be satisfied. Because most employers do match employee elective deferrals, satisfaction of the ACP is also relevant for most employers sponsoring a traditional Section 401(k). The ACP test has the same percentage rules as the ADP test.

Summary of ACP Rules

If ACP for non-HCE:	Maximum ACP for HCE is:
≤ 2%	2 × ACP of non-HCE
> 2%, but ≤ 8%	2% + ACP of non-HCE
> 8%	1.25 × ACP of non-HCE

A traditional Section 401(k) plan is appropriate when:

■ an employer wants to provide a qualified retirement plan for employees but can afford only minimal expense beyond existing salary costs [such a plan can be funded entirely from employee salary reductions, except for installation and administration (testing) costs];

■ employees are relatively young and have substantial time to accumulate retirement savings; and

■ employers want to encourage employees to save for their own retirement.

Pension Protection Act of 2006 (PPA) Automatic Enrollment in Traditional Section 401(k) Plans

Applicable to plan years beginning on or after January 1, 2008, PPA provides several incentives for sponsoring employers to adopt automatic enrollment in their Section 401(k) plans. Automatic enrollment, also known as a **negative election**, allows an employer to enroll employees in the Section 401(k) plan without the employees' consent, as long as the employees have the right to opt out of contributing. The PPA includes safe harbor rules that would relieve a **qualified automatic contribution arrangement (QACA)** from special non-discrimination testing, with lower required employer contributions than under the current safe harbor Section 401(k) plan rules. Such an arrangement will automatically qualify with Section 401(k) nondiscrimination testing if it:

■ provides for an automatic deferral percentage between 3% and 10% of employee compensation (if the automatic deferral percentage under the plan is less than 6%, a participant's automatic deferral percentage must be increased each year by 1% until reaching at least 6% of compensation);

■ provides an employer contribution to non-HCEs of either an employer match of 100% of the first 1% deferred plus 50% of the next 5% or a 3% profit-sharing contribution in lieu of the matching contribution;

■ provides that the employer contributions become 100% vested after the employee has completed no more than two years of service; and

■ requires that, within 30 days prior to enrollment (and annually thereafter), eligible employees must be given a written **Automatic Enrollment Notice** and a **Qualified Default Investment Notice** and allow the employees not to make any contributions, if they so choose.

In addition, under the PPA, non-safe harbor automatic enrollment arrangements will have additional time to test for discrimination (under the ADP or ACP tests) and, if needed, make corrective distributions (six months after the end of the plan year rather than the normal 2½ months).

PRACTICE
QUESTIONS   *Choose the best answer for each of the questions below.*

1. In a traditional Section 401(k) plan, which of the following must be considered in complying with the maximum annual additions limit?
1. Employee elective deferrals
2. Catch-up contributions for an employee age 50 or older
3. Qualified nonelective contributions
4. Qualified matching contributions

A. 1 and 2
B. 1, 2, and 4
C. 1, 3, and 4
D. 3 and 4

Answer: C. All of the above are counted against the annual additions limit except catch-up contributions for an employee age 50 or older. Such contributions are not taken into account for the annual additions limit or for purposes of ADP special nondiscrimination testing.

2. Janice, age 54, has an annual salary of $120,000 and participates in a traditional Section 401(k) plan sponsored by her employer. The plan provides for a 50% company match on the first 6% of an employee's salary deferred. If Janice makes the maximum elective deferral for 2015 (including catch-up contributions), what additional amount can her employer contribute on her behalf without exceeding the annual additions limit?

A. $25,900
B. $31,400
C. $30,900
D. $53,000

Answer: B. The company can contribute an additional $31,400 in 2015 on behalf of Janice, calculated as follows:

Maximum limit:	$53,000
Less regular elective deferral:	−$18,000
Less employer match:	−$ 3,600 ($120,000 × .06 × .50)
Additional amount:	$31,400

Janice's catch-up contributions of $6,000 in 2015 do not count against the annual additions limit.

Safe Harbor Section 401(k) Plan

Employers can avoid having to comply with special nondiscrimination testing (ADP and ACP tests) that apply to traditional Section 401(k) plans if the plan meets one of the safe harbor provisions under IRC Section 401(k)(12) and the Treasury Regulations. The **safe harbor Section 401(k) plan** permits a high level of elective deferrals by employees without annual discrimination testing. In addition, the safe harbor alternative is not subject to the top-heavy plan provisions. However, a mandatory minimum employer contribution is required in the safe harbor plan in which the employee must be 100% vested immediately. The two mandatory minimum employer contribution methods are:

- a nonelective contribution of 3% of compensation for all eligible employees (regardless of whether these employees are deferring salary into the Section 401(k) plan or not); or

- an employer matching contribution of 100% on the first 3% of non-HCE compensation plus a 50% match on the next 2% of non-HCE compensation (a total of 4%) for those non-HCEs who are actually deferring salary into the 401(k) plan. In tabular form, these matching contributions may be shown as follows:

Safe Harbor Basic Matching Formula

Employee Contribution as a % of Compensation	Employer Matching Contribution as a % of Compensation
0%	0%
1%	1%
2%	2%
3%	3%
4%	3.5%
5% or greater	4%

Many small businesses that wish to adopt a Section 401(k) plan will opt for the safe harbor arrangement because it is less expensive to operate and does not need to be tested annually. The plan permits a high level of salary deferrals by employees without annual discrimination testing. In addition, similar to any profit-sharing plan, hardship withdrawals and loans are permitted in the safe harbor Section 401(k), a characteristic that is important to a small businessowner and employee-participants.

PRACTICE
QUESTION   *Choose the best answer for the question below.*

1. Marten Publications has just implemented a safe harbor Section 401(k) plan. Which of the following may be avoided with the safe harbor arrangement?
   1. ADP test
   2. ACP test
   3. Top-heavy rules
   4. General nondiscrimination tests (coverage rules)

   A. 1 and 2
   B. 1, 2, and 3
   C. 1, 2, and 4
   D. 3 and 4

Answer: B. Safe harbor 401(k) plans are not required to comply with ADP, ACP, or top-heavy rules. However, as a qualified plan, it still must comply with the general nondiscrimination tests or coverage rules.

SIMPLE 401(k) Plan

There are two forms of savings incentive match plans for employees (SIMPLEs): a SIMPLE IRA plan and a **SIMPLE 401(k) plan**. The more prevalent of the two is the SIMPLE IRA, which will be discussed in the next unit. However, a Section 401(k) may also be structured as a SIMPLE plan for some employers. Employers with 100 or fewer employees earning $5,000 (or more) during the preceding year may adopt a SIMPLE 401(k) plan. The employer may not maintain any other qualified or employer-sponsored plan. However, if eligible, the employer can maintain a Section 457 plan (also discussed in the next unit) for the benefit of its employees. The SIMPLE 401(k), like the safe harbor option, is exempt from the special nondiscrimination testing that applies to the traditional Section 401(k) plan.

Employees who participate in a SIMPLE 401(k) may make elective deferrals similar to the traditional Section 401(k) plan. However, the maximum deferral limits are less than those permitted under a traditional Section 401(k) plan. For example, in 2015, employee elective deferrals to the SIMPLE 401(k) are limited to $12,500 with a catch-up contribution for those employees age 50 or older of $3,000. The employer-sponsor of the plan may match those elective deferral amounts up to 3% of employee compensation, or, alternatively, make a flat (nonelective) contribution of 2% of compensation for all eligible employees, even those employees who choose not to make elective deferrals. Unlike traditional Section 401(k) employer contributions for which vesting schedules are permissible, the employee is always 100% vested in the contributions made to a SIMPLE 401(k) by the employer.

Historically, the major advantage for employer implementation of the SIMPLE 401(k) option rather than the SIMPLE IRA was, as a qualified plan, it offered creditor protection of the assets within the plan. However, legislation has minimized this advantage in part. Specifically, subsequent to October 2005, the first $1 million of assets (inflation-adjusted) included in initially established IRAs of any type, including the SIMPLE IRA, are protected from creditor claims in the case of bankruptcy. This amount is unlimited for a rollover IRA holding a qualified rollover distribution from a qualified plan.

PRACTICE
QUESTION

Choose the best answer for the question below.

1. Tommy's Meat Market is a small business with only 20 employees. The business has adopted a SIMPLE 401(k) plan for the benefit of its employees. It now wishes to implement another plan on their behalf. Which one of the following plans, if any, may Tommy's Meat Market adopt immediately?

A. A simplified employee pension (SEP) plan
B. A traditional profit-sharing plan
C. A cash balance pension plan
D. None of the above

Answer: D. Because it has already established a SIMPLE 401(k) plan, Tommy's Meat Market may not have any other type of employer sponsored retirement plan. Some employers may be eligible to also have a Section 457 plan, but Tommy's Meat Market does not meet the criteria for establishing a Section 457 plan.

Roth 401(k) Plan

A **Roth 401(k) plan** is a type of Section 401(k) plan in which elective deferral contributions are permitted on an after-tax basis. A separate account is created for the Roth contributions and related earnings. The maximum contribution to such a plan is, as in the traditional Section 401(k), $18,000 (2015). Participants age 50 or older may contribute an additional $6,000 (for 2015) of after-tax dollars. If the employee also defers salary to a traditional Section 401(k) account, the total amount deferred under both the Roth and traditional Section 401(k) plans combined is limited to $18,000 and $6,000 catch-up (2015). Unlike the Roth IRA (to be discussed in Unit 5), the ability to make contributions to a Roth 401(k) is not phased out based on the taxpayer's AGI. Thus, high-income wage earners may find the Roth 401(k) option a very attractive retirement savings vehicle.

The major difference between the traditional Section 401(k) plan and the Roth 401(k) plan is the tax treatment of the contributions and distributions. Only the employer matching contributions (if any) and the related earnings associated with a Roth 401(k) are taxable. The employer contributions are made to a traditional Section 401(k) account on behalf of the employee. Employee contributions to the Roth 401(k), and earnings on such contributions, are generally tax free. The distribution of earnings from employee contributions is tax free if both of the following tests are met:

- The distribution must be made after a five-year period from the date of the first regular contribution to the Roth 401(k) plan.

- The distribution is made after the date on which the participant has attained age 59½ or becomes disabled, or it is made to a beneficiary of a deceased participant.

Minimum distribution rules that apply to traditional Section 401(k) plans also apply to Roth 401(k) accounts.

The following table is a comparison of the major characteristics of regular and Roth 401(k) plans.

Attribute	Traditional Section 401(k)	Roth 401(k)
Employee funding	Pretax	After-tax
Employer matching	Pretax	Pretax (to traditional Section 401(k) account)
Allowable employee contributions	$18,000 plus $6,000 catch-up (2015)	$18,000 plus $6,000 catch-up (2015) (less any contributions to traditional Section 401(k) plan)
Qualified distributions after age 59½ subject to tax?	Yes, all amounts	Only employer matching contributions and earnings
Minimum distribution requirement?	Yes, starting at age 70½ or date of retirement (unless >5% owner)	Yes, starting at age 70½ or date of retirement (unless >5% owner)
Rollover options	Tax free rollover to traditional IRA	Tax free rollover to another Roth 401(k) or Roth IRA

Section 401(k) plans that permit Roth contributions may allow participants to convert pre-tax amounts that qualify as eligible rollover distributions into Roth accounts within the same plan. The IRS has determined that the 10% early distribution penalty does not apply for this type of conversion. Upon distribution, all of the conversion rules apply. The mandatory 20% withholding from the conversion does not apply. The conversion amount is still taxable, but the taxpayer may pay the income tax from other funds.

Choose the best answer for the question below.

1. All of the following with respect to a Roth 401(k) are correct EXCEPT
   A.   the maximum elective deferral (younger than age 50 participant) to a Roth 401(k) is $18,000 for 2015
   B.   individuals age 50 or older may contribute an additional $6,000 to a Roth 401(k) for 2015
   C.   elective deferral contributions and catch-up contributions are made with after-tax dollars
   D.   the ability to make contributions to a Roth 401(k) is phased out based on the taxpayer's AGI

   Answer: D.   Unlike a Roth IRA, the ability to make contributions to a Roth 401(k) is not phased out based on the participant's AGI.

G. SAVINGS/THRIFT PLAN

LO 46.12   Describe the characteristics of a thrift plan and when it is appropriate for a business to choose.

A **savings/thrift plan** is a qualified defined contribution plan similar to a traditional profit-sharing plan except that it provides for and encourages after-tax employee contributions to the plan. The typical thrift plan provides for after-tax employee contributions with matching employer contributions. Pure thrift plans, featuring only after-tax employee contributions, have generally been replaced with the Section 401(k) type of plan.

The plan is most appropriate when:

- the employees are relatively young and have substantial time to accumulate retirement savings;

- the employees are willing to assume a degree of investment risk;

- there is a wide variation among employees in the need or desire for retirement savings; and

- the employer wants to supplement the company's defined benefit pension plan with a plan that features individual participant accounts.

H. SPECIAL RULES FOR SELF-EMPLOYED PLANS (KEOGH PLANS)

LO 47.3   Describe the limitations on contributions and benefits in qualified plans.

LO 48.7   Identify special rules applicable to a retirement plan for self-employed owners.

A **Keogh (self-employed) plan** is an employer-sponsored retirement plan that covers one or more self-employed individuals, such as a sole proprietor or a partner. It can be set up as any type of defined benefit pension, defined contribution, or tax-advantaged retirement plan. However, the three most common types of Keogh plans are profit-sharing, money purchase pension, and target benefit pension plans, all of which are defined contribution plans.

Member-owners of LLCs taxed as a sole proprietor or partnership are considered self-employed individuals for this purpose. A Keogh plan is fundamentally like any other qualified or tax-advantaged plan (it must comply with the same technical requirements) except for two differences.

- Self-employed individuals must calculate their retirement plan contribution based on earned income, or net earnings from self-employment, instead of W-2 income.

- Self-employed individuals must use a net contribution rate in determining their allowable contribution to a Keogh defined contribution plan (for example, a profit-sharing plan). This rate is calculated by dividing the plan contribution percentage by (1 + the contribution percentage). For example, the maximum contribution for a self-employed participant in a plan with a 25% contribution formula is 20% [.25 divided by (1 + .25)].

Earned income takes the place of compensation (W-2) income in applying the special rules applicable to Keogh plans. In calculating earned income of a self-employed individual, self-employment tax must be calculated, and a deduction of one-half of the self-employment tax must be taken before determining the Keogh deduction. This creates a circular calculation because the amount of self-employment tax (SE tax) deduction is not known before the calculation of earned income, and the amount of earned income cannot be derived without knowing the self-employment tax deduction. Following are the steps in determining the Keogh deduction.

1. Determine the net income of the business from Schedule C, IRS Form 1040, or the Schedule K-1 provided to the partner or the LLC member-partner.

2. Subtract the deductible amount of SE tax applicable from that income.

3. Multiply the result by the net contribution rate.

EXAMPLE Ken, a sole proprietor, earns $70,000 of net Schedule C income in 2015. Ken's business maintains a profit-sharing plan with a 25% contribution on behalf of all employees. Ken's deductible contribution as an owner-employee of the business is calculated as follows:

Schedule C income:	$70,000	
Less: deductible amount of SE tax paid:	(4,945)	[($70,000 × .9235 × .0765)]
Equals:	$65,055	
Multiply by net contribution rate:	× 0.20	
Maximum deductible contribution:	$13,011	

Note: The deductible amount of self-employment tax on Schedule C income of $118,500, the Social Security taxable wage base (2015), or less may be calculated using this shortcut method: ($70,000 × .9235 × .0765) = $4,945. See the 104: Income Tax Planning course to learn how to make this calculation when Schedule C income exceeds the taxable wage base.

Important concepts with respect to this contribution include the following:

- The net contribution rate of 20% is determined by dividing .25 by (1 + .25). If the plan contribution percentage was 15%, divide .15 by (1 + .15) for a net contribution rate of 13.04%.

■ This calculation applies only to the owner-employee of the business (or the self-employed individual); those individuals who work for the owner-employee (or the rank-and-file employee) are entitled to a full or unadjusted deductible contribution.

■ The deductible contribution for the owner-employee is an above-the-line deduction on IRS Form 1040.

PRACTICE
QUESTION

Choose the best answer for the question below.

1. The deductible contribution to a money purchase pension plan on behalf of a self-employed individual whose net income from self-employment is $20,000 and whose deductible SE tax is $1,413 is limited to

A. $3,000

B. $3,717

C. $4,714

D. $5,000

Answer: B. The maximum deductible contribution on behalf of the self-employed individual is $3,717, calculated as follows:

Schedule C income:	$20,000.00
Less: deductible self-employment tax:	($ 1,413.00)
Equals:	$18,587.00
Multiply by net contribution rate:	× 0.20 (.25 divided by 1.25)
Maximum deductible contribution:	$ 3,717.40

Remember that a money purchase pension plan has a maximum deductible contribution of 25% of employee covered compensation.

Keoghs Versus Other Qualified and Tax-Advantaged Plans

Keogh plans cover self-employed individuals who are not considered employees. The most important special rule for Keoghs is the definition of earned income. Earned income takes the place of compensation in applying the plan rules for Keoghs and is defined as the self-employed individual's net business income after all deductions, including the deduction for Keogh plan contributions. In addition, the IRS has ruled that the self-employment tax must be calculated, and a deduction of one-half of the self-employment tax must be taken before determining the Keogh deduction.

Life insurance can be used as an incidental benefit in a qualified plan covering self-employed individuals, but the tax treatment is different from that applicable to regular employees in a qualified plan. The entire cost of life insurance for regular employees is deductible as a plan contribution. Employees then include the value of the pure life insurance element as extra taxable compensation.

For a self-employed individual, the pure life insurance element of an insurance premium is not deductible. Only the portion of the premium that exceeds the pure protection value of the insurance is deductible. The pure protection value of the insurance is determined using Table 2001.

Regular employees have a cost basis (a nontaxable recovery element) in a plan equal to any Table 2001 costs if the plan distribution is made from the same life insurance contract on which the Table 2001 costs were paid. For a self-employed individual, however, the Table 2001 costs, although effectively included in income because they were nondeductible, are not includable in the cost basis.

PRACTICE
QUESTION   *Choose the best answer for the question below.*

1. Blake is a CFP® professional and was introduced to Karl by Blake's sister, Jan, today. Jan works at the bank that has Karl's business and personal accounts. When she refers a client to Blake, she is given a small finder's fee. Karl is the sole shareholder of a closely held corporation and is considering various profit-sharing plan alternatives for providing a qualified retirement plan to his employees and saving for his own retirement. He feels he needs the advice of a financial planning professional and likes what he has learned of Blake's services. What is Blake's next step in helping Karl choose the best profit-sharing plan alternative?

   A. Blake asks for all the documentation about Karl's personal financial status and gets detailed information on the company's finances, employee census, and more details on what Karl wants to accomplish with the retirement plan.

   B. Blake recommends a profit-sharing plan with a Section 401(k) feature to allow employees to also contribute to their own retirement.

   C. Blake discusses the financial planning process with Karl and explains the scope of services he will provide; he also discloses in writing his relationship to Jan and her finder's fee and issues a client engagement letter to Karl.

   D. Because Karl wants to choose a retirement plan for his corporation, Blake must decline to provide any services as he can only provide financial planning services to individuals and not entities.

   Answer: C. Blake is still in the very first step of the financial planning process and must make all regulatory and other disclosures now and provide an engagement letter with the scope of services he intends to provide to Karl. (Domain 1: Establishing and defining the client-planner relationship)

105 UNIT 3 POST-STUDY CHECKLIST

☐ Do I know how to differentiate between the different types of qualified plans and explain the basic provisions of each plan?

☐ Can I describe the main features of a defined contribution plan and identify its advantages and disadvantages?

☐ Can I describe the basic provisions of a traditional profit-sharing plan?

☐ Can I describe the general characteristics and types of Section 401(k) plans?

☐ Can I describe the characteristics of an age-based profit-sharing plan?

☐ Am I able to explain the features of a stock bonus plan and how it differs from other profit-sharing plans?

☐ Am I able to explain how to structure an employee stock ownership plan (ESOP) and where it is used in business and retirement planning?

☐ Am I able to explain the features of a new comparability plan and how it can satisfy the nondiscrimination rules?

☐ Can I describe the characteristics of a thrift plan and when it is appropriate for a business to choose?

☐ Do I know how to describe the limitations on contributions and benefits in qualified plans?

☐ Am I able to identify special rules applicable to a retirement plan for self-employed owners?

Am I able to define and understand the application of the following terms to financial planning?

☐ Actual contribution percentage (ACP) test

☐ Actual deferral percentage (ADP) test

☐ Age-based profit-sharing plan

☐ Automatic Enrollment Notice

☐ Cash or deferred arrangement (CODA)

☐ Cross-tested plan

☐ Defined contribution plan

☐ Elective deferral

☐ Employee stock ownership plan (ESOP)

☐ Financial needs test

☐ Hardship withdrawal

☐ HR-10 plan

☐ In-plan Roth rollover

☐ In-service distribution

☐ Keogh plan

☐ Leveraged ESOP (LESOP)

☐ Negative election

☐ Net unrealized appreciation (NUA)

☐ New comparability plan (NCP)

☐ Profit-sharing plan

☐ Qualified automatic contribution arrangement (QACA)

☐ Qualified default investment notice

☐ Qualified matching contributions

☐ Qualified nonelective contributions

☐ Resources test

☐ Roth 401(k) plan

☐ Safe harbor Section 401(k) plan

☐ Savings/thrift plan

☐ SIMPLE 401(k) plan

☐ Stock bonus plan

☐ Substantial and recurring

☐ Traditional Section 401(k) plan

Tax-Advantaged Plans and Nonqualified Plans

REFER TO

CFP® Certification Principal Topics – Retirement Planning, Qualified Plan Rules and Options

CFP® Certification Principal Topics – Retirement Planning, Other Tax-Advantaged Retirement Plans

CFP® Certification Principal Topics – Retirement Planning, Distribution Rules, Alternatives, and Taxation

Supplemental Readings Section of this 105 Retirement Planning Student Guide

(For specific assignments, refer to class syllabus.)

INTRODUCTION

This is the last of three units discussing employer-sponsored retirement plans. The plans addressed in this unit are best categorized as tax-advantaged plans rather than qualified plans. The term *tax-advantaged* means the plans have very similar requirements to qualified retirement plans, but the provisions of each plan are addressed in a separate Tax Code section other than Section 401, which applies to qualified plans.

Several of the plans addressed in this unit are essentially IRAs sponsored by a participant's employer. Among these plans are the simplified employee pension IRA (SEP IRA) and a savings incentive match plan for employees IRA (SIMPLE IRA). In addition, this unit will consider plans that may be established by public or private tax-exempt employers, such as the tax-sheltered annuity (known as a TSA or a Section 403(b) plan). Also discussed is the Section 457 plan that may be established for state and local government employees.

LEARNING OBJECTIVES

After completing this unit, you should be able to achieve the following learning objectives:

CFP® Certification Principal Topics – Retirement Planning, Qualified Plan Rules and Options

LO 47.4   Explain the rules for contributions to multiple retirement plans.

CFP® Certification Principal Topics – Retirement Planning, Other Tax-Advantaged Plans

LO 48.3   Describe the basic provisions of a simplified employee pension (SEP) and its suitability for a for-profit small business.

LO 48.4   Describe the basic provisions of a savings incentive match plan for employees (SIMPLE) IRA and its suitability for a for-profit small business.

LO 48.5   Explain the characteristics of the Section 403(b) plan for a tax-exempt employer and compare to a Section 401(k) plan.

LO 48.6   Discuss the differences between a Section 457 plan for private tax-exempt employers and such plans established for state and local government employees.

LO 48.8   Identify the types of tax-advantaged plans and the characteristics of each plan.

LO 48.9   Identify the characteristics of a SARSEP plan.

LO 48.10 Distinguish top-hat plans from qualified plans and tax-advantaged plans.

CFP® Certification Principal Topics – Retirement Planning, Distribution Rules, Alternatives, and Taxation

LO 52.1   Discuss premature distributions from a retirement plan and the exceptions allowed.

KEY TERMS

Nonqualified deferred compensation plans	SIMPLE
Salary reduction SEP (SARSEP)	Simplified employee pension (SEP) plan
Savings incentive match plan for employees (SIMPLE) IRA	Tax-advantaged
Section 403(b) plan	Tax-sheltered annuity (TSA)
Section 457 plan	Top-hat plans

A. TAX-ADVANTAGED PLANS VERSUS QUALIFIED PLANS

LO 48.8   Identify the types of tax-advantaged plans and the characteristics of each plan.

Tax-advantaged plans have nondiscrimination rules that differ from those that apply to qualified plans, although they generally avoid the issue entirely by requiring almost universal coverage. Nevertheless, tax-advantaged plans are more like qualified plans than other nonqualified plans and should not be confused with the nonqualified deferred compensation plans discussed in the *102: Insurance and Employee Benefits* course. Neither the 10-year averaging, special pre-1974 participation capital gain treatment nor the special net unrealized appreciation (NUA) treatment for employer stock distributions (discussed in Unit 6) is available for nonqualified plans, including the tax-advantaged plans discussed in this unit.

The following plans are tax-advantaged plans and have many similarities to qualified plans, especially regarding tax treatment:

■   Simplified employee pension plans (SEPs)

■   Traditional individual retirement annuities and accounts (traditional IRAs)

■   Roth IRAs

■   Savings incentive match plan for employees (SIMPLE)

■   Section 403(b) plans (TSAs)

Each plan makes the same promise to the plan participant—to pay the balance of the individual account at retirement. The distribution rules are essentially the same as those for qualified plans.

Nonqualified plans do not benefit from all of the tax advantages that apply to qualified plans or other tax-advantaged plans. These plans are generally discriminatory in favor of highly compensated employees. Nonqualified plans may supplement qualified plans and may defer taxes for the employee participants and are commonly referred to as top-hat plans.

B. SIMPLES

LO 48.4   Describe the basic provisions of a savings incentive match plan for employees (SIMPLE) IRA and its suitability for a for-profit small business.

LO 52.1   Discuss premature distributions from a retirement plan and the exceptions allowed.

Characteristics

There are two types of savings incentive match plans for employees, or **SIMPLEs**: SIMPLE IRAs and SIMPLE 401(k) (discussed in Unit 3). SIMPLE IRAs are not generally subject to the nondiscrimination and top-heavy rules applicable to qualified plans.

Employer contributions are deductible if made by the due date of the employer's tax return, including extensions, and are not subject to payroll taxes. Contributions made by employees are excludable from the employee's gross income for income tax purposes but are still subject to payroll taxes.

Plan assets for SIMPLEs cannot be rolled over into another plan (other than another SIMPLE) within two years of initial participation, and after-tax contributions are not allowed.

Eligibility for SIMPLEs

An employer is eligible to establish a SIMPLE if it:

■ has 100 or fewer employees on any day during the year who earned at least $5,000 during the preceding year (there is a two-year grace period for continuing a plan if the number of employees subsequently exceeds 100); and

■ does not maintain another employer-sponsored retirement plan, SEP plan, SARSEP plan, or Section 403(b) plan. An employer may, however, maintain a Section 457 plan and also have a SIMPLE plan if eligibility requirements are met for both plans.

Self-employed individuals can also establish SIMPLEs.

Employees who earned $5,000 or more during any two preceding years and are reasonably expected to receive at least $5,000 during the current year must be allowed to participate.

SIMPLE IRA

The **savings incentive match plan for employees (SIMPLE) IRA** is the second form of an employer-sponsored SIMPLE plan available to employees. A SIMPLE IRA is easy to adopt by using IRS Form 5304-SIMPLE or Form 5305-SIMPLE and is less expensive to administer than a qualified plan.

As with a SIMPLE 401(k), an employer that adopts a SIMPLE IRA plan may not maintain a qualified plan, Section 403(b) plan, or SEP plan at the same time. But, if pursuant to an elective bargaining agreement, the employer maintains a qualified plan or SEP plan solely for union employees, the employer may establish a SIMPLE plan for other employees, excluding those covered in the union plan. The plan must be effective January 1 of any year for which contributions are made, unless it is the first year of adoption, in which case the effective date may be any date between January 1 and October 1 of the applicable year. Employees may make an elective deferral into the plan as a percentage of compensation up to $12,500 (2015). In addition, individuals who have attained age 50 may make additional catch-up contributions of $3,000 (2015). Salary reduction contributions (elective deferrals) are subject to FICA and FUTA withholding, but employer contributions are not.

The employee is 100% vested in both elective deferrals and employer contributions, and the plan is not subject to nondiscrimination rules generally applicable to qualified plans.

Employers make contributions to the SIMPLE IRA using one of the following two formulas:

■ An employer match of up to 3% of employee compensation; the employer can match as little as 1% of employee compensation in no more than two out of five years

■ A 2% of compensation nonelective contribution for each eligible employee

There is, however, an operational oddity as these contribution rules are applied to a SIMPLE IRA. If the employer elects the 3% match, the covered compensation limit of $265,000 applicable to qualified plans in 2015 does not apply. Rather, the operative amount is $416,667 ($12,500 divided by .03). In the application of the compensation limit to all tax-advantaged plans, this is the only exception to the $265,000 limit. As an example, and alternatively, if the sponsoring employer of a SIMPLE IRA uses the nonelective 2% option, the covered compensation limit does apply, and no more than $265,000 of compensation may be taken into account.

Unlike the SIMPLE 401(k), a 25% premature withdrawal penalty applies to distributions made from a SIMPLE IRA during the first two years of plan participation. Also, as a form of IRA, the SIMPLE IRA may not purchase life insurance as a funding vehicle and participant loans are unavailable.

PRACTICE QUESTIONS   *Choose the best answer for each of the questions below.*

1. Jean, age 38, earns $280,000 annually as an employee for Junk Trash, Inc. Her employer sponsors a SIMPLE IRA retirement plan and matches employee contributions to the plan 100% up to 3% of compensation. What is the maximum contribution (combined employee and employer) that can be made to Jean's SIMPLE IRA plan in 2015?
    A. $8,400
    B. $11,500
    C. $18,850
    D. $20,900

    Answer: D.   The maximum contribution that may be made on Jean's behalf is $20,900 ($12,500 of employee elective deferrals and $8,400 of employer contributions). Junk Trash, Inc., has chosen to make a matching contribution up to 3% of compensation (the SIMPLE maximum). Thus, the covered compensation limit of $265,000 does not apply, and it can be matched based on Jean's total salary ($280,000 × .03 = $8,400).

2. Which one of the following plans is NOT permitted to invest in life insurance?
    A. A SIMPLE 401(k)
    B. A traditional profit-sharing plan
    C. A SIMPLE IRA
    D. An ESOP

    Answer: C.   A SIMPLE IRA is a form of IRA and, therefore, cannot invest in life insurance (in the plan's name). All of the other types of plans are qualified plans and are, within limits, permitted to invest in life insurance.

C. SIMPLIFIED EMPLOYEE PENSION (SEP) IRA

LO 48.3   Describe the basic provisions of a simplified employee pension (SEP) and its suitability for a for-profit small business.

A **simplified employee pension (SEP) plan** is an employer-sponsored IRA in which the employer agrees to contribute retirement monies on behalf of employees on a nondiscriminatory and fully vested basis. Such a plan is used most frequently by self-employed individuals, including sole proprietors, but may be established by any form of business entity.

The major advantage of a SEP plan is its simplicity. It may be adopted by completing a single IRS form, IRS Form 5305-SEP. However, if an employer wishes to adopt a model SEP using Form 5305-SEP, it may not currently maintain another qualified plan. The SEP provides a unique advantage in that it may be adopted and funded as late as the due date of the sponsoring employer's tax return, including extensions. Other plans may be funded by this same date, but, generally, must have been adopted prior to the end of the tax year for which contributions are being made. The account established for the participant(s) is totally portable, meaning it can be easily rolled to another IRA or qualified plan (presuming the receiving plan document allows for it). It is appropriate when the employer wants an alternative to a qualified plan because contributions are discretionary, and overall the plan is less expensive to operate. The participant may self-direct the investments in the IRA.

The major SEP plan requirements include the following.

- The plan must cover all employees who are at least 21 years of age and who have worked for the employer for three out of the preceding five years. Part-time service counts for purposes of this requirement.

- Contributions must be made on behalf of any employee whose compensation was at least $600 (2015) for the tax year for which the contribution is being made and who otherwise meet eligibility requirements.

- The plan may exclude employees who are members of unions (or any other collective bargaining unit) if they have their own retirement plan.

The limits for SEP plan contributions are higher than those of traditional IRAs and are similar to those of the qualified plans. Specifically, SEP plan contributions are limited to the lesser of:

- 25% of the employee's compensation [limited to the covered compensation amount of $265,000 (2015)]; or

- $53,000 (2015).

Top-Heavy Rules

SEP plans are treated as defined contribution plans when applying the top-heavy rules if at the determination date (the last day of the preceding plan year) the sum of the account balances for key employees exceeds 60% of the total of all account balances in the SEP plan. There is a special rule for the 60% test for SEP plans: when calculating the 60% test, the total of all employer contributions made to the SEP plan for the plan participants made be used instead of the participant account balances.

If the SEP plan is determined to be top-heavy then the employer must make a minimum contribution of 3% of the employee's compensation for each non-key employee plan participant.

Disadvantages

Some potential disadvantages of SEP plans are that:

- employees cannot rely on a SEP plan alone to provide adequate retirement benefits because the benefits are not significant unless the employer makes substantial, regular contributions to the SEP plan and the employer has no obligation to do so;

■ the employee bears the investment risk under the plan;

■ if an employer maintains a SEP plan and a qualified plan, contributions to the SEP plan reduce the amount that may be deducted for contributions to the qualified plan; and

■ the special rule for calculating deductible contributions on behalf of an owner-employee also applies to a SEP plan, as noted in the discussion of Keogh plans.

Tax Implications

An employer may deduct contributions to a SEP plan up to the contribution limit. Distributions to employees from the plan are treated as distributions from an IRA. As with an IRA, investments in collectibles and life insurance are not allowed. A 10% excise tax may be assessed to the employer on excess contributions. For the employee, an excess IRA contribution may be subject to a 6% excise tax.

Participation in a SEP plan counts as active participant status for purposes of determining the deductibility of separate IRA contributions. Neither the 10-year averaging nor the special net unrealized appreciation (NUA) treatment for employer stock distributions is available.

PRACTICE
QUESTIONS   *Choose the best answer for each of the questions below.*

1. For 2015, what is the maximum amount possible that may be contributed to a SEP plan on behalf of an individual participant?
    A. $12,500
    B. $18,000
    C. $25,000
    D. $53,000

    Answer: D.   For 2015, the maximum contribution to a SEP plan is the lesser of 25% of employee covered compensation or $53,000.

2. Which of the following statements with respect to SEP contributions made by an employer is(are) CORRECT?
    1. Contributions are subject to FICA and FUTA.
    2. Contributions are currently excludible from the employee's gross income.
    3. Contributions are subject to income tax withholding.
    4. Contributions are capped at $18,000 (2015).

    A. 1 only
    B. 1 and 3
    C. 2 only
    D. 2 and 4

    Answer: C.   Statement 2 is the only correct response. Contributions to a SEP plan are not subject to FICA, FUTA, or income tax withholding and are excluded from the employee's current income. The SEP plan contribution limit is the lesser of 25% of the employee's compensation or $53,000 (2015) and not the elective deferral limit of $18,000 (2015).

D. SALARY REDUCTION SEP (SARSEP)

LO 48.9   Identify the characteristics of a SARSEP plan.

As of January 1, 1997, employers can no longer establish a **salary reduction SEP (SARSEP)** plan. Some employees, however, still participate in still active SARSEP plans.

The SARSEP plan contribution limit for employees is limited to $18,000 (2015). Individuals who have attained age 50 may make a catch-up contribution of $6,000 (2015). Elective deferrals (salary reduction contributions) are subject to Social Security (FICA) and federal unemployment (FUTA) taxes.

E. TAX-SHELTERED ANNUITY (TSA)/SECTION 403(B) PLAN

LO 48.5   Explain the characteristics of the Section 403(b) plan for a tax-exempt employer and compare to a Section 401(k) plan.

A **tax-sheltered annuity (TSA)**, also known as a a **Section 403(b) plan** after the Internal Revenue Code of the same number and subsection, is a tax-deferred retirement plan that may only be adopted by certain private, tax-exempt organizations or Section 501(c)(3) organizations. Among the qualifying participants are public school employees, hospital employees, and church employees. Plan contributions are not currently taxable to the employees, and income taxes are deferred until the funds are distributed to the employee by the plan. TSA funding is limited either to annuity contracts or mutual funds. The annuities can be either group or individual contracts and can be either fixed or variable. The annuity contracts give participants some degree of choice as to investment strategy. Custodial accounts invested in mutual funds are another type of permitted investment in a Section 403(b) plan. Many plans allow for both mutual funds and annuities.

Section 403(b) plans must comply with many of the same reporting and auditing requirements that apply to Section 401(k) plans. Several years ago the IRS introduced major changes that have transformed Section 403(b) plans from an employee-controlled, tax-sheltered account to a fully integrated plan for which Section 501(c)(3) organizations will now have responsibility for plan development, investment provider choices, plan administration, and regulatory compliance.

Section 403(b) plans may be established similar to Section 401(k) plans, that is, on the basis of employee salary reduction contributions only or with accompanying employer matching. Salary reductions, but not employer matching contributions, are subject to FICA and FUTA payroll taxes. Two limitations apply:

■   If the employer contributes, the qualified plan defined contribution limit of the lesser of 100% of employee compensation (up to $265,000 in 2015) or $53,000 (2015) applies.

■   Maximum elective deferrals by employees are limited to $18,000 (2015).

There are two catch-up provisions that apply to a Section 403(b) plan participant:

■   The regular catch-up provision of $6,000 (2015) is for individuals age 50 or older.

■ A special catch-up provision whereby a participant who has worked for a qualifying employer for 15 years may increase his contribution limit by an amount equal to the lesser of

— $3,000,

— $15,000 reduced by amounts previously deferred under the special catch-up, or

— $5,000 multiplied by the employee's years of service with the employer less the sum of all prior salary deferrals.

If an employee is eligible for both the age 50+ catch-up and the special catch-up, catch-up deferrals will first be considered special catch-up deferrals (until the lifetime maximum is exhausted) before applying a catch-up deferral as an age 50+ catch-up deferral. For example, if an eligible participant wishes to make a $5,000 catch-up contribution and has not yet exhausted the $15,000 lifetime special catch-up amount, $3,000 of the contribution will be classified as special catch-up and $2,000 will be classified as age 50+ catch-up.

It is possible that a Section 403(b) participant age 50 or older with 15 years of service can contribute $27,000 in any one year ($18,000 as an elective deferral, $6,000 as a regular age 50+ catch-up, and $3,000 under the special catch-up rule).

Section 403(b) plans that permit Roth contributions may allow participants to convert pretax amounts that qualify as eligible rollover distributions into Roth accounts within the plan. The IRS has determined the 10% early distribution penalty does not apply for this type of conversion. Upon distribution, all of the conversion rules apply. The mandatory 20% withholding from the conversion does not apply. The conversion amount is still taxable, but the taxpayer may pay the income tax from other funds.

A common misconception is that a Section 501(c)(3) employer (as a tax-exempt organization) cannot establish a Section 401(k) plan. As a result of recent legislation, it can choose to establish a Section 401(k) or Section 403(b) plan (or, infrequently, both). However, a Section 403(b) plan has certain advantages over a Section 401(k) plan. Among them are:

■ a Section 403(b) plan is not generally subject to special (ADP and ACP) nondiscrimination testing (it is, however, subject to ACP testing if employer-matching or after-tax employee contributions are permitted);

■ a Section 403(b) plan sponsored by a governmental or church organization is not subject to ERISA reporting and disclosure requirements;

■ a Section 403(b) plan sponsored by a Section 501(c)(3) employer without substantial employer involvement (i.e., the plan is only a salary deferral plan and there is no employer contribution and actual employer involvement is minimal under ERISA rules) may not be subject to ERISA reporting and disclosure requirements (DOL will analyze the plan on a case-by-case basis for the exemption); and

■ the increased limit on salary reduction contributions applies for employees who have completed 15 years of service with qualifying employers.

Disadvantages

While Section 403(b) plans are a great source of retirement savings, they do have some disadvantages. For example, account balances at retirement age may be insufficient to provide adequate retirement amounts for employees who entered the plan at later ages. Although the ADP test does not apply, Section 403(b) plans must comply with the ACP test for matching contributions. Employees bear the risk for investments in their individual accounts, and individual stocks and bonds are not permitted as investments in Section 403(b) plans.

In summary, a TSA/Section 403(b) plan is most appropriate when:

- the employee works for a public or private tax-exempt employer;

- the employer wants to provide a tax-deferred retirement plan for employees with a minimum of administrative expenses;

- employees are willing to accept the investment risk and investment responsibility associated with the plan; and

- a plan similar to a Section 401(k) plan is desired by a nonprofit employer for the benefit of its employees.

PRACTICE
QUESTIONS   *Choose the best answer for each of the questions below.*

1. What is the maximum employee contribution limit (elective deferral) for a TSA in 2015, assuming no catch-up provisions apply?
- A. $3,000
- B. $12,500
- C. $53,000
- D. $18,000

Answer: D.   The employee elective deferral limit for 2015 to a TSA is $18,000.

2. Which of the following are permitted investments in a Section 403(b) plan?
1.   Variable annuity contract from an insurance company
2.   Growth stock mutual fund (open-end investment company)
3.   A self-directed brokerage account invested in individual stocks
4.   Whole life insurance

- A.   1 and 2
- B.   1 and 4
- C.   2 and 3
- D.   3 and 4

Answer: A.   Section 403(b) plan accounts must be invested either in annuity contracts (fixed or variable) or mutual funds (open-end investment companies). Such accounts may not be invested in individual stocks or whole life insurance.

F. TOP-HAT PLANS

LO 48.10   Distinguish top-hat plans from qualified plans and tax-advantaged plans.

Supplemental Executive Retirement Plans (SERPs) and **nonqualified deferred compensation plans** (discussed in the *102: Insurance Planning and Employee Benefits* course) are commonly referred to as top-hat plans because they are reserved for a select group of management or highly compensated employees. A top-hat plan may be either unfunded or funded by the employer. From the employee's standpoint, an unfunded plan means the employee assumes the risk that the employer may later refuse to pay benefits owed under the plan due to a merger, acquisition, insolvency, or other reason. An employee pays tax on the employer's unfunded top-hat plan contributions when the benefits are actually distributed or made available to the employee. If the plan is funded, however, an employer's contributions are includable in an employee's income in the year that the contributions are made.

Even though an unfunded top-hat plan is not a guarantee for the plan participant, an employer may still assure that funds are available by using financing vehicles like a rabbi trust, corporate-owned life insurance, or a secular trust. Similarly, an employer generally may not deduct contributions to a top-hat plan until the benefits are actually distributed or made available to the employee, which varies depending on whether the plan is funded or unfunded. With a funded plan, the employer is also subject to ERISA's participation, vesting, funding, fiduciary responsibility, and plan termination insurance rules.

In addition, a top-hat plan, even if unfunded, is subject to ERISA's reporting and disclosure requirements. Those requirements will be met if the plan administrator files a statement with the Department of Labor that includes all of the following.

■ The name and address of the employer

■ The employer's IRS identification number (EIN)

■ A statement declaring that the employer maintains the plan or plans primarily for the purpose of providing deferred compensation for a select group of management or highly compensated employees

■ A statement listing the number of such plans and the number of employees in each

The plan administrator must also provide plan documents to the Department of Labor upon request to the extent such documents exist.

G. SECTION 457 PLANS

LO 48.6   Discuss the differences between a Section 457 plan for private tax-exempt employers and such plans established for state and local government employees.

A **Section 457 plan** is a non-qualified deferred compensation plan established by a private tax-exempt employer (other than a church) or state or local government for the benefit of its employees. Amounts inside the plan grow income tax free until time of distribution.

Under Section 457 of the Tax Code, plans that include limits on the amounts deferred are subject to favorable income tax treatment; these are generally referred to as eligible Section 457 plans (or Section 457(b) plans). Plans providing greater deferral, generally designed for corporate executives (hence the discriminatory nonqualified nature of the plan), are referred to as ineligible plans (or Section 457(f) plans). For purposes of this course, we need be concerned only with eligible Section 457 plans.

As of 2011, Section 457 plans sponsored by state and local governments are permitted to have Roth accounts.

Employee elections to defer compensation under Section 457 must be made under an agreement entered into before earning the compensation. If so, the amount deferred annually cannot exceed the lesser of the elective deferral limit of $18,000 (2015), or 100% of the employee's compensation includable in gross income. In addition, employees who have attained age 50 in a governmental Section 457 plan may make additional catch-up contributions of $6,000 for 2015 as long as they have not also elected the three-year catch up provision for plan participants (to be discussed shortly).

To properly apply the provisions of IRC Section 457, we need to properly differentiate between governmental (state and local government) Section 457 plans and nongovernmental (non-church controlled private tax-exempt employer) Section 457 plans. For example, the regular catch-up provision for age 50 and older individuals is only available for participants in a governmental plan. Employees (or their beneficiaries) include Section 457 governmental plan distributions in income when they are paid; employees (or their beneficiaries) in private tax-exempt plans must include these distributions when there is no longer a substantial risk of forfeiture on their receipt (which may be earlier than when they are actually paid). These distributions are not subject to an early withdrawal penalty.

The special catch-up provisions that apply to either type of Section 457 plan are unique. During the participant's last three years of employment before the plan's normal retirement age, the limit on elective deferrals is increased to the lesser of:

■ twice the amount of the regular elective deferral limit ($36,000 in 2015); or

■ the sum of (a) the otherwise applicable limit for the year plus (b) the amount by which the applicable limit in the preceding years exceeded the participant's actual deferral for those years.

Thus, during the last three years before the plan's normal retirement age, a Section 457 plan participant may defer the greater of:

■ the elective deferral limit plus the regular catch-up amount; or

■ the elective deferral limit plus the amount permitted under the three-year catch-up provision.

> **EXAMPLE**   Jane, age 58, is a State of Kansas employee earning $60,000 per year. She participates in the Kansas governmental Section 457 plan and is within three years of the plan's normal retirement age of 60. Thus, for 2015 (and ignoring the summation limit), Jane can contribute a maximum of $36,000 to the plan ($18,000 of regular elective deferrals and $18,000 of special catch-up). Jane cannot take the age 50 and older catch-up amount of $6,000 in the same tax year she uses the special catch-up rule.

Taxation of Benefits

Section 457 plans are sponsored by tax-exempt entities, so contribution deductibility is not an issue for the employer. Assets in a Section 457 plan grow tax-deferred until they are withdrawn. Employees must include distributions from a Section 457 plan in their gross income when a distribution occurs. Distributions from a 457 plan are not subject to an early withdrawal penalty.

PRACTICE
QUESTION *Choose the best answer for the question below.*

1. All of the following statements are correct regarding a Section 457 plan EXCEPT
   A.   in 2015, an individual who has attained age 50 or older may generally make additional catch-up contributions of up to $6,000
   B.   it is a qualified plan of governmental units or agencies and non-church controlled, tax-exempt organizations
   C.   the participant contribution limit may be doubled in the last three years before the plan's normal retirement age
   D.   the time of taxable distribution depends on the type of plan and the eligible participant

Answer: B.   A Section 457 plan is not a qualified plan. Rather, it is a nonqualified deferred compensation plan of governmental units or agencies and non-church controlled tax-exempt organizations. In such a plan, the participant contribution limit may be doubled in the last three years before the plan's normal retirement age. This provision is unique to a Section 457 plan.

H. MULTIPLE PLAN LIMITS

LO 47.4   Explain the rules for contributions to multiple retirement plans.

In most instances, employers are not limited to just one type of qualified and/or tax-advantaged plan. For example, as mentioned, a Section 501(c)(3) employer may establish both Section 401(k) and Section 403(b) plans. However, with one exception, elective deferrals that may be made to multiple plans are limited by employee rather than by plan. Thus, the employee-participant must aggregate all elective deferrals from:

■   traditional and Roth Section 401(k) plans;

■   SIMPLE IRAs and SIMPLE 401(k)s (Note: SIMPLEs are subject to a lower deferral amount, and the employer can maintain only another SIMPLE plan);

■   SARSEP plans; and

■   Section 403(b) plans.

> **EXAMPLE**   Barbara works for two employers, both of which maintain Section 401(k) plans. If Barbara contributes $8,500 to Employer A's plan, she may then contribute only $9,500 to Employer B's plan (a total of $18,000).

The one exception to this aggregation rule is when the individual participates in one of the aforementioned plans and a Section 457 plan. When an individual participates in a Section 457 plan (governmental or nongovernmental) and any other type of qualified or tax-advantaged plan, the Section 457 participant may contribute an additional or second elective deferral amount up to $18,000 (2015). Also, participation in any form of a Section 457 plan is not considered active participation for purposes of the IRA deductibility rules (to be discussed in the next unit).

Choose the best answer for each of the questions below.

1. Tim, age 48, works for two private, tax-exempt employers. One has a Section 403(b) plan and one maintains a nongovernmental Section 457 plan. If Tim defers $10,000 into the Section 403(b) plan in 2015, how much can he separately defer into the Section 457 plan? (Assume he has sufficient compensation to fund both plans to the maximum.)

A. $8,000
B. $10,000
C. $18,000
D. $26,000

Answer: C.   Tim can separately defer the maximum of $18,000 into the Section 457 plan because Section 457 plan limits are not aggregated with the Section 403(b) plan limits.

2. Sara, age 51, has been working with Carol, a CFP® professional, in developing a plan for optimizing how she is saving for her retirement. Carol has developed a plan she feels will accomplish Sara's goals and has given it to her in a written document. Sara reviewed it and has returned to Carol's office to tell her she has accepted all of the recommendations. The plan has several parts, including changing her contributions to the Section 403(b) plan at her place of employment, and taking better advantage of the Section 457 plan that is also available to her. What is Carol's next step in assisting Sara in her retirement planning?

A.   Carol tells Sara how much she should defer each pay period in both the Section 403(b) and Section 457 plans.
B.   Carol should call the plan administrator for the plans at Sara's employer and get the forms for Sara to fill out.
C.   It is up to Sara to put Carol's recommendations in place, now that she has a good plan from a financial planning professional.
D.   Carol should create a prioritized timeline for implementation of the recommendations and explain how monitoring the implemented recommendations will be accomplished and by whom.

Answer: D.   Sara and Carol are in the implementation phase of the financial planning process. Carol should create a prioritized timeline for implementation of the recommendations and explain how monitoring the implemented recommendations will be accomplished and by whom. (Domain 6)

105 UNIT 4 POST-STUDY CHECKLIST

☐   Do I know how to explain the rules for contributions to multiple retirement plans?

☐   Can I describe the basic provisions of a simplified employee pension (SEP) plan and determine its suitability for a for-profit small business?

☐   Can I describe the basic provisions of a savings incentive match plan for employees (SIMPLE) IRA and determine its suitability for a for-profit small business?

☐   Am I able to explain the characteristics of the Section 403(b) plan for a tax-exempt employer and compare it to a Section 401(k) plan?

☐   Am I able to differentiate between a Section 457 plan for private, tax-exempt employers and such plans established for state and local government employees?

☐   Am I able to discuss premature distributions from a retirement plan and the penalty exceptions allowed?

Am I able to define and understand the application of the following terms to financial planning?

- ☐ Nonqualified deferred compensation plans
- ☐ Salary reduction SEP (SARSEP)
- ☐ Savings incentive match plan for employees (SIMPLE) IRA
- ☐ Section 403(b) plan
- ☐ Section 457 plan
- ☐ SIMPLE
- ☐ Simplified employee pension (SEP) plan
- ☐ Tax-advantaged
- ☐ Tax-sheltered annuity (TSA)
- ☐ Top-hat plans

Traditional and Roth IRAs

REFER TO

CFP® Certification Principal Topics – Retirement Planning, Other Tax-Advantaged Retirement Plans

CFP® Certification Principal Topics – Retirement Planning, Distribution Rules, Alternatives, and Taxation

Supplemental Readings Section of this 105 Retirement Planning Student Guide

(For specific assignments, refer to class syllabus.)

INTRODUCTION

Most financial planners and consumers have a general understanding of the role played by traditional and Roth IRAs in retirement planning. However, what may not be so widely understood are the limitations on the tax deductibility of contributions to a traditional IRA and the rules regarding conversions of a traditional IRA to a Roth IRA. This unit addresses both of these issues, as well as characteristics of both of these exceedingly important retirement planning vehicles.

While the term traditional IRA refers to either a personal IRA or a SEP IRA (discussed in Unit 4 of this course), the discussion of this unit will be confined to the personal type of IRA first created by the Employee Retirement Income Security Act of 1974 (ERISA).

Contributions made to a Roth IRA on a nondeductible basis within certain statutory limits result in 100% tax-free withdrawals if certain requirements are met. The compounding of these tax-free dollars over the years may be substantial, and a comparison should be made as to whether it is better to contribute to a traditional IRA or a Roth IRA. Even though the taxpayer-client may receive an income tax deduction for contributions made to the traditional IRA, this is not always the best alternative.

Distributions from both the traditional and Roth IRA will be covered in the next two units along with qualified plan distributions.

LEARNING OBJECTIVES

After completing this unit, you should be able to achieve the following learning objectives:

CFP® Certification Principal Topics – Retirement Planning, Other Tax-Advantaged Retirement Plans

LO 48.1 Explain the rules governing contributions to traditional IRAs and their income tax deductibility.

LO 48.2 Describe the basic provisions of the Roth IRA form and compare the attributes of the Roth IRA to those of the traditional IRA.

LO 48.11 Describe the contribution and distribution limits for Roth IRAs.

LO 48.12 Describe the conversion of a traditional IRA to a Roth IRA.

CFP® Certification Principal Topics – Retirement Planning, Distribution Rules, Alternatives, and Taxation

LO 52.1 Discuss premature distributions from a retirement plan and the exceptions allowed.

LO 52.2 Identify the options for taking distributions from a retirement plan.

LO 52.4 Explain the differences between an inherited IRA and a stretch IRA and when each is used.

LO 52.7 Describe the Roth IRA ordering rules for distributions.

LO 52.8 Discuss taxation and penalties on Roth IRA nonqualified distributions and the exceptions allowed.

KEY TERMS

Amortization method	Prohibited transaction
Annuity method	Required minimum distribution method
Early distribution penalty	Rollover IRAs
Individual retirement accounts	Roth IRAs
Individual retirement annuities	Spousal IRA
Inherited IRAs	Stretch IRA
Ordering rules	Traditional IRA

A. TRADITIONAL IRA CONTRIBUTION AND DEDUCTIBILITY RULES

LO 48.1 Explain the rules governing contributions to traditional IRAs and their income tax deductibility.

There are two types of **traditional IRAs**:

- **Individual retirement accounts** (usually funded with securities or investment products)

- **Individual retirement annuities** (funded with insurance products)

Both types of IRAs are subject to the following contribution limits for 2015 and beyond:

Taxable Year	Maximum Regular Contribution*	Maximum Catch-Up**
2015	$5,500	$1,000

*Lesser of 100% of earned income or this amount
**Individuals age 50 and older

Investment income earned on the assets held within either type of traditional IRA is not subject to federal income tax until withdrawn from the account. Minimum distribution rules generally require withdrawals to begin when the IRA owner attains age 70½. (No contributions can be made to the traditional IRA once an individual attains age 70½.) All distributions are taxable as ordinary income even though investment-type (capital) assets may be used to fund the account.

A **spousal IRA** of up to $5,500 (or $6,500 if spouse is age 50 or older) is permitted if the compensation limit is met by only one spouse. In effect, the spouse without earned income borrows compensation from the spouse with earned income to fully fund a traditional IRA.

Appropriate Application

Traditional IRAs are used when an individual wants to defer taxes on personal retirement investment income and shelter current compensation or earned income from taxation. They are also appropriate when long-term accumulation is an important financial objective, especially for retirement purposes. Traditional IRAs are an important supplement or alternative to a qualified pension or profit-sharing plan.

Advantages

For 2015, eligible individuals may contribute up to $5,500 to an IRA and possibly deduct this amount from their current taxable income (see "Deductibility Rules for a Traditional IRA," below). Individuals who have attained age 50 may make additional catch-up contributions. The additional catch-up amount for 2015 is $1,000 for each spouse age 50 or older. An income tax credit is allowed for certain taxpayers with respect to contributions to a traditional or Roth IRA. Investment income earned on the assets held in an IRA is not subject to federal income tax until it is withdrawn from the account.

Disadvantages

IRA withdrawals may be subject to a 10% early withdrawal penalty. Distributions are not eligible for 10-year forward averaging, pre-1974 participation capital gains treatment, or net unrealized appreciation (NUA) that applies to certain lump-sum distributions from qualified plans. Once an individual attains age 70½ (except in the case of a rollover IRA or Roth IRA), IRAs can no longer be established, and withdrawals from the account are required by April 1 of the year following the year the individual attains age 70½ (except in the case of a Roth IRA). All distributions from IRAs are ordinary income to the extent taxable.

Deductibility Rules for a Traditional IRA

There are three basic rules associated with the deductibility of contributions made to a traditional IRA:

■ If neither MFJ spouse is an active participant in an employer-sponsored retirement plan or if a single person is not an active participant, then contributions to a traditional IRA are deductible without regard to the participant's modified adjusted gross income (MAGI).

— Active participation in a defined benefit pension plan is considered when an employee is eligible to accrue benefits.

— Active participation in a defined contribution plan as well as a SIMPLE IRA, SEP IRA, or Section 403(b) plan is considered when an employer contribution or forfeiture is allocated to the participant's account or if the participant contributes an elective deferral. A taxpayer who participates in a Section 457 plan is not considered an active participant for purposes of determining deductibility of IRA contributions.

■ If both MFJ spouses are active participants (or if a single person is an active participant) in an employer-sponsored retirement plan, then deductibility of contributions is phased out based on the following MAGI ranges for during 2015:

— Single filing status: $61,000 to $71,000

— Married filing jointly status: $98,000 to $118,000

— Married filing separately status: $0 to $10,000

■ When one spouse is an active participant and one spouse is not an active participant, two separate phase-out thresholds are applicable. The phase-out for the active participant in 2015 is combined MAGI of $98,000–$118,000. The phase-out for the nonactive participant is combined MAGI of $183,000–$193,000.

> **EXAMPLE** Scott and Anne are married (married filing jointly) and have a combined MAGI of $120,000 in tax year 2015. Anne is an active participant in her company's Section 401(k) plan. Scott works for the state of Maine and participates in its Section 457 plan. Both Scott and Anne want to make a deductible contribution of $5,500 to their own traditional IRAs. Because Scott is not considered an active participant in an employer-sponsored plan (he participates in a governmental plan), his deduction will not begin to be phased out until the couple's MAGI reaches $183,000. As Scott and Anne's combined MAGI is only $120,000 for 2015, Scott is entitled to a full $5,500 deductible contribution. However, because Anne is an active participant, and their combined MAGI exceeds $118,000, none of her contribution will be nondeductible. Note that Anne may still contribute to her traditional IRA, but she cannot deduct any of the $5,500 contribution for 2015.

If a taxpayer's MAGI is between the beginning phase-out amount and the maximum phase-out amount, the allowable deductible amount is partially phased out. A phase-out percentage is applied, which is the amount of MAGI in excess of the applicable beginning phase-out range in relation to the total amount of phase-out range. For example, if a MFJ taxpayer, age 45, with MAGI of $103,000, who is also an active participant in an employer-sponsored plan, wishes to contribute to a traditional IRA, 25% of the deductible amount is phased out [$5,000 (excess MAGI) ÷ $20,000 (total phase-out range of $98,000–$118,000 in 2015) = 25%]. The maximum deductible contribution becomes $4,125 (1 – 25% × $5,500). The taxpayer may still contribute $5,500 to the IRA, but the deduction is limited to $4,125.

Earned income for purposes of the traditional IRA contribution deductibility rules does not include:

- rental income;

- interest or dividend income;

- pension, annuity, or deferred compensation income; or

- foreign earned income.

However, earned income for this purpose does include the receipt of alimony from an ex-spouse.

Prohibited Transactions

Generally, a **prohibited transaction** is the improper use of an IRA account or annuity by the individual or any disqualified person. The account fiduciary and members of the individual's family (spouse, ancestor, lineal descendant, and spouse of a lineal descendant) are examples of disqualified persons.

Prohibited transactions with an IRA include the following:

- Borrowing money from the IRA

- Selling property to the IRA

- Receiving unreasonable compensation for managing the IRA

- Using the IRA as security for a loan

■ Buying property for personal use (present or future) with IRA funds

Generally, if an individual or the individual's beneficiary engages in a prohibited transaction with the individual's IRA account at any time during the year, it will not be treated as an IRA as of the first day of the year. The individual (or beneficiary) must include the fair market value of all (or part, in certain cases) of the IRA assets in gross income for that year. The fair market value is the price at which the IRA assets would change hands between a willing buyer and a willing seller, when neither has any need to buy nor sell and both have reasonable knowledge of the relevant facts. The individual must use the fair market value of the assets as of the first day of the year he is engaged in the prohibited transaction. The individual also may have to pay the 10% tax on premature distributions.

If an individual borrows money against an IRA annuity contract, the individual must include the fair market value of the annuity contract as of the first day of the tax year in gross income. The individual also may have to pay the 10% additional tax on premature distributions. Also, if an individual uses a part of his IRA account as security for a loan, that part is treated as a distribution and is included in gross income. The individual may have to pay the 10% additional tax on premature distributions.

Allowable Investments in a Traditional IRA

Traditional IRA funds can generally be invested in any type of asset, with three specific exceptions:

■ Collectibles, such as stamps, coins, or antiques; however, certain types of U.S. -issued coins such as the American Eagle gold coin, are permissible

■ Life insurance policies

■ Any form of participant note or obligation; an IRA cannot make loans to an IRA participant

If a participant borrows from his traditional IRA, the entire interest in the account is considered a taxable distribution. If a portion of the IRA is instead pledged as collateral for a bank loan, then the portion of the account pledged is taxable.

Also, a traditional IRA cannot own S corporation stock as it is not a permissible shareholder under the S corporation rules.

An IRA owner cannot contribute more than his earned income for the year, except in the case of a spousal IRA. The total amount that may be contributed to all IRAs, traditional or Roth, deductible or nondeductible, is $5,500 per person, plus applicable age 50 and older catch-ups.

PRACTICE QUESTIONS   *Choose the best answer for each of the questions below.*

1. Jon and Mary are married, both age 33, and file a joint income tax return for the current year. Jon is self-employed as a business consultant and does not maintain a retirement plan through his business. Jon earns $120,000 of Schedule C income, and pays $15,659 in total self-employment taxes. Mary is a full-time homemaker and is not employed outside the home. What is the maximum deductible IRA contribution Jon and Mary can make, if any, for 2015?

   A. $0

   B. $4,000

   C. $5,500

   D. $11,000

Answer: D.   Neither Jon nor Mary is an active participant in an employer-sponsored retirement plan. Therefore, they can establish a spousal IRA and contribute (and deduct) a total of $11,000 (a maximum of $5,500 each) to a traditional IRA for 2015.

2.   Which of the following is a permissible investment in a traditional IRA?
1.   A mutual fund that invests exclusively in gold mining stock
2.   An international stock mutual fund
3.   An investment-grade work of art
4.   Gold coins minted by the U.S. Treasury

A.   1 and 2
B.   1, 2, and 4
C.   3 only
D.   3 and 4

Answer: B.   Collectibles are generally prohibited as an investment in a traditional IRA. Gold coins minted by the U.S. Treasury are an exception to this general rule. A mutual fund investing in gold mining stock is a permissible investment.

3.   Which of the following individuals may make a deductible contribution to a traditional IRA in 2015?

	Person	Filing Status	Modified Adjusted Gross Income (MAGI)	Covered by Employer Plan
1.	Jane	Single	$ 63,000	Yes
2.	Joe	Married	$110,000	No
3.	Betty	Single	$ 35,000	Yes
4.	Sue	Married	$ 45,000	Yes

A.   1 and 2
B.   2, 3, and 4
C.   3 and 4
D.   1, 2, 3, and 4

Answer: D.   All of these persons may make deductible contributions to a traditional IRA. Jane's MAGI is in the phaseout range for 2015, and she cannot deduct the full $5,500.

B. ROLLOVER, INHERITED, AND STRETCH IRAS

LO 52.2   Identify the options for taking distributions from a retirement plan.

LO 52.4   Explain the differences between an inherited IRA and a stretch IRA and when each is used.

The traditional IRA is a very popular retirement planning vehicle. In addition to holding personal contributions, a traditional IRA may be used to receive and distribute funds from a qualified plan (a rollover IRA). An inherited IRA is a specially titled account for which a nonspouse IRA beneficiary may use to defer taxation when inheriting IRA funds. A **stretch IRA** is an IRA that extends the tax deferral of earnings within the IRA beyond the lifetime of the person who originally established the IRA through the use of multigenerational beneficiary designations.

Rollover IRA

A rollover is a distribution of cash or other assets from one retirement plan to another retirement plan. Such a distribution is income tax free as long as the entire rollover contribution is made by the 60th day after the participant receives a distribution. Any amount not rolled over exceeding basis, if any, is treated for income tax purposes as a distribution and is taxable as ordinary income in the year distributed and may also be subject to a 10% premature distribution penalty.

A rollover may occur between a qualified or tax-advantaged plan and an IRA. Unlike an initially established traditional IRA, there is no dollar limit on the amount of contributions that may be made to a **rollover IRA**. In addition, under the Bankruptcy Act of 2005, all amounts in a rollover IRA are protected from the participant's creditors while within the confines of the rollover IRA (that is, not distributed to the participant). Any IRA rollovers must be reported on the participant's tax return for the year that the distribution is made. Tax-free rollovers between traditional IRA accounts are also allowed.

Inherited IRA

An **inherited IRA** is created when an IRA owner dies and leaves IRA funds to a non-spouse beneficiary. A nonspouse beneficiary (such as an adult child) may transfer the decedent's balance from a qualified plan, Section 403(b) plan, governmental Section 457 plan, or IRA to an inherited IRA, which is a specially titled IRA account, via a trustee-to-trustee transfer. Other contributions may not be made to the inherited IRA, and no additional rollovers may be made from or into the inherited IRA. All distributions in excess of basis, if any, from the inherited IRA are includable as income in the tax year it is received. Prior to 2007, the opportunity to roll over a deceased IRA owner's account balance was available only to a surviving spouse. This is a significant broadening of the inherited IRA opportunity, but, the nonspouse beneficiary must generally begin distributions from the inherited IRA in the year following the year of death of the owner. A surviving spouse beneficiary may continue to defer distributions until the surviving spouse attains age 70½. A spouse beneficiary of an IRA has the additional options of either rolling over the decedent's IRA balance to a personally owned IRA, treating the decedent's IRA as a personal IRA, or electing to be treated as the beneficiary rather than the owner.

PRACTICE QUESTION

Choose the best answer for the question below.

1. In 2015, is it possible for an adult child to roll over an inherited IRA?
   A.   Yes
   B.   No

Answer: A.   It is possible for a nonspouse beneficiary to roll over the deceased participant's balance in a qualified plan (or other qualifying plans) into an inherited IRA using a trustee to trustee direct transfer. However, the nonspouse beneficiary must generally begin receiving distributions immediately.

Stretch IRA

A **stretch IRA** extends or stretches the period of tax-deferred earnings within an IRA beyond the lifetime of the owner who originally established it, typically over several generations. Such an IRA allows the IRA owner's beneficiaries to name their own beneficiary at the owner's death, which may provide the longest permitted tax deferral period before all the assets in the IRA must be distributed. It is critical that the stretch IRA be established correctly before beginning distributions to optimize continued tax deferral.

> **EXAMPLE** Linda has a $1 million traditional IRA and names her 45-year-old son, Scott, as the primary beneficiary. Linda's grandson, Jim, is named as the contingent beneficiary. When Linda dies, Scott may elect to distribute Linda's IRA funds over his life expectancy, which is approximately 38 years. In addition, if Scott dies prematurely at age 50, Jim will still be able to elect to have the IRA distributed over the remaining 33 years of Scott's life expectancy. Thus, if Jim is age 20 when Scott dies, Jim will still receive the benefit of the IRA payout for another 33 years, with a minimum of taxable consequence.

For the stretch IRA concept to be most effective, the IRA owner's retirement income needs and additional retirement income sources are such that the IRA will not be significantly depleted during the owner's lifetime. Also, the concept is most effective when there exists significant age differences and, therefore, significant life expectancy differences between generations of beneficiaries.

C. PREMATURE DISTRIBUTION PENALTY AND EXCEPTIONS FOR A TRADITIONAL IRA

LO 52.1 Discuss premature distributions from a retirement plan and the penalty exceptions allowed.

Generally, distributions taken from a traditional IRA before the owner attains age 59½ are subject to an **early distribution penalty** of 10% of the taxable amount taken (in addition to income tax on the same). Distributions from a traditional IRA that include nondeductible contributions are subject to tax on a pro rata basis according to the following formula:

Nontaxable portion =

$$\left[\frac{\left(\begin{array}{c}\text{nondeductible contributions prior to current year} + \\ \text{all contributions for current year}\end{array}\right)}{\left(\begin{array}{c}\text{balances at end of current year} + \\ \text{distributions received in current year}\end{array}\right)}\right] \times \text{total distributions during current year}$$

However, there are notable exceptions to the imposition of this 10% penalty. If any of the following circumstances are associated with the distribution from the IRA, the penalty will not be imposed:

■ Attainment of age 59½

■ Total and permanent disability

■ Death

■ For medical expenses exceeding 10% of the owner's AGI (for taxpayers who have not attained age 59½)

■ To pay higher education costs for the taxpayer, spouse, child, or grandchild

■ To pay acquisition costs of a first home for the participant, spouse, child, or grandchild of the participant or spouse, up to a $10,000 lifetime maximum

■ To pay health insurance premiums if the owner is unemployed (the participant must file for unemployment compensation before this exception applies)

■ As a part of substantially equal periodic payments at least annually over the life expectancy of the owner, or the owner and a designated beneficiary; in addition, these payments, once begun, must continue for the greater of five years or until the owner attains the age of 59½

Transfers Incident to Divorce

If an IRA interest is transferred from a spouse or former spouse (transferor) to an individual (transferee) by reason of divorce or separate maintenance decree, the transfer is tax free if the transferred assets are deposited into the receiving spouse's IRA or qualified plan.

PRACTICE
QUESTION   *Choose the best answer for the question below.*

1. The premature distribution (10%) penalty does not apply to IRA distributions:
1. made after attainment of the age of 55 and separation from service
2. made for the purpose of paying qualified higher education costs for the owner's spouse
3. paid to a beneficiary after the death of the IRA owner who had not begun receiving minimum distributions

A. 1 only
B. 1 and 2
C. 2 only
D. 2 and 3

Answer: D.   The first statement is an exception for distributions from qualified plans. The second and third statements are correct exceptions to the imposition of the 10% penalty for early distributions made from an IRA.

D. ROTH IRA ELIGIBILITY AND CONTRIBUTION LIMITS

LO 48.2   Describe the basic provisions of the Roth IRA form and compare the attributes of the Roth IRA to those of the traditional IRA.

LO 48.11   Describe the contribution and distribution limits for Roth IRAs.

Roth IRAs are in many respects similar to traditional IRAs. For example, the list of permitted (and prohibited) investments is the same for both traditional and Roth IRAs. In addition, the definition of earned income is the same for both types of IRAs and the contribution limit is the same, $5,500 (2015) with an age 50+ catch up of $1,000. It is important to note that a taxpayer may own both a traditional IRA and a Roth IRA, but the maximum contribution is applied aggregately, not $5,500 (2015) for each account.

Roth IRAs permit only after-tax or nondeductible contributions to be made. If applicable holding period rules are met and a qualified distribution is made, these contributions plus the earnings generated thereon are entirely income tax free to the participant.

Only taxpayers with a modified adjusted gross income (MAGI) below certain levels are permitted to make contributions to a Roth IRA. For 2015, contributions are phased out for taxpayers with MAGIs as follows:

- Single: $116,000–$131,000

- Married filing jointly: $183,000–$194,000

- Married filing separately: $0–$10,000

Contributions to a Roth IRA may be made for years beyond when the owner has attained the age of 70½. In addition, required minimum distributions (RMD) do not apply during the owner's lifetime.

A qualified distribution (tax- and penalty-free distribution) is made from a Roth IRA when *both* of the following requirements are met:

- The distribution is made after a five-year holding period (which begins January 1 of the taxable year for which the first regular contribution is made to any originally-established Roth IRA or, if earlier, January 1 of the taxable year in which the first conversion contribution is made to a converted Roth IRA). For example, if a Roth IRA contribution is made in February 2016 for tax year 2015, the five-year holding period requirement timeline begins January 1, 2015. Note that a separate five-year period applies to each conversion, but is not applied separately for regular Roth contributions.

- The distribution is made because of one of the following circumstances:

  — The owner attains the age of 59½.

  — The owner dies, and payment is made to a beneficiary or estate of the owner on or after his death.

  — The owner becomes disabled.

  — Payment is made for a first-time home purchase of the owner, spouse, child, or grandchild (with a lifetime cap of $10,000 in amount).

Note the five-year holding period is an absolute requirement. Additionally, one of the other listed requirements must also be met. It is important to recognize that attainment of age 59½ is not an absolute requirement; it is one of the possible qualifying events. It is possible for a qualified distribution to occur prior to age 59½ if the five-year holding period is satisfied and death, disability, or first-time home purchase is the reason for distribution.

The five-year holding period is not re-determined when the Roth IRA owner dies. Thus, the beneficiary of the Roth IRA only needs to wait until the end of the original five-year period for the distribution to be treated as a qualified distribution.

PRACTICE QUESTION

Choose the best answer for the question below.

1. Jim and Janet are both 34, married, and file a joint tax return. Their MAGI for 2015 is $128,000. Janet has already made a $5,500 contribution to her traditional IRA and has made a contribution of $2,000 to their son's Coverdell Education Savings Account this year. What is the most that may be contributed, if any, to a Roth IRA for Jim and Janet for the year 2015 given these facts?
    A. $0
    B. $2,000
    C. $5,500
    D. $11,000

    Answer: C.   The maximum combined contribution to traditional and Roth IRAs (for an owner who is younger than age 50) is $5,500 per person annually for 2015. Therefore, Jim and Janet have a total of $11,000 to allocate between both forms of IRAs. Janet has already contributed the maximum amount to an IRA for her benefit; therefore, Jim can only contribute $5,500 to his own Roth IRA for the current year. Note that the $2,000 Coverdell contribution is not included in either the $5,500 (individual) or $11,000 (combined) limit.

E. CONVERSION OF A TRADITIONAL IRA TO A ROTH IRA

LO 48.2   Describe the basic provisions of the Roth IRA form and compare the attributes of the Roth IRA to those of the traditional IRA.

LO 48.12   Describe the conversion of a traditional IRA to a Roth IRA.

An amount in a traditional IRA may be converted to a Roth IRA. The amount converted must generally be from a traditional IRA that is rolled over to a Roth IRA within 60 days of the distribution. A direct rollover or direct trustee-to-trustee transfer is also allowed.

Any converted amount is treated as a taxable distribution from the traditional IRA and is included in the owner's gross income for the year in which the distribution occurs to the extent the amount exceeds basis, if any, in the traditional IRA. However, the 10% premature withdrawal penalty does not apply, regardless of the owner's age at the time of the conversion.

Additionally, a participant in a Section 401(k) plan, Section 403(b) plan, or a governmental Section 457 plan may elect to convert any eligible rollover distribution of non-Roth sums into an individual Roth account within the same plan if the plan offers a Roth account. The same tax rules apply to an in-plan conversion that apply to a traditional IRA to Roth IRA conversion.

The analysis of whether to convert a traditional IRA to a Roth IRA is not an easy one and requires a comprehensive tax and accounting analysis. However, if the tax due initially on conversion may be paid from assets other than the traditional IRA and the converted assets will remain in the Roth IRA for a relatively long period of time before withdrawal, the conversion is generally advisable. A financial planner should assist the client to determine if a conversion should, in fact, be made.

Aggregation Rule

The Tax Code requires that all deductible and nondeductible traditional IRAs are aggregated together and treated as one IRA for the purpose of calculating the basis of a distribution. Even if the nondeductible traditional IRA contributions are segregated in separate IRAs from the deductible traditional IRA contributions, the aggregation rules require that any distribution be treated as a partial return of nontaxable basis and a partial taxable distribution of contributions and earnings. Also, when calculating the nontaxable portion of the distributions made during a given tax year, all distributions in that year are also aggregated as though there was only one distribution in the year. The purpose of these rules is to prevent a taxpayer from choosing to convert or distribute only the nontaxable portion of a traditional IRA and leaving the taxable contributions and earning untouched. Once the IRAs are combined, the basis in the distribution is allocated as follows:

Nontaxable portion =

$$\left[\frac{\left(\begin{array}{c}\text{nondeductible contributions prior to current year} +\\ \text{all contributions for current year}\end{array}\right)}{\left(\begin{array}{c}\text{balances at end of current year} +\\ \text{distributions received in current year}\end{array}\right)}\right] \times \text{total distributions during current year}$$

E X A M P L E   Aggregation rule Mike has a traditional deductible IRA with a balance of $50,000. He also has a separate traditional IRA with a balance of $10,000, which is comprised of $9,000 of nondeductible contributions and $1,000 of earnings. Mike converted $9,000 to a Roth IRA this year and would like to identify it as the $9,000 of nondeductible contributions because it has already been taxed and he wants to avoid including the $9,000 in his gross income.

The aggregation rules require Mike to combine both of his IRAs into one and allocate the basis to the conversion distribution:

$$[\$9,000 \div (\$50,000 + \$1,000 + \$9,000)] \times \$9,000 = \$1,350$$

Mike can allocate only $1,350 of nontaxable basis to the $9,000 conversion.

F. TAXATION OF NONQUALIFIED DISTRIBUTIONS FROM A ROTH IRA

LO 48.2   Describe the basic provisions of the Roth IRA form and compare the attributes of the Roth IRA to those of the traditional IRA.

LO 52.1   Discuss premature distributions from a retirement plan and the penalty exceptions allowed.

LO 52.7   Describe the Roth IRA ordering rules for distributions.

LO 52.8   Discuss taxation and penalties on Roth IRA nonqualified distributions and the exceptions allowed.

An amount distributed from a Roth IRA is treated as being made according to the **ordering rules** applicable to a Roth IRA:

■ From regular (after-tax) contributions

■ From conversion contributions, on a first-in-first-out (FIFO) basis

— The order of the distribution of conversion amounts is first, from amounts taxable at conversion, and then second, from amounts nontaxable (basis) at conversion

■ From earnings generated from the plan investments

The significance of these ordering rules may be seen when determining the taxation of withdrawals from a Roth IRA that does not meet the five-year holding period. These are commonly known as nonqualified distributions and may involve regular or converted contributions or earnings from those contributions (or all three).

A distribution that is not a qualified distribution from a Roth IRA is taxable as income to the extent the distribution exceeds the owner's cumulative regular and conversion contributions. The 10% early withdrawal penalty will apply to any distribution from a Roth IRA that is includable in the owner's gross income unless an exception to the IRA penalty applies. In addition, the penalty may apply to a nonqualified distribution, even if the distribution is not included in income, if the distribution is attributable to an IRA conversion contribution within five years of the conversion.

> **EXAMPLE** Trevor, age 45, converts $20,000 to a Roth IRA (#1) in Year 1 and $15,000 to a Roth IRA (#2) in Year 3. No other contributions to either Roth are subsequently made. In Year 7, a $30,000 distribution is made to Trevor that is not a qualified distribution. As a result, the distribution is taxed under the ordering rules as $20,000 from the Year 1 conversion contribution (#1) and $10,000 from the Year 3 conversion contribution (#2) that were includable in gross income when converted. As a result, for Year 7, no amount is includable in Trevor's gross income, but because $10,000 is allocable to a conversion contribution made within the previous five years (and no exception applies), that amount is subject to the 10% penalty. Thus, Trevor pays a penalty of $1,000 ($10,000 × .10) on the total $30,000 distribution.

Note that all distributions from an individual's Roth IRAs made during one taxable year (in the example above, Year 7) are aggregated for purposes of the ordering rules.

When evaluating the tax treatment of a distribution from a Roth IRA, it is helpful to analyze the tax and penalty elements separately.

■ Is the distribution qualified?

■ Does a penalty apply?

myRA Retirement Savings Account

A new type of Roth IRA has been developed by the U.S. Treasury Department. The myRA account will be available to employees through employers, allowing contributions via payroll deduction on an after-tax contribution basis. While anyone may open an account at a sponsoring employer, the myRA is targeted for low to middle income workers who may not have access to an employer-sponsored retirement plan. Accounts may be established with any payroll deduction amount and will be subject to regular Roth IRA contribution limits and rules. The myRA will earn interest at the same rate as the Government Securities Investment Fund in the Thrift Savings Plan for federal employees. Participation is subject to income thresholds. Once a participant's account balance has reached $15,000, or after 30 years, the account must be transferred to a regular Roth IRA.

Distributions to Charity

Donations from a donor-taxpayer's individual retirement accounts (IRAs) and Roth IRAs (to the extent includable in the donor's income under the qualified distribution rules for Roth account distributions) to qualifying public charities are included in the donor-taxpayer's taxable income. The donor-taxpayer is allowed a corresponding charitable deduction for the donation on the donor-taxpayer's income tax return. This charitable deduction amount is subject to the rules on the limitations of charitable contributions by a taxpayer (explained in the *104: Income Tax Planning* course).

PRACTICE
QUESTIONS   *Choose the best answer for each of the questions below.*

1. Roth IRA distributions are required to be treated as occurring in a specific order. Which of the following sequences correctly states this order?
  A. Contributions, conversions, earnings
  B. Conversions, earnings, contributions
  C. Contributions, earnings, conversions
  D. Earnings, contributions, conversions

  Answer: A.   Under the ordering rules, regular contributions are distributed first, followed by conversion contributions and, finally, earnings. Distributions made from all Roth IRAs are aggregated for purposes of the rules.

2. Ally, who is age 35, converted a $90,000 traditional IRA to a Roth IRA in 2014. Her adjusted basis in the traditional IRA is $18,000. She also made a contribution of $4,000 to the same Roth IRA in 2014. If Ally takes a $4,000 distribution from her Roth IRA during 2015, how much total federal tax, if any, including penalties, is due as a result of the distribution? (Assume that Ally is in a combined 30% marginal tax rate.)

A. $0
B. $200
C. $620
D. $915

Answer: A.   Although the distribution is not a qualified distribution, it will not be taxable because it is treated as coming from the regular Roth IRA contributions first (here, $4,000 in 2014). Because the $4,000 is not includable in gross income, nor does it relate to a conversion within the last 5 years, it will not be subject to the 10% penalty.

105 UNIT 5 POST-STUDY CHECKLIST

☐ Can I explain the rules governing contributions to traditional IRAs and their income tax deductibility?

☐ Do I know how to describe the basic provisions of the Roth IRA form and compare the attributes of the Roth IRA to those of the traditional IRA?

☐ Am I able to discuss premature distributions from a retirement plan and the penalty exceptions allowed?

☐ Am I able to identify the options for taking distributions from a retirement plan?

☐ Can I explain the differences between an inherited IRA and a stretch IRA and when each is used?

Am I able to define and understand the application of the following terms to financial planning?

☐ Amortization method	☐ Prohibited transaction
☐ Annuity method	☐ Required minimum distribution method
☐ Early distribution penalty	☐ Rollover IRAs
☐ Individual retirement accounts	☐ Roth IRAs
☐ Individual retirement annuities	☐ Spousal IRA
☐ Inherited IRAs	☐ Stretch IRA
☐ Ordering rules	☐ Traditional IRA

6

Plan Distributions— Part I

REFER TO

CFP® Certification Principal Topics – Retirement Planning, Qualified Plan Rules and Options

CFP® Certification Principal Topics – Retirement Planning, Distribution Rules, Alternatives, and Taxation

Supplemental Readings Section of this 105 Retirement Planning Student Guide

(For specific assignments, refer to class syllabus.)

INTRODUCTION

One of the most frequent issues dealt with by a financial planner is how to maximize the effectiveness of distributions from a qualified plan, an IRA, or both. Distributions may be selected to create the cash flow security of an annuity or a lump-sum distribution or rollover. The retiree must choose a proper retirement plan distribution strategy to accommodate lifestyle needs while distributing as little as possible to save on income taxes. IRS regulations have somewhat resolved this issue in requiring only a minimum amount of payment to be made for tax purposes (known as a required minimum distribution), although the retiree is permitted to withdraw more if needed. Balanced against these considerations is the anticipated life expectancy of the client and the optimal withdrawal rate to ensure that the client does not outlive her total retirement fund or lump-sum capital that has been accumulated.

In this unit, the consequences of plan distributions during the participant's lifetime are addressed. The next unit (Unit 7) will cover distributions made subsequent to the participant's death. Post-death distribution issues are not a concern if all or most of a participant's benefits have been used up during her lifetime. However, if a spouse is named as beneficiary of a participant's retirement plan, there are certain qualified plan rules which must be followed.

LEARNING OBJECTIVES

After completing this unit, you should be able to achieve the following learning objectives:

CFP® Certification Principal Topics – Retirement Planning, Qualified Plan Rules and Options

LO 47.6   Explain the rules for loans to participants in qualified plans, Section 403(b) plans, and governmental Section 457 plans.

CFP® Certification Principal Topics – Retirement Planning, Distribution Rules, Alternatives, and Taxation

LO 52.2   Identify the options for taking distributions from a retirement plan.

LO 52.3   Define the terms required beginning date (RBD) for making a retirement plan distribution and the required minimum distribution (RMD).

LO 52.5   Describe a qualified domestic relations order (QDRO) and know where it can be used.

LO 52.6   Explain the income tax implications of a retirement plan lifetime distribution options.

LO 52.9   Calculate the required minimum distribution (RMD) for a given client assuming specified facts.

LO 52.10   Explain the income tax penalty for failure to take a required minimum distribution (RMD) from a retirement plan or IRA.

LO 52.11   Identify the early distribution penalty exceptions.

LO 52.12   Explain when the income tax penalty is applied to a retirement plan distribution.

KEY TERMS

10-year forward averaging	Net unrealized appreciation (NUA)
50% excise tax	Pre-1974 capital gain treatment
Annuity	Required beginning date (RBD)
Direct transfer	Required minimum distribution (RMD)
Early distribution penalty	Rollover
Lump-sum distribution	Uniform Lifetime Table

A. ALLOWABLE LIFETIME DISTRIBUTION OPTIONS

LO 52.2   Identify the options for taking distributions from a retirement plan.

LO 52.6   Explain the income tax implications of a retirement plan lifetime distribution options.

In the case of a qualified retirement plan, there are three basic distribution options that may be available, depending on plan provisions:

■ A **lump-sum distribution**

■ An **annuity** or other form of periodic payment

■ A **rollover** or **direct transfer**

Lump-Sum Distribution

Generally, distributions from qualified plans are taxed as ordinary income. Special tax treatment may be available when a distribution meets the qualifications for lump-sum distribution treatment. The special tax treatments available are:

■ 10-year forward averaging;

■ pre-1974 capital gain treatment; and

■ net unrealized appreciation.

Typically, only defined contribution types of qualified plans offer a lump-sum payout option. A lump-sum distribution is a distribution from a qualified plan of a participant's entire interest in the plan that occurs within one tax year.

There are three conditions that must be met for a lump-sum distribution to qualify for favorable income tax treatment. These conditions include the following:

■ The distribution must represent the entire amount of the employee's benefit in the plan.

■ An election must be made by the participant, or in the case of the participant's death, by the estate, within one year of the receipt of the distribution.

■ The distribution must be due to one of the following:

  — The employee dies.

  — The employee attains the age of 59½.

  — The employee separates from service (this triggering event is not possible in the case of a self-employed individual).

  — The employee becomes disabled.

In addition, for a lump-sum distribution to be eligible for 10-year forward averaging or pre-1974 capital gain treatment, the employee must have participated in the plan for at least five taxable years before the tax year of distribution (unless the lump-sum distribution is payable because of the participant's death).

Because pre-1974 capital gain treatment and 10-year forward averaging are both techniques tied to an eligible birth date of before January 2, 1936, the utility of these treatments becomes less relevant every year. In practice, the financial planner will have few clients who receive lump-sum distributions that qualify for these techniques. For the CFP® certification examination, it is recommended the student understand the two treatments conceptually, but it is unlikely the actual calculations will be tested.

10-Year Forward Averaging

A plan participant receiving a qualifying lump-sum distribution is eligible to elect **10-year forward averaging** if the participant was born before January 2, 1936.

Using 10-year forward averaging, the income tax payable on the lump-sum distribution is calculated by determining the tax attributable to an amount equal to one-tenth of the total taxable distribution after taking into account a specified minimum distribution allowance. This calculated amount is then multiplied by 10 to determine the total tax due on the distribution. The benefit of the method is that the participant-taxpayer will avoid taxation at higher income tax rates. However, the averaging tax calculation is based on 1986 income tax rates and not on current (2015) income tax rates. Thus, the tax on the lump-sum distribution is not always lower under the 1986 rates, and working through a separate calculation is the only way to determine if the 10-year method is indeed advantageous for a client.

Pre-1974 Capital Gain Treatment

A qualified plan participant born before January 2, 1936, who is receiving a qualifying lump-sum distribution may also benefit by electing **pre-1974 capital gain treatment**. This election allows the taxpayer to treat the portion of a lump-sum distribution attributable to pre-1974 participation in a qualified plan as long-term capital gain rather than ordinary income. The long-term capital gain portion is taxed at 20%, not at current long-term capital gain tax rates. The taxpayer must compare his current marginal income tax rate with the applicable 20% rate in evaluating the pre-1974 capital gain treatment election.

The portion of the lump-sum distribution eligible for pre-1974 capital gain treatment is determined by multiplying the total lump-sum distribution by a calculated ratio. The applicable ratio is determined by dividing the participant's number of months of pre-1974 participation in the qualified plan by the participant's total number of months of participation in the plan. The remaining lump-sum portion not eligible for pre-1974 capital gain treatment is taxed as ordinary income and may be eligible for 10-year forward averaging if the taxpayer otherwise qualifies.

Net Unrealized Appreciation

The **net unrealized appreciation (NUA)** tax concept has already been discussed several times in this educational course. A taxpayer who receives a lump-sum distribution consisting at least partially of employer stock will not be liable for income tax on the net unrealized appreciation portion of the distribution until the stock is sold or otherwise disposed of. Further, the NUA portion of the stock is taxed at long-term capital gains rates, as opposed to ordinary income tax rates, upon disposition.

NUA is defined as the excess of the FMV of employer securities distributed over the cost or basis of the securities to the trust, typically the total value of the securities at the time of employer contribution to the plan. This cost or basis of the securities is taxed as ordinary income in the year of distribution. The NUA portion at the time of the lump-sum distribution will always be taxed as LTCG, regardless of the holding period after the lump-sum distribution. Note that if the taxpayer otherwise qualifies, the ordinary income portion of the distribution may be eligible for 10-year forward averaging treatment.

EXAMPLE Bryan received a lump-sum distribution of 10,000 shares of stock from his employer's stock bonus plan valued at $1 million. The value of these shares contributed over the years was $250,000 (basis to the trust). Thus, $750,000 ($1 million – $250,000) is treated as NUA and is not taxed currently on distribution. The basis amount of $250,000 is taxed as ordinary income in the year of the lump-sum distribution. Bryan's adjusted basis in these shares now equals $250,000 (the amount of the ordinary income taxed at distribution event). When Bryan subsequently sells the stock, the $750,000 NUA amount is taxed as long term capital gain and any appreciation on the shares that has occurred after the lump-sum distribution date will be subject to capital gains tax (either short term or long term depending on how long he holds the shares before selling).

Note that, in the event employer stock is distributed from a qualified plan before the participant's death, the NUA portion does not receive a step-up in basis. Rather, it is treated as income in respect of a decedent (IRD), to be discussed in the *106: Estate Planning* course of this program. Any additional appreciation in the stock, once removed from the plan, is eligible for a step-up in basis at the employee's death under the step-up to fair market value rules in effect on the date of the participant's death. As a result, the basis of the stock to the beneficiary is usually equal to the FMV of the stock at the participant's death, less the amount that is treated as NUA.

EXAMPLE Continuing with the previous example, now assume Bryan dies with the FMV of the stock equal to $2 million. The adjusted basis of these shares to Bryan's heirs is now $1,250,000 or the FMV of the stock ($2 million) less the amount treated as NUA ($750,000).

PRACTICE QUESTION

Choose the best answer for the question below.

1. A lump-sum distribution made from a qualified plan may be eligible for the following favorable tax treatments EXCEPT
   A. 10-year forward averaging for individuals born before January 2, 1936
   B. 5-year forward averaging for individuals born before January 2, 1936
   C. capital gains treatment on the portion of distribution allocable to pre-1974 contributions
   D. NUA on employer securities portion of distribution

   Answer: B. Five-year forward averaging is not an available tax treatment for lump-sum distributions to any qualified plan participant.

Annuity or Other Periodic Payment

The second basic option for distributions from qualified retirement plans is the **annuity** or other periodic payment option. An annuity distribution received from a qualified plan is taxable as ordinary income to the extent that it exceeds the allocated portion of the employee's basis. If the employee has no basis in the plan created by after-tax contributions, the full amount of each annuity distribution is taxable as ordinary income when received.

A simplified method of taxing annuity distributions payable from a qualified plan is now required by law. Under this method, the participant recovers the basis, if any, as of the annuity starting date in level amounts over the number of anticipated monthly payments. Except in the case of payments that are made for a fixed period (rather than over the life expectancy of the participant or a spouse), the anticipated payments are determined under IRS tables. The calculation of exclusion amount of the annuity payment (tax-free portion) is covered in both the *102: Insurance Planning and Employee Benefits* and *104: Income Tax Planning* courses.

All pension plans (such as traditional defined benefit, cash balance, and money purchase pension plans) must provide for two forms of survivorship annuities for spouses: the qualified preretirement survivor annuity (QPSA) and the qualified joint and survivor annuity (QJSA). These will be discussed in more detail in Unit 7. Profit-sharing type plans (traditional profit-sharing, Section 401(k) plan, stock bonus plan, and ESOPs) generally are not required to provide these types of annuities, although they can, and often, do.

Direct Transfers and Rollovers

Qualified plan participants and IRA owners may transfer plan assets between plans, without current taxation, through direct transfers and rollovers.

A **direct transfer** (or trustee-to-trustee transfer) occurs when the trustee or other custodian who holds the assets making up the participant's accrued benefits transfers some or all of those assets directly to the trustee or custodian of another retirement plan or IRA. A direct transfer is important because such a transfer is not subject to the 20% mandatory tax withholding that is otherwise applicable to qualified plan distributions.

Any taxable eligible rollover distribution paid from an employer-sponsored retirement plan directly to the plan participant is subject to a mandatory income tax withholding of 20%, even if the participant intends to roll it over later. If the distribution is subsequently rolled over, the participant must add funds from other sources equal to the amount withheld, or the withheld amount itself is subject to current income taxation and a possible early withdrawal penalty. The 20% mandatory tax withholding is not applicable to IRA distributions. If the participant adds funds equaling the 20% withholding amount and rolls over the entire original amount distributed from the plan to another retirement plan or IRA, none of the distributed amount is included in the participant's gross income. The income tax withheld is added to any other federal income tax withholding amounts for that tax year and may be refundable to the taxpayer when the IRS Form 1040 is filed for the tax year depending on what the taxpayer's taxable income is and if enough has been previously withheld to cover the resulting income tax liability.

Qualified plan participants and IRA owners may also transfer assets tax free through **rollovers**. Generally, a rollover is a distribution from a qualified plan or IRA that the taxpayer subsequently contributes to another qualified plan or IRA within 60 days of receipt of the distribution. The rollover is free from current taxation if completed within 60 days of receipt of the distribution. A taxpayer may make only one tax-free rollover within a one-year period to an IRA or the IRA into which the first rollover was made even if the taxpayer has multiple IRAs. The limit is one tax-free IRA rollover when the rollover is not a trustee-to-trustee rollover. This is a disadvantage when compared to a direct transfer, as the number of direct transfers that may be made in a one-year period is not limited.

The following are rules that apply to all rollovers and direct transfers:

- Both the transferor and transferee plans must satisfy statutory requirements for treatment as an eligible retirement plan or IRA, as the case may be.

- Required minimum distributions (RMDs) and hardship withdrawals may not be rolled over.

In addition, a distribution from a qualified plan, a Section 403(b) plan, or a Section 457 plan may not be rolled over if it is made by reason of the substantially equal periodic payment exception to the 10% premature distribution penalty rules.

Rollovers and direct rollovers are allowed among all qualified plans, Section 403(b) plans, IRAs, and Section 457 plans. The following chart summarizes allowable rollovers.

Allowable Rollovers

Type of Distribution	Rollover Allowed to a:
1. From qualified plan	Qualified, Section 403(b), or Section 457 plan or IRA
2. From Section 403(b) Plan (TDA)	Qualified, Section 403(b), or Section 457 plan or IRA
3. From Section 457 Plan (governmental)	Qualified, Section 403(b), or Section 457 plan or IRA
4. Pursuant to a qualified domestic relations order (QDRO)	Qualified, Section 403(b), or Section 457 plan or IRA
5. From SIMPLE IRA (after 2 years of participation)	Qualified, Section 403(b), or Section 457 plan or IRA
6. From SIMPLE IRA (during first 2 years of participation)	SIMPLE IRA only
7. From Section 457 plan (nongovernmental)	Section 457 plan only
8. From after-tax contributions to a qualified plan or Section 403(b) plan	IRA, Section 403(b), or a direct transfer to a defined contribution or defined benefit plan (separate account)
9. From after-tax contributions to an IRA	IRA only

While plans are required to provide participants with the option of rolling over distributions by transferring them directly to another plan or IRA, there is no requirement that the transferee plan must accept the rollover contribution. Thus, before assuming that one qualified plan distribution may be rolled to another qualified plan, it is best to check.

Participants can make direct transfers of distributions from their qualified plans, Section 403(b) plans, and governmental Section 457 plans to Roth IRAs. Any such transfer is subject to the Roth IRA conversion rules in effect at the time of the rollover. There is no modified adjusted gross income limit for taxpayers making conversion transfers.

Finally, an employee-participant is not required to roll over the entire amount received from a qualified plan. The participant may roll over only a portion. To the extent of the amount rolled over properly, the distribution is non-taxable and is not counted as a contribution to a recipient plan (annual additions limit) or IRA (annual limit). Alternatively, the taxable portion of any amount not rolled over properly is treated as an ordinary distribution and also is not eligible for special 10-year averaging treatment (if the participant otherwise qualifies for this benefit).

So Which Do I Take?

The threshold question for any qualified plan participant who has any of the three distribution options—lump-sum, annuity, or rollover—available to the client is "which one do I choose?" There is no one simple answer to this question as it depends on a number of factors, including future income tax rates. But there are some basic questions to be considered:

■ How will the benefit be used by the participant? For example, if the plan offers a lump-sum distribution payout, and the participant wants to buy a vacation home with his retirement benefit, the lump-sum distribution may be the best choice but the tax consequences of doing so should be considered.

■ Does the participant need the principal of the retirement benefits or just the income to support his anticipated retirement lifestyle? If choosing the lump-sum distribution or rollover option, the participant assumes the risk of superannuation or the risk of outliving his money. This is not an issue if an annuity or periodic payment is taken, so long as it is not over a fixed period rather than over the participant's life.

■ What is the amount of the retirement distribution? Certainly from a tax standpoint, either the annuity or rollover is best here because taxes need to be paid immediately (and all at once) if a lump-sum distribution is chosen. If the lump-sum distribution option is available to participants, a majority of participants take it.

■ What is the anticipated life expectancy of the participant? The amount to which a rollover distribution accumulates is dependent on a longer participant life expectancy. As a general rule, the younger the participant is when separating from service (and generally eligible for a distribution), the more advantageous is the rollover option so as to achieve maximum compounding of tax-deferred dollars.

Note that IRS 1099-R statements report withdrawals and distributions from IRAs and retirement plans. These amounts should be reported on line 15 of IRS Form 1040 (Individual Tax Return), even if they are not taxable. If the IRA was rolled over, enter the amount rolled over on line 15a and write the word "Rollover" next to line 15b.

PRACTICE
QUESTION

Choose the best answer for the question below.

1. Jack, age 65, has received a lump-sum distribution of his Section 401(k) plan balance of $500,000. Jack wants to combine the proceeds from the sale of his personal residence with $50,000 from his lump-sum distribution to purchase a new home in the city close to his daughter and his grandchildren. He wants to rollover the balance to his IRA as he is still within the 60-day rollover window. What affect will reducing his distribution by $50,000 have on his rollover plans?

   1. Jack must rollover the entire lump-sum distribution within 60 days of its receipt or the entire $500,000 will be included in his gross income.

   2. Jack will have to include the $50,000 in gross income in the year of the distribution.

   3. Jack can make a rollover of $450,000 with no penalty as long as he is within the 60 day time window.

   4. Jack will not be able to use 10-year forward averaging for this distribution.

   A. 1 only

   B. 2 and 3

   C. 2, 3, and 4

   D. 1 and 4

Answer: C.   Statement 1 is incorrect. If Jack rolls over less than the entire $500,000 distribution, only the amount not rolled over is included in his gross income. Statements 2, 3, and 4 are correct. Jack will have to include $50,000 in gross income this year and the remaining balance of the distribution can still be rolled over as long as he does it within 60 days of the distribution. Jack is too young to qualify for 10-year forward averaging.

B. REQUIRED BEGINNING DATE FOR REQUIRED MINIMUM DISTRIBUTIONS

LO 52.3   Define the terms required beginning date (RBD) for making a retirement plan distribution and the required minimum distribution (RMD).

LO 52.6   Explain the income tax implications of a retirement plan distribution option.

LO 52.9   Calculate the required minimum distribution (RMD) for a given client assuming specified facts.

LO 52.12   Explain when the income tax penalty is applied to a retirement plan distribution.

Generally, the **required beginning date (RBD)** for the first distribution from a qualified plan, Section 403(b), or Section 457 plan (or IRA) must be made by April 1 of the year following the year in which the participant (or owner of the IRA) attained age 70½. In subsequent years, the distribution must be made by December 31 of that year. Because of this, it is possible to delay distributions to April 1 of the year subsequent to when the participant attains age 70½. However, if doing so, there must be two distributions in that calendar year (with the second distribution occurring on or before December 31 of that year). If the client postpones the first year's **required minimum distribution (RMD)** into a year where two RMDs are taken, the two RMDs are now calculated using different account balances. Specifically, the postponed first-year RMD is based on the participant's plan or IRA account balance as of the end of the year preceding the first distribution year, whereas the second RMD is based on the account balance as of the end of the first distribution year. Different divisors or distribution periods must be used in calculating the amount of RMD that is necessary. This raises the planning question: should a taxpayer delay the first distribution to the subsequent year? As a general rule, the answer to this question is no. In that the majority of the distributions will most likely be taxed as ordinary income, taking two required minimum distributions in the same tax year may serve to increase, perhaps substantially, the overall marginal tax rate for the client on all income for the year.

Participants in qualified plans, Section 403(b) plans, and governmental Section 457 plans may defer the required beginning date until April 1 following the year of actual retirement, if the participant continues to work after attaining age 70½. In other words, in these types of plans (not any type of IRA), the participant's required beginning date for distributions is the later of April 1 following the year in which the participant attained age 70½ or actually retired. This exception is not available, however, if the participant is a greater than 5% owner of the business sponsoring the retirement plan. Thus, self-employed businessowners are subject to the normal age 70½ rule.

> **EXAMPLE** Bruce is a 50% partner, along with his brother, in Brothers Barbecue. He attains age 70½ in 2015. Thus, he must begin taking distributions from the Brothers Barbecue profit-sharing plan no later than April 1, 2016, even though he may plan to continue working full time at the restaurant. Had Bruce not been a greater than 5% owner, he could have elected to defer commencement of RMD until April 1 of the year following his actual retirement date.

After distributions are required to begin from a qualified plan, Section 403(b) plan, governmental Section 457 plan, or IRA, if sufficient amounts are not withdrawn, a 50% excise tax is imposed on the difference in the amount of minimum distribution that should have been made and the amount of distribution that was actually made.

C. CALCULATING REQUIRED MINIMUM DISTRIBUTIONS (RMDS)

LO 52.9 Calculate the required minimum distribution (RMD) for a given client assuming specified facts.

The RMD for any given year is calculated by dividing the participant's account balance as of the close of business on December 31 of the preceding year by an applicable divisor or distribution period. This divisor is determined by referencing the participant's age, as of December 31 of the distribution year, in an IRS Table known as the **Uniform Lifetime Table**. This table is always used to determine the RMD of a plan participant or IRA owner with one exception: if the participant's designated beneficiary on the plan or IRA is the participant's spouse and this spouse is more than 10 years younger than the participant, then the actual joint life expectancies of the respective spouses may be used. The following table is a reproduction of the Uniform Lifetime Table.

Table for Determining Applicable Divisor for Minimum Distributions (Minimum Distribution Applicable Divisor)*

Age	Applicable Divisor	Age	Applicable Divisor
70	27.4	93	9.6
71	26.5	94	9.1
72	25.6	95	8.6
73	24.7	96	8.1
74	23.8	97	7.6
75	22.9	98	7.1
76	22.0	99	6.7
77	21.2	100	6.3
78	20.3	101	5.9
79	19.5	102	5.5
80	18.7	103	5.2
81	17.9	104	4.9
82	17.1	105	4.5
83	16.3	106	4.2
84	15.5	107	3.9
85	14.8	108	3.7
86	14.1	109	3.4
87	13.4	110	3.1
88	12.7	111	2.9
89	12.0	112	2.6
90	11.4	113	2.4
91	10.8	114	2.1
92	10.2	115	1.9

*Use this table if the beneficiary is 1) someone other than spouse, or 2) a spouse that is no more than 10 years younger than the participant.

The complexity in using this table does not come from referencing the divisor number. Instead, it comes from determining the distribution period number for the first several years of RMDs. For example, if your client attained age 70½ before July 1 of any given year, he will be age 71 (70½ plus six months) by the end of that year, and you would use a divisor or distribution period of 26.5 from the Uniform Lifetime Table. Alternatively, if your client did not turn age 70½ until the last half of any given year (after June 30), he will only be age 70 at the end of that year, and you would use a divisor or distribution period of 27.4.

> **EXAMPLE** Joe attained the age of 70½ in May 2015. Because Joe will be 71 years old on December 31, 2015, his divisor or distribution period is 26.5 years. If his IRA account balance is $500,000 on December 31, 2014, (remember to use the prior year's account balance), his RMD will be $18,868 ($500,000 divided by 26.5). This is the result even though Joe can delay his 2015 RMD until April 1, 2016, if he so chooses. (Note: If Joe took two distributions in 2016, his second RMD, required to be taken by December 31, 2016, would be calculated by dividing his December 31, 2015, account balance by 25.6 because he would be 72 years old on December 31, 2016.)

Finally, it is important to recognize that the Uniform Lifetime Table is designed to liquidate your client's account balance over the joint-and-survivor life expectancy and a hypothetical beneficiary who is no more than 10 years younger than the participant, recalculated annually. For retired individuals who need their RMDs to support themselves in their accustomed standard of living throughout their retirement years, this should be comforting and an excellent reason not to take more than the RMD in any one year.

PRACTICE
QUESTIONS

Choose the best answer for each of the questions below.

Answer questions 1–3 from the following facts:

Marian, who turned age 70½ on June 30, 2015, owns 10% of ABC Company. She has accumulated $5 million in ABC's stock bonus plan as of December 31 of the previous year (2014) and $5.5 million as of December 31, 2015. Distribution periods are as follows:

Age	Applicable Divisor
70	27.4
71	26.5
72	25.6

1. What is the required minimum distribution (RMD), if any, Marian must receive for 2015?
   A. $0
   B. $182,482
   C. $188,679
   D. $207,547

   Answer: C.   The minimum distribution that must be received for 2015 is calculated by dividing Marian's account balance on December 31, 2014, ($5 million) by the factor for age 71 (26.5). This results in an RMD of $188,679 ($5 million divided by 26.5).

2. If Marian receives a distribution of $180,000 during 2015, how much in penalties, if any, will she be required to pay on her 2015 tax return?
   A. $0
   B. $1,241
   C. $4,340
   D. $13,774

   Answer: A.   Marian may defer her first RMD until April 1, 2016. Therefore, she has until April 1, 2016 to distribute the balance of her RMD for 2015 without incurring a penalty.

3. Which of the following statements regarding Marian is CORRECT?
   A. If she continues to work for ABC Company, she is permitted to defer her RMD until after she retires.
   B. She can roll her account balance over into a rollover IRA when she terminates employment.
   C. If she rolls her account balance into a rollover IRA and she does not commingle the funds with other IRA funds, she is permitted to use 10-year forward averaging on the entire balance.
   D. If she takes her RMD by April 1 of next year, she will not be required to take any other distributions next year.

   Answer: B.   The only statement that is correct is that Marian may roll her account balance to a rollover IRA when she separates from service. She is a greater than 5% owner of ABC Company; therefore, she is not allowed to defer her RMD until after she retires. It is not possible to use 10-year forward averaging with an IRA distribution. Finally, if she waits until April 1 of the next year to take her 1st RMD, she must take a 2nd distribution by December 31 of that same year.

D. PREMATURE DISTRIBUTION PENALTY AND EXCEPTIONS FOR QUALIFIED PLANS AND SECTION 403(B) PLANS

LO 52.3   Define the terms required beginning date (RBD) for making a retirement plan distribution and the required minimum distribution (RMD).

LO 52.5   Describe a qualified domestic relations order (QDRO) and know where it can be used.

LO 52.6   Explain the income tax implications of lifetime retirement plan distribution options.

LO 52.11   Identify the early distribution penalty exceptions.

LO 52.12   Explain when the income tax penalty is applied to a retirement plan distribution.

Like IRAs, distributions taken from a qualified or Section 403(b) plan before the owner attains age 59½ are subject to an **early distribution penalty** of 10% on the taxable portion of the distribution (in addition to income tax). However, also like IRAs, there are notable exceptions to the imposition of this 10% penalty. If any of the following circumstances are the reason for the distribution from a qualified plan, the penalty will not be imposed:

- Made on or after the attainment of age 59½

- Made because of the owner's total and permanent disability

- Made to the owner's beneficiary or estate due to the owner's death

- Made as a part of substantially equal periodic payments at least annually over the life expectancy of the owner, or the owner and a designated beneficiary; in addition, these payments, once begun, must continue for the greater of five years or until the owner attains the age of 59½

- Made for medical expenses exceeding 10% of the owner's AGI for taxpayers who have not yet attained age 59½

- Made after separation from service from the employer after attainment of age 55

- Made to a qualifying family member under a qualified domestic relations order (QDRO) (QDROs are discussed in the next unit), a domestic relations order, or a separate maintenance agreement. Note that six of these exceptions are the same as for IRAs as mentioned in the previous unit. However, the separation from service after attainment of age 55 exception is applicable only to qualified plan distributions. Furthermore, the IRA premature distribution exceptions for higher education costs, first-time home buyer costs, and paying for health insurance premiums while the owner is unemployed, do not apply to distributions made from qualified plans.

Choose the best answer for the question below.

1. Which of the following distributions from a qualified plan would NOT be subject to the 10% early withdrawal penalty, assuming the participant has not attained age 59½ at the time of the distribution?

1. Distribution for higher education costs for the taxpayer, spouse, child, or grandchild
2. Distribution made to a qualifying family member under a QDRO
3. Distribution made after separation from service from the employer after attainment of age 55
4. Distribution to pay employer-sponsored health insurance premiums on a pretax basis

A. 1, 2, and 3
B. 1 and 4
C. 2 and 3
D. 3 and 4

Answer: C.   Only Statements 2 and 3 are correct. Statement 1 is incorrect because the exception to the 10% premature distribution penalty for higher education expenses only applies to IRAs and not qualified plans. Statement 4 is incorrect because the health insurance premium provision only applies (under the medical expense exception) if payments are made on an after-tax basis or for a private (not employer-sponsored) plan.

E. LOANS FROM QUALIFIED PLANS, SECTION 403(B) PLAN AND GOVERNMENTAL SECTION 457 PLANS

LO 47.6   Explain the rules for loans to participants in qualified plans, Section 403(b) plans, and governmental Section 457 plans.

To allow plan participants access to a portion of their vested retirement plan funds without incurring income tax or penalties, some plans allow provisions for plan loans. However, no type of IRA-funded plan may allow loans. The most common type of plan to provide loan provisions is the traditional Section 401(k) plan. Occasionally, Section 403(b) TSA plans and governmental Section 457 plans may allow loans. If the plan allows for loans, the tax code rules regarding repayment of the loan must be adhered to closely or the loan may become a taxable distribution. Such a distribution results not only in income tax due, but in a 10% penalty, if made before the participant attains age 59½.

All loans from a qualified, Section 403(b), or governmental Section 457 plan must be repaid within five years with interest. The only exception to this rule is when a plan loan is made to allow the participant to acquire a dwelling to be used as a principal residence. In this case, the loan must be repaid over a reasonable period of time (with the timeframe determined by the plan sponsor). In addition, all loan repayments must be made in level installments at least quarterly.

Generally, plan loans are limited to one-half the vested account balance of the plan participant, not to exceed a dollar cap of $50,000. However, when the vested account balance is currently less than $20,000, loans up to $10,000 are available without regard to the one-half the vested account balance rule. The following table summarizes the maximum plan loans that are available based on the participant's account balance.

Vested Account Balance of Participant	Maximum Loan Amount Available
$10,000 or less	Vested account balance
$10,001–$20,000	$10,000
$20,001–$100,000	50% of vested account balance
More than $100,000	$50,000

The maximum loan balance may also be reduced further by any loan balance the participant had in the one-year period preceding the loan. If not for this provision, participants could unjustly take advantage of the five-year repayment rule by waiting until the last possible date for repayment and then immediately re-executing the loan.

> ✱ **EXAMPLE** Four years ago, Sharon borrowed $50,000 from her qualified plan. Last year, she made the final payment of $10,000 to satisfy the plan loan obligation. Sharon now has a vested account balance of $300,000 and wants to borrow another $50,000. Because of the loan reduction rule, Sharon may only borrow $40,000. The $50,000 maximum loan amount must be reduced by $10,000, the outstanding loan balance in the prior year.

Finally, interest on a plan loan is generally treated for income tax purposes as consumer interest, meaning it is nondeductible. However, if the loan is secured by the participant's principal residence, the interest is considered qualified residence interest and it is deductible if the participant itemizes expenses when filing his federal income tax return. However, if a loan is made to a key employee, as defined by top-heavy rules, the interest is always treated as consumer interest and is nondeductible even if the loan is secured by the key employee's principal residence.

PRACTICE
QUESTIONS   *Choose the best answer for each of the questions below.*

1. Which one of the following retirement plans generally has loan provisions?
    A. Defined benefit pension plans
    B. Money purchase pension plans
    C. Section 401(k) plans
    D. SEPs

    Answer: C.   Defined benefit and money purchase pension plans do not generally have loan provisions. SEPs are a type of IRA and, therefore, cannot have loan provisions. Loan provisions are established in the plan document and are common for plans that have elective deferrals, such as a Section 401(k) and Section 403(b) plan.

2. Mark and Julie are both age 58 and have come to their financial planner, Jack, a CFP® professional, for advice. Mark has been laid off from his current position. He expects to be recalled to work within 6 months as the layoff is to allow new machinery to be installed, after which time manufacturing will start again. In the meantime unemployment benefits are not enough to meet their current financial needs. The couple is afraid of depleting their retirement assets to fill the gap but do not know what else to do. Mark has a SEP plan account at his old employment with a balance of $360,000. Julie has a Section 401(k) at her place of employment with a plan balance of $280,000 and it has loan provisions. They have no mortgage on their home and their savings is currently being depleted by living expenses since Mark ceased working. Which of the following is the best recommendation for Jack to make to the couple?

   A. Take a distribution from Julie's Section 401(k) plan for 6 months of expenses.
   B. From Mark's SEP plan, take substantially equal payments until Mark attains age 59½.
   C. Julie should take a loan from her Section 401(k) plan for the minimum amount needed.
   D. Mark and Julie should obtain a line of credit using their personal residence as collateral.

   Answer: C.   Julie should take a loan from her Section 401(k) plan for the minimum amount needed. There would be no early distribution penalty and it can be repaid over time. As long as the loan is repaid before she retires, it will not reduce their retirement assets, which is a concern the couple has. If she took a distribution instead of a loan, there would be a 10% early distribution penalty. If Mark takes the substantially equal payments from his SEP, they must continue for the greater of 5 years or until he attains age 59½. This will reduce their retirement assets, which they wanted to avoid. While it may be possible to obtain a line of credit using the home as collateral, the decrease in income and the fact that they are having difficulty living on one income as it is makes it unlikely they could qualify. (Domain 4: Developing the recommendations)

105 UNIT 6 POST-STUDY CHECKLIST

☐   Can I explain the rules for loans to participants in qualified plans, Section 403(b) plans, and governmental Section 457 plans?

☐   Am I able to identify the options for taking distributions from a retirement plan?

☐   Am I able to identify the required beginning date (RBD) for making a retirement plan distribution and calculate the required minimum distribution (RMD) for a given client assuming specified facts?

☐   Do I know how to describe a qualified domestic relations order (QDRO) and know where it can be used?

☐   Can I explain the income tax implications of a retirement plan distribution option?

Am I able to define and understand the application of the following terms to financial planning?

☐ 10-year forward averaging	☐ Net unrealized appreciation (NUA)
☐ 50% excise tax	☐ Pre-1974 capital gain treatment
☐ Annuity	☐ Required beginning date (RBD)
☐ Direct transfer	☐ Required minimum distribution (RMD)
☐ Early distribution penalty	☐ Rollover
☐ Lump-sum distribution	☐ Uniform Lifetime Table

Plan Distributions—
Part II

REFER TO

CFP® Certification Principal Topics – Retirement Planning, Retirement Needs Analysis

CFP® Certification Principal Topics – Retirement Planning, Distribution Rules, Alternatives, and Taxation

No Supplemental Readings for Unit 7 of 105 Retirement Planning Student Guide

(For specific assignments, refer to class syllabus.)

INTRODUCTION

This is the second of the two units on qualified plan and IRA distributions. This unit focuses on post-death distribution issues and the choice of beneficiary by the plan participant or IRA owner. The issues discussed in this unit are, in part, estate planning issues (rather than pure retirement planning issues), and it is best to work with an estate planning attorney to answer any detailed questions and to draft or at least review all beneficiary designation forms.

The choices of beneficiary for a qualified plan or IRA are primarily those listed below:

■ A younger individual (so as to spread the taxable impact of the distribution)

■ The participant's surviving spouse

■ A qualified charity

■ Older individuals

■ A trust for the benefit of the surviving spouse

■ The participant's estate

LEARNING OBJECTIVES

After completing this unit, you should be able to achieve the following learning objectives:

CFP® Certification Principal Topics – Retirement Planning, Retirement Needs Analysis

LO 44.3   Describe the choice of beneficiary considerations as they relate to a qualified plan or IRA.

CFP® Certification Principal Topics – Retirement Planning, Distribution Rules, Alternatives, and Taxation

LO 52.2   Identify the options for taking distributions from a retirement plan.

LO 52.3   Define the terms required beginning date (RBD) for making a retirement plan distribution and the required minimum distribution (RMD).

LO 52.5   Describe a qualified domestic relations order (QDRO) and know where it can be used.

LO 52.13   Identify the distribution options for different identified beneficiaries of a qualified plan or IRA.

LO 52.14   Identify the post-death options for taking distributions from a Roth IRA.

LO 52.15   Describe the automatic survivor benefit method of taking distributions from a retirement plan (QJSAs and QPSAs).

KEY TERMS

Beneficiary

Designated beneficiary

Five-year rule

Nonspouse beneficiary

Qualified domestic relations order (QDRO)

Qualified joint and survivor annuity (QJSA)

Qualified preretirement survivor annuity (QPSA)

Qualifying public charities

Qualifying trust

Remaining life expectancy

Surviving spouse

A. CHOICE OF BENEFICIARY FOR A QUALIFIED PLAN OR IRA

LO 44.3   Describe the choice of beneficiary considerations as they relate to a qualified plan or IRA.

LO 52.3   Define the terms required beginning date (RBD) for making a retirement plan distribution and the required minimum distribution (RMD).

LO 52.13   Identify the distribution options for different identified beneficiaries of a qualified plan or IRA.

The choice of **beneficiary** for a qualified plan or IRA is not nearly as simple as most individuals may think. Most married individuals automatically name their spouse the beneficiary (which is a favored option under current law) and think little about what happens if the spouse does not survive the participant. The choice for unmarried individuals is not as simple.

The manner in which qualified plan or IRA benefits are distributed depends on several questions:

■   Is there a designated beneficiary of the plan or account?

■   Have required minimum distributions (RMDs) already begun at the time of the participant-owner's death?

Under the Treasury Regulations, a **designated beneficiary** means any individual designated as a beneficiary by the participant or owner. The period for determining a designated beneficiary is as of September 30 of the year following the year of the participant-owner's death. If a designated beneficiary is determined as of this date, the beneficiary's interest is generally distributed over the longer of:

■   the beneficiary's life expectancy, beginning in the year following the participant-owner's death, reduced by one for each subsequent year (known as the minus one method); or

■   either the **five-year rule** or the **remaining life expectancy** of the participant-owner, determined as of his date of death, reduced by one for each subsequent year [depending on whether RMDs have or have not begun as of the participant-owner's death, or in other words, whether death has occurred before the required beginning date (RBD) for RMDs or after].

If no designated beneficiary is determined by September 30 of the year following the year of the participant-owner's death, the interest is distributed as follows:

■   Death before required beginning date: no longer than five years

■   Death after required beginning date: the remaining life expectancy of the participant-owner, reduced by one for each subsequent year

If the **surviving spouse** is the beneficiary, these general rules regarding a designated or nondesignated beneficiary do not apply as the surviving spouse has a different set of rules. If more than one beneficiary is designated with respect to a participant-owner as of the September 30 date, the designated beneficiary with the shortest life expectancy is the measuring life for purposes of determining the distribution period. Special rules apply if the participant-owner's benefit is divided into separate accounts as of the date of death and the beneficiaries of each account differ. These rules will be discussed later in this unit.

In all of these designation rules, the September 30 date of the year following the year of the participant-owner's death is used so a distribution may be calculated and made by the statutory deadline of beginning qualified plan or IRA distributions by December 31 of the year following the year of the participant-owner's death.

Surviving Spouse as Beneficiary

The participant-owner's spouse has more favorable tax alternatives available regarding required post-death distributions than any other individual beneficiary because a surviving spouse beneficiary may elect to be treated as the account owner or as the designated beneficiary. As mentioned, while other beneficiaries must begin taking required distributions by December 31 of the year after the participant's death, the spouse (if the sole beneficiary) generally has other options, depending on whether or not death of the participant spouse occurred before or after the required beginning date (RBD) for required minimum distributions (RMDs). This applies to the participant's balance in a qualified plan, Section 403(b) plan, governmental Section 457 plan, or IRA.

Death Before the Required Beginning Date (RBD)

If the surviving spouse is the sole beneficiary of the plan, the surviving spouse can receive distributions over the surviving spouse's own remaining single-life expectancy, recalculated each year. Distributions must begin in the year in which the owner would have attained age 70½.

The surviving spouse can also roll the plan balance over and defer distributions until the surviving spouse attains age 70½. This election may be made only if the surviving spouse is the sole beneficiary. The surviving spouse can also elect to distribute the entire account balance within five years after the year of the owner's death (five-year rule). This election can be made only if the plan provisions allow the five-year rule.

Death After the Required Beginning Date

If the surviving spouse is the beneficiary of the plan, the surviving spouse can receive distributions over the surviving spouse's own remaining single-life expectancy, recalculated each year. Distributions must begin in the year following the year of death. The surviving spouse can also roll over the plan balance and defer distributions until the surviving spouse attains age 70½. This election may be made only if the surviving spouse is the sole beneficiary.

PRACTICE QUESTIONS   *Choose the best answer for each of the questions below.*

1. Stan is age 70 and his wife, Kris, is age 64. If Stan dies, what is the best option for his IRA if Kris wants to delay distributions as long as possible?
   A. Roll over his IRA to her IRA and take distributions based on her own required beginning date (age 70½).
   B. Keep the assets in his IRA and take distributions when Stan would have reached age 70½.

   Answer: A.   Because Kris is younger than Stan, she should roll over his IRA proceeds to her IRA and delay taking the proceeds until she attains age 70½ based on her life expectancy.

2. Continuing with the facts of Question #1, assume that Kris dies instead of Stan. What is Stan's best option for her IRA if he wants to delay distributions as long as possible?

    A. Roll over her IRA to his IRA and take distributions based on his own required beginning date (age 70½).

    B. Keep the assets in her IRA and take distributions when Kris would have reached age 70½.

Answer: B.   Now the preferable option is reversed. Stan should keep the assets in her IRA and take distributions when Kris would have been age 70½ based on his life expectancy.

Nonspouse as Beneficiary

A **nonspouse beneficiary** is an individual, not an entity, who is also not the surviving spouse of the decedent. As with the spousal beneficiary, distribution options depend on whether death of the participant-owner occurred before or after the required beginning date (RBD) for required minimum distributions (RMDs). This applies to the participant's balance in a qualified plan, Section 403(b) plan, governmental Section 457 plan, or IRA.

Death Before The Required Beginning Date

If the beneficiary is an individual other than the surviving spouse, the distribution period is the remaining life expectancy of the designated beneficiary. Life expectancy is calculated using the age of the designated beneficiary in the year following the year of the decedent's death, reduced by one for each subsequent year. The beneficiary can also elect to distribute the entire account balance as a single lump sum or in installments but fully distributed before the end of the fifth year following the year of the participant-owner's death (five-year rule). This installment election can be made only if the plan provisions allow the five-year rule following the owner's death. The account must be fully distributed either as a single lump sum or in installments but fully distributed before the end of the fifth year following the year of the participant-owner's death.

Death After The Required Beginning Date

For a nonspouse beneficiary, the distribution must be distributed at least as rapidly as the longer of remaining life expectancy of the designated beneficiary or the owner's life expectancy that would have been applicable for RMD purposes. Life expectancy is calculated using the age of the designated beneficiary in the year following the year of the employee's death, reduced by one for each subsequent year. The beneficiary may still elect a single lump-sum distribution.

Nonspouse beneficiaries are permitted to rollover death benefits from a qualified plan, Section 403(b) plan, governmental Section 457 plan, or IRA using a direct trustee-to-trustee transfer into an inherited IRA, which is a specially titled IRA account. No other contributions or rollovers may be made to the inherited IRA, and no rollovers may be made from the inherited IRA. Taxable distributions from the inherited IRA are includable in the income for the tax year it is received. Distributions still must be taken by the nonspouse beneficiary over the nonspouse's lifetime.

The direct trustee-to-trustee transfer to an inherited IRA is permitted whether death occurred before or after the required beginning date.

Qualifying Trust as Beneficiary

If a **qualifying trust** is named as beneficiary, the beneficiaries of the trust will be treated as a designated beneficiary so long as:

■ the trust is valid under state law;

■ the trust is irrevocable or will become so on the participant's death (such as revocable living trust);

■ the beneficiaries of the trust are identifiable from the trust instrument; and

■ appropriate documentation has been provided to the plan administrator (for example, a copy of the trust document is given to the plan administrator at or before the participant's death).

Assuming all these requirements are met, the trust can then use the life expectancy of the oldest trust beneficiary as the measuring life upon which to calculate the minus one method. If the qualified plan permits a life expectancy (annuity) payout, a young, sole beneficiary may receive many years of continued income tax deferral after the participant's death. In addition, this same stretching effect may be obtained by distributing the assets from an IRA to a younger beneficiary (through what is known as a trusteed IRA). This type of IRA may restrict the primary beneficiary's access to the account after the participant's death, and the participant can also name a successor beneficiary to receive what is left in the account after the primary beneficiary's death.

If the trust beneficiary is an older individual, he can still use the life expectancy payout (stretch) method but will not realize as much income tax deferral as a younger beneficiary because of his shorter life expectancy.

Qualifying Charity as Beneficiary

When individuals donate from their individual retirement accounts (IRAs) and Roth IRAs (to the extent the IRA or Roth IRA is taxable) to **qualifying public charities**, they must include the distributions as taxable income. There is a corresponding charitable deduction for the donation allowed the donor-taxpayer on the income tax return, subject to the rules of the limitations on charitable contributions by a taxpayer.

While a charity is treated as a nondesignated beneficiary for purposes of the post-death RMD rules, and a five-year payout is generally required, there is no income tax due on the benefit because a qualifying charity is a tax-exempt entity. In addition, an unlimited deduction is allowed for transfer (estate and gift) tax purposes if the charity is named as the sole beneficiary at the participant's death.

Estate as Beneficiary

It is usually not prudent to name the decedent's estate as the beneficiary of any qualified plan or IRA benefits. This is generally because of the post-death RMD rules and the income tax rules.

An estate cannot be treated as a designated beneficiary. Benefits payable to the estate have to be distributed under the five-year rule (either as a single lump sum or in installments, but fully distributed before the end of the fifth year following the year of the participant-owner's death) if death occurs before the required beginning date. If death occurs after the required beginning date, a single lump-sum distribution is still available, but any installment payments must continue over the deceased participant's remaining distribution period, reduced by one each year. The application of either of these rules (as compared to the stretching-out effect possible with a designated beneficiary) is usually not advantageous.

From an income tax perspective, the drawback of naming the estate as beneficiary is that an estate reaches the highest marginal income tax bracket after generating just $12,300 (2015) of taxable income. This is to be compared to an individual beneficiary designation where the individual does not reach the top marginal income tax bracket in 2015 until taxable income of $413,200 (single) or $464,850 (MFJ) is generated.

Separate Accounts as Beneficiary

For purposes of the post-death RMD rules, separate accounts are portions of a participant-owner's benefit representing the separate interests of beneficiaries under the plan as of the participant's date of death. The applicable distribution period is determined for each of these accounts, whereby each beneficiary is permitted to use his own life expectancy, only if the separate account is established no later than December 31 of the year following the participant's death. If these accounts are not established by this date, the life expectancy of the oldest beneficiary of all the accounts must be used (of course, then not permitting the maximum stretching effect that would otherwise be possible).

Regulations state that if a qualifying trust is the beneficiary of the participant's plan interest, separate account treatment is not available to the trust beneficiaries. The IRS has repeatedly stated the establishment of separate shares does not entitle multiple beneficiaries of the same trust to use their own life expectancy as the applicable distribution period. Rather, the life expectancy of the oldest trust beneficiary (the shortest life expectancy) must be used.

Summary of the Post-Death Required Minimum Distribution (RMD) Rules

The following is a summary of the RMD rules subsequent to a participant-owner's death and depending on whether death has occurred before or after the required beginning date for starting these distributions.

Beneficiary	Death Before Required Beginning Date	Death After Required Beginning Date
No designated beneficiary (includes charity, decedent's estate, and trusts with no designated beneficiary)	5-year rule	Remaining distribution period of decedent, reduced by one each year
Nonspouse beneficiary*	1) Remaining life expectancy of the beneficiary in the year following the year of death, reduced by one for each subsequent year, or 2) Elect 5-year rule, if plan provisions allow	Remaining life expectancy of the beneficiary in the year following the year of death, reduced by one for each subsequent year (may use owner's, if longer, had death not occurred)
Spouse beneficiary	1) Distributions over spouse's remaining single life expectancy, beginning in the year the decedent would have attained age 70½, 2) Roll over and treat as spouse's own, or 3) Elect 5-year rule, if plan provisions allow	1) Distributions over spouse's remaining single life expectancy, beginning in the year following the year of death, or 2) Roll over and treat as spouse's own

*A nonspouse beneficiary in a qualified plan, Section 403(b) plan, governmental Section 457 plan, or IRA also may roll over an inherited amount into an inherited IRA, preserving the right to take distributions over the nonspouse beneficiary's remaining life expectancy.

PRACTICE
QUESTIONS   *Choose the best answer for each of the questions below.*

1. Matt has died and named only his adult daughter, Suzie, as the designated beneficiary of his quali-fied plan account balance. Matt had not begun making RMDs from this account because he died at age 62. When must Suzie begin taking distributions from Matt's account to stretch the balance over her life expectancy?

    A.   By September 30 of the year following the year of Matt's death

    B.   By December 31 of the year of Matt's death

    C.   By December 31 of the year following the year of Matt's death

    D.   Whenever the plan document specifies that she must begin taking distributions

    Answer: C.   Suzie must begin taking distributions by December 31 of the year following the year of Matt's death. Otherwise, distributions must be made according to the five-year rule.

2. Valerie, an unmarried individual, recently died at age 74, leaving behind an IRA with a FMV of $200,000. She began taking RMDs after attaining age 70½ and correctly reported the same on her income tax returns. Before her death, Valerie named her granddaughter, Dawn, as the designated beneficiary of her IRA. Now that Valerie has died, Dawn has come to you for advice with respect to how these IRA benefits should be distributed. What do you tell her?

   A. Dawn can roll the IRA over into an inherited IRA and take distributions beginning at age 70½.

   B. In the year following Valerie's death, Dawn must begin taking distributions from the IRA over Valerie's remaining single-life expectancy.

   C. In the year following Valerie's death, Dawn must begin taking distributions from Valerie's IRA based on Dawn's remaining life expectancy, reduced by 1 each subsequent year.

   D. As a nonspouse beneficiary, Dawn must take a lump-sum distribution by the end of the year.

   Answer: C.   Because minimum distributions had already begun at the time of Valerie's death, Dawn must begin taking distributions (in the year following Valerie's death) based on Dawn's remaining life expectancy, reduced by one for each subsequent year (the minus one method). Dawn could roll over the IRA into an inherited IRA via a direct transfer but cannot wait until she is 70½ to take the distributions.

B. AUTOMATIC SURVIVOR BENEFITS (QJSAS AND QPSAS)

LO 52.2   Identify the options for taking distributions from a retirement plan.

LO 52.15   Describe the automatic survivor benefit method of taking distributions from a retirement plan (QJSAs and QPSAs).

Under ERISA, all defined benefit plans and those defined contribution plans that are subject to minimum funding standards (for example, money purchase and target benefit pension plans) must offer automatic survivor benefits. These automatic survivor benefits are in the form of:

■ a **qualified joint and survivor annuity (QJSA)**; and

■ a **qualified preretirement survivor annuity (QPSA)**.

These automatic survivor benefits may also apply to any other defined contribution plan (such as a Section 401(k) plan) unless:

■ the plan provides that, at the participant's death, his vested account balance will be paid in full to the surviving spouse;

■ the participant does not elect payments in the form of a life annuity; and

■ with respect to such participant, the plan is not a direct or indirect transferee of a plan to which the automatic survivor annuity requirements apply.

The automatic survivor benefit rules do not apply to IRAs but do apply to Section 403(b) plans that match employee elective deferrals.

Plans that are subject to the automatic survivor benefit requirements must provide that, unless waived by the participant with the written consent of her spouse, retirement benefits will be paid in the form of a QJSA. This means an annuity for the life of the participant, with a survivor annuity for the life of her spouse that is not less than one-half (nor greater than 100%) of the amount of the annuity payable during the life of the participant. In addition, such plans must provide that if a vested participant dies before the annuity starting date, leaving a surviving spouse beneficiary, benefits will be paid in the form of QPSA. This means an annuity for the life of the surviving spouse of the participant under which payments are to begin no later than the month in which the participant would have reached the earliest retirement age under the plan and is the actuarial equivalent of not less than one-half of the participant's vested account balance as of the date of her death.

To elect any option that eliminates an automatic survivor benefit for a married participant's spouse, the participant and the spouse must consent on a notarized written form to waive the spousal right to the QJSA or QPSA.

PRACTICE
QUESTION   *Choose the best answer for the question below.*

1. All of the following forms of qualified plans must generally provide for a QJSA form of benefit EXCEPT
   A.   a cash balance pension plan
   B.   a money purchase pension plan
   C.   an ESOP
   D.   a target benefit pension plan

Answer: C.   Of the plans listed, only an ESOP is not subject to the minimum funding standards because a profit-sharing plan does not fund for or promise a benefit in the form of a pension. Thus, it is generally exempt from the rules that mandate the QJSA form of benefit.

C. QUALIFIED DOMESTIC RELATIONS ORDER (QDRO)

LO 52.5   Describe a qualified domestic relations order (QDRO) and know where it can be used.

In general, under ERISA, a qualified plan benefit cannot be assigned or alienated by a participant, voluntarily or involuntarily, while it is not in payable status. This provides for creditor protection of the benefit. There is one major exception to this rule involving the claims of spouses and dependents in domestic relations situations (divorce or separate maintenance) known as a **qualified domestic relations order (QDRO)**.

A QDRO is a decree, order, or property settlement under state law relating to child support, alimony, or marital property rights that assigns all or part of a participant's plan benefits to an alternate payee. An alternate payee includes (most commonly) a spouse or former spouse, child, or other dependent of the participant. The order may be executed with respect to benefits payable under a qualified plan, Section 403(b) plan, and governmental Section 457 plan.

■   Distributions made from a qualified plan to an alternate payee pursuant to a QDRO or other court order are still subject to income tax but are exempt from the 10% premature distribution penalty.

Additionally, an alternate payee who is the former spouse of the participant, and who receives a distribution by reason of a QDRO or other court order, may roll over the distribution in the same manner as if she were the participant (including to her own IRA).

IRAs and Annuities

A matrimonial court may also issue a domestic relations order, decree, property settlement, or other order that can have the same effect on an IRA or annuity that a QDRO has on a qualified plan. IRAs and annuities are assets that are subject to division or assignment when separating property of divorcing taxpayers. In some states, all that is needed is a notarized separation agreement by the parties for the assignment of the IRA to be effective. For the national exam, understand that the QDRO and domestic relations orders are able to assign the ownership of part or all of a participant's balance in the retirement asset.

D. ROTH IRA POST-DEATH DISTRIBUTIONS

LO 52.2   Identify the options for taking distributions from a retirement plan.

LO 52.3   Define the terms required beginning date (RBD) for making a retirement plan distribution and the required minimum distribution (RMD).

LO 52.14   Identify the post-death options for taking distributions from a Roth IRA.

It is important to remember that there are no lifetime RMD requirements (unlike those that apply to other retirement accounts) for Roth IRAs. In addition, contributions may still be made to a Roth IRA after the owner attains age 70½. These two attributes alone make a Roth IRA a very powerful wealth accumulation vehicle that is only made stronger if qualified distributions are made because they are entirely free of income tax.

If a Roth IRA owner dies, the minimum distribution rules that apply to traditional IRAs apply as though the Roth IRA owner died before the required beginning date applicable to traditional IRAs. Generally, the entire interest in the Roth IRA must be distributed by the end of the fifth calendar year after the year of the owner's death, unless the interest is payable to a designated beneficiary over the life or life expectancy of the designated beneficiary. In this case, the entire interest must be payable over a period no greater than the designated beneficiary's life expectancy, and distributions must begin before the end of the calendar year following the year of death. If the sole beneficiary is the spouse, she can either delay distributions until the decedent would have reached age 70½ or treat the Roth IRA as her own.

If a distribution to a beneficiary occurs before completion of the five-year period that would have determined qualified distributions had the owner not died, the distribution is generally includable in the beneficiary's gross income to the same extent it would have been included in the owner's income had it been distributed to the IRA owner when he was alive. The 10% additional tax on early distributions does not apply because the distribution was made to the beneficiary as a result of the IRA owner's death.

▍105 UNIT 7 POST-STUDY CHECKLIST

- ☐ Can I describe the choice of beneficiary considerations as they relate to a qualified plan or IRA?
- ☐ Am I able to identify the options for taking distributions from a retirement plan?
- ☐ Am I able to identify the required beginning date (RBD) for making a retirement plan distribution and calculate the required minimum distribution (RMD) for a given client assuming specified facts?
- ☐ Can I describe a qualified domestic relations order (QDRO) and know where it can be used?

Am I able to define and understand the application of the following terms to financial planning?

- ☐ Beneficiary
- ☐ Designated beneficiary
- ☐ Five-year rule
- ☐ Nonspouse beneficiary
- ☐ Qualified domestic relations order (QDRO)
- ☐ Qualified joint and survivor annuity (QJSA)

- ☐ Qualified preretirement survivor annuity (QPSA)
- ☐ Qualifying public charities
- ☐ Qualifying trust
- ☐ Remaining life expectancy
- ☐ Surviving spouse

Social Security

REFER TO

CFP® Certification Principal Topics – Retirement Planning, Social Security (Old Age, Survivor, and Disability Insurance, OASDI)

Supplemental Readings Section of this105 Retirement Planning Student Guide

(For specific assignments, refer to class syllabus.)

▌INTRODUCTION

A part of nearly every American's retirement planning is the government-sponsored retirement program known as Social Security. When adopted in the 1930s (largely as a result of the Great Depression), Social Security was intended only to supplement an individual's retirement savings, but over the years, it has become much more than that. For many Americans, Social Security is the base of financial protection when earnings are lost due to retirement, disability, or death.

This unit discusses the basics of the Social Security system, including who is covered (and not covered), payment into the system, how benefits are calculated, what types of benefits are available, and the taxation of those benefits. Benefit eligibility is largely determined according to whether an individual is fully or currently insured under the system. Those terms will be defined in this unit and examples given with respect to resulting available benefits.

The taxation of Social Security benefits was first mentioned in the *104: Income Tax Planning* course.

LEARNING OBJECTIVES

After completing this unit, you should be able to achieve the following learning objectives:

CFP® Certification Principal Topics – Retirement Planning, Social Security (Old Age, Survivor, and Disability Insurance, OASDI)

LO 45.1   Explain how the Social Security program is funded.

LO 45.2   Analyze a given situation to determine eligibility of an individual for Social Security benefits and identify types and amounts of benefits that are available under the system.

LO 45.3   Describe what is meant by the term primary insurance amount (PIA) and how benefits are calculated under the Social Security program.

LO 45.4   Explain the effect on benefits of employment prior to and after attaining full retirement age (FRA).

LO 45.5   Explain the taxation of Social Security benefits under current law.

LO 45.6   List who is covered and who is excluded from the Old Age, Survivors, and Disability Insurance Program.

LO 45.7   Analyze a given situation to determine eligibility of an individual for Social Security benefits.

KEY TERMS

Average indexed monthly earnings (AIME)

Currently insured

Disability benefit

Federal Insurance Contributions Act (FICA)

Fully insured

Full retirement age (FRA)

Maximum family benefit

Medicare

Old age, survivors, and disability insurance (OASDI) program

Primary insurance amount (PIA)

Retirement benefits

Self-employment (SE) tax

Social Security

Survivors benefits

Taxable wage base

A. FUNDING OF THE SOCIAL SECURITY PROGRAM

LO 45.1   Explain how the Social Security program is funded.

Technically, **Social Security** is known as the **old age, survivors, and disability insurance (OASDI) program**. It was created through the Social Security Act of 1935 and is designed to protect eligible workers and their dependents from financial loss resulting from death, disability, and the risk of superannuation (running out of money during the participant's lifetime). Approximately 95% of all U.S. workers participate and are covered by the program.

Social Security is funded through a series of taxes paid by the participant and participant's employer, commonly referred to as payroll taxes. Accordingly, an employee will pay a **Federal Insurance Contributions Act (FICA)** tax of 7.65%, and the employer will separately pay 7.65%, for a combined total of 15.3%. A self-employed individual must pay both the employer and employee portions of the FICA tax, known as the **self-employment (SE) tax**.

Of this amount, the employer share of 7.65% may be separately broken down into a tax of 6.2% specifically dedicated to Social Security and 1.45% for **Medicare** funding. The employee share of 7.65% may be separately broken down into a tax of 6.2% specifically dedicated to Social Security and 1.45% for **Medicare** funding. In 2015, Social Security taxes are paid on wages up to the **taxable wage base** of $118,500. There is not a taxable wage base cap associated with Medicare funding, thus the compensation against which the 1.45% tax is assessed is unlimited in amount.

Beginning in 2013, a 0.9% Additional Medicare Tax applies to taxpayers whose compensation exceeds stated threshold amounts. For more information, *see 104: Income Tax Planning* course.

PRACTICE
QUESTION   *Choose the best answer for the question below.*

1.   Social Security is funded through
   1.   employee payroll taxes
   2.   employer payroll taxes
   3.   sales tax
   4.   self-employment tax

   A.   2 only
   B.   1 and 2
   C.   1, 2, and 4
   D.   2 and 3

   Answer: C.   Employee and employer payroll taxes and self-employment tax are the sources of funding for Social Security. Sales tax does not fund Social Security.

B. COVERAGE IN AND EXCLUSIONS FROM THE SOCIAL SECURITY PROGRAM

LO 45.2   Analyze a given situation to determine eligibility of an individual for Social Security benefits and identify types and amounts of benefits that are available under the system.

LO 45.6   List who is covered and who is excluded from the Old Age, Survivors, and Disability Insurance Program.

Almost all employees pay into and are covered by the Social Security program. These include the following:

- Employees of private, for-profit companies

- Self-employed individuals

- Employees of tax-exempt organizations

- Members of the armed services

- Approximately 75% of state and local government employees (Note: some public school teachers employed by state or local school districts do not pay into the system and are not covered)

- Federal civil service workers hired after 1983, including members of Congress (Note: federal civil service workers hired after this date also participate in a system known as the Federal Employees Retirement System, or FERS)

The major exceptions to coverage in the Social Security program are:

- certain federal civil service workers;

- approximately 25% of state and local government employees (Note: each state and local government unit with a pension plan decides whether to elect Social Security coverage; some have not);

- railroad workers covered under the federal Railroad Retirement Act; and

- some other exceptions.

While not covered for Social Security purposes, these workers are covered by Medicare if they separately meet those rules (discussed in the *102: Insurance and Employee Benefits* course).

There are also some special provisions under the Social Security program. These individuals may or may not be covered depending on whether or not certain other circumstances exist. These special provisions include the following:

- Household or domestic employees—if a household worker is paid above a specified amount ($1,900 annually for 2015), Social Security and Medicare taxes must be withheld from their wages. The law exempts household workers younger than the age of 18 who are students or who have another principal occupation.

- Agricultural workers—an agricultural worker is general covered by Social Security and wages subject to payroll taxes if paid at least $150 or more in the calendar year for farm work or if the employer pays at least $2,500 for farm labor for all employees for the year.

■ Family workers—if a taxpayer is self-employed and hires her spouse, parent, or child age 18 or older in the course of the self-employed business, that employment is covered. Alternatively if, for example, the child is younger than 18, and is employed in the taxpayer's unincorporated business, he is not covered.

PRACTICE
QUESTION   *Choose the best answer for the question below.*

1. Which of the following groups of employees are NOT covered under Social Security?
   A. Members of Congress
   B. Railroad workers
   C. Members of the armed forces
   D. Employees of tax-exempt organizations

Answer: B.   Railroad workers are covered under the federal Railroad Retirement Act and have their own retirement system. They are not covered under the Social Security program.

C. BENEFIT ELIGIBILITY

LO 45.2   Analyze a given situation to determine eligibility of an individual for Social Security benefits and identify types and amounts of benefits that are available under the system.

The type of benefits for which a worker covered by Social Security is eligible depends on whether the worker is considered fully insured or currently insured.

Fully insured coverage is necessary to qualify for most benefits and consists of 40 credits of coverage (effectively, 10 working years under the system) or one credit for each year over age 21. In 2015, a worker earns one credit of coverage for every $1,220 of compensation earned, up to a maximum of four credits per year. A worker is fully insured for life once 40 credits of coverage have been earned.

A fully insured worker is generally eligible for the following benefits:

■ Retirement benefits

■ Spousal retirement benefits

■ Surviving spouse benefit for widow(er) age 60 or older

■ Surviving spouse benefit caring for a dependent child (if spouse is caring for dependent child younger than age 16)

■ Dependent benefit

■ Dependent parent benefit (if parent is age 62 or older)

■ Lump-sum death benefit of $255

Currently insured coverage is a more limited form of coverage and eligibility for benefits than fully insured status. Currently insured coverage is achieved if the worker has earned six credits of coverage during the 13 calendar quarters ending with the calendar quarter in which the individual died, most recently became eligible for disability benefits, or became entitled to retirement insurance benefits. Again, a credit of coverage is obtained if the worker has compensation of at least $1,220 in 2015.

A currently insured worker is generally eligible only for the following benefits:

■ Surviving spouse caring for a dependent child

■ Dependent benefit

■ Lump-sum death benefit of $255

There is also a separate qualification requirement to receive disability income benefits from the Social Security program. To qualify for disability benefits under the program, the worker must be so severely impaired, physically or mentally, that she cannot perform any substantial gainful activity. In addition, this impairment must be expected to last at least 12 months or result in death. Disability benefits under the program are not payable to workers disabled solely because of alcoholism or drug addiction.

Presuming the definition of Social Security disability is met, a worker must also have earned a minimum number of credits of coverage based on the worker's year of birth and a portion of the credits must have been earned in recent years.

D. HOW ARE BENEFITS CALCULATED?

LO 45.3   Describe what is meant by the term *primary insurance amount* (PIA) and how benefits are calculated under the Social Security program.

All benefit amounts paid under the Social Security program are based on an amount known as the worker's **primary insurance amount (PIA)**. A worker's PIA is calculated using his **average indexed monthly earnings (AIME)**, which is based on the worker's life-time earnings history. As previously mentioned, annual earnings in excess of the Social Security taxable wage base are not considered ($118,500 for 2015). The Social Security Administration will generally calculate both the AIME and PIA for the worker and, indeed, is required by law to send the worker an annual statement which includes his PIA estimate.

The PIA is the amount payable to any worker based on attainment of **full retirement age (FRA)**, which is age 65 for workers born before 1938. Beginning with workers born in 1938, the FRA gradually increases from age 65, reaching age 67 for workers born in 1960 and later. If the worker starts his retirement benefit early under the Social Security program (for example, at age 62), it will be actuarially less than the PIA available at FRA. When taking retirement benefits early, the PIA is reduced five-ninths of 1% per month for each of the first 36 months that the worker takes benefits before his FRA, plus five-twelfths of 1% for each month in excess of 36 months. This results in a reduction of 30% in PIA if the worker is born in 1960 or later and elects to take retirement benefits at the earliest possible age of 62.

E. TYPES AND AMOUNTS OF BENEFITS AVAILABLE UNDER SOCIAL SECURITY

LO 45.2   Analyze a given situation to determine eligibility of an individual for Social Security benefits and identify types and amounts of benefits that are available under the system.

The types and amounts of benefits available under Social Security depend on whether the worker is fully insured or currently insured. The benefits are retirement, survivor, and disability income.

Retirement Benefits

The following individuals are eligible to receive **retirement benefits** based on the employment record of the Social Security insured worker:

■ The retired worker (at age 62 or older)

■ The spouse of the retired worker (at age 62 or older) (Note: the spouse at FRA is entitled to receive 50% of the worker's PIA, otherwise, it is 32.5–35%)

■ The divorced spouse who is age 62 or older and was married to the worker for at least 10 years and is unmarried, if the worker is at least age 62 (whether retired or not)

■ An unmarried child who is under age 18, under age 19 if still in high school, or at any age if the child became disabled before age 22

■ A spouse currently taking care of a dependent child under the age of 16

■ A parent currently taking care of a dependent child who became disabled before the age of 22

Survivors Benefits

The following survivors are eligible to receive **survivors benefits** based on the employment record of the Social Security insured worker:

■ Surviving spouse benefit for widow(er) age 60 or older

■ A disabled widow(er) age 50 or older

■ A surviving spouse currently taking care of a dependent child under the age of 16

■ An unmarried child under age 18, under age 19 if still in high school, or at any age, if the child became disabled before age 22

■ A dependent parent age 62 or older

A lump-sum death benefit of $255 is also payable to any surviving spouse or child of the Social Security worker or eligible child of the Social Security worker. Only one $255 death benefit is payable per worker. For example, if the death benefit was paid to the surviving spouse, it would not be available to an eligible child. If there was no surviving spouse, only one dependent child would be eligible to receive the benefit.

Disability Benefits

The following individuals may receive income from a **disability benefit** from the Social Security program based on the worker's employment record. The definition of fully insured differs slightly when considering disability benefits:

■ The disabled worker (Note: the disability benefit is equal to 100% of the worker's PIA or retirement benefit)

■ The spouse of the disabled worker

■ An unmarried child (of the disabled worker) under age 18 or under age 19 if still in high school

■ An unmarried child (of the disabled worker) of any age who became disabled before attaining age 22

Maximum Family Benefit

There is a limit on the total amount of benefits that members of one family may receive based on the worker's employment record, called a **maximum family benefit**. The limitation is based on a separate table provided by the Social Security Administration. This limitation applies before any reduction for early retirement or any increase for late retirement but does not apply if both the husband and wife receive only a retirement benefit based on their own respective employment records. The amount payable to a divorced spouse is also not included in the limitation, except if the surviving divorced spouse qualifies for benefits only on the basis of caring for a dependent child of the worker.

Summary of Basic Social Security Coverage and Benefits (% of PIA)
(All Are Subject to Family Maximum Dollar Benefits and Assume Normal Retirement Age.)

Beneficiaries	Retirement Insurance	Disability Insurance[1]	Survivorship Insurance[2]	
Required Credit to Earn Coverage FICA must be paid on $1,220 (2015) of earnings to receive one Social Security credit (a maximum of 4 credits may be earned each year)	Required to be fully insured (40 credits)	If < age 24, 6 credits. If < age 31, credits in at least half the quarters available since age 21. If ≥ age 31, fully insured and credits in at least 20 of the last 40 quarters.	Fully insured (F.I. definition and status is different than the one required for retirement benefits.)	Currently insured credits in at least 6 of last 13 quarters
Covered Worker	100% at NRA[3]	100%	Deceased (none)	Deceased (none)
Spouse NRA Age 62 Age 60	50% 32.5%–35% N/A	50% 35% N/A	100% 82.9% 71.5%	0 0 0
Child < 18	50%	50%	75%	75%
Spouse if Caretaker of Child < 16 or disabled	50%	50%	75%	75%
Dependent Parents ≥ Age 62	N/A	N/A	75–82.5%[4]	N/A
Divorced Spouse[5]	Same as spouse	Same as spouse	Same as spouse	N/A

1. A blind person need not be fully insured to receive benefits; special rules apply.
2. Plus a death benefit of $255 to spouse or dependent child, if fully or currently insured.
3. NRA = normal retirement age. Also referred to by Social Security Administration as FRA—full retirement age.
4. 75% each if two dependent parents; 82.5% if one dependent parent.
5. The divorced spouse must have been married at least 10 years to the worker and not have remarried before age 60. This is not subject to a family maximum.

PRACTICE
QUESTIONS   *Choose the best answer for each of the questions below.*

1. Glen, now deceased, was divorced after 12 years of marriage. He had two dependent children, ages 4 and 6, who are cared for by their mother, age 45. Glen's mother, age 70, also survived him. At the time of Glen's death, he was currently, but not fully, insured under Social Security. What are Glen's survivors entitled to as a benefit under the Social Security program?

    1. A lump-sum death benefit of $255
    2. A children's benefit
    3. A surviving spouse benefit to take care of a dependent child
    4. A dependent parent's benefit

    A. 1 only
    B. 1, 2, and 3
    C. 2 only
    D. 2, 3, and 4

    Answer: B.   A lump-sum death benefit of $255 is payable. The children's benefit is payable because Glen was currently insured. Glen's divorced spouse (the children's mother) is entitled to a caretaker's benefit for caring for his children. His mother is only entitled to a benefit if Glen was fully insured.

2. Which of the following unmarried, dependent children is eligible for a survivors benefit from Social Security based on the employment record of his fully insured parent?
    A. A 19-year-old child who is disabled
    B. A 19-year-old child still in high school
    C. A 19-year-old child in junior college
    D. A 19-year-old child who lives away from home

    Answer: A.   Only the 19-year-old child who is disabled (became disabled before age 22) is entitled to a survivors benefit. If the child was under age 19 and still in high school, he would also be entitled to a survivors benefit based on the parent's PIA.

F. EMPLOYMENT PRIOR TO AND AFTER FRA

LO 45.4   Explain the effect on benefits of employment prior to and after attaining full retirement age (FRA).

A worker who has attained full retirement age (FRA) will not experience a reduction in Social Security benefits if the worker continues to have earned income after claiming Social Security retirement benefits. However, a limit on earnings from employment applies to workers or beneficiaries under the FRA if Social Security benefits are being received. This earnings limit is a retirement earnings test and is a separate issue from income taxes on Social Security benefits (to be discussed shortly). In 2015, a worker-beneficiary who is eligible to receive retirement benefits (age 62), but who has not yet achieved FRA, is only able to earn a maximum of $15,720 per year before a loss of benefits will occur. If a worker-beneficiary earns more than this amount, $1 in Social Security benefits will be withheld for every $2 in earnings above the limit. There is a special monthly test that may be applied in the first year of retirement. Under this special test, earnings prior to the month of retirement are not considered in the annual limit and the retiree may receive benefits in a given month if he does not earn more than one-twelfth of the annual earnings limit in that month. For example, a worker may have earned $50,000 in the months prior to retirement but may begin to receive benefits each month at retirement as long as the worker's earned income is below one-twelfth of the applicable annual limit. After the first year in retirement, if the worker has not yet attained FRA, the annual earnings limit will apply.

If a worker-beneficiary attains FRA in 2015, he can earn $41,880 in the months immediately before the month in which FRA is attained with no reduction in benefits. If earnings exceed this amount, then $1 in Social Security benefits is withheld for every $3 the worker-beneficiary earns above $41,880. The annual earnings limit no longer applies once a worker has attained FRA. Benefits will not be reduced, regardless of earned income.

G. TAXATION OF SOCIAL SECURITY BENEFITS

LO 45.5   Explain the taxation of Social Security benefits under current law.

Social Security retirement beneficiaries with significant total incomes may be required to include up to 85% of their Social Security benefits as income for federal income tax purposes. Special step-rate thresholds determine the amount of Social Security retirement benefits that must be included in income for federal income tax purposes.

- The first threshold or base amount is $25,000 of provisional income for all single, unmarried taxpayers and $32,000 of provisional income for married taxpayers filing jointly (Note: this threshold amount is $0 for married taxpayers filing separate returns and who do not live apart for the entire taxable year).

- The second threshold or base amount is $34,000 of provisional income for all single, unmarried taxpayers and $44,000 of provisional income for married taxpayers filing jointly (Note: the same limitation of $0 also applies for married taxpayers filing separate returns and not living apart).

If the first threshold is exceeded in any taxable year, generally 50% of the amount by which the Social Security benefits exceed the threshold is subject to income tax. If the second threshold is exceeded in any taxable year, generally 85% of the amount by which the Social Security benefits exceed the (second) threshold is subject to income tax. However, this amount cannot exceed the smaller of:

- 85% of the actual Social Security benefits received in any taxable year; or

- 50% of the benefits plus 85% of any excess over the second threshold.

An example is given below.

Provisional income is the beneficiary's modified adjusted gross income (MAGI) plus one-half of the Social Security or tier 1 railroad retirement benefits. In turn, MAGI is the beneficiary's adjusted gross income plus any tax-exempt interest, including interest earned on savings bonds used to finance higher education, amounts excluded under an employer's adoption assistance program and any foreign earned income or foreign previously excluded.

Note: The example below is to aid the student in understanding the application of the thresholds. It is not expected that the student will have to calculate the taxable Social Security income for a taxpayer. Knowledge of the theory, however, may be tested.

E X A M P L E   In 2015, Ted and Alice, both age 70, have AGI of $50,000 as shown on their IRS Form 1040. They also have received $3,000 of municipal bond interest and have been paid $20,000 in Social Security benefits in 2015. They file as married filing jointly. Accordingly, $17,000 of their total of $20,000 Social Security benefits received is subject to income tax (at their 2015 marginal income tax rate), calculated as follows.

Preliminary Form 1040 AGI:	$50,000
+ Municipal bond interest:	$ 3,000
MAGI	$53,000
+ 50% of $20,000 in Social Security benefits:	$10,000
Provisional income:	**$63,000**
Excess provisional income over first threshold ($32,000):	$31,000
Excess provisional income over second threshold ($44,000):	$19,000

Social Security benefits included in AGI for the tax year is the lessor of:

50% of excess provisional income over first threshold plus 35% of excess over second threshold (.50 × $31,000 + .35 × $19,000):	$22,150
85% of benefits (.85 × $20,000):	**$17,000**
50% of benefits, plus 85% of excess over second threshold (.50 × $20,000 + .85 × $19,000):	$26,150

The lessor of these three figures, $17,000, is added to the preliminary AGI of $50,000, resulting in AGI on Form 1040 to be $67,000.

PRACTICE
QUESTION   *Choose the best answer for the question below.*

1. Which of the following is included when calculating the provisional income for purposes of Social Security benefits taxation?
A.   Dividends from stock
B.   Municipal bond interest
C.   50% of Social Security benefits received
D.   Each of these is included

Answer: D.   Dividends from stock are included as income when calculating AGI (which is the first step to calculating the total provisional income). Then, municipal bond interest and 50% of Social Security benefits received are added back.

105 UNIT 8 POST-STUDY CHECKLIST

☐   Am I able to explain how the Social Security program is funded?

☐   Do I know how to analyze a given situation to determine eligibility of an individual for Social Security benefits and identify types and amounts of benefits that are available under the system?

☐   Can I describe what is meant by the term primary insurance amount (PIA) and how benefits are calculated under the Social Security program?

☐   Am I able to explain the effect on benefits of employment prior to and after attaining full retirement age (FRA)?

☐   Am I able to explain the taxation of Social Security benefits under current law?

Am I able to define and understand the application of the following terms to financial planning?

☐   Average indexed monthly earnings (AIME)

☐   Currently insured

☐   Disability benefit

☐   Federal Insurance Contributions Act (FICA)

☐   Fully insured

☐   Full retirement age (FRA)

☐   Maximum family benefit

☐   Medicare

☐   Old age, survivors, and disability insurance (OASDI) program

☐   Primary insurance amount (PIA)

☐   Retirement benefits

☐   Self-employment (SE) tax

☐   Social Security

☐   Survivors benefits

☐   Taxable wage base

9

Plan and Investment Considerations for Retirement Plans

REFER TO

CFP® Certification Principal Topics – Retirement Planning, Key Factors Affecting Plan Selection for Businesses

CFP® Certification Principal Topics – Retirement Planning, Investment Considerations for Retirement Plans

Supplemental Readings Section of this 105 Retirement Planning Student Guide

(For specific assignments, refer to class syllabus.)

INTRODUCTION

This unit reviews the selection of an appropriate retirement plan for a given type of business. It is important for a planner to gather comprehensive information about a client company, including details about the goals and motivations for having an employer-sponsored retirement plan and then work to match the goals with the best type of plan suited to deliver the objectives of the client company or business owner. The majority of plans are for for-profit enterprises, although two types of plans, the Section 403(b) plan and Section 457 plan, may only be established for tax-exempt (nonprofit) entities. We have discussed the differences between qualified and tax-advantaged plans, but you should also remember that a nonqualified plan may be established for the benefit of certain valued, selected employees (such as corporate executives). The types of nonqualified plans and the characteristics of each are discussed in the *102: Insurance and Employee Benefits Planning* course.

LEARNING OBJECTIVES

After completing this unit, you should be able to achieve the following learning objectives:

CFP® Certification Principal Topics – Retirement Planning, Key Factors Affecting Plan Selection for Businesses

LO 50.1   Identify factors that should be considered before implementing a qualified or tax-advantaged plan for a business.

LO 50.2   Evaluate a given situation to select the most appropriate type of retirement plan for a given client or businessowner.

CFP® Certification Principal Topics – Retirement Planning, Investment Considerations for Retirement Plans

LO 51.1   Determine the suitability of an investment for a given retirement plan.

LO 51.2   Explain the effect time horizon of an investment option has on its inclusion as a plan asset.

LO 51.3   Discuss the diversification of investments in retirement plans.

LO 51.4   Explain the fiduciary considerations of employer-sponsored retirement plans.

LO 51.5   Discuss the unrelated business taxable income (UBTI) rules.

LO 51.6   Explain the rules of using life insurance in a qualified plan.

LO 51.7   Identify the types of assets appropriate as retirement plan investments.

LO 51.8   Discuss the effect of investment risk in retirement plans.

LO 51.9   Explain the characteristics used in determining appropriate investment vehicles for employer-sponsored retirement plans.

LO 51.10   Discuss taxation where life insurance is used as an asset in a retirement plan.

KEY TERMS

100 times test	Pure protection cost
Incidental benefit test	Retirement savings need
Investment risk	Table 2001 cost
Liquidity	Unrelated business taxable income (UBTI)
Percentage test	

A. RETIREMENT PLAN SELECTION FOR BUSINESSOWNERS

LO 50.1   Identify factors that should be considered before implementing a qualified or tax-advantaged plan for a business.

LO 50.2   Evaluate a given situation to select the most appropriate type of retirement plan for a given client or businessowner.

In many instances, the decision whether to implement a retirement plan for a business comes down to the threshold question, can we afford not to? A primary reason why the implementation of a retirement plan is important is because it makes business sense. Retirement plans of any sort have become popular and are potentially advantageous for a number of reasons. A business must proceed with implementing a plan or risk being left behind competitively.

Factors to Consider in Determining the Type of Retirement Plan to Be Adopted

There are four primary factors that should guide the financial planner in recommending any type of retirement plan for a businessowner client.

- The owner's retirement savings need—the larger the sum of money the owner needs to save for personal retirement needs, the larger the annual amount needed to reach this goal. The annual savings needed for the owner's retirement may exceed the defined contribution plan annual additions dollar limit ($53,000 in 2015), influencing the owner to possibly adopt a defined benefit, age-weighted profit-sharing or target benefit defined contribution plan.

- The owner's current age—the closer the owner is to the desired retirement date, the more immediate the owner's savings need will be. The owner will also probably wish to deposit money in a personal retirement account as quickly as possible. Again, this may indicate the need to implement some form of defined benefit plan or age-weighted profit-sharing or target benefit defined contribution plan.

- The owner's attitude toward investment risk (for the owner and the employees)—in defined contribution plans, the employee assumes the investment risk. In defined benefit plans, the employer assumes this risk. The owner-employer may not wish to assume the risk of investment for the employees. This may sway the financial planner toward the implementation of a defined contribution type plan or tax-advantaged retirement plan.

- The current financial condition of the business—the ability to sustain annual plan contributions will be critical in choosing between any type of pension plan versus any profit-sharing plan for the business. For example, while some defined contribution profit-sharing plans allow for flexible employer plan contributions, all defined benefit plans and defined contribution pension plans require mandatory annual funding. If the current or foreseeable business cash flow will not support a mandatory plan contribution, the financial planner should orient his client's thinking away from a pension plan and toward a profit-sharing plan approach.

EXAMPLE Assume Marshall owns a small company with the following census information.

Employee	Age	Total Compensation	Covered Compensation
Marshall	30	$180,000	$180,000
Jack	30	$ 20,000	$ 20,000
Patty	35	$ 20,000	$ 20,000
John	30	$ 20,000	$ 20,000
Totals		$240,000	$240,000

What type of retirement plan would you recommend if Marshall wanted to provide the maximum annual benefit for himself?

Marshall can provide the maximum benefit for himself by implementing a Section 401(k) plan in conjunction with a profit-sharing or stock bonus plan. The Section 401(k) plan would allow employee deferrals on top of the regular 25% maximum plan limit up to the annual additions limit of $53,000 (2015). A 25% employer contribution for Marshall would be $45,000. Because the maximum annual additions limit is $53,000 in 2015, Marshall could contribute an additional $7,000 elective deferral ($53,000 – $45,000), assuming ADP tests are met. However, the administrative expenses of a Section 401(k) plan for such a small employee group could outweigh the $8,000 additional benefit for Marshall and should be considered. Another Section 401(k) alternative to consider could be a safe harbor Section 401(k) plan. A safe harbor design would eliminate ADP testing but would require mandatory contributions by the company and immediate vesting of company contributions. The advantages and disadvantages of each plan would need to be analyzed.

What other types of retirement plans might Marshall implement if he decided against the Section 401(k) plan?

A SEP or profit-sharing plan could certainly be appropriate, depending on other objectives, such as vesting, participation, and so forth. Either plan could be integrated with Social Security.

Either a defined contribution pension plan or a profit-sharing plan would allow a deductible contribution of up to 25% of covered compensation.

How would your recommendation change if Marshall were age 55?

Because Marshall would be significantly older than the rest of the employees, an age-weighted (cross-tested) type plan may be appropriate. Alternatively, a defined benefit plan would allow higher contributions for Marshall compared with the remaining employees.

> ✳**E X A M P L E** Assume Marshall and Jack own a small company with the following census information.
>
> | Employee | Age | Compensation |
> |----------|-----|--------------|
> | Marshall | 55 | $180,000 |
> | Jack | 30 | $160,000 |
> | Patty | 35 | $ 20,000 |
> | John | 30 | $ 20,000 |
> | Total | | $380,000 |
>
> How does the age difference between the owners of the business affect the retirement plan selection?
>
> Because one owner is older and one owner is younger, an age-weighted plan will provide greater benefits to Marshall over Jack. Using a profit-sharing plan or a money purchase pension plan, however, both owners could receive annual additions up to $53,000 (2015). In addition, a defined benefit plan also could be added to provide higher benefits. They also could use a new comparability plan with one of the classes as owners.

Review and Select Among Available Plans

As with any financial planning opportunity, the planner must know the universe of alternatives that is available to satisfy the client's goals. In retirement planning for the businessowner, these are the various types of qualified and tax-advantaged plans. It is fortunate that in recent years, eligibility for these types of plans has been standardized such that all are generally available to a business entity, no matter what the form. The only notable exceptions to this statement are:

■ stock bonus plans and ESOPs, which may not be adopted by unincorporated entities such as a sole proprietorship or partnership;

■ Section 403(b) plans, which may only be adopted by Section 501(c)(3) nonprofit organizations; and

■ Section 457 plans, which may only be adopted by private tax-exempt organizations and state or local government entities.

With these exceptions, all forms of qualified or tax-advantaged plans are generally permitted for all forms of business entity.

The following table briefly summarizes the major types of retirement plans available to a for-profit businessowner and their distinguishing characteristics.

Type of Plan	Easily Understood by Employees?	Who Assumes Investment Risk?	Does Plan Favor Older Participants?	Does Plan Permit Elective Deferrals?*
Traditional defined benefit pension plan	No	Employer	Yes	No
Cash balance pension plan	No (but perhaps easier to understand than traditional defined benefit pension plan)	Employer	No	No
Traditional profit-sharing plan (without Section 401(k) feature)	Maybe	Employee	Maybe (if age-weighted)	No
Profit-sharing plan with Section 401(k) feature	Maybe	Employee	No	Yes, $18,000
Money purchase pension plan	Yes	Employee	No	No
Target benefit pension plan	No	Employee	Yes	No
SEP IRA	Yes	Employee	No	No
SIMPLE IRA	Yes	Employee	No	Yes, $12,500
SIMPLE 401(k)	Maybe	Employee	No	Yes, $12,500

*Contributions are the maximum amount of employee pretax contributions for calendar year 2015; catch-up contributions are also permitted for individuals age 50 or older.

> **EXAMPLE** ABC Company would like to implement a retirement plan for the benefit of its employees. It has the following business objectives:
>
> - Attract and retain employees
> - Allow the employer to make all initial contributions to the plan using company stock
> - Allow for integration of the plan with Social Security
>
> Therefore, with no more information than this, any type of pension plan would not be appropriate because it does not permit more than 10% of plan assets to be invested in employer securities. Nor is an ESOP appropriate because it cannot be integrated with Social Security. Finally, a SEP or SIMPLE IRA would not be appropriate because employer contributions would have to be made in cash.
>
> After eliminating other possible plans, the most advantageous type of retirement plan to meet ABC's objectives would likely be a stock bonus (profit-sharing type) plan.

PRACTICE
QUESTIONS   *Choose the best answer for each of the questions below.*

1. The goal of RDF Company is to maximize retirement benefits to the highly compensated employees of the company. These employees also happen to be the oldest employees. Which one of the following plans best accomplishes this goal, assuming a new plan is to be implemented?
   A. An age-based profit-sharing plan
   B. A money purchase pension plan
   C. A target benefit pension plan
   D. A traditional defined benefit pension plan

Answer: D. The traditional defined benefit pension plan favors older participants and generally allows larger contributions than other plans. While age-based profit-sharing and target benefit plans also favor older participants, they are limited by the annual additions dollar limit that applies to all defined contribution type plans ($53,000 in 2015).

2. Which of the following types of plans may be structured to provide for deferral of taxable income for retirement?
    1. Nondeductible traditional IRA
    2. Roth IRA
    3. SIMPLE 401(k) plan
    4. Nonqualified deferred compensation plan

    A. 1 and 3
    B. 1, 3, and 4
    C. 2 and 3
    D. 1, 2, 3, and 4

    Answer: D. Each of these individual accounts or plans may be structured to provide for deferral of taxable income, although in different ways.

3. Charles is a 30-year-old CPA with his own tax practice. For most of the year, he works by himself, preparing and reviewing income tax returns. For the last 5 years, he has hired 3 part-time employees to assist him during the busy season. Each of these employees works approximately 200 hours, earning an average salary of $3,000. Charles would like to establish a retirement plan that would allow him to save for his own retirement, without significant administrative costs. Which one of the following plans would be most appropriate for Charles?
    A. SEP IRA
    B. Traditional Section 401(k) plan
    C. SIMPLE IRA
    D. Section 457 plan

    Answer: C. A SEP IRA is incorrect because it would require coverage of all of Charles's part-time employees. A traditional Section 401(k) plan is incorrect because the plan would involve special nondiscrimination testing and annual filing of the Form 5500 series. A Section 457 plan is incorrect because it is available only for certain, private tax-exempt organizations. A SIMPLE IRA would be the most appropriate plan because it involves little administrative costs and would meet Charles's retirement planning goals.

4. Jack, a CFP® professional, has a client, age 45, who is the sole proprietor of a small company with 5 employees. The client has given Jack an employee census and requested that Jack recommend a retirement plan that will fit in with the client's desire to retire at 62 and also help retain employees. The company has historically had positive cash flows. Jack has developed recommendations for plans using a variety of scenarios for his client and written a plan. What does Jack do next?
    A. Jack presents the recommendations to his client and clearly explains his findings and the alternatives available.
    B. Jack should mail the written plan to the client and wait to hear from him.
    C. Jack creates a prioritized plan to implement his recommendations.
    D. Jack calls a third party administrator to set up the plan Jack has recommended.

    Answer: A. Jack presents the recommendations to his client and clearly explains his findings and the alternatives available. Jack cannot create a plan to implement his recommendations until he has discussed the recommendations with his client, obtained feedback, and verified his client's acceptance of his recommendations. Jack cannot call anyone to assist in setting up a plan until one has been agreed upon by his client. (Domain 5: Communicating the recommendations)

B. INVESTMENT CONSIDERATIONS FOR RETIREMENT PLANS

LO 51.1   Determine the suitability of an investment for a given retirement plan.

LO 51.2   Explain the effect time horizon of an investment option on its inclusion as a plan asset.

LO 51.3   Discuss the diversification of investments in retirement plans.

LO 51.4   Explain the fiduciary considerations of employer-sponsored retirement plans.

LO 51.7   Identify the types of assets appropriate as retirement plan investments.

LO 51.8   Discuss the effect of investment risk in retirement plans.

LO 51.9   Explain the characteristics used in determining appropriate investment vehicles for employer-sponsored retirement plans.

The foremost consideration in determining the composition of assets in which a qualified or tax-advantaged retirement plan should invest in is who bears the investment risk: the employer or employee. In an individual account defined contribution type of plan, the investment risk is assumed directly by the employee. As a result, sponsors of such plans typically provide participants with a choice of investment vehicles, among them fixed income investments, common stock, mutual funds, real estate, and, sometimes, employer stock. The employee is often permitted to self-direct contributions among a number of assets or mutual funds, usually with very little assistance from the employer or employer's plan representatives.

In contrast, the investment risk under a pooled account defined benefit type of plan is assumed almost entirely by the plan sponsor-employer. Accordingly, because this type of plan typically promises some fixed amount of benefit to the participant at the date of his retirement (and for which this benefit requires mandatory funding), an employer is usually somewhat conservative in its choice of investment assets to fund the plan. In addition, the necessity of developing a written investment policy standard (under ERISA) to assist in the meeting of investment objectives is usually much more critical for those employer sponsors who have decided to implement a defined benefit type of qualified retirement plan.

There are four primary characteristics of any investment vehicle that need to be considered in assessing the asset's potential suitability as a retirement plan asset. These are:

- the investment's stability in value;

- its ability to preserve the future purchasing power of the plan participant;

- the liquidity of the investment; and

- the investment's tax advantages (for example, it makes little sense to put a tax-advantaged investment, such as a municipal bond, within a tax-deferred investment vehicle, such as a qualified retirement plan).

When determining **liquidity** of an investment choice, liquidity can be defined as the ability to sell or redeem an investment quickly and at a known price without significant loss of principal (*see 103: Investment Planning*). While some investment choices can easily be converted to cash (e.g., mutual funds), they cannot always meet this definition. Broadly, as with any investment, these factors may be categorized generally as characteristics of expected return and risk. They are relevant for each of the following five major classes of retirement plan assets:

■ Money market instruments

■ Fixed income assets (including bonds and guaranteed investment contracts, or GICs)

■ Common stocks (including employer stock)

■ Mutual funds

■ Real estate

In tabular form, following is a summary of all of these types of assets and their appropriateness/use in a qualified or tax-advantaged retirement plan.

Asset Class	Appropriateness/Use in Retirement Plan	Characteristics of Asset Risk	Expected Return Considerations
Money market instruments	Use primarily for liquidity purposes	Low risk; safety of principal; liquid	Minimal rate of expected return
Corporate and government bonds	Use to fund future fixed obligations	Moderate risk; inflation protection lower; not liquid	Higher (fixed) rate of return than money market
Guaranteed investment contracts (GICs)	Use to fund future fixed obligations—common in defined benefit plans	Low risk; guaranteed payments; liquid	Real rate of return similar to bonds (fixed income)
Common stock	Use to generate capital appreciation and some income	Highest risk; inflation protection; not liquid	Highest historical rates of expected return (but volatile)
Employer stock	Use primarily as employee incentive	Higher risk; lack of diversification	Return tied to corporate earnings
Mutual funds	Use primarily for diversification purposes	Diversification minimizes systematic risk	Comparable historical return to that of stock (consider expenses)
Real estate (direct and indirect)	Use as inflation hedge in some plans	Highest risk depending on location; not liquid	Real rate of return may be comparable to common stock

PRACTICE
QUESTION

Choose the best answer for the question below.

1. What type of investment is generally appropriate to hold within any form of tax-deferred retirement plan?
    A. Zero-coupon bond
    B. Municipal bond
    C. Nondividend paying common stock
    D. Limited partnership interest generating unrelated business taxable income (UBTI)

    Answer: A.   Because zero-coupon bonds generate phantom income, they are generally appropriate to hold as an asset within any form of tax-deferred retirement plan. A nondividend paying common stock would convert a capital gain to an ordinary income asset if owned by a retirement plan although the growth of the stock would be beneficial. A limited partnership may or may not be preferable based on its amount of generated UBTI, to be discussed later in this unit.

C. LIFE INSURANCE IN A QUALIFIED RETIREMENT PLAN

LO 51.6   Explain the rules of using life insurance in a qualified plan.

LO 51.7   Identify the types of assets appropriate as retirement plan investments.

LO 51.10   Discuss taxation where life insurance is used as an asset in a retirement plan.

Life insurance can be purchased as an asset by a qualified plan (but not by any type of IRA). The advantage of purchasing life insurance by the retirement plan is twofold—1) it can satisfy the need for additional life insurance protection for the owner of a small business, and 2) it can generate an immediate income tax deduction for the payment of the life insurance premiums (as qualified plan contributions) that may not otherwise be possible.

The amount of life insurance that may be held inside a qualified plan is limited under law. These are known as the **incidental benefit rules** of life insurance investment, and the amount of insurance held by the plan must meet one of the following two tests:

- The **percentage test**—under this test, the aggregate contributions paid for a life insurance policy owned by the plan on the lives of the plan participants may not exceed a certain percentage of the employer contributions to the plan as follows:

    — For the purchase of a whole life policy, no more than 50% of the employer contributions to the plan may be used.

    — For the purchase of any other life insurance policy (for example, term or universal life), no more than 25% of the employer contributions to the plan may be used.

Defined contribution plans use the percentage test rules in determining whether they have achieved compliance with the incidental benefit rules.

- The **100 times test**—under this test, the life insurance limitation is based on a ratio of the death benefit paid by the policy to the expected monthly benefit of the employee-participant payable by the plan. Specifically, using the 100 times test, the death benefit payable from the life insurance policy cannot exceed 100 times the expected monthly benefit for the employee-participant.

Defined benefit plans typically use the 100 times test rules in determining whether they have achieved compliance with the incidental benefit rules.

Tax Issues During Lifetime

If a qualified plan owns life insurance on the life of a participant, the participant must include in his income the **pure protection cost** of life insurance provided by the plan. The pure protection element amount is measured by the difference between the policy face amount and the policy cash value. The amount of inclusion in taxable income is the lesser of the actual cost of the insurance to the qualified plan or the **Table 2001 cost** as determined by a table in the Treasury Regulations. This amount is also treated as nontaxable basis to the employee-participant once distributions begin to be made from the plan.

Tax Issues at Death

Taxation of an insured death benefit received by a beneficiary of the plan participant may be summarized as follows.

■ The total of all Table 2001 costs (or, if lower, the actual insurance cost to the qualified plan) may be recovered tax free from the plan death benefit.

■ The pure insurance element of the plan death benefit is income tax free to the participant's beneficiaries (as life insurance proceeds).

■ The remainder of the distribution is taxable as a qualified plan distribution.

PRACTICE
QUESTION   *Choose the best answer for the question below.*

1. Which of the following statements regarding the incidental benefit rules of life insurance owned by a qualified plan is(are) CORRECT?
I.   For defined contribution plans, no more than 25% of the plan's assets may be in the form of universal life insurance.
II. For defined benefit plans, the life insurance death benefit cannot exceed 100 times the expected monthly benefit for an employee.

A.   I only
B.   II only
C.   Both I and II
D.   Neither I nor II

Answer: B. For defined contribution plans, no more than 25% of the employer contributions to the plan can be used to purchase universal life insurance. Statement II is correct.

D. UNRELATED BUSINESS TAXABLE INCOME (UBTI)

LO 51.5   Discuss the unrelated business taxable income (UBTI) rules.

Unrelated business taxable income (UBTI) generally means the gross income derived from any unrelated trade or business regularly carried on by the retirement plan, less any deductions directly connected with carrying on this trade or business. It is generated by the qualified plan trust and usually arises from property acquired with any funds that are borrowed by the trust. The major exception to the purchase of securities with borrowed money is employer securities that are purchased by an ESOP, as this is a specific ERISA exception to the UBTI rules.

The following items are excluded, however, from the calculation of UBTI (and do not count against the $1,000 per year exclusion):

■ Dividends, interest, and royalties

■ Rents from rental real estate owned by the trust

■ All gains or losses from the disposition of property, with certain exceptions

■ Certain amounts received from controlled entities and foreign corporations

Choose the best answer for the question below.

1. Which of the following statements with respect to UBTI is(are) CORRECT?

    I.   Employer securities purchased by an ESOP with borrowed funds give rise to UBTI.

    II. Dividends, interest, and royalties received by the qualified plan trust are included in the computation of UBTI.

    A. I only

    B. II only

    C. Both I and II

    D. Neither I nor II

Answer: D.   Employer securities purchased by an ESOP with borrowed funds do not give rise to UBTI, as this is a specific exception to the UBTI rules. Dividends, interest, and royalties are excluded from the calculation of UBTI, so that statement is also incorrect.

Beginning in 2015, an additional funding choice may be offered to IRA owners and Section 401(k) plan participants. The additional choice is referred to as a "longevity annuity" and will allow participants to allocate the lesser of 25% or $125,000 (2015) in their account to the purchase of a deferred annuity from which payments begin at an older age. The annuity allocation provides a stream of income to the participant for the balance of a participant's lifetime once payments commence. The funds allocated to the longevity annuity will not be considered in the calculation of required minimum distributions at age 70½.

105 UNIT 9 POST-STUDY CHECKLIST

☐ Am I able to identify factors that should be considered before implementing a qualified or tax-advantaged plan for a business?

☐ Do I know how to evaluate a given situation to select the most appropriate type of retirement plan for a given client or businessowner?

☐ Do I know how to determine the suitability of an investment for a given retirement plan?

☐ Am I able to explain the effect time horizon of an investment option has on its inclusion as a plan asset?

☐ Can I discuss the diversification of investments in retirement plans?

☐ Am I able to explain the fiduciary considerations of employer-sponsored retirement plans?

☐ Can I discuss the unrelated business taxable income (UBTI) rules?

☐ Am I able to explain the rules of using life insurance in a qualified plan?

☐ Am I able to identify the types of assets appropriate as retirement plan investments?

Am I able to define and understand the application of the following terms to financial planning?

☐ 100 times test	☐ Pure protection cost
☐ Incidental benefit test	☐ Retirement savings need
☐ Investment risk	☐ Table 2001 cost
☐ Liquidity	☐ Unrelated business taxable income (UBTI)
☐ Percentage test	

Retirement Needs Analysis

REFER TO

CFP® Certification Principal Topics – Retirement Planning, Retirement Needs Analysis

No Supplemental Readings for Unit 10 of 105 Retirement Planning Student Guide

(For specific assignments, refer to class syllabus.)

INTRODUCTION

Like financial planning in general, planning for retirement is a process rather than a one-time event. The retirement planning process parallels that of the six-step personal financial planning process, but in the analysis and evaluation step, a calculation is usually done to quantify how much money a client needs to meet the desired retirement income goals. As a part of this calculation, certain economic assumptions are made, including the rate of inflation before and during the retirement income period. In addition, an assumed total rate of return is used, as well as (and this is likely the most critical input) a life expectancy factor for the client once retirement age is attained.

The actual retirement needs analysis calculation has been presented before, most notably in the time value of money section of the first course in this program (*101: Fundamentals and Ethical Considerations*), but it is essentially a three-step process and will be reviewed in this unit.

LEARNING OBJECTIVES

After completing this unit, you should be able to achieve the following learning objectives:

CFP® Certification Principal Topics – Retirement Planning, Retirement Needs Analysis

LO 44.1   Perform a retirement needs analysis taking into account various assumptions such as inflation rate, retirement period, life expectancy, income sources, and other variables.

LO 44.2   Determine financial needs during the retirement period and calculate future values.

LO 44.4   Explain various patterns of work-to-retirement transitions and phased retirement.

LO 44.5   Discuss the various assumptions such as inflation rate, retirement period, life expectancy, income sources, and other variables used in retirement needs analysis.

LO 44.6   Determine financial needs during the retirement period and calculate future value of the projected first-year retirement income need.

LO 44.7   Determine whether to use a serial or a level payment approach to fund a future retirement need.

LO 44.8   Review alternatives when client is unable to meet the retirement savings goal.

LO 44.9   Determine financial needs during the retirement period and calculate future values when utilizing current retirement assets.

KEY TERMS

Bridge employment

Capital needs analysis

Capital preservation approach

Capital utilization approach

Level payment approach

Rate of Inflation

Rate of investment return

Retirement needs analysis

Serial payment approach

Wage replacement ratio (WRR)

A. ASSUMPTIONS FOR RETIREMENT PLANNING

LO 44.1   Perform a retirement needs analysis taking into account various assumptions such as inflation rate, retirement period, life expectancy, income sources, and other variables.

LO 44.5   Discuss the various assumptions such as inflation rate, retirement period, life expectancy, income sources, and other variables used in retirement needs analysis.

There are three primary assumptions made in any **retirement needs analysis** calculation. They are:

■   the anticipated annual rate of inflation;

■   the projected rate of annual investment return; and

■   the client's age at retirement and anticipated life expectancy.

Rate of Inflation

Projecting future inflation rates is inherently problematic, but since 1926, the Consumer Price Index (CPI) has averaged approximately 3% per year. Under the rule of 72, this means prices will double every 24 years (72 divided by 3) and is a good example of how a planner may impress upon the client the need to save with inflation-adjusted dollars.

However, the **rate of inflation** for retiree-senior citizens may well be higher than 3% per year. This is primarily because of the rising cost of health care in the United States. It is best to assume a higher annual rate of inflation in the retirement savings need analysis calculation of about 4–5% annually.

Rate of Investment Return

With respect to an assumed **rate of investment return**, most planners tend to use a flat average annual rate of return, which has the disadvantage of not taking into consideration the annual volatility of the return. Additionally, most estimates tend to be based on past performance, which may not be accurate when planning for extended periods in the future.

Taxes also impact the investment return actually achieved. Before retirement, the planner may use a before-tax rate of return in the assumptions, particularly if tax-advantaged savings vehicles (such as a traditional or Roth IRA) are used in the planning process. However, at the time of either optional or required retirement plan distributions, the client's anticipated effective income tax rate is very important. This rate should be a blend of the client's federal and state marginal income tax rates but should be projected based only on current rates because it is not feasible to accurately predict future income tax rates.

Client's Projected Retirement Age and Anticipated Life Expectancy

Like inflation and investment return rates, projecting a client's life expectancy (time in the retirement period) is very difficult. While actuarial life expectancy tables are of some assistance (for example, the actuarial factor applied from the required minimum distribution table is 27.4 at a client's age 70), these tables do not take into account family health history or, more importantly, how healthy (or unhealthy) the client is at the date of retirement.

In addition, if the client has a considerably younger spouse, certainly the spouse's much longer life expectancy needs to be considered. Whatever actuarial table is used to determine the life expectancy of any individual client, it is likely prudent to add a factor of between 5–10 years to the specified expectancy to provide a cushion for the client (or spouse) outliving the anticipated norm. Lifestyle is also an assumption to be considered when planning for a client's retirement. Does the client want to travel during retirement? Does the client plan on maintaining his current lifestyle or making changes in the retirement years? The costs associated with the lifestyle choices the client makes should be included in the retirement planning assumptions.

The analysis can be recalculated any time there is a significant change in the circumstances of the client. One-year changes in tax rates should not trigger a recalculation (such as a temporary change in FICA rates or income tax tables). Significant life events (e.g., marriage, divorce, births, deaths, or employment, health, and income changes) should be the major triggers considered.

B. FINANCIAL NEEDS AT RETIREMENT

LO 44.2   Determine financial needs during the retirement period and calculate future values.

LO 44.6   Determine financial needs during the retirement period and calculate future value of the projected first-year retirement income need.

On the path to determining how much the client should be saving to accomplish retirement income goals, the planner must first determine the lump-sum capital amount necessary to fund the projected income need over the entire retirement period. Thus, a two-step calculation is required.

1. Adjust or inflate the projected first-year retirement income need (expressed in present value dollars) to future dollars at the time of retirement.

2. Calculate the total retirement fund needed (lump-sum capital amount) to meet the projected income demands. To do this, the planner must calculate the present value of an annuity due using an inflation-adjusted rate of return.

Retirement needs tend to be 60–80% of preretirement income to maintain the individual's preretirement lifestyle. This percentage is called the **wage replacement ratio (WRR)**.

The savings rate required beginning at age 25 to achieve a 60–80% wage replacement ratio is approximately 10% of gross income. This figure is significantly higher than the typical personal savings rate in the U.S., which has been approximately 5% for many years. The process of analyzing the accumulation of sufficient resources for retirement is called **capital needs analysis** or retirement needs analysis.

E X A M P L E   Your client, Steve, estimates he will need $60,000 annual income in today's dollars when he retires 10 years from now. He assumes a 4% annual rate of inflation, a 7% after-tax rate of return on available investments, and a 20-year retirement period. His total retirement fund needed to support this standard of living is $1,374,075, calculated as follows.

1. The client's first year retirement income need is $88,815.

    PV = −$60,000

    $i = 4$

    $n = 10$

    FV = $88,815

2. The total capital required to support this need for 20 years is $1,374,075.

    In BEGIN mode (the client will make annual withdrawals at the beginning of each year)

    PMT = −$88,815

    FV = 0

    $n = 20$

    $i = 2.8846$ [(1.07 ÷ 1.04) − 1] × 100

    $PV_{AD} = \$1,374,075$

Often, there is another critical question that should be asked of the client during this stage of the retirement needs analysis process. Is the client comfortable using both the principal and income from the lump-sum capital amount to meet the retirement income needs or, alternatively, does the client wish to use only the income for living expenses (leaving the principal intact for transfer to any heirs)? Normally, for all but the very wealthy, the answer to this question is that the client must use both the principal and income to support the retirement income need. Accordingly, most retirement needs analysis calculations assume a **capital utilization approach**; nevertheless, be aware that the alternative calculation is to assume a **capital preservation approach**, a method that will require even more total capital to be accumulated at a client's projected date of retirement. The capital preservation approach maintains the original capital balance needed at the retirement date for the entire life expectancy. In the previous capital utilization approach example, the capital needed at retirement was calculated to be $1,374,075. In the capital preservation approach, this amount is then discounted at the expected investment return rate over the expected retirement period, and the result is added to the original capital utilization value. The sum is the amount of capital needed at retirement to generate the desired retirement income and leave a balance at life expectancy equal to the original capital utilization value. In our example, the capital preservation approach value becomes $1,729,162. The two-step calculation is as follows:

FV = $1,374,075

n = 20

i = 7

PV = –$355,087 (additional capital needed for capital preservation)
    $1,374,075 + $355,087 = $1,729,162

Note: The example is illustrated with the calculator set for 1 P/YR. If your calculation result does not match the example, check your calculator to be sure it is set for 1 P/YR.

C. FUTURE VALUE OF ACCUMULATED RESOURCES

LO 44.2   Determine financial needs during the retirement period and calculate future values.

LO 44.9   Determine financial needs during the retirement period and calculate future values when utilizing current retirement assets.

It is necessary to determine how much, if any, of the required lump-sum capital amount will be satisfied through the future growth of available client assets or resources. Unfortunately, many clients have very little already saved that may be dedicated to their retirement income goals. A planner's first responsibility is to assist the client in implementing a periodic savings program. However, if some assets have already been set aside at the time of performing the retirement needs analysis, the value of these assets should be included in the calculation on an after-tax basis. Including the existing funds can result in a lower calculated current savings amount needed or, perhaps, provide the client with the flexibility to consider a capital preservation approach instead of a capital utilization approach.

> **EXAMPLE** In the previous example, it was determined that the total capital required to support Steve's retirement need for 20 years is $1,374,075. Now assume that Steve has already dedicated a total of $450,000 to the retirement income goals. What is the future value of this amount in 10 years at a 7% after-tax rate of investment return?
>
> PV = –$450,000
>
> i = 7
>
> n = 10
>
> FV = $885,218.1108
>
> As a result, we can now subtract the available amount of resources ($885,218) from the capital requirement need of $1,374,075. This yields a projected deficit at retirement of $488,857 ($1,374,075 – $885,218).

In considering the amount of accumulated resources, some clients will want the financial planner to consider Social Security retirement benefits, while others will not. However, while Social Security retirement benefits are the foundation of retirement income for some (particularly lower income) workers, Social Security will generally not meet a client's total retirement needs. Therefore, it is prudent to prepare a conservative savings program based on the capital needed using only personal savings and employer-sponsored benefits.

D. RETIREMENT NEEDS ANALYSIS CALCULATIONS

LO 44.7   Determine whether to use a serial or a level payment approach to fund a future retirement need.

How much does a client need to save on an annual basis to meet a retirement income goal (and support the client's retirement lifestyle)? In the second example, the client had already set aside certain available resources ($450,000) to assist in meeting the desired retirement income goal. However, if no (or very little) resources have been dedicated to this goal, the initial savings need would be much greater. In addition to this analysis, we must also consider whether the client wishes to use a level or **serial payment approach** when saving for retirement. While most clients may want to use a **level payment approach**, the financial planner should also make the clients aware that a serial payment calculation is more realistic as it takes into account the effects of inflation.

Level Payment Approach

Returning to the first client example (needing $60,000 per year for 20 years in today's dollars, retiring 10 years from now), the client needs to save $99,451.75 annually to accumulate his retirement lump-sum capital need of $1,374,075 as calculated below. Note that the uneven cash flows method is used. The keystroke input for the HP10BII is as follows:

1)   Determine PV of future need

   0 CFj

   0 CFj

   9 shift Nj

   60,000 CFj

   20 shift Nj

   $[(1.07 \div 1.04) - 1] \times 100 = 2.8846$ I/YR

   shift NPV 698,507.46

2) Determine end-of-year payment required

In END mode

PV = $698,507.46

$i = 7$

$n = 10$

FV = 0

PMT = –$99,451.75

Serial Payment Approach

In a serial payment approach, an initial or first-year savings amount is calculated and then increased each year by inflation, anticipating an increase in the client's income at that same rate. The difference in the calculation between this approach and the previous approach is that the interest rate used in Step 2 is the inflation-adjusted interest rate.

> **EXAMPLE** Using the same example, solve for a first-year serial payment of $84,661 as follows.
>
> **Step 1:**
>
> 0 CFj
>
> 0 CFj
>
> 9 shift Nj
>
> 60,000 CFj
>
> 20 shift Nj
>
> [(1.07 ÷ 1.04) – 1] × 100 = 2.8846 I/YR
>
> shift NPV 698,507.46
>
> **Step 2: (after clearing the calculator)**
>
> In END mode
>
> PV = $698,507.46
>
> $n = 10$
>
> $i = 2.8846$ [(1.07 ÷ 1.04) – 1] × 100
>
>   (Note an inflation-adjusted return is used in step 2, unlike the level payment approach.)
>
> FV = 0
>
> PMT = –$81,404.92
>
> $81,404.92 × 1.04 = $84,661

Note that what has been calculated is the first serial (increasing) savings payment. Because the client is assumed to make payments at the end of the year, adjust the result ($81,404.92) to the value or the serial payment that will be made at the end of the first year by multiplying the payment by (1+ the inflation rate).

Compare the resulting payments under both approaches. The annual payments made in the early years under the serial payment approach will be less than that calculated using the level payment approach. However, as the client nears retirement, the annual payment required under the serial payment approach will exceed that required using the level payment alternative.

PRACTICE
QUESTIONS   *Choose the best answer for each of the questions below.*

1. A client has determined an annual retirement income need of $40,000 per year in today's dollars. In performing a retirement needs analysis, the client wants you to assume a 5% annual inflation rate, an 8% after-tax return, and a 20-year retirement period. The client plans to retire in 12 years. What is the annual payment needed at the end of each year to meet the client's retirement income goal using a level payment savings approach?
   A. $46,264
   B. $58,697
   C. $71,834
   D. $54,349

   Answer: B.   The annual level savings payment needed by your client to meet her retirement income goal is $58,697, calculated using the following 2-step process.

   Step 1:
   0 CFj
   0 CFj
   11 shift Nj
   40,000 CFj
   20 shift Nj
   [(1.08 ÷ 1.05) − 1] × 100 = 2.8571 I/YR
   shift NPV 442,347.8801

   Step 2:
   In END mode
   PV = $442,347.88
   FV = 0
   n = 12
   i = 8
   PMT = −$58,697

2. Using the same facts as Question #1, what is the annual serial payment amount required at the end of the 1st year by the client?
   A. $46,264
   B. $58,697
   C. $44,061
   D. $44,979

Answer: A. The annual serial payment needed by your client to meet her retirement income goal is $46,264 using the following 2-step process.

Step 1: Result from Question 1: NPV of $442,347.88

Step 2:
In END mode
PV = $442,347.88
$n = 12$
$i = 2.8571$ $[(1.08 \div 1.05) - 1] \times 100$
FV = 0
PMT= −$44,061
$44,061 × (1 + .05) = $46,264

E. METHODS OF SAVING FOR RETIREMENT

LO 44.8   Review alternatives when client is unable to meet the retirement savings goal.

After performing a retirement needs analysis and calculating the necessary capital needed, it is important to evaluate the various retirement savings alternatives available to the client. The client should review his employer-sponsored retirement plan benefits. For example, if he is not participating in an employer-sponsored Section 401(k) plan, deferring some salary to take advantage of the probable employer savings match is an excellent option. In addition, increasing elective deferrals to such a plan is worth considering. If the individual is self-employed, the importance of establishing and contributing to a tax-advantaged retirement plan (such as a simplified employee pension (SEP) or a solo Section 401(k)) cannot be overstated. Other methods of taking advantage of employer-sponsored alternatives include nonqualified deferred compensation (NQDC) and equity-based compensation exercisable at an employee's projected retirement date.

There are also individual savings plan alternatives that may be implemented by the client. Popular among these are the traditional IRA and the Roth IRA, but there are also insurance-backed retirement products, such as deferred fixed or variable annuities as well as cash value life insurance policies. Finally, there are taxable account alternatives, including investment portfolios structured to provide primarily capital appreciation (stocks) and fixed income (bonds). If it is determined the client is unable to meet the retirement savings goal, the client then has five alternatives:

- Retire later (or not at all)

- Save more

- Reduce the retirement income needs

- Restructure the asset allocation of the investment portfolio to increase investment return (while assuming additional investment risk)

- Some combination of the available alternatives

The most common choice is a combination of retire later and save more. The client should review his employer-sponsored retirement plan benefits.

PRACTICE
QUESTION   *Choose the best answer for the question below.*

1. All of the following are commonly thought of as methods of saving for retirement EXCEPT
   A.   the traditional deductible IRA
   B.   the Roth IRA
   C.   a Section 529 plan
   D.   a Section 401(k) plan

Answer: C.   A Section 529 plan is commonly used in the college education savings process and not as a method of saving for retirement.

F. TRANSITIONS TO RETIREMENT

LO 44.4   Explain various patterns of work-to-retirement transitions and phased retirement.

As clients approach retirement age, many questions and concerns can arise. Often, one of clients' biggest concerns is the sufficiency of retirement income. Post-retirement income is often considerably less than during the working years. Whether or not it is sufficient depends on many factors, such as investment returns, inflation, health issues, and the client's spending habits in retirement.

A planner can assist the client by helping to construct a budget that illustrates the relationship of post-retirement expenses to the level of retirement income. This can alleviate some of the anxiety clients may feel by the unknown and can give them a sense of control over their retirement planning.

In addition to financial concerns, many retirees find the sudden lack of a place to go and a schedule to meet disconcerting. They may feel uneasy without the validation of having a place to go every day where they are valued and productive. Easing into retirement can lessen the difficulty. By cutting their hours gradually for some time prior to retirement and reducing their role in the workplace (i.e., winding down) the transition into retirement is less stressful for many clients.

Bridge employment is a job that helps ease this transition. When a client is not ready to completely retire, feels safer having additional income, or must make up for a shortfall in retirement assets, a part- or full-time bridge job may be the answer. Even though bridge jobs seldom have the same compensation level clients enjoyed preretirement, there are many opportunities to use the employment to satisfy other interests clients have and allow them to put their talents to work.

When discussing with a client the possibility of post-retirement employment, the planner should take advantage of the various agencies available to counsel retirees in their area. For those with a college degree, it is possible that teaching in the public or private arenas would be a good fit. Entry level positions in different fields can provide any income needed as well as the social interaction the retiree was used to during his previous employment.

Once fully retired, clients may find they still need the opportunity to be in contact with others on a daily basis that they would miss if they fully retired and left the workforce. These clients often see the onset of retirement as an opportunity to learn a new skill, start a second career, volunteer in causes that are important to them, or travel.

If clients are concerned about becoming isolated in their later years and additional retirement funds aren't needed, planners may want to suggest that clients volunteer for a cause they support or where their help is truly needed. The Retired Senior Volunteer Program (RSVP) in a client's area can offer clients many options to help others, as can churches or other religious and civil organizations.

Actually retiring can be a complicated and emotional event for clients. However, presenting some of these options can help them make a smoother transition so they can enjoy their retirement years.

PRACTICE QUESTION

Choose the best answer for the question below.

1. Mike and Sara are a married couple, each age 30, who file jointly for income tax purposes. Many of their assets, but not their retirement plans, are jointly owned. Sara has approached Jack, a CFP® professional, for retirement planning advice. Jack has requested multiple documents needed in the planning process but Mike, as a joint owner of some of those assets, has declined to participate in the retirement planning process or to provide information. Sara would be Jack's only client. What does Jack do next?

   A. Jack must inform Sara of the types of information he requires and how it will impact his ability to fulfill the engagement.

   B. Jack cannot have only 1 spouse as a client and must terminate the engagement.

   C. Jack should ask Sara to obtain the information he needs without Mike's knowledge.

   D. Jack should call Mike and try to persuade him to give him the information he needs for the engagement.

   Answer: A. *Rules of Conduct 3.3* states "A certificant shall obtain the information necessary to fulfill his or her obligations. If a certificant cannot obtain the necessary information, the certificant shall inform the prospective client or client of any and all material deficiencies." Before Jack can determine whether or not he can continue with Sara as a client he must clearly advise her of the documentation he needs to satisfy the engagement. If it is then unavailable, then, the scope of the engagement must be altered to accommodate, or the engagement terminated, depending on what documentation is unavailable. (Domain 8: Practicing within professional and regulatory standards)

---

105 UNIT 10 POST-STUDY CHECKLIST

☐ Am I able to perform a retirement needs analysis taking into account various assumptions such as inflation rate, retirement period, life expectancy, income sources, and other variables?

☐ Do I understand how to determine financial needs during the retirement period and calculate future values?

☐ Can I explain various patterns of work-to-retirement transitions and phased retirement?

Am I able to define and understand the application of the following terms to financial planning?

☐ Bridge job	☐ Rate of Inflation
☐ Capital needs analysis	☐ Rate of investment return
☐ Capital preservation approach	☐ Retirement needs analysis
☐ Capital utilization approach	☐ Serial payment approach
☐ Level payment approach	☐ Wage replacement ratio (WRR)

Case Study

Case studies are a principal part of the national CFP® Certification Examination. The Allen case study below will allow you to become familiar with the presentation and layout of a case study. The questions and answers following this case study will give you a sampling of the Fundamentals and Ethical Considerations subject matter that may be tested on the national CFP® exam.

You will see the Allen case study in the 101 through 106 courses. Questions and answers presented in each course will focus on the subject matter of that course. After studying the Allen case in all six education courses, you should be well prepared for the 107 Financial Plan Development Course, a CFP Board requirement for all students matriculating in the education program after December 31, 2011.

These case study facts and the practice questions that follow will allow you to become familiar with case studies, which are found on the CFP® Exam. After completing this case study section, you will also be required to complete the Case Study exam, which will present a different set of case study facts, but will be of a similar format.

Case Study Approaches

Generally, there are two approaches you can use for case studies, the Case Facts Analysis Approach and the Question Review Approach.

Case Facts Analysis Approach

Read the case carefully and slowly, making sure that you pay attention to detail. Particularly note age, marital status, number of children and grandchildren, net worth, and income levels. These variables will give you a good idea of what the case is about. Anticipate questions and make notes. When a topic is presented, make a mental or written note of that topic. When additional information is provided on that topic later in the case, a question regarding that topic usually appears unless the additional information negates the question.

Read each question and the answers provided. Answer the easy questions first, followed by the more complex questions. Calculation questions (e.g., probate estate, education funding, capital needs analysis, minimum distributions, and mortgage qualification) can be time consuming. Go back to them later.

Question Review Approach

Read the questions quickly. Make notes. Answer any questions that do not require reading the case, then read the case only looking for the answers to the questions asked.
Follow these steps:

1. Read the last line of the question.

2. Make notes.

3. Answer all questions that can be answered without reading the case. Record your answers.

4. Read the case to answer the questions that involve specific case facts. Record your answers.

5. Make sure all questions are answered.

6. Review the answers.

Michael and Marie Allen Case Study

Michael and Marie Allen have come to you, a financial planner, for help in developing a plan to accomplish their financial goals. You are a Series 7 registered representative and hold insurance licenses for life and health insurance and variable contracts.

The Allens have been reading about various financial planning services and want to consider having a "fee-only" based arrangement with you. They ask if you are a "fee-only" planner and if you can work with them on that basis. They have great hope for their future; however, after having a conversation about investing with one of their neighbors, they have recently realized that they are not as financially comfortable as they would like to be at this point in their lives. Assume today is January 1, 2015.

Personal Background and Information

The Allens

Michael and Marie have been married for 12 years. They have two children, Max and Sam. Michael has a son, Alex, and a daughter, Abby, from a previous marriage.

Michael Allen (Age 45)

Michael is a vice president of Asher Bank and Trust. He has been employed there for 12 years and has an annual salary of $70,000.

Marie Allen (Age 40)

Until Sam was born, Marie was an architect with a local design firm. She has been uncertain when she would resume her career until recently when the top architecture firm in the city, Wright and Associates, approached her about joining the firm as a part-time independent contractor. Marie has a high level of skill using architectural design software, and Wright and Associates wants her to help with high-end design projects. Marie's earnings from the part-time work are expected to be at least $50,000 annually. Marie is excited to accept the position because she feels she has the time with Sam now attending school full days.

Family

- Alex is 20 years old and is a junior at State University on a partial scholarship, 500 miles from Michael and Marie. When not boarding at school, he lives with his mother, Nicole. During the summers, Alex works at Asher Bank and Trust as an intern and lives with Michael and Marie. Nicole and Michael have agreed that Nicole may claim Alex as a dependent.

- Abby, 16 years old, lives in another state with her mother and attends public school. She has aspirations to study at The Juilliard School upon graduation and has applied for a scholarship. She is also Nicole's dependent for income tax purposes.

- Max is 10 years old and attends Woodridge Academy, a private school. He plays the trombone in the school band and attends band camp each summer. Max also plays on the school's basketball team.

- Samantha (Sam) is 7 years old and is in second grade at Woodridge Academy. She meets with a private tutor once a week to get help with her reading skills.

■ Carol, Michael's mother, died within the past month at the age of 70 and her estate is currently in probate. She had been in poor health and living with Michael and Marie the past two years and had been using her investments to meet her living expenses. Michael is the sole beneficiary and executor of Carol's estate.

■ Grant and Rose, Marie's parents, are in good health and have agreed to pay for Max and Sam's tuition through the 8th grade. They are retired and travel year-round. Marie is their only child. Marie mentions to you that her parents want to know if there are any gift tax consequences for them paying tuition for Max and Sam. They are also interested in making additional gifts for education, and Marie asks you what she should tell her parents.

■ Nicole, Michael's ex-wife, who lives in another state, is an attorney for the Department of Justice. There is currently no child support agreement for Abby.

Personal and Financial Goals

■ Help Alex pay for his college expenses

■ Assist Abby with tuition and expenses when she begins college in two years

■ Save for college tuition for Max and Sam

■ Evaluate investment and insurance risks and improve risk management

■ Pay off all debt by retirement

■ Retire at the age of 62 with 80% of preretirement salary at retirement

■ Prepare proper wills and an estate plan

The Allens have asked you to comment and offer recommendations on any area of their current finances you feel has a weakness or vulnerability or presents an opportunity for improvement in reaching their goals.

Economic Information

The Allens expect medical inflation to be 5% annually and the annual inflation rate to average 3% over both the short and long terms. The present average interest rate on their credit cards is approximately 16%. The risk-free rate is 3.25%, and the Allens' required rate of return is 8%.

Current mortgage rates are 6% for 30-year fixed mortgages and 5.5% for 15-year fixed mortgages. Closing costs will approximate 3% of any mortgage refinanced and will be paid separately. Michael and Marie feel this is an opportune time to refinance their home mortgage. Given their goals, they have asked you to evaluate available mortgage options and make a recommendation. Their credit score is good, but they are concerned whether or not they will be able to meet some of the standard financial ratio tests required to qualify for a new mortgage.

Insurance Information

Health Insurance

The entire family is insured under Michael's company plan, which is a major medical plan with a $500 per person deductible, an 80/20 coinsurance clause, and a family annual stop-loss limit of $2,500. Michael's employer pays 100% of the health insurance premium.

Life Insurance

Michael has a group term life insurance policy with a face amount of $60,000 provided by his employer. Michael is not a highly compensated employee. The policy beneficiary is Marie. The premium of $9 per month is paid by his employer. The Section 79 table cost per $1,000 of protection is $0.15 for Michael's age.

Recently, one of their neighbors, who was the same age as Marie and had three very young children, died prematurely. After the Allens saw firsthand the financial stress of the surviving spouse, they decided it was time to have you create a life insurance needs analysis for them. They want to know what type of information you need from them to help you prepare your life insurance recommendations.

Disability Insurance

Michael has a private disability income insurance policy with an own occupation definition of disability and a 30-day elimination period. Based on the provisions of the policy, in the event Michael is disabled, the benefit is $2,700 per month until Michael's normal retirement age, defined as Michael's retirement age under the Social Security Act on the date of his disability. The annual premium is $761 and is paid by Michael.

Homeowners Insurance

The Allens have a HO-3 policy with dwelling extension and replacement cost on contents. There is a $1,000 deductible. The annual premium is $950.

Automobile Insurance

The Allens have automobile liability and bodily injury coverage of $100,000/$300,000/$100,000. They have both comprehensive coverage (other than collision) and collision. The deductibles are $250 (comprehensive) and $500 (collision), respectively. The annual premium is $900.

The Allens are not entirely happy with their auto and homeowners insurance carrier due to a dispute over hail damage last year. Michael has asked you what you think of their carrier and if you can get the Allens a better rate on their coverages.

Investment Information

The only investments the Allens have outside of the retirement plan are the ABC stock inherited by Marie from her grandmother in 2014 and the college fund certificates of deposit.

The Allens have had little investment experience but consider themselves to have a moderate risk tolerance (7 on a scale of 10), given their ages and long-term goals.

ABC stock has paid a steady dividend of $3.50 per share. The dividend is expected to grow at a constant rate of 5% per year into the foreseeable future. Given the Allens' required rate of return , they have asked you to determine if the stock is overpriced or underpriced in the secondary market.

The Allens are concerned that ABC stock may substantially decline in price in the near future. They want to know which investment strategies would best protect their position in ABC over the next 60 days.

Income Tax Considerations

Michael and Marie tell you that they are in the 15% federal income tax bracket. They pay $820 annually in state and local income taxes. The Allens want to know the income tax implications of Marie returning to work as an independent contractor. The majority of Marie's work will be done at home, and the Allens are currently remodeling a guest bedroom as office space for Marie.

The Allens have also asked you if there are any income tax consequences related to the life insurance and health insurance for which Michael's employer pays the premiums.

Retirement Information

Michael wants to retire at age 62 with income equal to 80% of his preretirement income. He expects to receive Social Security benefits of $24,000 (in today's dollars) for himself and $12,000 for Marie (in today's dollars) at full retirement age 67. They will receive 70% of Michael's full benefit at age 62 but only 32.5% of Michael's full benefit for Marie at early retirement. With Marie returning to work, she may earn a higher benefit on her own work record.

The bank offers a Section 401(k) plan in which Michael is an active participant. The bank matches contributions dollar for dollar up to 3% of Michael's salary. Michael currently defers 3% of his salary.

The Allens want to know the amount of required capital, after considering Social Security, to support their retirement goal.

Marie wants to know what type of retirement plan would allow her to contribute the most for retirement on a tax-favored basis if her work with Wright and Associates generates sufficient income.

Education Information

Max is 10 years old and currently attending fifth grade at Woodridge Academy, which he will attend through high school. Michael and Marie have $2,500 in CDs that they contribute to once a year ($500 each year) for Max. This account will be used for college and is in Max's name.

Samantha (Sam) is 7 years old. She is in second grade at Woodridge Academy and will attend the academy through high school. Michael and Marie have $1,000 in CDs to which they contribute once a year ($500 each year) for Sam. This account will be used for college and is in Sam's name.

Michael and Marie invested in CDs for Max and Sam's college educations; the CDs are owned by Michael and Marie. The rate of return on this college fund is 6%, and the current balance is $15,000. Michael and Marie would also like to be able to send their children to school for five years instead of the traditional four years. The extra year could be used to pursue a graduate degree.

The current cost of college (including room, board, tuition, and books) is $15,000 per year per child. They expect their children to start college at the age of 18. The Allens expect an educational CPI of 5%.

To this point, the Allens have had limited resources to save for college for the children. They intend to assist Alex and Abby the best they can out of current cash flows and want to know the best way to do so from a tax perspective and what other college funding resources may be available to consider. Additionally, they would like to know the amount of annual savings required to provide for college for Max and Sam.

Gifts, Estates, Trusts, and Will Information

Michael's will leaves everything to Marie conditioned on a six-month survivorship clause, otherwise, equally in separate trusts for the four children.

Marie does not have a will.

Michael has questions regarding several assets in Carol's estate:

- A nonqualified variable annuity consisting of an initial investment of $50,000 made in 1994. The current value of the annuity is $126,000, and Michael is the sole primary beneficiary. If Michael chooses to take the entire $126,000 in a lump-sum distribution to help refinance the mortgage, what would be the tax consequence?

■ A universal life insurance policy with a stated face amount of $100,000. The policy had a cash surrender value of $18,000 and Carol had paid total premiums of $15,000. They policy had an outstanding policy loan of $5,000 at the time of her death. Carol had elected death benefit option B at the time the policy was issued. Michael wants to know the amount he will receive from the policy after taxes.

■ A nonqualified fixed annuity in which she had invested a total of $40,000. This contract was purchased in 1996 and has a current value of $93,000. Michael is the sole beneficiary. He decided to take the life income option on this portion of his inheritance to help out with the entertainment section of the budget. Michael's life expectancy is 35 years, and he is to receive $500 per month for the rest of his life. He has asked how much of this monthly distribution is taxable.

■ A Roth IRA with an account balance of $50,000 into which contributions of $30,000 had been made over the past 10 years, Carol maintained the account. Michael would like to make this account part of their retirement savings and has asked about his options regarding this account and the respective income tax treatment of those options.

■ A mutual fund valued at $30,000 at the time of Carol's death. Carol invested $10,000 initially in the mutual fund, and the fund had generated $5,000 in dividends and capital gains (all reinvested in the fund) over the 10 years she had held the fund. Michael is considering liquidating the fund once ownership is established in his name and wants to know the tax consequences of this transaction.

■ Michael also has asked you to brief him on the general responsibilities he has as executor of his mother's estate.

STATEMENT OF CASH FLOWS
Michael and Marie Allen
For the Year 2015 (Expected)

INFLOWS

Salary and Schedule C Income

Salary - Michael	$ 70,000	
Schedule C Income—Marie	50,000	
Total Salary and Schedule C Income		**$120,000**

Investment income

Interest (taxable)	$ 900	
Dividends	150	
Total investment income		$ 1,050
TOTAL INFLOWS		**$ 121,050**

OUTFLOWS

Savings

Reinvestment interest/dividends	$ 1,050	
Section 401(k) plan elective contribution	2,100	
College fund CDs	1,000	
Total savings		$ 4,150

Ordinary living expenses

Food	$ 6,000	
Clothing	3,600	
Child care	600	
Entertainment	1,814	
Utilities	3,600	
Auto maintenance	2,000	
Church contributions	3,500	
Total ordinary living expenses		$ 21,114

Other payments

Section 401(k) loan repayment	$ 1,703	
Credit card payments[1]	960	
Mortgage payments[2]	21,954	
Boat loan[3]	3,040	
Total payments		$ 27,657

Insurance premiums

Automobile	$ 900	
Disability	761	
Homeowners	950	
Total insurance premiums		$ 2,611

Tuition and education expenses		$ 1,000

Taxes

Federal FICA and withholding	$ 22,855	
State and city income tax	1,320	
Property tax (principal residence)	1,000	
Total Taxes		$ 25,175

TOTAL OUTFLOWS		**$ 81,707**
NET CASH FLOW (SURPLUS)		**$ 39,343**

[1] Credit card payments: Principal $345; Interest $615
[2] Mortgage payments: Principal $1,234; Interest $20,720
[3] Boat loan payments: Principal $1,493; Interest $1,547

STATEMENT OF FINANCIAL POSITION
Michael and Marie Allen
January 1, 2015

ASSETS[1]

Liquid assets

JT Checking account	$ 1,500	
JT Savings account	1,000	
Total liquid assets		$ 2,500

Investments

S2 ABC stock (100 shares)[2]	$ 13,000	
JT Certificates of deposit (college fund)	15,000	
S1 Section 401(k) vested plan balance	43,000	
Total investments		$ 71,000

JT Personal real estate – residence		$250,000

Other personal assets

JT Automobiles	$ 15,000	
JT Boat	20,000	
JT Jewelry	13,500	
JT Furniture/household	60,000	
Total other personal assets		$108,500

TOTAL ASSETS		**$432,000**

LIABILITIES[3] AND NET WORTH

Current liabilities

JT Credit cards		4,000

Long-term liabilities

S1 Section 401(k) plan loan[4]	$ 7,000	
JT Mortgage on residence[5]	197,888	
JT Boat loan	13,559	
Total long-term liabilities		$218,447

TOTAL LIABILITIES		**$222,447**
ALLEN FAMILY NET WORTH		**$209,553**
TOTAL LIABILITIES AND NET WORTH		**$432,000**

S1 – Michael Allen; S2 – Marie Allen; JT – jointly owned by Michael and Marie Allen

Other notes to the Statement of Financial Position:

[1] Assets are stated at fair market value.

[2] The ABC stock was inherited from Marie's grandmother on November 15, 2014. Her grandmother originally paid $20,000 for it on October 31, 2014. The fair market value at her grandmother's death was $12,000.

[3] Liabilities are stated at principal only.

[4] The proceeds from the Section 401(k) plan loan were used to pay off the auto loan, which had a higher interest rate.

[5] Note that some statements of financial position may show the current year's mortgage liability as a current liability. However, the total liability may also be listed as a long-term liability, as done in this case.

Allen Case Study – Practice Questions

1. Michael and Marie are committed to reducing living expenses to be able to save more for retirement. The couple is not counting any possible income from any potential part-time earnings for Marie as that income is not yet realized. Assuming they create the necessary discretionary income, what is the total maximum deductible contribution they can make to a traditional IRA together for 2015?

   a. $0
   b. $5,500
   c. $9,000
   d. $11,000

2. Michael's employer, Asher Bank and Trust, is considering making an additional profit-sharing contribution to the bank's Section 401(k) plan for 2015. What is the maximum amount of additional profit-sharing contribution the bank could make on behalf of Michael for 2015?

   a. $13,800
   b. $15,900
   c. $48,800
   d. $53,000

3. A rival bank across town has been aggressively recruiting Michael. If Michael leaves Asher Bank and Trust, which of the following statements regarding the tax status of his outstanding loan from his Section 401(k) plan is(are) correct if Michael cannot make arrangements to pay off the loan?

   1. The loan balance continues to be tax free because Michael is essentially borrowing from himself.
   2. Michael may roll over the outstanding loan to an IRA.
   3. The outstanding loan is subject to income tax if not repaid.
   4. The outstanding loan may be subject to an additional 10% excise penalty.

   a. 1 only
   b. 1 and 2
   c. 3 only
   d. 3 and 4

4. If Michael should leave Asher Bank and Trust and he elects to take a lump-sum distribution of his Section 401(k) balance, which of the following statements is(are) CORRECT?

   1. Michael may elect 10-year forward averaging to reduce his tax liability on the lump-sum distribution.
   2. Michael may elect a tax-free direct transfer of the lump-sum distribution to an IRA, less the 20% mandatory withholding.
   3. Michael may take receipt of the lump-sum distribution, and as long as he rolls over the distribution within 60 days to an IRA, the rollover is tax free and not subject to the 20% mandatory withholding.
   4. If Michael's new employer's qualified plan allows, he may be able to directly transfer the lump-sum distribution to the new plan without being subject to the mandatory 20% withholding.

   a. 1, 2, and 3
   b. 2 and 3
   c. 3 and 4
   d. 4 only

5. If Michael died today, which family members may be eligible for Social Security survivor benefits based on Michael's PIA, assuming he is fully insured?

    a. Marie, Max, Sam, and Alex
    b. Max and Sam
    c. Max, Sam, Alex, and Abby
    d. Marie, Max, Sam and Abby

6. Assuming Michael's income increases by 3% per year between now and age 62, what lump sum will be necessary at the date of retirement to provide Michael's goal of 80% of preretirement income for 25 years in retirement without considering Social Security? Assume the Allens' required rate of return in the calculation.

    a. $839,790
    b. $1,388,038
    c. $1,400,000
    d. $2,313,975

7. Michael and Marie have been working with you, a CFP® professional, for some time on their financial plans for retirement. You have presented your recommendations to the Allens and a timeline for implementation has been created. The Allens now inform you that Marie is considering working as an independent contractor doing architecture consulting part-time with Wright and Associates. She feels this would be a good way to help increase the amount they save for retirement. Marie is considering adopting a qualified profit-sharing plan as a self-employed individual. What do you do next to assist the couple in their retirement planning and the potential changes?

    a. You discuss and evaluate the effects this possible new employment will have on the recommendations already implemented and redefine the scope of the engagement, if appropriate.
    b. You must return to the developing the recommendations phase of the planning process because the Allens' circumstances will change.
    c. Marie's plans have no effect on any retirement planning already accomplished because it will only add to the couple's retirement assets.
    d. Because the Allens' circumstances will change, you must procure a new client engagement letter for the couple.

8. Michael is considering executing an additional loan from his Section 401(k) plan. What is the maximum loan amount he could currently execute?

    a. $10,000
    b. $14,500
    c. $21,500
    d. $43,000

9. Michael is considering a second, part-time job, teaching evenings at a community college. The college offers a Section 403(b) plan. Assuming Michael would earn $20,000 per year teaching, what is the maximum elective deferral he could make to the Section 403(b) plan?

    a. $12,500
    b. $15,900
    c. $18,000
    d. $20,000

10. If Michael died today, what is the total lump-sum death benefit that would be paid by Social Security to his family?

    a. $255
    b. $510
    c. $1,020
    d. $1,275

Allen Case Study Answers

1. **D.** The maximum deductible contribution for the Allens to a traditional IRA for 2015 is $11,000 ($5,500 each). Michael is an active participant in a qualified plan, but his AGI is below the MFJ phaseout of $98,000. If Marie has no earned income in 2015, she can make an IRA contribution based on Michael's earned income, and her AGI for these purposes is below the nonparticipant spouse AGI limit of $183,000.

2. **C.** The maximum additional profit-sharing contribution the employer could make for Michael in 2015 is $48,800. The maximum annual additions limit in 2015 is $53,000. The annual additions limit includes employer contributions and employee elective deferrals. Michael makes elective deferrals of 3% ($2,100), and the employer matches this amount 100% ($2,100). The total elective deferrals and employer contributions is $4,200, so the employer could make an additional profit-sharing contribution of $48,800 ($53,000 – $4,200).

3. **D.** Statements 3 and 4 are correct. Michael cannot roll over the loan to an IRA. The loan becomes fully taxable if not repaid and may be subject to an additional 10% excise penalty.

4. **D.** Only statement 4 is correct. Statement 1 is incorrect because Michael is not eligible to elect 10-year forward averaging. He does not meet the age requirement. Statement 2 is incorrect because if a direct transfer to an IRA is elected, the distribution is not subject to 20% mandatory withholding. Statement 3 is incorrect because even if the distribution is rolled over into an IRA within 60 days, the 20% mandatory withholding still applies if Michael takes receipt of the distribution prior to the rollover.

5. **D.** Marie, Max, Sam, and Abby are eligible for benefits. Alex is not eligible because he is over age 18. Carol is not eligible because she does not qualify as a dependent of Michael.

6. **B.** The lump sum needed at the date of retirement to support Michael's goal (without considering Social Security) is $1,388, 038.

   Step 1:
   $70,000 × 80% = $56,000
   $56,000 +/– PV
   17 N
   3 I/YR
   Solve FV
   $92,559

   Step 2:
   BEG mode
   $92,559 PMT
   25 N
   [(1.08 ÷ 1.03) – 1 × 100] = 4.8544 I/YR
   0 FV
   Solve PV
   $1,388,038

   Solution using the uneven cash flows method:
   $92,559 CFj
   $92,559 CFj
   24 shift Nj
   [(1.08 ÷ 1.03) – 1 × 100] = 4.8544 I/YR
   Shift NPV
   $1,388,038

7. **A.** You discuss and evaluate the effects this possible new employment will have on the recommendations already implemented and redefines the scope of the engagement, if appropriate. The monitoring phase of the financial planning process is when changes in a client's circumstances are evaluated and the plan is changed to accommodate the new circumstances. A new letter redefining the scope of the engagement may be needed. (Domain 7)

8. **B.** Normally, with a vested account balance of $43,000, Michael would be eligible to make a loan from his Section 401(k) account in the amount of 50% of his vested account balance ($21,500). However, the $7,000 outstanding loan must be deducted from this maximum loan amount, leaving $14,500 as the maximum loan currently available.

9. **B.** If permitted by the plan, Michael could defer $15,900. The elective deferral limit in a Section 403(b) plan is $18,000 (2015), but Michael already defers $2,100 into his Section 401(k) plan at Asher Bank and Trust. The combined elective deferral limit between plans is $18,000, so the most Michael could defer into the Section 403(b) plan is $15,900 ($18,000 – $2,100).

10. **A.** The total lump-sum death benefit payable by Social Security is $255. The amount is fixed and is not based on the number of family members eligible for survivor benefits.

Appendix 1— Retirement Plan Characteristics and Features

Having discussed some of the more typical objectives of businessowners in considering the establishment of a retirement plan, we now turn to the key characteristics and features of the various retirement plans previously discussed. The following table contains a summary of those key characteristics and features.

			Defined contribution plans							Defined Benefit Plans	
	Simplified employee pension (SEP) (tax-advantaged plan)	SIMPLE IRA (tax-advantaged plan)	Section 401(k) plan (regular)	Profit sharing plan	Money purchase pension plan	Target benefit plan	Savings/ match or thrift plan	Stock bonus plan	Employee stock ownership plan (ESOP)	Traditional defined benefit plan	Cash balance pension plan
Key advantage	Easy to set up and maintain	Salary reduction plan with little administrative paperwork	Permits higher level of salary deferrals by employees than other retirement vehicles	Permits employer to make large contributions for employees	Permits employer to make large contributions for employees	Plan formula does not allow employer discretion in contributions. Hybrid of DB and money purchase plan	Generally only a supplement to a 401(k) plan.	Benefit paid in employer stock rather than cash	Stock bonus plan which employer can use for borrowing from bank or other financial institution	Provides a fixed, pre-established benefit for employees	Provides a stated account balance at retirement in hypothetical individual accounts.
Employer eligibility	Any employer with one or more employees	Any employer with 100 or fewer employees that does not currently maintain another plan	Any employer with one or more employees	Any employer with one or more employees	Any employer with one or more employees	Any employer with one or more employees	Any employer with one or more employees	Any corporation but only C corporations are eligible for all related tax benefits	Any corporation but only C corporations are eligible for all related tax benefits	Any employer with one or more employees	Any employer with one or more employees
Employer's role	Set up plan by completing IRS Form 5305-SEP. No annual filing requirement for employer.	Set up plan by completing IRS Form 5304-SIMPLE or 5305-SIMPLE. No annual filing requirement for employer. Bank or financial institution processes most of the paperwork.	No model form to establish. May need professional advice. Annual filing of Form 5500 required. Also may require annual nondiscrimination testing to ensure plan does not discriminate in favor of HCEs.	No model form to establish. May need professional advice. Annual filing of Form 5500 required.	No model form to establish. May need professional advice. Annual filing of Form 5500 required.	No model form to establish. May need professional advice. Annual filing of Form 5500 required.	No model form to establish. May need professional advice. Annual filing of Form 5500 required.	No model form to establish. May need professional advice. Annual filing of Form 5500 required.	No model form to establish. May need professional advice. Annual filing of Form 5500 required.	No model form to establish. Professional advice necessary. Annual filing of Form 5500 required. Actuary must determine annual contributions.	No model form to establish. Professional advice necessary. Annual filing of Form 5500 required. Actuary must determine annual contributions.
Contributors to the plan	Employer contributions only	Employee salary reduction contributions and employer contributions.	Employee salary reduction contributions and/or employer contributions.	Annual employer contribution is discretionary	Employer contributions are fixed.	Employer contributions that are not discretionary	After-tax employee contributions and employer matching	Primarily employer but employees may contribute also	Primarily employer but employees may contribute also	Primarily funded by employer.	Usually only the employer.

Employer-Sponsored Retirement Plan Characteristics and Features

Retirement Plan Characteristics and Features (continued)

	Simplified employee pension (SEP) (tax-advantaged plan)	SIMPLE IRA (tax-advantaged plan)	Defined Contribution Plans							Defined Benefit Plans	
			Section 401(k) plan (regular)	Profit sharing plan	Money purchase pension plan	Target benefit plan	Savings/match or thrift plan	Stock bonus plan	Employee stock ownership plan (ESOP)	Traditional defined benefit plan	Cash balance pension plan
Maximum annual contribution (per participant)	Up to 25% of compensation or a maximum of $53,000 in 2015	Employee: Up to $12,500 in 2015 plus catch-up contributions Employer: Either match employee contributions 100% of first 3% of compensation (can reduce to as low as 1% in any 2 of 5 years); or contribute 2% of each eligible employee's compensation	Employee: $18,000 in 2015; plus catch-up contributions Employer/Employee combined: Up to lesser of 100% of compensation or $53,000 in 2015; employer can deduct amounts that do not exceed 25% of aggregate compensation for all participants.	Contributions per participant up to lesser of 100% of compensation or $53,000 in 2015; employer can deduct amounts that do not exceed 25% of aggregate compensation for all participants	Contributions per participant up to lesser of 100% of compensation or $53,000 in 2015; employer can deduct amounts that do not exceed 25% of aggregate compensation for all participants	Contributions per participant up to lesser of 100% of compensation or $53,000 in 2015; employer can deduct amounts that do not exceed 25% of aggregate compensation for all participants	Employee contributions not deductible. Employer contributions deductible as long as plan remains qualified.	Contributions per participant up to lesser of 100% of compensation or $53,000 in 2015; employer can deduct amounts that do not exceed 25% of aggregate compensation for all participants	Same as stock bonus plan except C corporation ESOP can deduct amounts that do not exceed 25% of aggregate compensation for amounts used to repay loan principal, with no limit on amounts used to pay interest	Actuarially determined contribution; annual benefit capped at $210,000 (2015)	Actuarially determined contribution; pay credit (% of compensation) plus an interest credit based on employer-guaranteed return on investment; annual benefit capped at $210,000 (2015)
Contributor's options	Employer can decide whether to make contributions year-to-year	Employee can decide how much to contribute. Employer must make matching contributions or contribute 2% of each employee's compensation	Employee can elect how much to contribute pursuant to salary reduction agreement. Employer can make additional contributions including possible matching contributions as set by plan terms.	Employer makes contributions as set by plan terms. Employee contributions (if allowed) as set by plan terms.	Employer makes contributions as set by plan terms. Employee contributions (if allowed) as set by plan terms.	Employer makes contributions based on actuarially-determined formula in 1st year and then held constant. Must make annual contributions in amount per plan formula.	After-tax employee contributions must meet ACP test. Employer contributions can meet ACP or one of 2 additional tests.	Employer makes contributions as set by plan terms. Employee contributions (if allowed) as set by plan terms.	Employer makes contributions as set by plan terms. Employee contributions (if allowed) as set by plan terms.	Employer required to make contributions as set by plan terms.	Employer required to make contributions as actuarially-determined.
Minimum employee coverage requirements payroll deduction traditional IRA (tax-advantaged plan)	Must be offered to all employees at least 21 years old, employed by employer for 3 of last 5 years, and had earned income of $600 (2015)	Must be offered to all employees who have earned income of at least $5,000 in any prior 2 years and are reasonably expected to earn at least $5,000 in current year	Generally must be offered to all employees at least 21 years old who worked at least 1,000 hours in a previous year	Generally must be offered to all employees at least 21 years old who worked at least 1,000 hours in a previous year	Generally must be offered to all employees at least 21 years old who worked at least 1,000 hours in a previous year	Generally must be offered to all employees at least 21 years old who worked at least 1,000 hours in a previous year	Generally must be offered to all employees at least 21 years old who worked at least 1,000 hours in a previous year	Generally must be offered to all employees at least 21 years old who worked at least 1,000 hours in a previous year	Generally must be offered to all employees at least 21 years old who worked at least 1,000 hours in a previous year	Generally must be offered to all employees at least 21 years old who worked at least 1,000 hours in a previous year	Generally must be offered to all employees at least 21 years old who worked at least 1,000 hours in a previous year

Retirement Plan Characteristics and Features (continued)

	Simplified employee pension (SEP) (tax-advantaged plan)	SIMPLE IRA (tax-advantaged plan)	Defined Contribution Plans							Defined Benefit Plans	
			Section 401(k) plan (regular)	Profit sharing plan	Money purchase pension plan	Target benefit plan	Savings/match or thrift plan	Stock bonus plan	Employee stock ownership plan (ESOP)	Traditional defined benefit plan	Cash balance pension plan
Withdrawals, loans, and payments	Withdrawals permitted anytime subject to Federal income taxes; early withdrawals subject to tax penalty	Withdrawals permitted anytime subject to Federal income taxes; early withdrawals subject to tax penalty	Withdrawals permitted after a specified event occurs (e.g., retirement, plan termination, etc.). Plan may permit loans and hardship withdrawals; early withdrawals subject to penalty tax.	Withdrawals permitted after a specified event occurs (e.g., retirement, plan termination, etc.). Plan may permit loans and hardship withdrawals; early withdrawals subject to penalty tax.	Payment of benefits after a specified event occurs (e.g., retirement, plan termination, etc.). Plan may permit loans; early withdrawals subject to tax penalty.	Target benefit not guaranteed. Depends on investment return. Distributions subject to normal rules for qualified plan distributions.	Generally offer liberal employee withdrawal & plan loan provisions. Distributions must comply with qualified plan distribution rules.	Distributions subject to same rules applicable to all qualified plans; employee has "put option" if receives stock not traded on established market (employer must repurchase under fair valuation formula and by independent appraiser). Net unrealized appreciation is deferred until sale of stock.	Same as stock bonus plan plus employees age 55 or over and participants for at least 10 years, have annual election to diversify investments in their accounts (25% of balance for first six years and 50% in last year). Net unrealized appreciation is deferred until sale of stock.	Payment of benefits after a specified event occurs (e.g., retirement, plan termination, etc.). Plan may permit loans; early withdrawals subject to tax penalty.	Payment of benefits after a specified event occurs (e.g., retirement, plan termination, etc.). Plan may permit loans but usually does not due to additional administrative burden; early withdrawals subject to tax penalty.
Vesting	Contributions are immediately 100% vested	Employer and employee contributions are immediately vested 100%	Employee salary deferrals are immediately 100% vested. Employer contributions may vest over time according to plan terms.	Employer contributions may vest over time according to plan terms. Employee contributions if any are immediately 100% vested.	Employer contributions may vest over time according to plan terms. Employee contributions if any are immediately 100% vested.	Employer contributions may vest over time according to plan terms. Employee contributions if any are immediately 100% vested.	Employer matching contributions must vest in same accelerated manner as applicable to top-heavy plans	Employer contributions may vest over time according to plan terms. Employee contributions if any are immediately 100% vested.	Employer contributions may vest over time according to plan terms. Employee contributions if any are immediately 100% vested.	Right to benefits may vest over time according to plan terms.	Right to benefits may vest over time according to plan terms.
Maximum 2015 salary deferral		$12,500	$18,000								
Maximum 2015 catch-up		$3,000	$6,000								
Subject to compensation limit of $265,000 in 2015[1]		No	Yes	Yes	Yes	Yes	Yes	Yes	Yes	Yes	

[1]Maximum compensation on which 2015 contribution can be based is $265,000.

Appendix 2—The Retirement Planning Process

Retirement planning clients range from those who are many years away from retirement to those who are either just at the point of retirement or already retired. In addition, their circumstances may vary significantly. For instance, a businessowner may be able to build his retirement funding through his business while a key executive may be in a position to negotiate meaningful retirement benefits. Other employees may not be able to influence the benefits provided by their employers. Further, certain clients may have considerable personal assets outside of their employer, while others will have very little other than company-provided retirement benefits and Social Security.

Moreover, retirement planning may not only involve the skills of a competent financial planner but also may require the services of an attorney specializing in estate planning as well as an employee benefits expert and/or investment manager. However, it is usually the financial planner who will provide the major portion of the retirement planning services. To do this effectively, the financial planner follows a prescribed retirement planning process involving six steps. The **six-step financial planning process** is based on the eight job task domains:

1. Establishing and defining the client-planner relationship (Step 1)

2. Gathering information necessary to fulfill the engagement (Step 2)

3. Analyzing and evaluating the client's financial status (Step 3)

4. Developing the recommendations (Step 4)

5. Communicating the recommendations (Step 4)

6. Implementing the recommendations (Step 5)

7. Monitoring the recommendations (Step 6)

8. Practicing within the professional and regulatory standards (Throughout steps 1-6)

In the following sections, we will discuss these six general steps of the retirement planning process. It should be noted that while the steps reviewed here are in the retirement planning context, they are the same for all parts of financial planning.

Step 1: Establishing and Defining the Client-Planner Relationship

In this first stage of the retirement planning process, the client and the planner identify the specific services to be provided by the planner. This involves educating the client as to her needs and the appropriateness of specific services to address those needs. This also requires that the client place a high degree of trust in the planner.

In the initial step, the planner and the client mutually define the scope of the engagement. The **scope of the engagement** is the universe of services that the planner and the client agree is necessary and appropriate and that the financial planner is qualified and willing to provide. The scope may include the entire array of retirement planning services or may be limited to specific activities. The process of mutual definition of the scope of the engagement is designed to provide realistic expectations for both parties. While there is no requirement that the scope of the engagement be in writing, it is normally a prudent practice for legal and ethics disclosure purposes. If an engagement letter is not executed by the parties, the financial planner should prepare file memoranda that document any oral understandings about the engagement objectives; the scope of the services provided; the roles and responsibilities of the financial planner, the client, and other advisors; compensation arrangements; and scope limitations and other constraints. Also, it is important for both the client and the financial planner to realize that the scope of the engagement may, after initial mutual definition, be revised by mutual agreement.

In mutually defining the scope of the engagement, the client and the financial planner may agree to so-called segmented (or modular) retirement planning rather than comprehensive retirement planning. In segmented retirement planning, the scope of the engagement is limited to a specific subject area or areas. For instance, a client who does not currently have nor is projected to accumulate significant assets may not need the services of a separate estate planning attorney. On the other hand, a reasonably wealthy client who has never used the services of a financial planner may require comprehensive retirement planning in which all of the major aspects of retirement planning are evaluated.

Step 2: Gathering Client Data Necessary to Fulfill the Engagement

Having established and defined the client-planner relationship in Step 1 and having determined the scope of the engagement includes retirement planning services, the second step of the retirement planning process is to determine a client's personal and financial goals, needs, and priorities and to gather appropriate quantitative information and documents relevant to the client's personal financial situation. In gathering client data, it is important to draw a distinction between **qualitative** and **quantitative** information obtained from or about the client. Examples of *qualitative* data include the client's personal and financial goals, needs, priorities, time horizon, and risk tolerance. Such data are considered qualitative in that they are subjective and, therefore, require a judgment on the part of the client rather than constituting objective, factual data.

Examples of *quantitative* information include copies of wills, trust documents, recent income tax returns, employer's current statement of employee benefits, investment account statements, copies of insurance policies currently in force, statements of projected social insurance benefits, ages and current health of client family members, fair market value of assets owned, personal financial statements (including a statement of personal financial position and a personal cash flow statement), credit history, and so forth. All of these items constitute objective, factual data that can be expressed in quantitative terms. Depending upon the type of client engagement and its scope, the financial planner will need to make a determination as to what quantitative information is both sufficient and relevant to the particular engagement. This information may be obtained either directly from the client or through other sources by interviews, questionnaires, data-gathering forms, client records, or other documents. Data-gathering forms may also be useful in garnering such qualitative information as the client's anticipated retirement date, where the client intends to reside during retirement, whether the client will work part time during retirement, and whether the client anticipates significant changes in lifestyle during retirement.

Benefit Plan Information

In order to provide competent retirement planning, a planner needs to obtain complete information about all employee benefit plans in which the client and the client's spouse are currently participating or have ever participated. This includes not only qualified or non-qualified retirement plans but also other benefit plans such as health insurance, life insurance, or the use of employer athletic or health clubs during retirement. The planner should rely solely on the plan documents rather than the client's understanding of the benefits provided by the plans involved. In that regard, plans subject to the provisions of the Employee Retirement Income Security Act of 1974 (ERISA) are required to provide each participant with a Summary Plan Description (SPD). This document contains much useful information about such topics as early retirement, normal retirement age, deferred retirement, payout options available at retirement, terms that may trigger a loss of benefits, and the procedures for filing claims against the plan.

As for qualified plans, the employer must provide an individual benefit statement at least annually. These statements must, at a minimum, show the employee/client his accrued benefit and vesting status, but other information, such as an estimate of the employee's Social Security benefit and death benefits payable to spouses or other beneficiaries, may also be included. For non-ERISA plans, documentation of the plan may be difficult or impossible to obtain. In these cases, the planner should refer to the employer's benefits manual or other similar information.

Finally, the planner needs to estimate the benefits the client will receive from government benefits such as Social Security, veterans' benefits, and the like.

Personal Financial Statements

In constructing or reviewing a statement of financial position (or personal balance sheet), the planner must ascertain that the included assets are stated at fair market value rather than at historical book value. This is especially true in the case of closely held businesses. Equally as important as determining a current value is the problem of determining whether the small business interest will continue as an income source during retirement.

It is essential that the planner not overlook the client's liabilities. The client's traditional debt obligations are usually easily determinable. However, some obligations may not appear on the statement of personal financial position, such as future alimony, child support or outstanding property settlement payments, state or federal tax liabilities, or legal judgments. Clients may also be reluctant, or even embarrassed, to offer information about some of these obligations.

The planner will then need to identify those client assets potentially available to generate retirement income. Generally, it is useful to categorize these assets as investment assets, investment real estate assets, tax-deferred savings, and before-tax savings. As a general rule, investment assets, including such items as securities, money market accounts, limited partnership interests, and mutual funds, are originally funded with after-tax dollars and are, therefore, presumed to be liquidated for retirement needs. Income earned on these assets is assumed to be taxable each year, and such assets are assumed to be liquidated without the payment of income taxes, except to the extent that they have appreciated in value since acquisition.

Real estate assets that will be sold at retirement should be included in the available retirement resources at their estimated sale price less the income taxes and other expenses payable upon sale and any mortgage indebtedness at that time. Mortgage indebtedness amounts at retirement can be calculated on a financial function calculator.

The original invested amounts in tax-deferred savings vehicles funded with after-tax dollars will be recovered tax free upon distribution, but the earnings on the invested funds will be subject to income taxation. Examples of this type of asset are nondeductible IRAs, thrift plans, single or flexible premium annuities, and life insurance cash values.

Savings funded through income tax deductions (e.g., deductible IRAs) and/or by employer contributions to a retirement plan (e.g., Section 401(k) plans and Section 403(b) plans) are usually fully taxable upon distribution.

The amount of income needed in retirement is often determined by applying a ratio or percentage to the client's preretirement income. Typically, these income replacement percentages have ranged from 70–80%. However, it can vary widely from one individual to another. While a planner may use typical income replacement ratios to weigh the reasonableness of a client's retirement income goal, a client's retirement income goal should not be determined based solely on such ratios. Rather, the planner needs to thoroughly analyze the client's personal cash flow statement to assess both current and expected retirement expenses. The accuracy of the retirement savings need calculation (discussed in Step 3) depends on the accuracy of the estimated retirement expenditures that reflect the client's retirement goals and bear a reasonable relationship to preretirement expenditures. In determining the reasonableness of the estimated retirement expenditures, the planner should determine that the level of housing, health care, insurance, entertainment and travel, and pension expenses have been adjusted from the preretirement levels to reflect what is anticipated during retirement.

Retirement Planning Assumptions

Another part of the data-gathering step is the determination, by both the planner and the client, of the retirement planning assumptions. Key among these assumptions is the anticipated investment return on those assets earmarked for retirement. Most planners tend to use a flat average annual rate of return, which has the disadvantage of not taking into consideration the volatility of the return. Volatility can have a major impact on the actual average rate of return. For instance, if a planner were to use a 10% average annual return on a client's portfolio, each $1,000 would grow to about $1,611 in five years. If instead, the portfolio was to earn 20% in each of the first three years, 5% in the fourth, but then was to lose 15% in the fifth year, the average return is still 10%, but each $1,000 has then only grown to about $1,542. One can construct other scenarios in which the average return over five years is 10% but yet the amount accumulated does not equal the amount that accumulates using a 10% year-over-year return.

Without much question, one of the greatest threats to a retiree's economic independence during retirement is inflation. Inflation gradually erodes a retiree's purchasing power over the retirement period. For instance, if we assume the total of a retiree's pension income and Social Security benefit are exactly equal to the retiree's required retirement income in the first year of retirement, that inflation averages 4% per year, and that the retiree's pension income is not indexed for inflation (as is Social Security), after 10 years, the retiree's retirement income will cover only about 75% of the retiree's retirement income requirement. After 25 years of retirement, her income will cover only 50% of her needs.

Projecting future inflation rates is problematical; however, some general guidelines may be useful. For instance, from December 1950 to December 1992, the average compound increase in prices was 4.2%. Subsequent to 1992, inflation has averaged less than 3%. As a result, some planners may want to use 3–4% annual increase for the long term, but other more cautious and conservative planners may choose a higher rate. Of course, another issue is that the consumer price index (CPI) is made up of a market basket of about 12 categories of goods and services purchased by the average consumer. Unfortunately, a specific client is not "average." His personal rate of inflation may vary significantly from the CPI due to regional variations from the national rate, the heavy weighting of housing prices in the CPI, and personal buying habits. Moreover, retirees generally purchase more services than goods, and services have escalated in price more quickly than have goods. Underestimating the actual inflation rate will cause a significant shortfall in retirement income.

In addition to the anticipated investment return and the rate of inflation, the planner and the client need to make a reasonable assumption about the client's age at retirement and life expectancy. While historically an individual's retirement age tended to be linked with the start of Social Security benefits (age 65, until recently), in recent years, a large percentage of individuals have instead retired early. In fact, today the average retirement age of American workers is age 62. Factors that have contributed to this earlier retirement age are health issues, job elimination, or corporate downsizing under early retirement incentive programs.

With regard to how long an individual can expect to live, even mortality table data are at best only rough estimates in light of the fact that slightly more than one-half of people of a given age will live *beyond* the life expectancy for their age. For instance, consider a couple in which the male is age 65 and the female is age 62 having individual life expectancies of about 15 and 21 years, respectively. However, from a mathematical (or statistical) standpoint, these individuals have more than a 50% chance of living beyond their respective life expectancies. This is because the median age of death is the age when a person has exactly a 50/50 chance of surviving for that person's mortality-table life expectancy. For the 65- and 62-year-old couple, the median number of years until death is 15.7 and 22 years, respectively. This illustrates the inadvisability of using median ages of death. By reference to the same mortality table from which the foregoing life expectancies are derived, one can ascertain that the 65-year-old male has a 25% probability of surviving nearly 22 years to age 86.9 and a 10% chance of surviving almost 27 years to age 91.8. In comparison, the 62-year-old female has a 25% chance of surviving almost 28 years to age 90.9 and a 10% chance of surviving about 34 years to age 96.2. Consequently, the client needs to decide how much risk she is willing to incur that she will outlive her retirement income.

In the case of married couples, using the life expectancy of the spouse whose life expectancy is longer will result in underestimating the length of the couple's retirement income needs. Strangely enough, the average number of years until the second death of two persons is *longer* than the individual life expectancy of either person alone.[1] In fact, according to *National Vital Statistics Reports*, Vol. 51, No. 3, December 19, 2002, the average number of years until the second death of a husband and wife both age 65 is about 23.3 years, whereas the husband and wife have individual life expectancies of 16.3 years and 19.2 years, respectively. This is more than four years longer than the life expectancy of the wife, individually. Accordingly, planners should generally use *joint* (second-to-die) life expectancies (defined as the average number of years until both spouses will have died) rather than *joint-and-survivor* life expectancies in determining the average number of years of retirement income required for a married couple. In the case of the couple discussed earlier in which the male is 65 and the female is 62, use of joint-and-survivor life expectancies will result in half of such couples exhausting their retirement fund about one year early, one-fourth depleting their funds about six years prematurely, and one-tenth running out of money almost 11 years too soon. This also illustrates the necessity to use conservative estimates of life expectancy. Indeed, some people will likely be retired for more years than the number of years they actually worked.

A final key assumption is the client's anticipated effective income tax rate during retirement. This rate should be a blend of the client's federal and state income tax rates and should be based on only current income tax rates (because no one can hope to accurately predict future rates).

The data gathering step of the retirement planning process is the one in which the client and the planner mutually identify retirement income needs as well as the resources or assets that are currently allocated and presumably available for meeting these needs.

---

1   *Tools & Techniques of Financial Planning*, by Leimberg, Satinsky, Doyle, and Jackson, 7th edition, The National Underwriter Company, 2004, Chapter 29, page 397.

Step 3: Analyzing and Evaluating the Client's Current Financial Status

Having gathered the client's qualitative and quantitative retirement data, the planner is now ready to move to the stage in which he analyzes and evaluates the client's financial status and degree of preparedness for retirement. This involves the calculation of the client's retirement savings need. This calculation involves the following six steps.

1. Develop an estimate of the value, at the time of retirement, of those assets designated as being available for retirement.

2. Develop an estimate of the after-tax value of the assets in Step 1 by subtracting the estimated income taxes payable upon the anticipated sale or taxable distribution of such assets.

3. Determine if there is a first-year anticipated deficit or surplus of retirement income, based only on inflation-adjusted income sources.

4. Determine the amount of the retirement fund necessary to generate annual income growing annually with inflation that is adequate to offset any first-year retirement income deficit as determined in Step 3.

5. Calculate the additional amount of savings needed to create the retirement fund determined in Step 4.

6. Calculate the additional annual savings required to accumulate the necessary retirement fund.

Step 1: Develop an estimate of the value, at the time of retirement, of those assets designated as being available for retirement.

In this first step of the retirement savings need determination, the present value of the assets categorized in the data gathering stage (Step 2) of the retirement planning process as investment assets, real estate assets, tax-deferred savings, and before-tax savings is converted to a future value. In order to make this conversion, we need to know the current market value of each of these assets, their assumed growth rates, and the number of years until retirement. Again, this information was obtained in Stage 2 of the retirement planning process. This step involves performing a future value calculation on a financial function calculator where the current market value is PV, the growth or appreciation rate is I/YR, and the number of years until retirement is N. For example, an asset having a current market value of $100,000 that is anticipated to grow in value at a compound rate of 5% per year for the next 10 years until retirement will have a future value at retirement of $162,889, calculated using the following keystrokes on the HP 10BII calculator:

$$100,000 +/- \text{ PV; } 5 \text{ I/YR; } 10 \text{ N; FV} = 162,889$$

It is important to remember that the calculations to this point compute the future value of current asset balances only. It is assumed, for this purpose, that no further deposits/additions are made to these assets.

In those cases where the client has an *ongoing* savings/investment program, the value of such savings/investments at the time of retirement must be calculated and added to the future value of the assets that have already accumulated and been calculated previously. In order to determine the future value of the client's future annual savings on a financial function calculator, the assumed annual level savings amount is treated as PMT, the assumed earnings rate on such annual savings amounts is treated as I/YR, and the number of years until retirement is treated as N. For example, $5,000 of level annual savings invested at 6% per year for 12 years will have a future value at retirement of $84,350, calculated using the following keystrokes on the HP 10BII calculator:

$$5,000 +/- \text{PMT}; 6 \text{ I/YR}; 12 \text{ N}; \text{FV} = 84,350$$

This amount would then be added to the amount determined as the future value of the already existing assets, calculated earlier.

Step 2: Develop an estimate of the after-tax value of the assets in Step 1 by subtracting the estimated income taxes payable upon the anticipated sale or taxable distribution of such assets.

Because of the impact of income taxation, the amounts calculated in Step 1 will most likely *not* be available in full at retirement. When these assets are distributed or sold at retirement, income tax will probably be due at that time. These anticipated income taxes must be subtracted from the future value of the assets calculated in Step 1 to arrive at the net amount of available resources (after taxes). Not all assets will necessarily be liquidated at retirement, especially those that are providing an acceptable return. However, for purposes of the retirement savings need calculation, it is assumed that all investment assets will indeed be liquidated at retirement. This assumption is made so that a later comparison may be made between total available retirement assets and total required retirement assets.

To determine the income taxes payable upon liquidation of each of the major categories of retirement assets, the following procedures should be employed.

- **Investment Assets**—Those investment assets that have earned only interest or dividends (have experienced no capital growth) will not be taxed at distribution; however, common stock and mutual funds will be taxed at capital gains rates to the extent they have increased in value since acquisition (anticipated future value less tax basis). The estimated capital gains taxes payable at retirement are then subtracted from the future before-tax value to arrive at the net proceeds at the date of retirement.

- **Real Estate Assets**—To determine the taxable portion of such assets sold at retirement, calculate the difference between the projected sales price and the property's income tax basis and subtract any projected selling expenses. Then apply the capital gains tax rate to determine the projected tax due. Subtract this from the projected before-tax future value to arrive at the net proceeds at date of retirement. If the asset involved is the retiree's personal residence, special tax rules apply, and up to $500,000 (for a married couple filing jointly) of the taxable gain may be excluded from taxation, presuming the taxpayer meets the qualifying requirements. Where property is mortgaged, be sure to reduce the after-tax proceeds by any projected mortgage balance at retirement.

- **Tax-Deferred Savings**—Only the earnings that have accumulated tax deferred are taxable at distribution. Subtract the cost basis (the total after-tax dollars invested) from the projected future value at retirement to determine the taxable gain, and then apply the applicable regular income tax rate to this amount to arrive at the income tax due at retirement. Then subtract the estimated income taxes due from the projected future value to arrive at the net proceeds at date of retirement.

- **Before-Tax Savings**—Inasmuch as these assets were funded with before-tax dollars and have accumulated earnings on a tax-deferred basis, they will be fully taxable upon distribution. On the other hand, a lump-sum distribution from a qualified retirement plan may be rolled over into an IRA and withdrawn over the owner's lifetime, thus deferring taxation. However, as discussed earlier, the assumption here is that this distribution is still taxable at retirement. Step 2 includes only lump-sum distributions from retirement plans—not annual benefits. Annual benefits are included in income under Steps 3 and 5.

■ **Future Savings/Investments**—To convert these amounts to an after-tax basis, use the procedures just described for the appropriate category of investment discussed in the previous bullets.

All of the assets that have been converted to an after-tax basis should now be totaled to arrive at the net future value of assets available to the client at her date of retirement.

Step 3: Determine if there is a first-year anticipated deficit or surplus of retirement income, based only on inflation-adjusted income sources.

In this step, only projected annual income (such as retirement plan benefits) that is adjusted annually during retirement for inflation is considered. Generally, retirement plan benefits are *not* adjusted annually for increases in the cost of living, so such benefits will not be considered in this step. Level annual retirement plan benefits will be considered in Step 5.

To arrive at the retirement income shortfall, subtract any annual inflation-adjusted retirement income sources from the projected retirement income need as determined in Stage 2 of the retirement planning process. The amount remaining is the annual retirement income deficit that must be met either by income from the client's retirement funds or level (as opposed to inflation-adjusted) sources of retirement income (or both). In rare circumstances, a client will have a surplus (rather than a deficit) of annual retirement income over his retirement income needs. This means the client does not need to use retirement assets to generate retirement income. Again, this is a situation that few planners will actually encounter.

Step 4: Determine the amount of the retirement fund necessary to generate annual income, growing annually with inflation, adequate to offset any first-year retirement income deficit as determined in Step 3.

In Step 4, the planner computes the lump-sum amount necessary to fund the projected annual income deficits over the entire retirement period. But before doing so, the planner must first adjust the projected first-year retirement income deficit, which at this point is expressed in today's dollars, to future dollars at the time of retirement. To make this calculation, let PV equal the present value of the retirement income deficit (in today's dollars), let N equal the number of years until retirement, and let I/YR equal the assumed inflation rate. For example, if PV is \$20,000 per year, N is 10 years, and I/YR is 4%, the calculation on the HP 10BII calculator is as follows:

$$20,000 +/- PV; 10 N; 4 I/YR; FV = 29,605$$

Having adjusted the projected first-year retirement income deficit to its value at the time of retirement, the planner is now ready to calculate the amount of the retirement fund needed to meet this projected income deficit. One complicating factor, however, is that this projected first-year retirement income deficit needs to increase annually with inflation. Consequently, the next calculation called for is known as the present value of an annuity due (PVAD). One of the key assumptions behind this calculation is that the amount of the fund calculated will be totally depleted at the end of the projected retirement period through the use of both principal and income to fund the annually inflated income deficit. This is known as the **capital utilization** approach, as contrasted with the **capital preservation** approach where only income is used and principal is not consumed. We will discuss these alternative approaches in greater depth later in this unit.

In order to perform the PVAD calculation, the planner first needs to determine the **inflation-adjusted yield**. While the planner is concerned with both the anticipated annual after-tax return on investments (i) and the expected annual inflation rate (r), unfortunately, the calculator will accommodate only one I/YR. Therefore, these two rates must be incorporated into a single inflation-adjusted rate. Intuitively, one would simply subtract the inflation rate from the investment return rate and use the difference as the inflation-adjusted rate. However, from a theoretical standpoint, the inflation-adjusted rate must be calculated with use of the following formula:

$$\text{I/YR (inflation-adjusted rate)} = [(1 + i) \div (1 + r) - 1] \times 100$$

For example, if the anticipated annual after-tax return on investments is 7% and the expected annual inflation rate is 3%, the inflation-adjusted rate is 3.88%, calculated as follows:

$$[(1 + .07) \div (1 + .03) - 1] \times 100 = [1.07 \div 1.03 - 1] \times 100 = [1.0388 - 1] \times 100$$
$$= .0388 \times 100$$
$$= 3.88$$

Having calculated the inflation-adjusted rate of return, the planner is now ready to perform the PVAD calculation to determine the retirement fund needed to meet the projected annual income deficit. Before doing so, however, the planner needs to recognize that a retiree will need to have access to her annual retirement income at the *beginning*, as opposed to the *end*, of each year during retirement. This is what makes the annual retirement income stream an annuity due rather than an ordinary annuity (where payments are made/received at the end of each year).

To perform this calculation, the planner needs to know the first-year retirement income deficit that will increase each year due to inflation (*PMT*), the inflation-adjusted rate of return as described earlier (*I/YR*), and the number of years of retirement (*N*). For example, if the first-year annual retirement deficit is $15,000, the inflation-adjusted rate of return is 3.88 (as calculated previously), and the number of years in actual retirement is 25, the retirement fund necessary to meet the inflation-adjusted retirement income deficit is $246,540, calculated as follows on the HP 10BII calculator:

BEGIN mode; 15,000 +/– PMT; 3.88 I/YR; 25 N; PV = 246,540

Step 5: Calculate the additional amount of savings needed to create the retirement fund determined in Step 4.

Prior to completing this step, the planner needs to have a discussion with the client as to his feelings about his retirement funds. Is the client comfortable using both the principal and the income from those funds to meet retirement income need or, alternatively, does the client wish to use only the income from those funds to provide his retirement income need, leaving the principal intact for possible transfer to his heirs or as a hedge against living beyond his life expectancy?

As discussed previously, these two approaches are known as **capital utilization** and **capital preservation**. The results of the calculations in Step 5 will vary significantly depending on which of these two approaches is used. As one would surmise, the capital utilization approach (in which capital is fully depleted) requires a much *smaller* retirement fund than that required under the capital preservation (use of fund earnings only) approach. On the other hand, as the retirement period increases, the gap between the amount required in the retirement fund under these two approaches narrows.

Of course, everyone would like to be able to accumulate enough retirement assets to live on the interest alone and never have to liquidate the principal amount. For all but the very rich, this is not a realistic option. Most retirees will have to deplete their retirement funds to varying degrees.

Calculations Using the Capital Utilization Approach   To perform this calculation effectively, the planner begins with the amount of the retirement fund necessary to offset the projected retirement income deficit, as determined in Step 4. From this amount, the planner subtracts the total assets identified as available for retirement, which includes currently owned assets and the projected value of the client's existing savings program at the time of retirement, as determined in Step 2. Also subtracted is the present value of level (non-inflation-adjusted) retirement benefits referred to in Step 3. In order to calculate the present value of level retirement benefits, the benefits must first be adjusted for inflation between today and the assumed retirement date (unless already expressed in retirement period dollars). Then, to calculate the present value of these level retirement benefits, we use *PMT* to represent the level annual retirement benefit amount expressed in retirement period dollars; *N* to represent the number of years of retirement; and *I/YR* to represent the investment return rate. For example, if *PMT* is $15,000 per year, *N* is 25 years, and *I/YR* is 7%, we solve for *PV* by using the following HP 10BII keystrokes:

BEGIN mode; 15,000 +/– PMT; 25 N; 7 I/YR; PV = 187,040

After reducing the retirement fund necessary to offset the projected retirement income deficit by both the total assets identified as being available for retirement and the present value of the anticipated level retirement benefits, the amount remaining is the additional savings need at retirement under the capital utilization approach.

One final adjustment is then to remove the effect of inflation from the additional savings need at retirement (we will perform this calculation in Step 6). This is accomplished by using *FV* as the additional savings need at retirement, *N* as the number of years until retirement, and *I/YR* as the inflation rate. For example, if we assume that *FV* is $100,000, *N* is 10 years, and *I/YR* is 7% per year, *PV* (the present value of the additional savings need at retirement) is $50,835 calculated on the HP 10BII as follows:

100,000 FV; 10 N; 7 I/YR; PV = 50,835

Calculations Using the Capital Preservation Approach   Again, in this calculation, the planner begins with the amount of the retirement fund necessary to offset the projected retirement income deficit, as determined in Step 4. However, the retirement resources available under the capital preservation approach are calculated a bit differently than under capital utilization. Accordingly, we again start with the total assets identified as available for retirement, which includes currently owned assets and the projected value of the client's existing savings program at the time of retirement, as determined in Step 2. However, from this amount, we then subtract the assets required to be preserved to determine the asset resources that are available. To this amount, we add two additional items: (1) the present value of the level annual income stream from the assets preserved, which is calculated by first multiplying the assets preserved by the investment return percentage to arrive at the level annual income stream and then calculating its present value over the retirement period using the after-tax investment return and (2) the present value of any level retirement benefits to be paid, as calculated under the capital utilization approach. The sum of these three items equals the total resources available.

Next, we subtract from the retirement fund, necessary to offset the projected retirement income deficit, the total resources available as calculated in the previous paragraph. The remainder is the additional savings need at retirement. Finally, as we did under the capital utilization approach, we must remove the effect of inflation from the additional savings need at retirement (again, we will perform this calculation in the upcoming Step 6). This is accomplished by using FV as the additional savings need at retirement, N as the number of years until retirement, and I/YR as the inflation rate. For example, if we assume that FV is \$150,000, N is 10 years, and I/YR is 7% per year, PV (the present value of the additional savings need at retirement) is \$76,252, calculated on the HP 10BII as follows:

$$150,000 \; FV; \; 10 \; N; \; 7 \; I/YR; \; PV = 76,252$$

Step 6: Calculate the additional annual savings required to accumulate the necessary retirement fund.

In this final step of the retirement savings need calculation, we need to, again, separately discuss the procedures employed under both the capital utilization and capital preservation approaches.

Calculations Using the Capital Utilization Approach   What we are attempting to do in this step is calculate the annually increasing serial savings amount required to accumulate the additional savings need at retirement, previously computed in Step 5. We will assume that the annual savings amounts will occur at the end of each year, meaning we will be determining the present value of an ordinary annuity (PVOA), rather than an annuity due (PVAD). To perform this calculation, we need to begin with the amount of the additional savings need at retirement for the capital utilization approach as deflated for the effect of inflation, as computed in Step 5. Using this amount as FV, N as the number of years until retirement, and I/YR as the inflation-adjusted annual investment return (calculated in the manner described in Step 4), we calculate the PMT (or the annually increasing serial savings amount required to accumulate the additional savings need at retirement). For example, if FV is \$300,000, N is 10 years, and I/YR is 3.88 (using the same assumptions as we did in Step 4—an after-tax investment return of 7% and an inflation rate of 3%), then the PMT is \$25,127, calculated as follows:

$$\text{END mode}; \; 300,000 \; FV; \; 10 \; N; \; 3.88 \; I/YR; \; PMT = 25,127$$

What we have just calculated is the first serial (increasing) savings payment *before* any adjustment for inflation. Because we will be making our savings payments at the *end* of each year, we need to, therefore, adjust this first payment to its value at the end of the first year by multiplying it by (1 + the inflation rate). This is the amount of the first-year serial savings payment to be made at the end of the year.

If instead of using annually increasing savings amounts, the client prefers to make a fixed, level savings payment at the end of each year that will not increase annually, a different calculation is required. If you recall, in Step 5, we calculated the additional savings need required at retirement under both the capital utilization and capital preservation approaches and then deflated this amount to remove the effect of inflation. For purposes of this level payment calculation, however, we must not use the deflated amount, but rather the additional savings need at retirement unadjusted for inflation from Step 5. Letting this amount equal FV, letting N equal the number of years until retirement, and letting I/YR equal the after-tax investment return (rather than the inflation-adjusted return because we are no longer adjusting the annual savings amounts for inflation), we solve for PMT, the level savings payment invested at the end of each year. For example, if FV is \$350,000, N is 10 years, and I/YR is 7%, PMT is \$25,332, calculated as follows:

$$\text{END mode; } 350{,}000 \text{ } FV; \text{ } 10 \text{ } N; \text{ } 7 \text{ } I/YR; \text{ } PMT = 25{,}332$$

Calculations Using the Capital Preservation Approach   Under the capital preservation approach, the calculations for Step 6 are *identical* to those we just performed under the capital utilization approach. Accordingly, simply follow the instructions provided under the capital utilization approach using the amounts calculated under the capital preservation approach in previous steps.

Step 4: Developing and Presenting the Recommendations

After having determined the retirement savings need in Step 3 of the retirement planning process, using the six-step retirement savings need calculation process, the planner is now in a position to evaluate alternative courses of action for the client and then develop definitive recommendations for a retirement savings program. In doing so, the planner may need to consider multiple assumptions and conduct research or consult with other professionals. The result of this analysis may be a single alternative, multiple alternatives, or no alternative to the client's current course of action. Clearly, the financial planner needs to evaluate such alternatives with a clear understanding of his level of competency and legal authority. The development and evaluation of alternatives is a highly subjective activity, and it is doubtful that any two financial planners will identify exactly the same alternatives.

After identifying and evaluating possible alternatives, the planner is now ready to develop recommendations that may be expected to reasonably achieve the client's goals, needs, and priorities. The planner must be satisfied that there is sufficient relevant information to form the basis for any recommendations made. Relevant information may include an understanding of the client's goals, existing financial situation, the resources available for achieving the goals, nonfinancial factors, and external factors. Any resulting recommendations must, therefore, be consistent with and directly affected by the:

- mutually defined scope of the engagement;

- mutually defined client goals, needs, and priorities;

- quantitative data provided by the client;

- personal and economic assumptions made;

- financial planner's analysis and evaluation of the client's current situation; and

- any alternatives selected by the financial planner.

One possible result of the recommendations made is that the client may now need to revise one or more retirement lifestyle goals.

When the Client is a Businessowner

If the client is the owner of a closely held business, it may be advantageous for the client to establish a qualified retirement plan. Some of the reasons for establishing such a plan include the following:

■ The business obtains an income tax deduction for contributions made to the plan.

■ The plan participant pays no income taxes when the employer makes the plan contributions but instead defers such taxation until plan benefits are distributed.

■ The funds used for plan contributions come from the business, rather than from the owner's personal funds, and, therefore, do not affect his personal cash flow.

■ If the plan permits employees to make pretax contributions, the amounts contributed by the employees avoid current taxation.

Use of a qualified retirement plan as a savings program option will necessitate upward adjustment of the retirement savings required at retirement age to add the taxes payable upon distribution from the plan at retirement. Another way to express this is that a larger before-tax amount must be accumulated so the after-tax amount available to the client equals the retirement savings need. This adjustment is made by dividing the after-tax savings need calculated in Step 5 of the retirement planning process by (1 minus the client's effective tax rate), resulting in the before-tax retirement savings required at retirement age. Then, using this amount, the planner can recalculate the annual savings requirement necessary to accumulate the before-tax retirement savings required. This calculation was performed for the after-tax retirement savings required in Step 6 of the retirement planning process. In performing this recalculation, the planner needs to use the estimated before-tax savings need and a before-tax investment return (rather than an after-tax return) because of the fact that the return will be shielded from current taxation inside the qualified plan trust.

Of course, the amount recalculated as the annual savings requirement necessary to accumulate the before-tax retirement savings required at retirement age, as discussed in the previous paragraph, needs to be evaluated for feasibility. It may be that the closely held business does not currently have adequate cash flow to make plan contributions in this amount.

When the Client is an Employee Rather than a Businessowner

In this situation, the planner needs to refer to the information gathered about employer-provided qualified plans in Step 2 of the retirement planning process. If the clients are a married couple, such information must be obtained for both spouses. Then the planner needs to determine how much each spouse can contribute to his or her respective qualified plan. In addition, the planner needs to evaluate whether the spouses qualify to contribute to IRAs on either a deductible or non-deductible basis.

So much of making a recommendation regarding how to effectively take advantage of an employer's qualified retirement plan(s) is understanding the client's situation, including such information as the client's annual retirement savings need, the client's disposable income as reflected in the personal cash flow statement, the client's age, the client's budgeting and savings skills, salary, marginal income tax bracket, investment plan, and other client goals and objectives. The client's annual retirement savings need must be compared to the client's disposable income (excess of cash inflows over cash outflows) from the client's personal cash flow statement. The amount of the client's disposable income will, therefore, be an important factor in determining the type of plan that will fulfill the client's need. Moreover, tax-deductible contributions to a qualified retirement plan require less cash flow than do after-tax contributions. Clients who have difficulty saving on a regular basis may need a plan that automatically deducts, through a payroll deduction plan, contributions from their salaries.

The amount of a client's salary may also affect her ability to make the maximum contribution to specific types of plans. Likewise, clients in high marginal income tax brackets will benefit more from before-tax contributions and the tax deferral of annual earnings inside the fund.

Finally, the planner needs to look at the client's other investments, outside of qualified retirement plans, to strike a reasonable portfolio balance. The investment options offered by certain plans may not be appropriate for the specific client. When making this determination, the planner also needs to consider penalties or fees associated with particular investment options, such as ongoing management fees, back-end loads on mutual funds, and deferred sales charges on annuities.

Client goals and objectives and the related time horizons for these goals may also drive the type of plan(s) recommended. For example, if client goals such as an extended vacation, college funding, home remodeling, or an automobile purchase will affect the client's future cash flow, it needs to be factored into the choice of retirement savings vehicle. In these instances, perhaps the client needs to consider installing or accessing a qualified plan that provides for in-service distributions, such as a plan loan.

Presenting the Recommendations

After evaluating alternatives and developing recommendations, the financial planner must now communicate with the client and assist the client in making an informed decision. It is recommended that such communications be in writing and include a summary of the client's goals and significant assumptions, a description of any limitations on the work performed, the recommendations made, and a statement that projected results may not be achieved.

The financial planner is obligated to make a reasonable effort to assist the client in understanding his current situation, the recommendation(s) being made, the rationale for the recommendation(s), and the expected impact on the ability of the client to achieve his goals, needs, and priorities. Note that the financial planner is *not* responsible for making the client understand these issues, but she *is* required to make a reasonable effort in helping the client understand them. Some of the factors the client needs to understand are:

- material personal and economic assumptions;

- interdependence of recommendations;

- advantages and disadvantages of each recommendation;

- risks; and

- time sensitivity.

The client needs to appreciate the sensitivity of changes in personal and economic conditions on the results that may be achieved by the recommendation(s). New tax laws, a change in family status, loss of or change in job or career, actual versus anticipated investment returns, and the client's health could all have a significant effect on the degree of achievement of the client's goals, needs, and priorities under a particular recommendation.

The financial planner also has an obligation to disclose, if necessary, any conflicts of interest that may have resulted from the recommendation(s) made. For instance, if the financial planner is recommending the purchase of a large quantity of securities or mutual funds from which the financial planner will receive a material amount of compensation, this must be disclosed to the client before the client acts on the recommendation.

In summary, the planner needs to analyze the client's total financial and personal situation to determine how certain factors will be affected by the choice of particular qualified retirement plans or IRAs. The planner should also provide the client with the information just discussed so the client can make an informed decision. The presentation of recommendations presents a good opportunity for the financial planner to determine whether her recommendations meet the expectations of the client, whether the client is motivated to act on the recommendations, and whether the recommendations may need revision.

Step 5: Implementing the Recommendations

After the retirement planning recommendations have been developed, presented to the client, and accepted by the client, the planner and the client must mutually agree on the responsibilities for implementing the recommendations, consistent with the scope of the engagement. It is essential that the client take responsibility for accepting or rejecting the retirement planning recommendations and for either implementing them personally or delegating implementation to others. Regardless of the level of assistance, implementation decisions are made by the client, *not* by the planner. If the planner is to provide implementation services, the specific services must be mutually agreed upon by the client and the planner. This may involve revision of the scope of the engagement. Some of the responsibilities that may be assumed by the planner include the following:

- Identifying activities necessary for the plan's implementation

- Determining the division of activities between the planner and the client

- Establishing the selection criteria for selecting and referring to other professionals

- Coordinating with other professionals

- Sharing information as authorized

- Selecting and securing products and/or services

This is another time at which the planner may be obliged to disclose conflicts of interest, sources of compensation, or material relationships with other professionals or advisers that have not been disclosed previously. For instance, if the planner refers the client to other professionals or advisers, the planner is obligated to indicate the basis for the referral, including any direct or indirect compensation that he may receive as a result. This team of other professionals or advisers may include a financial planner, tax preparer, attorney, plan administration firm, and/or an actuary. The planner, however, should be the team leader in coordinating the efforts of each professional involved.

It is entirely possible that the planner may have been selected to implement the recommendations of another retirement planning professional (such as the tax preparer). This will require the planner to revert back to Step 1 in the retirement planning process to mutually define with the client the scope of the engagement, including such matters as the extent to which the planner will rely on any information, analysis, or recommendations provided by others.

In implementing the retirement planning recommendations, not only is the planner obligated to select any appropriate products and services consistent with the client's goals, needs, and priorities, but he also needs to reasonably investigate and evaluate those products and services. Different retirement planners might select different products or services for the same client, both of which may be suitable for the client and capable of achieving the client's goals, needs, and priorities. Clearly such a selection is subjective.

Step 6: Monitoring the Recommendations

The final step in the retirement planning process is the monitoring of retirement planning recommendations implemented in Step 5. The planner needs to mutually define with the client the responsibilities for periodic monitoring of the implemented retirement planning recommendations. If the client wants the planner to monitor the plan progress and the degree of success achieved by the implementation of the retirement planning recommendations, this needs to be agreed upon between the parties. Such an agreement should also specify exactly what is to be monitored, the frequency of monitoring, and how the results will be communicated to the client.

In determining a client's progress toward achieving established retirement planning goals, the planner should (1) ascertain whether all recommended actions to achieve the goals have been undertaken; (2) measure and evaluate the actual progress toward achievement of the goals; and (3) identify developments in the client's circumstances and in external factors that have affected the retirement planning recommendations. The client and planner also need to anticipate that the factors affecting the client's retirement savings program will change during the preretirement years. For example, the client may decide to revise her retirement planning goals, she may lose her job, or a second wage earner may enter the workforce. Moreover, interest rates, inflation, and other market factors may materially impact the client's retirement savings program. The planner should communicate to the client, typically in writing, an evaluation of progress toward achieving the client's retirement planning goals.

In certain cases, the results of monitoring may give rise to the re-initiation of earlier steps in the retirement planning process and modification of the scope of the engagement. This illustrates the point that retirement planning is an *ongoing process*, not a single transaction or series of transactions. Monitoring can, thereby, result in starting and restarting the process at various points in the process.

Job Task Domain 8: Practicing within Professional and Regulatory Standards (Throughout Steps 1-6)

Job task domain 8 encompasses all six steps of the financial planning process. It is not Step 7 but should be integral to each step of the process as a financial planner works with a client. Whether a client requires comprehensive planning, the services required are strictly limited, or any combination of services, CFP® professionals are required to practice within the professional and regulatory standards set by CFP Board.

CFP® professionals agree to abide by *CFP Board's Standards of Professional Conduct* at all times, especially during the financial planning process. These standards include a *Code of Ethics and Professional Responsibility*, *Rules of Conduct*, *Financial Planning Practice Standards*, and *Candidate Fitness Standards*. CFP Board enforces the Standards through a process outlined in its *Disciplinary Rules and Procedures*.

Supplemental Reading—Qualified Plan Requirements and Regulatory Plan Considerations

EXCLUSIVE BENEFIT RULE

One of the basic requirements for tax qualification of a retirement plan is that it be established for the exclusive benefit of the employer's employees or their beneficiaries (not just corporate executives and businessowners). In fact, none of the plan's trust corpus or income may be used for, or diverted to, purposes other than for the exclusive benefit of employees or their beneficiaries.

MINIMUM PARTICIPATION STANDARDS

Another set of requirements that qualified retirement plans must meet is the minimum participation standards of IRC Section 410. These include the "age and service" requirements that the plan establishes as conditions of participation in the plan and the "overall coverage" and "participation" requirements. Section 410 does not permit a plan to require an employee to complete a period of service with the employer (or employers) maintaining the plan extending beyond the *later of*:

■ the date on which the employee attains age 21; or

■ the date on which the employee completes one year of service.

Certain plans are subject to special rules. For example, a plan that provides 100% vesting after meeting a requirement of not more than two years of service is considered to satisfy the minimum participation standards. Also, a plan maintained exclusively for employees of a tax-exempt educational institution, which provides 100% vesting after meeting a requirement of at least one year of service, may substitute age 26 for age 21 in the foregoing requirements.

A qualified plan must provide that any employee who has satisfied the minimum age and service requirements specified in the previous paragraph, and who is otherwise entitled to participate in the plan, must commence participation in the plan no later than the *earlier of*:

■ the first day of the first plan year beginning after the date on which such employee satisfied such requirements; or

■ the date six months after the date on which the employee satisfied such requirements.

A "year of service" means a 12-month period during which the employee has not less than 1,000 hours of service.

In addition to the age and service requirement, a qualified retirement plan must meet one of three alternative overall coverage and participation tests under IRC Section 410(b).

■ **Percentage test**—the employer-sponsor of the qualified plan must cover at least 70% of the nonhighly compensated employees. Plans that do not meet the percentage test must meet one of the two following tests.

■ **Ratio test**—the plan must benefit at least 70% of the nonhighly compensated employees *or* the plan must benefit a percentage of nonhighly compensated employees that is at least 70% of the percentage of highly compensated employees benefiting under the plan.

■ **Average benefit percentage test**—the plan must benefit a nondiscriminatory classification of employees, and the average benefit, as a percentage of compensation, for all nonhighly compensated employees of the employer must be at least 70% of the average benefit for highly compensated employees. Note that the average benefit test is a two-part test. Not only must the plan meet the nondiscriminatory classification part of the test but it must also meet the 70% average benefit test.

Just to make an already complex set of rules even more complex, a *defined benefit plan* must meet an additional coverage requirement known as the 50/40 test in order to be qualified. A defined benefit plan must benefit the lesser of

■ 50 employees; or

■ 40% of all eligible employees.

If the employer has five or fewer employees and maintains a defined benefit plan, then at least two employees must be covered (or, if there is only one employee, that employee).

OTHER NONDISCRIMINATION REQUIREMENTS

Contributions to or benefits from a qualified plan must *not* discriminate in favor of "highly compensated employees," as that term is defined in IRC Section 414(q). Section 414(q) defines a "highly compensated employee" as any employee who (1) was a 5% owner (defined in IRC Section 416(i)(1)) at any time during the year or the preceding year or (2) for the preceding year had compensation from the employer in excess of $120,000 (in 2015), and, if the employer so elects, was in the top-paid group of employees for such preceding year. An employee is in the top-paid group of employees for any year if such employee is in the group consisting of the top 20% of the employees when ranked on the basis of compensation paid during such year. The following employees may be excluded in determining the top-paid group:

■ Employees with less than six months of service

■ Employees who normally work less than 17½ hours per week

■ Seasonal employees who normally work not more than six months during any year

■ Employees under the age of 21

■ Except as provided by regulations, union employees

■ Nonresident aliens with no U.S. earned income

Compensation, as defined in IRC Section 415(c)(3), is the compensation of the participant from the employer for the year and includes elective deferrals and other amounts contributed or deferred by the employer at the election of the employee, which is not includable in the gross income of the employee. As discussed previously, if there is evidence that retirement benefits were the subject of good-faith bargaining between employee representatives and the employer (or employers), union employees covered by a collective bargaining agreement are excluded for this purpose. Also excluded are employees who are nonresident aliens and who receive no earned income from the employer, which constitutes income from U.S. sources.

In classifying employees for retirement plan purposes, a classification is not considered discriminatory merely because it is limited to salaried or clerical employees. In addition, contributions or benefits of, or on behalf of, the employees under the plan are permitted to bear a uniform relationship to the compensation of such employees. For example, if an employee receives a benefit of 8% of his compensation, regardless of the amount of his compensation, such a benefit formula is not considered to discriminate against low-paid employees. Moreover, a plan is not considered discriminatory merely because the contributions or benefits of, or on behalf of, the employees under the plan favor highly compensated employees.

In testing for nondiscrimination, defined contribution plans (discussed later in this unit) are normally tested under the contributions test but may be tested using the benefits test. This is known as cross testing of a plan. Defined benefit plans must meet a general test or a uniformity requirement and one of three safe harbors. These tests will be discussed in more detail later in these readings. The defined benefit tests compare the rate at which benefits accrue for highly compensated employees to the rate benefits accrue for other employees.

VESTING REQUIREMENTS

A qualified plan must meet the requirements of IRC Section 411 relating to minimum vesting standards. Generally, this means an employee's right to her normal retirement benefit is nonforfeitable upon the attainment of her normal retirement age. At all times, an employee's accrued benefit on her *own* contributions is nonforfeitable (100% vested). With regard to *employer* contributions, a plan must provide for either five-year vesting (100% vesting after completing five years of service; otherwise known as cliff vesting) or three- to seven-year vesting (20% vesting with three years of service, 40% vesting with four years of service, 60% vesting with five years of service, 80% vesting with six years of service, and 100% vesting with seven or more years of service; otherwise known as graded or graduated vesting).

In counting years of service for purposes of determining an employee's vested rights, the plan may disregard, among other years of service, years of service before age 18, years of service during a period for which the employee elected not to contribute to a plan requiring employee contributions, years of service during any period for which the employer did not maintain the plan (or predecessor plan), or years of service during which there was a break in service. A one-year break in service is a calendar year, plan year, or other 12-consecutive-month period designated by the plan during which a participant has not completed more than 500 hours of service. The significance of a one-year break in service is that the employer is *not* required to take into account years of service before the break in service until an employee has completed a year of service *after* his return to work. Also, if a participant has five consecutive one-year breaks in service, the employer is *not* required to take into account years of service *after* the five-year period for purposes of determining the nonforfeitable percentage of his accrued benefit derived from employer contributions that accrued before the five-year period.

Normal retirement age is defined in Section 411 as the time a plan participant attains normal retirement age under the plan or the later of:

- the time a plan participant attains age 65; or

- the fifth anniversary of the time a plan participant commenced participation in the plan.

Accelerated vesting rules apply to employer-matching contributions, which are contributions made by an employer on account of employee contributions or elective deferrals or forfeitures allocated on the basis of employee contributions, matching contributions, or elective deferrals. With regard to these contributions, a plan must provide for either three-year vesting (100% vesting after completing three years of service, otherwise known as cliff vesting) or two- to six-year vesting (20% vesting with two years of service, 40% vesting with three years of service, 60% vesting with four years of service, 80% vesting with five years of service, and 100% vesting with six or more years of service; otherwise known as graded or graduated vesting). This same accelerated vesting schedule also applies to top-heavy plans, discussed later in this unit.

PLANS COVERING OWNER-EMPLOYEES AND TOP-HEAVY PLANS

If a plan provides contributions or benefits for employees, some or all of whom are owner-employees, the plan must provide that contributions on behalf of any owner-employee may be made only with respect to the earned income of such owner-employee that is derived from the trade or business with respect to which such plan is established. For this purpose, an owner-employee is an employee who either owns the entire interest in an unincorporated trade or business or, in the case of a partnership, is a partner who owns more than 10% of either the capital interest or the profits interest in such partnership.

Special rules apply to so-called top-heavy plans. A top-heavy defined benefit plan is one in which, as of the determination date for a plan year, the present value of the cumulative accrued benefits under the plan for key employees exceeds 60% of the present value of the cumulative accrued benefits under the plan for all employees. A top-heavy defined contribution plan is one in which the aggregate of the accounts of key employees under the plan exceeds 60% of the aggregate of the accounts of all employees under the plan. The definition of a key employee is *not* the same as that of a highly compensated employee, discussed under Other Nondiscrimination Requirements earlier in these readings. Instead, Section 416(i) defines a key employee as an employee who, at any time during the plan year, is one of the following:

- An officer of the employer having an annual compensation greater than $170,000 (in 2015)

- A 5% owner of the employer

- A 1% owner of the employer having an annual compensation from the employer of more than $150,000

A top-heavy plan or a plan which may become top-heavy must meet the requirements of IRC Section 416. Section 416 requires top-heavy plans to meet either three-year, 100% vesting (cliff vesting) or six-year graded vesting, both of which were described previously in this unit. In addition, top-heavy plans must meet the minimum benefits or contribution requirements of Section 416. For defined benefit plans, the accrued benefit derived from employer contributions of each participant who is a non-key employee, when expressed as an annual retirement benefit, must not be less than the applicable percentage of the participant's average compensation for years in the testing period. The applicable percentage is the *lesser of*:

- 2% multiplied by the number of years of service with the employer; or

- 20%.

A participant's testing period is the period of consecutive years (not exceeding five) during which the participant had the greatest aggregate compensation from the employer.

In the case of defined contribution plans, the employer contribution for a year for each participant who is a non-key employee in a top-heavy plan must be not less than 3% of such a participant's compensation.

INTEGRATION WITH SOCIAL SECURITY

A qualified plan must provide, in the case of a participant or beneficiary who is receiving benefits under the plan or a participant who is separated from the service and has nonforfeitable rights to benefits, that such benefits are *not* decreased by reason of any increase in Social Security benefit levels or any increase in the Social Security wage base. However, it *is* permissible to integrate a plan's benefit or contribution formula with Social Security. A plan that is integrated with Social Security normally provides greater contributions or benefits for higher-paid employees whose compensation is greater than the Social Security taxable wage base. This is because lower-paid employees receive a higher percentage of their total retirement benefit from Social Security than do higher-paid employees. As a result, a disparity exists between lower-paid employees and higher-paid employees with regard to the contributions or benefits provided by the plan. The allowable size of this difference in contributions or benefits between those for highly compensated employees and those for nonhighly compensated employees is known as the permitted disparity, and it cannot exceed certain statutory limits.

For defined benefit plans, there are two methods of integrating plan benefit formulas with Social Security—the excess method and the offset method. In the case of the excess method, the plan establishes a level of compensation known as the integration level and then provides benefits for compensation in excess of the integration level that are *greater than* those provided for compensation below the integration level. The integration level may be established at either a certain dollar amount or by use of a formula. However, a plan's integration level may not exceed an amount known as covered compensation, determined from an IRS covered compensation table or, alternatively, from an IRS rounded covered compensation table. In addition to limiting the integration level, the Internal Revenue Code and related regulations limit the size of the disparity between the benefit as a percentage of compensation above and below the integration level. A plan's base benefit percentage is the percentage of compensation that is below the integration level, while the excess benefit percentage is the percentage of compensation above the integration level. Under IRC Section 401(l)(4)(A), the excess benefit percentage cannot exceed the base benefit percentage by more than the maximum excess allowance. The maximum excess allowance, with respect to any single year of service with the employer taken into account under the plan, is three-fourths of a percentage point (0.75%). With respect to total benefits, the maximum excess allowance is three-fourths of a percentage point multiplied by the participant's years of service (not to exceed 35 years) with the employer taken into account under the plan. In addition, the maximum excess allowance may never exceed the base benefit percentage.

Here are some examples to illustrate how the defined benefit plan *excess method* of Social Security integration works.

E X A M P L E Franks Manufacturing Company's defined benefit pension plan has an integrated formula providing an annual benefit of 28% of final average annual compensation plus 24% of compensation above the plan's integration level. Jason Martin, born in 1949, is a participant in the plan who retires in 2015. Jason's final average compensation is $60,000. The integration level is $48,000. To determine Jason's annual retirement benefit, we make the following calculations:

28% of final average compensation of $60,000, or $16,800

24% of $12,000 ($60,000 – $48,000), or $2,880

The total benefit is, therefore, $19,680 ($16,800 + $2,880).

E X A M P L E Now assume that a defined benefit pension plan provides a benefit of 1.25% of compensation below the integration level for each year of service. Applying what we just learned about the maximum excess allowance, the excess benefit percentage cannot exceed 2% (1.25% + .75%). So for a participant with 35 years of service, if the plan provides a benefit of 28% of final average compensation below the integration level, it cannot provide more than 54.25% of compensation above the integration level (0.75% × 35 years = 26.25% + 28% = 54.25%). We then need to check for the other limitation (that the maximum excess allowance may be no greater than the base percentage). In the case of the Franks plan from the previous example, the maximum excess allowance (the difference between the excess and base percentage) cannot exceed 28%. Therefore, the maximum excess allowance is 56% (28% + 28%). The Franks plan uses 28% as its base percentage and 24% as its excess percentage for a maximum excess allowance of 52% (which meets both tests just discussed).

A defined benefit plan that uses the *offset method* reduces the benefit attributable to employer contributions for each participant by an amount specified in the plan. Under the offset method of Social Security integration, a defined benefit plan's benefit formula is reduced either by a fixed amount or a formula amount (limited by the Code and regulations) that takes into account a participant's Social Security benefits. However, the offset method does not employ an integration level as does the excess method. Instead, the plan must provide that a participant's accrued benefit attributable to employer contributions may not be reduced (by reason of the offset) by more than the maximum offset allowance, with benefits based on average annual compensation. The maximum offset allowance for any year of service with the employer taken into account under the plan is three-fourths of a percentage point, and for total benefits, three-fourths of a percentage point multiplied by a participant's years of service (not to exceed 35 years). Moreover, in no event may the maximum offset allowance exceed 50% of the benefit, which would have accrued without regard to the offset reduction. This means, for example, that a plan formula of 50% of final average compensation using an offset for Social Security must provide at least 25% of final average compensation to even the lowest-paid participant.

A defined contribution plan may use *only* the excess method in integrating for Social Security benefits. In such a plan, the excess contribution percentage may *not* exceed the base contribution percentage by more than the *lesser of*

■ the base contribution percentage; or

■ 5.7 percentage points or the old-age insurance portion of the Social Security tax, as may be adjusted from time to time, whichever is greater.

Accordingly, an integrated plan, allocating employer contributions plus forfeitures at the rate of 15.7% of compensation above the integration level, would have to provide at least a 10% (15.7 − 5.7) allocation for compensation below the integration level. Defined contribution plans, however, go to great lengths to determine the actual optimum integration level to maximize benefits for higher-paid employees and stay within the limitations imposed by law.

BENEFIT AND CONTRIBUTION LIMITATIONS

IRC Section 415 establishes the limits on benefits and contributions for qualified plans. For defined benefit plans, a participant's annual benefit may not exceed the *lesser of*:

■ $210,000 (for 2015); or

■ 100% of the participant's average compensation (not exceeding $265,000 for 2015) for the participant's three consecutive years of highest compensation.

This maximum annual benefit is actuarially reduced when retirement benefits are paid before age 62 and increased when paid after age 65. However, if certain requirements are met, a minimum annual benefit of $10,000 may be provided by the plan. The benefit limit and the compensation limit are reduced in the case of participants with less than 10 years of service with the employer. A participant's annual benefit is defined as a benefit payable annually in the form of a straight life annuity (with no ancillary benefits) under a plan to which employees do not contribute and under which no rollover contributions are made.

For defined contribution plans, annual additions (contributions and other additions) with respect to a participant may not exceed the *lesser of*:

■ $53,000 (for 2015); or

■ 100% of the participant's compensation (not exceeding $265,000, for 2015).

The term *annual additions* is the sum for any year of (1) employer contributions, (2) employee contributions, and (3) reallocated forfeitures. Participants who will be at least 50 years of age by the end of the tax year are also permitted to make catch-up contributions to most employer-sponsored defined contribution plans, including a Section 401(k) plan, a SEP plan, a SIMPLE plan, a 403(b) plan, and a 457 plan. The maximum amount of the catch-up contributions, however, depends on the type of plan established by the employer. Note: eligible catch-up contributions are not considered in the application of the annual additions limit.

LIMITATIONS ON ELECTIVE DEFERRALS

A plan that permits elective deferrals must limit the amount of such annual deferrals to the limitation specified in IRC Section 402(g)(1)(A). This limitation is $18,000 in 2015. There is a greater limitation for plan participants age 50 or older by the end of the taxable year (known as catch-up contributions). Such participants may contribute an additional $6,000 in 2015.

CONTRIBUTION DEDUCTION LIMITS

In the case of a defined benefit plan, an employer may claim an income tax deduction for contributions to the plan to the extent of the *greater of*:

■ an amount determined actuarially as provided in IRC Section 404(a); or

■ the amount required to satisfy the minimum funding standards of IRC Section 412.

Employers may deduct contributions to profit-sharing and stock bonus types of defined contribution plans to the extent of 25% of total aggregate covered compensation or payroll. Compensation includes elective deferrals to a qualified plan, Section 403(b) plan, Section 457 plan, SEP plan, SIMPLE, or a Section 125 flexible spending account plan. Also, in determining the total amount that the employer has contributed to a plan, elective deferrals are *not* required to be included. Here is an example to illustrate the deduction limitation for a plan that allows for employee elective deferrals.

> **EXAMPLE** Assume that Marshall Manufacturing's participating employees make elective deferrals to Marshall's Section 401(k) plan in the amount of $15,000. The total annual payroll cost for all plan participants in the current plan year is $150,000. Accordingly, Marshall may claim an income tax deduction for $37,500 (25% of $150,000). Note that the gross payroll cost does not need to be reduced by the $15,000 of elective deferrals before applying the 25% limitation. Also note that the $37,500 income tax deduction calculated above does not need to be reduced by the $15,000 of elective deferrals. Accordingly, Marshall may contribute and deduct an employer contribution of $37,500 plus the $15,000 of elective deferrals made by its employees for a total deduction of $52,500.

Some employers offer both defined benefit and defined contribution plans. In such event, the employer deduction limit is the *greater of*

■ 25% of the compensation of all participants; or

■ the amount necessary to satisfy the minimum funding standards for the defined benefit plan.

In the situation where an employer contributes to a plan an amount greater than the deduction limits, the excess contributions are subject to a 10% penalty.

TIME LIMIT FOR MAKING PLAN CONTRIBUTIONS

Defined benefit plan contributions must be paid within 8½ months after the end of the plan year. If the defined benefit plan fails to meet the funding requirements for a particular plan year, it must pay the deficiency in quarterly payments during the next plan year. Defined contribution pension plan contributions are due within 2½ months of the end of the plan year. This deadline, however, may be extended up to six months. If an employer fails to meet the minimum funding requirements, it is subject to penalties. As discussed earlier, however, profit-sharing plans are not subject to the minimum funding requirements and are, therefore, extremely flexible in this regard.

FIDUCIARY OBLIGATIONS

An employer must tread carefully when sponsoring a qualified retirement plan. While an employer's officers or shareholders may serve as plan trustees, they must function in the legal capacity of a *fiduciary* and meet strict requirements that protect the interest of the plan participants and beneficiaries. Unlike employees, the employer is subject to penalties for borrowing from the plan as a breach of its fiduciary duty to the plan participants and beneficiaries.

REGULATORY JURISDICTION OR AUTHORITY

The U.S. Department of Labor (DOL) is given its jurisdiction or authority to act in Title I of ERISA, which also spells out the reporting and disclosure requirements that both pension and welfare types of employee benefit plans must meet. Generally, an employee benefit plan is covered by ERISA *unless* it is specifically exempted by ERISA or the related regulations. The Internal Revenue Service tax qualification rules are found in Title II of ERISA, as subsequently codified in the Internal Revenue Code beginning in IRC Section 401. Moreover, ERISA created the Pension Benefit Guaranty Corporation (PBGC) as a federal insurance agency to assure that promised retirement benefits payable via a defined-benefit type of plan are in fact paid (within statutory limits).

Some of the pension and welfare plans exempted from ERISA include the following:

■ Governmental (federal, state, or local) or governmental organization plans

■ Religious organization plans except those that elect ERISA coverage

■ Plans for nonresident aliens maintained outside the United States

■ Unfunded excess benefit plans (a type of nonqualified deferred compensation plan)

■ Workers' compensation, unemployment compensation, or disability insurance law plans (maintained solely to comply with such laws)

PENSION PLANS UNDER ERISA

A pension plan is defined more broadly under ERISA than under the Internal Revenue Code. In general, a pension plan under ERISA is any employee benefit plan that involves deferral of an employee's compensation until her retirement date or later (without regard to the method used to calculate contributions to the plan, the method used to calculate benefits under the plan, or the method used to distribute benefits from the plan) or, alternatively, provides retirement income to employees. The foregoing definition encompasses all qualified pension, profit-sharing, stock bonus, and similar qualified plans. Even certain types of nonqualified deferred compensation plans are included but may be exempted from most of ERISA's requirements. A top-hat plan, as an unfunded nonqualified plan maintained by an employer primarily for the purpose of providing deferred compensation for a select group of management or highly compensated employees, is exempt from all of ERISA's provisions except its reporting and disclosure requirements and its administrative and enforcement provisions. A top-hat plan satisfies the former requirement by providing plan documents, upon request to the DOL and by filing a simple, one-time statement about the arrangement with the DOL. The DOL has not yet clarified the definition of "highly compensated" for this purpose.

Nonqualified deferred compensation plans not meeting one of these ERISA exemptions must generally comply with most of the ERISA provisions applicable to qualified pension plans, including the vesting, fiduciary, minimum funding, and reporting and disclosure requirements.

Other than the foregoing exemptions specified in ERISA itself, the DOL issues regulations granting partial exemptions or special treatment for certain pension-like plans. For example, a severance pay plan does *not* have to comply with the reporting and disclosure requirements for pension plans but must comply with the more limited reporting and disclosure requirements for welfare plans. Specifically, reporting and disclosure to the DOL must occur if

- payments are not directly or indirectly dependent on the employee retiring;

- total payments under the plan are not more than twice the employee's annual compensation during the year immediately preceding the separation from service; and

- all payments to any employee are generally completed within 24 months of separation from service.

A supplemental payment plan providing additional benefits to retirees to cover the cost of inflation also need not comply with numerous ERISA requirements under DOL regulations. SEP and SIMPLE IRAs, as well as IRC Section 403(b) plans (TSAs), may be either exempt from ERISA's reporting and disclosure requirements or subject to lesser requirements. Refer to the applicable readings discussing plan types for a brief discussion of ERISA requirements that must be met by various types of retirement plans.

See Exhibit 2.1 for the reporting and disclosure requirements that must be met by pension plans. The principal requirements that all such plans must satisfy include the following:

- The **Summary Plan Description (SPD)**, which describes the major provisions of the plan to participants in understandable language. An SPD must be furnished to participants within 120 days of the creation of a plan or 90 days after a new participant enters an existing plan. Supplements to the SPD are also required in the event that plan provisions are revised. While DOL regulations specify what must be contained in an SPD, there is no prescribed form for filing such document. Filing of an SPD with the DOL is only required if requested by the DOL.

- The **Annual Report** (Form 5500 series), which includes financial information and is due by the end of the seventh month after the plan year ends. The report includes financial statements as well as an actuary's report (if a defined benefit plan) and information relative to any insurance contracts held by the plan.

- The **Summary Annual Report (SAR),** which summarizes the financial information from the annual report for the purpose of providing plan participants with such information within nine months of the end of the plan year.

- An **Individual Accrued Benefit Statement** within 30 days, if requested by a plan participant, only once per year.

EXHIBIT 1.1 Major Reporting and Disclosure Requirements for Pension Plans

I. Governmental Filings

Form	Description	Who Must File	When to File	Where to File
5500	Annual Return/Report of Employee Benefit Plan	Plan administrator	On or before last day of seventh month after available—file Form 5558	Address indicated in instructions to Form 5500
5500EZ	Annual Return of One-Participant (Owners and Their Spouses) Plans	Plan administrator. May be filed for plans that cover only an individual or an individual and spouse who are the owners of a business. May also be filed for partnership plans that cover only partners or partners and their spouses.	Same as Form 5500	Address indicated in instructions to Form 5500EZ
Schedule A (Form 5500)	Insurance Information	Plan administrator, where any plan benefits are provided by an insurance company or similar organization	Attachment to Form 5500	Same as Form 5500
Schedule B (Form 5500)	Actuarial Information	Plan administrator of defined benefit plan subject to minimum funding standards	Attachment to Form 5500	Same as Form 5500
Schedule C (Form 5500)	Service Provider and Trustee Information	Plan administrator	Attachment to Form 5500	Same as Form 5500
Schedule E (Form 5500)	ESOP Annual Information	Plan administrator	Attachment to Form 5500	Same as Form 5500
Schedule G (Form 5500)	Financial Schedules	Plan administrator	Attachment to Form 5500	Same as Form 5500
Schedule P (Form 5500)	Annual Return of Fiduciary of Employee Benefit Trust	Trustee or custodian of qualified trust or custodial account (begins running of statute of limitations)	Attachment to Form 5500	Same as Form 5500
Schedule SSA (Form 5500)	Annual Registration Statement Identifying Separated Participants with Deferred Vested Benefits	Plan administrator, if plan had participants who separated with deferred vested benefits during the plan year	Attachment to Form 5500	Same as Form 5500
Schedule T (Form 5500)	Qualified Pension Plan Coverage Information	Plan administrator	Attachment to Form 5500	Same as Form 5500
PBGC Form 1-ES	Estimated Premium Payment (base premiums for plans with 500 or more participants)	Plan administrator or sponsor of defined benefit plan (with 500 or more participants) subject to PBGC provisions	Within two months after the end of the prior plan year	Pension Benefit Guaranty Corporation P.O. Box 7247-7426 Philadelphia, PA 19170-7426
PBGC Form 1	Annual Premium Payment	Plan administrator or sponsor of defined benefit plan subject to PBGC provisions	Within eight months after the end of the prior plan year	Pension Benefit Guaranty Corporation P.O. Box 7247-7426 Philadelphia, PA 19170-7426

EXHIBIT 1.1 Major Reporting and Disclosure Requirements for Pension Plans (continued)

II. Disclosure to Pension Plan Participants

Item	Description	Who Must Provide	When Provided
Notice of Preretirement Survivor Benefit	Written explanation of preretirement survivor annuity, participant's right to make an election (or revoke election) to waive the annuity, spouse's rights, and effect of election or revocation	Plan administrator of plan required to provide	Within period beginning on first day of plan year in which participant attains age 32 and ending with close of plan year in which participant attains age 34. Election must be made within the period beginning on the first day of the plan year in which the participant attains age 35 and ending with the participant's death. For individuals who become participants after age 32, plan must provide explanation within three years of first day of plan year they become participants.
Notice of Joint and Survivor Benefit	Written explanation of joint and survivor annuity, right to make election to waive the annuity, right to revoke waiver, effect of election or revocation, and rights of the spouse	Plan administrator of plan required to provide	Within reasonable period before annuity starting date. Election must be made no sooner than 90 days before the annuity starting date.
Notice to Terminated Vested Participants	Same information as provided to IRS on Schedule SSA (Form 5500) concerning participant's accrued benefit. Statement must include notice if certain benefits may be forfeited if the participant dies before a particular date.	Plan administrator	No later than due date for filing Schedule SSA (Form 5500)
Individual Accrued Benefit Statement	Statement of participant's benefit accrued to date based on the latest available data. Statement must include notice of certain benefits; may be forfeited if the participant dies before a particular date.	Plan administrator	Within 30 days of participant's request. Need not be provided more than once in a 12-month period.

Source: *Tools & Techniques of Employee Benefit and Retirement Planning*, 9th edition, Stephan R. Leimberg and John J. McFadden, The National Underwriter Company, 2005. Used with permission.

Finally, Title IV of ERISA covers the plan termination insurance provisions and imposes various reporting and disclosure obligations on certain defined benefit pension plans. This information is provided to the Pension Benefit Guaranty Corporation (PBGC) pursuant to its role of insuring and protecting pension benefits for participants and beneficiaries.

PROHIBITED TRANSACTIONS BY A PLAN FIDUCIARY

ERISA requires that a plan fiduciary act solely in the best interest of the retirement plan participants or, under Title I of that act, be prepared to incur *personal liability* if certain prohibited transactions are permitted to take place. There are six prohibited transactions between a retirement plan trust and a so-called disqualified person, such as a plan fiduciary. They are as follows:

- The sale, exchange, or leasing of any property

- The lending of money or extending of any credit

- The furnishing of goods, services, or facilities

- The transfer to or use of plan assets by a fiduciary

- A fiduciary dealing with plan income or plan assets for his own interest

- A plan fiduciary receiving consideration for his own account from a party in a plan transaction involving plan income or plan assets

For each transaction that is prohibited under ERISA, there is currently imposed personally on the plan fiduciary a penalty tax of 15% on the amount involved for each year until the transaction is corrected. An *additional 100% tax* is imposed if the transaction is *not corrected* within a period of 90 days after the mailing of a deficiency notice by the IRS.

In part because of the punitive nature of the tax on prohibited transactions between a retirement plan and a plan fiduciary, it is, therefore, necessary to identify who is considered a fiduciary under the provisions of ERISA. Quite simply, a fiduciary is defined as any person who does the following:

- Exercises any discretionary authority or control over the management of the plan

- Exercises any authority or control over the management or disposition of the plan's assets

- Offers investment advice for a fee or other compensation with respect to plan funds or property

- Has any discretionary authority or responsibility in the plan's administration

Accordingly, this definition includes the plan sponsor (usually the employer), plan administrator, plan trustee, any investment adviser providing services to the plan for a fee, and certain officers and directors of the employer. On the other hand, individuals whose duties are purely ministerial (e.g., the accountant who files certain reporting or tax forms on behalf of the plan) are *not* considered to be plan fiduciaries. It is also interesting to note that the DOL has ruled that broker/dealers who regularly provide only general research concerning securities to its customers, including ERISA plans, are *not* rendering investment advice. Rather, individualized advice that serves as the primary reason for a plan investment decision appears to be the triggering event for determining fiduciary liability.

Once fiduciary status is determined, certain obligations or responsibilities attach. One of these, the obligation to act solely in the interest of plan participants and beneficiaries, has already been mentioned. However, there are others. Among these is the requirement to act with the care, skill, prudence, and diligence that a prudent person who is familiar with such matters would use under the circumstances then prevailing—the so-called prudent person rule. A fiduciary is also responsible for diversifying plan investments so as to minimize the risk of large losses unless it is clearly prudent not to diversify. Nevertheless, the practical, present-day standard for evaluating a fiduciary's prudence in investing plan assets is one of conduct and not a test of the result of the performance of the investment. As a final prudence requirement, the fiduciary must comply with the documentation requirements of the plan and must invest only in assets subject to the jurisdiction of U.S. courts. This latter requirement does not preclude investing in international securities; it simply requires that the assets be held in a manner such that the U.S. courts may take jurisdiction (e.g., not held in an offshore trust).

A particularly interesting aspect of fiduciary responsibility is the obligation to attempt to achieve superior plan investment performance. This obligation has come into potential conflict with the multiplicity of present-day defined contribution plans (e.g., a Section 401(k) plan) permitting employees to direct the investment of their own individual accounts. Under these plans, employers and other plan fiduciaries are exempt from liability for investment returns that result from participant choices, provided that participants are given the opportunity to exercise control over the assets in their accounts and can choose from a broad range of categories. This exemption from potential liability is specified in ERISA Section 404(c) and regulations specifying how and in what situations the employer will be protected from any liability for the bad investment decisions of its employees. For example, safe harbor provisions have been enacted protecting plan sponsors who offer at least three diversified categories of investments with materially different risk and return characteristics. The Department of Labor has also issued interpretive guidance to help the employer/sponsor distinguish between investment education for its employees (which will *not* subject the employer to potential liability) and investment advice (which probably *will* result in liability).

Since December 2001, a managed account option is now available for participants in defined contribution plans. Specifically, prior to that time, participants in self-directed Section 401(k) retirement plans were beseeching employers/plan sponsors to assist with investment decisions. However, as noted, employers were restricted by ERISA from offering investment advice. In addition, employers often hesitated in providing this service for fear of assuming fiduciary liability for poorly performing investment choices by their employees. To lessen this conflict, the DOL relaxed its regulations to provide for the managed account option. The practical implementation of this option permits employee/participants in Section 401(k) plans to choose among money managers at several well-known investment companies (mutual funds) to advance the employees' retirement fund accumulation and wealth-building goals.

Finally, as a part of the regulatory considerations involved in the implementation and administration of a qualified retirement plan, several additional pieces of legislation need to be mentioned. The first is the Age Discrimination in Employment Act (or ADEA) that protects plan participants from discrimination on the basis of age. Specifically, under ADEA, an employee cannot be required to contribute more to a qualified plan simply because she has attained the age of 40 or older. The second is Title VII of the Civil Rights Act of 1964 that prohibits discrimination against participants on the basis of sex or sex-related conditions, such as pregnancy. A difference in the amount of employer plan contributions or benefits provided a participant is also prohibited when based solely on gender.

2

Supplemental Reading–Defined Benefit and Other Pension Plans

DEFINITION, PURPOSE, AND PROS AND CONS OF DEFINED BENEFIT PENSION PLANS

For tax purposes, a defined benefit pension plan is *always* classified as a qualified employer pension plan. A pension plan provides for the payment of definitely determinable benefits to employees over a period of years, usually for life, after retirement. The determination of the benefits to be paid and the contributions that must be made in order to provide those benefits cannot be dependent on the employer's profits. In addition to a retirement benefit, a pension plan may provide for the payment of a pension due to disability or for the payment of death benefits. However, a pension plan may not provide for the payment of layoff benefits or benefits for illness or accident, except for retired employees. Unlike defined contribution plans, employer contributions to a defined benefit pension plan are *not* allocated to separate accounts for employees. Rather, a defined benefit pension plan guarantees a specific level of benefit at a participant's retirement.

An employer that assumes an obligation to provide a meaningful level of retirement income to all of its eligible employees and to allocate a higher level of contributions to older key employees would tend to select a defined benefit plan. A defined benefit plan would also be indicated where the principal(s) in a small professional practice wishes (wish) to defer the maximum amount possible for retirement and at the same time obtain the largest income tax deduction permissible for his (their) practice.

Some of the positive attributes of defined benefit plans include:

- maximization of contributions for older HCEs;

- guarantee of benefits by both the employer and the Pension Benefit Guaranty Corporation (PBGC), discussed later in this unit;

- tax deferral of retirement savings; and

- provision of a meaningful benefit to older employees who enter the plan with only a few years left until their retirement.

The downside of defined benefit plans includes:

- the high cost of establishing and operating such plans;

- the complexity of such plans and the challenge of communicating to employees how their benefits are determined;

- the lack of a meaningful benefit for employees who leave the employer before retirement;

- the lack of flexibility in making required annual contributions even when employer profit or cash flow is inadequate to do so; and

- the assumption of the investment risk by the employer, sometimes resulting in larger annual employer contributions.

▌DEFINED BENEFIT PLAN DESIGN AND OPERATION

Under a defined benefit plan, each participant's retirement benefit is defined and guaranteed in terms of dollars or as a replacement for some percentage of preretirement compensation from the employer sponsoring the plan. The term compensation may be defined in terms of average career wages or final employment years' wages.

Under the **career average method**, the employee's compensation over the years of plan participation is averaged, with some portion of that average replaced by the plan during retirement. Clearly, this method suffers from its failure to keep up with wage inflation and to replace a portion of the compensation being earned at or near retirement.

The **final average method** is more favorable to employees because it determines the retirement benefit as a percentage of their compensation immediately preceding their retirement. Typically, a participant's final three to five years of service are considered in computing the final average (commonly referred to as the *high five* or *high three*). This method provides plan participants with protection against inflation. In most cases, a worker's wages are highest in the final years of employment with the plan sponsor. Of course, under either the career average or final average method, only the first $265,000 (in 2015) of each employee's compensation may be taken into account in calculating the average.

Once a method of determining a participant's average compensation has been chosen, one of the following four types of **benefit formulas** *must* be selected.

- **Flat amount formula**   Under a flat amount formula, all employees normally receive the same monthly dollar amount of retirement benefit regardless of preretirement compensation and/or years of service. For example, all covered employees receive a monthly pension of $750 beginning at their normal retirement age (e.g., age 65), reduced by some plans for employees with less than a minimum number of years of service as specified in the plan document. This formula fails to take into account the level of each employee's preretirement compensation. However, in the rare case where the level of compensation of covered employees is within a narrow range, the formula may provide some degree of equity.

- **Flat percentage of earnings formula**   Benefits for covered employees are expressed as a flat percentage of compensation (either using career average or final average). For example, a benefit of 45% of salary may be paid at the normal retirement age. This formula is more commonly associated with plans using the final average compensation method and in plans in which most participants earn relatively low salaries. As with the flat amount formula, the plan may reduce benefits for those participants not completing a minimum number of years of service. In plans where the key employees are relatively old, this type of benefit formula may also be very advantageous to those employees.

- **Flat amount per year of service formula**   Under this formula, benefits are expressed as a stated dollar amount for each year of service to the employer. For example, this type of formula may provide $25 per month for each year in which the employee worked 1,800 hours or more. Accordingly, a participant with 30 years of service would receive a benefit of $750 per month ($25 × 30). Many defined benefit plans impose minimum years of service and minimum hours of service per year for a participant to be considered covered as a full-time employee. Accordingly, participants not meeting these minimums will have their benefits reduced. On the other hand, a participant who does satisfy the minimum years of service requirement with at least 1,000 hours of service per year is entitled to some level of benefit under the flat amount per year of service formula.

■ **Percentage of earnings per year of service or unit credit or unit benefit formula**
A participant's retirement benefit is based on a benefit credit for each year of covered service. Typically, benefit credits operate differently for past service years versus future service years. The amount credited for the past years' service is normally lower than that credited for future years' service. Past service refers to years of a participant's service to the employer prior to the implementation of the defined benefit plan. For example, a defined benefit plan may credit only 0.75% for each year the employee worked before the plan's inception, then 1.5% for each year of service following the plan's inception. The advantage of this formula is that it considers both compensation and years of service and, therefore, tends to favor the businessowner who typically has more years of service than the average employee. However, those hired only a few years before retirement receive a smaller amount of benefit because they are able to accumulate only a minimal number of years of service (even those with high salaries). This type of benefit formula, therefore, is most appropriate for an employer with a large disparity in participant compensation.

These formulas may also be integrated with Social Security benefits to provide a reasonable level of retirement income for all employees by taking into account their anticipated Social Security benefits. The effect of Social Security integration is to adjust the employer's total plan contributions by reason of these benefits.

Having selected both the method for determining average compensation and the benefit formula to be employed, a defined benefit plan must then be funded by the employer with periodic (usually quarterly) deposits calculated by an actuary to provide assurance that the plan will have sufficient funds to pay the promised benefit as each participant retires. The goal is to accumulate an amount of money for each participant that is capable of providing the promised benefit over the remaining lifetime of the participant. Certain defined benefit plans may also purchase an annuity for each retiring participant in order to discharge their continuing obligation to each participant.

An actuary performs a time value of money calculation to determine the size of the fund needed for each participant and, in turn, the periodic deposit the employer will have to make to accumulate this fund. There are many factors to be considered in the actuarial calculations. Some factors are relatively easy to determine, such as the age and sex of each participant and the benefit payable to each participant at normal retirement age.

However, other actuarial factors must be estimated or assumed. For example, the rate of return on plan investments is not knowable in advance and must, therefore, be projected over the relevant time frame. Higher rates of return will result in lower employer contributions, and lower rates of return will result in higher employer contributions. Another factor requiring reasonable estimation is the extent of both voluntary and involuntary employee turnover. Greater turnover rates will result in fewer employees receiving full retirement benefits and, hence, lower contributions by the employer. Conversely, lower turnover rates will result in more employees receiving full retirement benefits and, hence, higher contributions by the employer. The estimation of the employee turnover rate is greatly influenced by the average age of the employee population because younger employee populations generally have higher turnover rates. An additional factor is the rate of mortality among the employee population. Employees dying prior to their normal retirement age will, of course, *not* receive a full retirement benefit, resulting in lower employer contributions. Similarly, morbidity (or disability) rates must be estimated to predict how many employees will become disabled prior to normal retirement age and accordingly receive early distributions from the plan. A final factor to be considered is the number of employees who will retire at or before their normal retirement age. Clearly, as the actual results over the years differ from the estimates for these various factors, adjustments need to be made to the periodic employer contributions to be sure that the plan is adequately funded or, alternatively, not overfunded.

DEFINED BENEFIT PLAN CONTRIBUTIONS

Annual contributions to a defined benefit pension plan by the employer must meet **minimum funding standards** under IRC Section 412. The purpose of these standards is to ensure that the employer will have provided sufficient funding to pay benefits to participants. In general, a funding standard account must be maintained by the plan to determine the amount of annual contributions required from the employer. Such funding standards apply to all qualified pension plans, including defined benefit, money purchase, and target benefit plans.

ERISA does not allow an employer to fund a pension plan on a pay-as-you-go method (where pension payments are funded only as they become due), nor does it allow a terminal funding method (where the entire value of a retirement annuity is funded immediately at retirement). Instead, only actuarial cost methods (whereby the cost of the projected benefits is funded over the service period of the employee) are required. Minimum funding includes amortization of past service liability as well as current plan costs. In determining the minimum funding standard for any tax year, amortized amounts are credited for investment gains in excess of projected experience and for decreases in pension liabilities. For instance, the funding requirements as applied to a money purchase pension plan are satisfied if the promised contributions are made in each year.

The IRS may temporarily waive the requirement for a particular year in the event of business hardship. The funding requirements are not qualification requirements. However, failure to meet and correct the minimum funding requirements for a defined benefit plan will subject the employer to a special 10% excise tax. The tax for underfunding is generally limited to the year of actual underfunding. The employer is also required to notify participants and beneficiaries that the plan did not meet its required minimum funding standards. If an employer fails to make such notification, the employer is liable for a penalty of up to $100 per day from the date of the failure as well as any other relief the court may order.

The deadline for making funding contributions may be extended for up to one year in the event of a presidentially declared terrorist action. Also, the Treasury may waive interest and penalties for up to one year.

DEFINED BENEFIT PLAN VESTING

In the case of a defined benefit plan, the vested benefit is not one determined at the termination of a participant's employment. Rather, the benefit is defined in terms of payments once reaching normal retirement age under the plan. Accordingly, an employee must usually wait until normal retirement age to receive the present value of her vested benefit. Under a defined contribution plan, a participant's accrued benefit is the participant's account balance. Under a defined benefit plan, however, a participant's accrued benefit is determined by the manner of accrual as specified by the plan.

There are three general classes of vesting:

- those relating to situations calling for full and immediate vesting,

- those relating to the minimum vesting schedules for IRC Section 411(a)(2), and

- those relating to compliance with the IRC Section 401(a)(4) nondiscrimination requirements.

The situations that require full and immediate vesting are the attainment of normal retirement age, employee contributions, and the complete or partial termination of, or discontinuance of contributions to, a plan. The minimum vesting schedules of Section 411(a)(2) include five-year cliff vesting and three- to seven-year graded vesting, as well as three-year cliff vesting and two- to six-year graded vesting for top-heavy plans and those plans that feature employer matching contributions. Finally, even if a plan adopts one of the two statutory vesting schedules, it is possible that a pattern of abuse under the plan may exist (e.g., dismissal of lower-paid employees prior to vesting in their accrued benefits). Therefore, determination of whether a plan actually discriminates in favor of HCEs is based on all the facts and circumstances. If a plan is found to be discriminatory, it is not considered as having met the required vesting schedules.

DEFINED BENEFIT PLAN LIMITS

Since 1975, there has been a limit on the annual benefit that may be payable from the interest of a participant in a qualified defined benefit plan or in a tax-sheltered annuity arrangement (TSA) of the defined benefit variety. This limit is a qualification requirement, meaning that a defined benefit plan may not qualify for the favorable tax treatment unless so provided for in the plan. Finally, not only must the plan language so provide, but if tax qualification is to be maintained, benefits paid must also not exceed the limit in actual practice.

The limit is expressed in terms of the maximum annual payment under a single-life annuity. If a benefit is not paid in the form of a single life annuity, the limitation is converted to the actuarial equivalent of such an annuity. The limit is the *lesser of*:

- 100% of the participant's average compensation for the three consecutive years for which compensation is the highest (compensation limit); or

- a dollar amount indexed for increases in the cost of living (dollar limit)($210,000 in 2015).

If an employee is covered by both a defined benefit plan and a defined contribution plan maintained by the same employer (or related employers), there is a special overall limitation.

NONDISCRIMINATION REQUIREMENTS OF DEFINED BENEFIT PLANS

IRC Section 401(a)(4) requires only that a plan not discriminate in relation to benefits or contributions, but not both. Generally, this requires defined benefit plans to demonstrate that they do not discriminate with benefits. A plan is not considered to be discriminatory merely because its benefits bear a uniform relationship to total employee compensation. That is, just because the highly compensated group members receive a larger absolute amount of benefits does not automatically mean that discrimination exists. Rather, discrimination with respect to benefits is based strictly on the amount provided as a percentage of compensation.

Three safe harbors are available for determining whether benefits from a defined benefit plan are nondiscriminatory. If a plan does not satisfy one of these three safe harbors, it must then pass the general test for nondiscrimination. A plan must satisfy all of the following requirements, however, if it is to take advantage of these safe harbors.

The same benefit formula applies to all employees in the plan:

- Annual benefits provided to all employees are payable in the same form, commencing at the same uniform normal retirement age, and are the same percentage of average annual compensation (computed over at least a three-year period) or the same dollar amount for all employees in the plan who will have the same number of years of service at normal retirement age. Further, the annual benefit must equal the employee's accrued benefit at normal retirement age and must be the normal retirement benefit under the plan.

- Regarding an employee with a given number of years of service at any age after normal retirement age, the annual benefit commencing at the employee's age is the same percentage of average annual compensation or the same dollar amount that would be payable commencing at normal retirement age to an employee who had the same number of years of service at normal retirement age.

- Each subsidized optional form of benefit is available to substantially all employees in the plan.

- The plan must not be a contributory plan (i.e., no employee contributions).

- Each employee benefit must be accrued over the same years of service that are taken into account in applying the benefit formula.

The three safe harbor tests are quite technical and are beyond the scope of this text. As discussed previously, if a defined benefit plan does not satisfy any of the three safe harbors, it must pass the general nondiscrimination test for benefits. This test is met if each rate group under the plan satisfies the minimum coverage requirements of IRC Section 410(b). Again, the details of this test are very technical and beyond the scope of this text.

REPORTING REQUIREMENTS OF DEFINED BENEFIT PLANS

ERISA imposes several reporting and disclosure requirements on defined benefit plan administrators. Because ERISA divides the jurisdiction over employee benefit plans among the IRS, the Department of Labor (DOL), and the Pension Benefit Guaranty Corporation (PBGC), certain reporting requirements are required by all three entities. In addition, ERISA requires that certain disclosures concerning benefits be provided or made available to plan participants and beneficiaries. To reduce duplication of reporting, the IRS, DOL, and PBGC have designed consolidated annual return/report forms. These annual report forms, filed with the IRS, generally satisfy the annual reporting requirements of all three government agencies.

The 5500 series of forms, including information concerning the plan's qualification, operations, and financial condition, must be filed annually with the IRS. Each of the 5500 series is due by the end of the seventh month after the plan year-end (July 31 for calendar-year plans). An automatic extension of 2½ months may be obtained by filing IRS Form 5558 by the normal due date. The DOL may also assess a civil penalty of up to $1,100 per day against the plan administrator for failure or refusal to file an annual report. Form 5500 is used by plans having more than 100 participants. Form 5500-C/R is used by plans with fewer than 100 participants. Form 5500-EZ is filed annually by a one-participant pension benefit plan. Plan administrators must attach to the appropriate form the applicable schedules. Schedule B is for actuarial information while Schedule H is for large plan financial information and

Schedule I is for small plan financial information. Schedule R is required for defined benefit plans otherwise subject to IRC Section 412. Schedule SSA provides details of plan participants who have separated from service with a deferred vested benefit that was neither paid nor forfeited. Large plans must also submit separate audited financial statements.

With regard to reports to the DOL, the Taxpayer Relief Act of 1997 eliminated the requirement that plan administrators automatically file Summary Plan Descriptions (SPDs), separate plan descriptions with certain prescribed information, and summaries of material modifications with the DOL. However, many of these documents must now be furnished to the DOL upon request.

Regarding reports to the PBGC, an annual return for the payment of termination insurance premiums is required for all defined benefit plans subject to PBGC insurance.

TERMINATION OF DEFINED BENEFIT PLANS

The PBGC uses the premiums collected from defined benefit plans to maintain a fund to guarantee certain benefits to participants of pension plans, in the event that the plan's assets are insufficient to pay its promised benefits. As discussed previously, one of the reportable events is the intent to terminate a plan. In the event of a voluntary termination by the plan sponsor, the PBGC determines whether the plan has sufficient assets to pay its guaranteed benefits when they become due. If so, the PBGC gives approval to the termination but remains otherwise uninvolved. On the other hand, if plan assets are insufficient to meet the promised benefits, and the employer request qualifies as a so-called distress termination, the PBGC will step in as the plan trustee and administer the payment of benefits. In this case, however, the sponsor remains liable to the PBGC for any shortfall, up to a statutory limitation.

The PBGC may also force the *involuntary* termination of a plan, although it does not often exercise this power. It may do so in the following situations:

■ The plan has not met the minimum funding requirements of IRC Section 412.

■ The plan is unable to pay benefits when due.

■ The plan has made a distribution of $10,000 or more to a substantial (10%) owner and immediately afterward has unfunded vested liabilities.

■ The possible long-run loss to the PBGC is expected to increase unreasonably if the plan is not terminated.

The PBGC does not guarantee the payment of *all* benefits promised under a plan. Rather, it guarantees only those *basic* pension benefits vested at termination of the plan, up to a maximum amount. The guaranteed benefit is payable in the form of a monthly straight life annuity commencing at age 65. The maximum monthly benefit is limited to the *lesser of*:

■ one-twelfth of the participant's average annual compensation from the employer during his highest five consecutive years; or

■ an otherwise specified limitation ($5,011 for 2015).

The employer is liable to the PBGC for the amount of unfunded guaranteed benefits as of the termination date. If the liability exceeds 30% of the net worth of the employer (and members of the same controlled group), the PBGC provides commercially reasonable terms for the liability in excess of 30% of the employer's net worth. If the employer refuses to pay the amount of its liability, the PBGC may attach a lien on the employer's property.

Normally, a 50% excise tax is imposed on excess plan assets that revert to an employer from a terminating overfunded defined benefit plan, after benefits have all been paid out to participants. Under certain circumstances, if the excess assets are placed in a qualified replacement plan established by the employer, the excise tax is lowered to 20%.

DEFINED BENEFIT PLANS VERSUS DEFINED CONTRIBUTION PLANS

As the reader has learned previously, qualified plans are divided into two major categories—defined contribution and defined benefit plans. The fundamental difference between defined contribution and defined benefit plans is that under defined benefit plans, the employer has the risk and obligation to make sufficient contributions to the plan to insure that the benefits due to the participant/employee are actually paid. Benefits are typically in the form of a monthly retirement pension based on levels of compensation and years of service. Contributions to the plan are actuarially calculated to provide the promised benefits and are not allocated to individual accounts.

Alternatively, under a defined contribution plan, the employee/participants are not entitled to any particular level of benefits, and the amount of benefits received is dependent upon the amount of contributions that the employer and employee make to the individual account of each participant as well as the earnings thereon. Forfeitures that are allocated to each individual account are also included. The employee, not the employer, bears the risk as to the amount of benefits that will be received under a defined contribution plan. Other differences between the two types of plans are that:

- typically, the benefits under defined contribution plans such as a Section 401(k) CODA plan are more portable (i.e., may be moved to other plans if changing jobs) than with defined benefit plans; and

- employees, in many cases, control how contributed funds are invested under defined contribution plans (e.g., a self-directed employee plan), whereas, in defined benefit plans, the investment decisions are made by the qualified plan trustee.

These plan differences, other tax factors, and certain demographic factors, have led to a tremendous *increase* in the percentage of employers offering defined contribution plans. In recent years, many major employers have converted their defined benefit plans to cash balance plans. Most likely, this is due to the fact that the conversions reduce (and, in some cases eliminate for one year or more) future amounts that employers must contribute to the plan. The general impact of the conversion is a reduction in the amount that must be contributed on behalf of *older* workers. This occurs because contributions into cash balance plans are made more evenly over time (therefore, benefiting younger workers), as contrasted to the traditional defined benefit plan where employer contributions increase as a worker nears retirement.

Defined benefit plans result in the deferral of more tax-deductible contributions than a defined contribution plan as the employees age. According to Stephan R. Leimberg and John J. McFadden in their book *Tools & Techniques of Employee Benefit and Retirement Planning*, a defined benefit plan is more advantageous than a defined contribution plan for tax deferring the maximum amount of retirement savings needed, once an employee attains the ages of 45 to 50.

Finally, it is possible for an employee to participate in *both* a defined benefit plan and a defined contribution plan of the same employer. ERISA originally limited the benefits available under both plans to a so-called combined plan formula. However, this limit was repealed effective for plans established after 1999, making it now possible to obtain the maximum benefit payable under both types of plans. Nonetheless, as a practical matter, Tax Code Section 404(a)(7) still imposes an overall 25% of covered payroll limit (or the required funding for the defined benefit plan, if greater) on total annual employer deductions for the two plans.

CASH BALANCE PENSION PLAN DESIGN

While a cash balance pension plan is technically a qualified defined benefit plan, it actually combines the features of a defined benefit plan and a defined contribution plan. As mentioned in the introductory section, traditional defined benefit pension plans define the benefit as a monthly payment in the form of a life annuity. Cash balance pension plans define the benefit in terms of a guaranteed account balance at retirement; however, a participant may take the benefit either as an annuity or a lump-sum distribution.

The plan sponsor creates a hypothetical account for each participant and makes two types of credits to each account at least annually. The first type of credit is referred to as a pay credit, calculated as a certain percentage (as provided in the plan document) of a participant's annual compensation. This credit may or may not be integrated with Social Security benefits.

The other type of credit is an interest credit or employer-guaranteed return on investment adhering to a formula specified in the plan. Typically, this rate is set at a very conservative level so the employer will be able to easily achieve it; however, a participant's account may be credited with a rate exceeding the guaranteed minimum if such a rate is actually achieved. Certain plans tie the guaranteed rate to U.S. government bonds or to a rate specified by the PBGC. If the guaranteed minimum rate is not achieved, the employer then must make up the shortfall.

The crediting of the pay credit and interest credit to a participant's hypothetical account is analogous to the actual allocation of contributions and earnings to a participant's account under a defined contribution plan. That is why the cash balance pension plan is said to combine the features of a defined benefit plan and a defined contribution plan.

PURPOSE, ADVANTAGES, AND DISADVANTAGES OF CASH BALANCE PENSION PLANS

A cash balance pension plan will prove most beneficial to an employer whose workforce is made up mostly of younger workers who have the advantage of many years to accumulate a meaningful amount of retirement savings. Employers with a sizeable workforce consisting primarily of middle-income workers are able to allocate plan administrative costs over a large number of participants. This type of plan is especially advantageous in those cases where employees are apprehensive about the security of their retirement accumulation. Finally, sponsors of traditional defined benefit plans who want to enhance the benefit for younger workers and spend less on older participants' benefits will find conversion to a cash balance plan to be attractive.

As a qualified retirement plan, a cash balance plan offers the advantage of tax-deferred savings and, for plan participants born before January 2, 1936, 10-year income tax averaging for lump-sum plan distributions. From the standpoint of the employee/participant, investment risk is borne by the employer/plan sponsor, and plan benefits (like those of other defined benefit plans) are guaranteed by the Pension Benefit Guaranty Corporation. Plans with 25 or more participants are generally required to pay PBGC premiums. Moreover, cash balance plans are relatively easy to explain to employees, with younger employees tending to favor them over the traditional form of defined benefit plans.

Some of the attributes of cash balance plans include the following:

- Older plan participants generally receive lower benefits than they enjoyed under a traditional defined benefit plan, which, of course, is one of the main reasons to convert to a cash balance plan.

- Cash balance pension plans involve somewhat more administrative burden than defined contribution plans but are not as complex in design and administration as traditional defined benefit plans.

- Because the employer assumes the investment risk in cash balance plans, administrative costs tend to be higher.

- Due to the fact that the employer guarantees a particular balance at retirement, the services of an actuary are required to determine the annual cost.

- Unlike defined contribution plans, there are no actual individual participant accounts, and participants have no voice in the selection of investments.

- Cash balance pension plans, like money purchase pension plans and profit-sharing plans, may accumulate meaningful funds for participants' retirement, but they offer the additional advantage of the employer's guaranteed minimum investment return.

- Cash balance pension plans do not provide guaranteed benefits for participants, but they are much easier to design and administer than traditional defined benefit plans.

- While participant loans are permitted in a cash balance plan, most employers normally do not offer them because of the additional administrative burden caused by the lack of actual individual participant accounts.

INCOME TAX IMPLICATIONS OF CASH BALANCE PENSION PLANS

As a qualified retirement plan, cash balance pension plans offer the normal income tax benefits. Contributions are deductible by the employer as made. Employee/participants receive a deferral of taxation until the funds are withdrawn and may receive a maximum annual benefit of the lesser of $210,000 (in 2015) or 100% of the participant's high three-year average preretirement compensation. In addition, the normal distribution rules apply, with certain premature withdrawals subject to penalties.

Cash balance pension plans also must comply with the minimum funding rules of IRC Section 412. As a defined benefit plan, cash balance pension plans are subject to the mandatory insurance coverage provided by the Pension Benefit Guaranty Corporation (PBGC) and, accordingly, must pay the required premiums to the PBGC. Moreover, cash balance pension plans are subject to additional ERISA reporting and disclosure requirements to participants, including the Summary Plan Description, Summary of Material Modification, Summary Annual Report, and other required notices. Finally, an income tax credit (business tax credit) of up to $500 may be available for the qualified costs of starting up such a plan.

MONEY PURCHASE PENSION PLAN

A qualified pension plan is ordinarily a defined benefit plan because of the fact that the amount of retirement benefits to be paid to the participants is a determined amount, and the contributions to fund such benefits are determined by an actuary. In fact, Regulation 1.401-1(b)(i) states the following:

A pension plan within the meaning of Code Sec. 401(a) is a plan established and maintained by an employer primarily to provide systematically for the payment of definitely determinable benefits to his employees over a period of years, usually for life, after retirement. Retirement benefits generally are measured by, and based on, such factors as years of service and compensation received by the employees. The calculations of the amount of retirement benefits and the contributions to provide such benefits are not dependent upon profits... A plan designed to provide benefits for employees or their beneficiaries to be paid upon retirement or over a period of years after retirement will, for purposes of Code Sec. 401(a), be considered a pension plan if the employer contributions under the plan can be determined actuarially on the basis of definitely determinable benefits, or, as in the case of money purchase pension plans, such contributions are fixed without being geared to profits.

The quoted regulation states that money purchase pension plans are pension plans. They are so classified because their benefits, by virtue of a fixed contribution formula, are actuarially predictable. Money purchase pension plans, which are defined contribution plans, are the *only* exception to the general rule that pension plans are defined benefit plans.

Definition, Purpose, and Pros and Cons

As already discussed, a money purchase pension plan is a defined contribution qualified plan under which the employer is obligated to make definitely determinable annual contributions to the account of each participant in the plan. Unlike a profit-sharing plan, an employer's annual contributions to a money purchase pension plan are fixed, nondiscriminatory, and not based on profits or some other criteria. For example, under a money purchase pension plan, the plan may require that the employer contribute 5% of each participating employee's wages, regardless of whether the employer shows a profit for the year. As a result, money purchase pension plans have the advantage of being easily understood by participants.

There are numerous reasons why an employer may choose to establish a money purchase pension plan. As mentioned, one factor is that such plans are easily grasped by employees (e.g., we will deposit 5% of your compensation in your account each year) and are not difficult to operate. Also, if the employer has a relatively young labor force and wishes to encourage employment longevity, required annual contributions may be made over a substantial period of time so that they accumulate to a meaningful retirement nest egg for each employee. Another reason why an employer may consider creation of a money purchase pension plan is that the investment risk is transferred to the employees rather than being borne by the employer.

A money purchase pension plan offers tax-deductible annual employer contributions of up to 25% of the total covered payroll of the employees covered under the plan and the tax deferral on earnings characteristic of qualified plans. Annual additions to each participant's account are limited to the lesser of

- 100% of the participant's compensation; or

- $53,000 (in 2015), as indexed.

Moreover, participants in a money purchase pension plan may also reap the advantage of favorable investment results in their individual accounts or, alternatively, suffer the ill effects of poor investment choices.

However, participants who enter the plan when they are older will *not* have adequate time for the employer's required annual contributions to accumulate a meaningful retirement fund. The same result will occur where an employer adopts a money purchase pension plan when the key employees are reasonably close to retirement age. The disparity in retirement account balances between employees with many years of service and employees with significantly less years of service may be mitigated somewhat by the size of annual salary increases. Nevertheless, where annual salary increases have been relatively large, this disparity in account balances is smaller, whereas the reverse is true where salary increases have been more conservative.

Due to the limitation on annual additions, HCEs in a money purchase pension plan typically receive a much smaller contribution as a percentage of total compensation than NHCEs. This is the result of the $53,000 cap (in 2015) on individual contributions and the limitation on the amount of compensation that may be taken into account for this purpose ($265,000 in 2015).

Another potentially negative factor in implementing a money purchase pension plan is that a participant's ultimate account balance at retirement is very sensitive to the actual investment return earned on her account. A difference of a few percentage points in the actual investment return may mean a significant difference in the size of one's account balance at retirement.

Finally, an employer adopting a money purchase pension plan is subject to the minimum funding requirements and must make annual contributions to the plan regardless of whether the employer has adequate profits or cash flow. If the employer contributes less than the minimum required amount (the amount specified by the plan's contribution formula) a penalty may be imposed on the amount of the shortfall.

Contributions

Under the law, employer contributions under a money purchase pension plan are a specified percentage of a participant's compensation (up to a maximum of 25%). For example, a plan's formula may call for 10% of the first $100,000 of annual compensation and 15% of earnings in excess of $100,000. Amounts contributed each year may not discriminate in favor of HCEs with only the first $265,000 of compensation of each participant (in 2015) taken into account in determining employer contributions.

An employer may contribute and take advantage of an income tax deduction for up to 25% of the payroll of participants covered by the plan. However, the limitation on annual additions to a participant's account is the lesser of $53,000 (in 2015) or 100% of the participant's annual compensation. Some money purchase pension plans incorporate into their contribution formula a factor for employee service with the employer; this may result in discrimination in favor of HCEs and threaten the overall tax qualification of the plan.

Plans that use uniform allocation formulas for making contributions to participants' accounts may take advantage of various safe harbors to avoid discrimination in actual plan operation. For instance, plans may satisfy the general nondiscrimination test for defined contribution plans, restructure the relevant HCE and NHCE groups, or use cross-testing in plan design (e.g., test defined contribution plans on the basis of benefits rather than contributions) and vice versa for defined benefit plans.

Money purchase pension plans may also be integrated with Social Security benefits. This permits higher rates of employer contributions (within a permitted disparity) for compensation *above* the so-called integration level than for compensation rates *below* that level.

Finally, salary reductions (elective deferrals) are *not* permitted in a money purchase pension plan as they are in a profit-sharing, SARSEP, SIMPLE, or Section 403(b) plan. After-tax employee contributions are permissible but may easily run afoul of the nondiscrimination rules and are, therefore, understandably less popular.

Vesting

As a type of defined contribution plan, a new money purchase pension plan must use an accelerated vesting schedule, typically either a two- to six-year graded schedule or a three-year cliff vesting schedule. Plan forfeitures left by non-vested or only partially vested plan participants terminating employment may be used to reduce future employer contributions or added to the accounts of remaining participants. As with contributions, if forfeitures are added to the accounts of remaining participants, they must also be allocated in a nondiscriminatory fashion and are usually tied to participants' compensation, rather than current account balances.

Distributions

As with any defined contribution plan, benefits payable under a money purchase pension plan are based on a participant's account balance at the time the benefit payments are to begin. A participant's account balance is composed of:

- employer contributions;

- any forfeitures allocated to the participant's account; and

- employee contributions.

Benefits are normally distributed when a participant's employment is terminated or at the participant's normal retirement age (as specified in the plan). The Tax Code requires a qualified pension plan to provide the accrued benefit payable to a participant, who does not die before the annuity starting date, in the form of a qualified joint and survivor annuity (QJSA). If the participant dies before the annuity starting date and has a surviving spouse, a qualified survivor annuity must be provided to the participant's surviving spouse. However, if a participant otherwise has the written consent of his spouse, he may elect a lump sum or some form of installment option.

Unlike profit-sharing plans, money purchase pension plans are generally *not* permitted to make in-service distributions before termination of employment, with an exception being for participants who have attained age 62. The portion of a participant's account balance attributable to employer contributions or earnings on the invested funds may not be distributed until the participant dies, retires, becomes disabled, terminates her employment, or the plan is terminated. Certain early distributions are subject to penalties.

TARGET BENEFIT PENSION PLAN

A target benefit pension plan is similar to a money purchase pension plan because the amount of employer contributions allocated to each participant is determined under a plan formula that does not allow employer discretion. Further, the plan is designed to generate the amount necessary to provide, for each participant, a specific benefit of the type provided by a defined benefit plan (i.e., a monthly pension). In other words, the benefit that the participant actually receives (and that the plan is legally obligated to provide) is based on the participant's account balance, but the objective is for the account balance to provide a specified periodic benefit. Target benefit plans are treated as defined contribution plans.

Definition, Purpose, and Pros and Cons

Although the term is used only once in the Internal Revenue Code, and is not defined in the Code, there are frequent references in IRS regulations and rulings to target benefit pension plans. A target benefit pension is a retirement plan that is a hybrid of a defined benefit pension plan and a money purchase pension plan. Under a target benefit pension plan, a target age-weighted, defined benefit is established, and contributions are determined by actuarial assumptions to fund the target benefit. Subsequently, after the initial plan contribution formula is established, no adjustments are made to that formula. In that respect, the plan is a defined contribution plan. Many of the other features of a target benefit pension plan are similar to those of money purchase pension plans. Consequently, the pros and cons of a target benefit pension plan are very much the same as those of a money purchase pension plan.

Contributions

As discussed previously, a contribution formula adequate to fund the target (but not guaranteed) benefit is determined by actuarial assumptions and, once calculated, is held constant thereafter. As a defined contribution plan, a target benefit pension plan is subject to the same contribution, deduction, and annual additions limitations as a money purchase pension plan.

A target benefit pension plan is required, under the minimum funding requirements, to make annual contributions in the amount specified in the plan formula. Penalties are applicable for failure to make the minimum annual contributions outlined in the plan. Also, like other defined contribution plans, the investment risk in a target benefit pension plan rests with the participant, not with the employer.

Employer contributions are tax deductible when made, as long as the plan continues to be qualified (i.e., as long as it meets the eligibility, vesting, funding, and other requirements). The employee is not taxed on contributions and plan earnings until withdrawn.

Vesting

A target benefit pension plan is subject to the normal vesting requirements imposed on defined contribution plans.

Distributions

As discussed previously, the benefit from a target benefit pension plan is *not* guaranteed, and, unlike the traditional defined benefit pension plan, a participant's ultimate benefit from a target benefit pension plan depends on the plan's investment return. Because the retirement benefit is not guaranteed, a target benefit pension plan is not required by law to use the services of an actuary every year.

SAVINGS/MATCH OR THRIFT PLAN

While popular in the past as a free-standing qualified plan, the savings or thrift plan is now generally employed only as a *supplement to* a Section 401(k) plan. The most common form of savings or thrift plan features after-tax employee contributions and employer-matching contributions.

TRADITIONAL DEFINED BENEFIT PLAN VERSUS CASH BALANCE PENSION PLAN VERSUS DEFINED CONTRIBUTION PLAN

In a traditional defined benefit plan, the contribution is determined on an actuarial basis, whereas with a cash balance pension plan, it is determined as a percentage of compensation, including actuarial aspects (as a result of the employer guarantee feature). A defined contribution plan simply uses a specific percentage of compensation.

In the case of both a traditional defined benefit plan and a cash balance pension plan, the investment risk is borne by the employer, while with a defined contribution plan the investment risk is borne by the employee. Similarly, in the case of a traditional defined benefit plan and a cash balance pension plan, a participant has no voice in the choice of plan investments. In a defined contribution plan, a participant usually has a broader choice of investments and greater participation in choosing those investments.

Social Security benefit integration is available in all three types of plans.

Both traditional defined benefit plans and cash balance plans are subject to PBGC coverage and premiums, while defined contribution plans are not.

Section 401(k) features are only available in a profit-sharing type of defined contribution plan—not in a traditional defined benefit plan or in a cash balance pension plan.

Only a traditional defined benefit plan is designed to provide an adequate retirement benefit to older participants. Neither the cash balance pension plan nor the defined contribution plans are likely to provide an adequate benefit for such participants.

Finally, administrative costs are typically much higher for traditional defined benefit plans and cash balance pension plans than for defined contribution plans. The exception to this is where the defined contribution plan offers Section 401(k) features or grants employees investment discretion, which in turn, drives up the administrative costs of offering such plans.

Supplemental Reading—Profit-Sharing and Other Defined Contribution Plans

DEFINITION, PURPOSE, AND PROS AND CONS OF PROFIT-SHARING PLANS

Under the Tax Code, a profit-sharing plan is a plan established and maintained by an employer to provide for the participation in his profits by his employees or their beneficiaries. The plan must provide a definite predetermined formula for allocating the contributions made to the plan among the participants and for distributing the funds accumulated under the plan after a fixed number of years, the attainment of a stated age, or upon the prior occurrence of some event such as layoff, illness, disability, retirement, death, or severance of employment. A formula for allocating the contributions among the participants is definite if, for example, it provides for an allocation in proportion to the basic compensation of each participant. A plan (whether or not it contains a definite predetermined formula for determining the profits to be shared with the employees) does not qualify under Section 401(a) if the contributions to the plan are made at such times or in such amounts that the plan in operation discriminates in favor of officers, shareholders, persons whose principal duties consist in supervising the work of other employees, or highly compensated employees.

A profit-sharing plan is a qualified defined contribution plan under which the employer makes contributions on behalf of participating employees using a definite predetermined formula that may, in part, be based on profits but is not required to be based on profits. The main advantage of such a plan is its flexible contributions for employers whose profits vary significantly from year to year. The benefits receivable by the participants (or beneficiaries) depend on the amounts contributed (in a nondiscriminatory manner), any earnings on the contributed amounts, and forfeitures allocated to the participants' individual accounts. Normally, a participant's account balance is distributed as a lump sum under the plan when the employee terminates her employment.

A profit-sharing plan not only provides flexibility in annual contributions but may also function as an incentive for employees to increase both employer profits and, ultimately, their own account balances. Such plans are best suited to an employer whose employees are relatively young and, therefore, tend to earn less, have many years before retirement to accumulate a retirement fund, and have a long time horizon over which they can afford to take increased investment risk. A profit-sharing plan sometimes works well in tandem with a defined benefit plan to balance out the overall investment risk to which participants are subject.

In addition to contribution flexibility (even when there are no current or accumulated profits), a profit-sharing plan offers ease and lower cost of design and administration as compared to defined benefit and some other types of plans. On the other hand, older participants entering such a plan may not accrue meaningful benefits before retirement, particularly in light of the employer's ability to reduce or eliminate contributions (within limits). In fact, *all* participants in such plans are *not guaranteed* any particular benefit. Moreover, the accounts of highly compensated employees, such as owners or key employees, are allocated contributions that represent a relatively smaller proportion of their compensation than those allocated to lower-paid employees. Participants bear the investment risk in such plans.

PROFIT-SHARING PLAN CONTRIBUTIONS

As a defined contribution plan, a profit-sharing plan may allow annual contributions, called the *annual additions limit*, (employer contributions, employee contributions, and forfeitures) to a plan participant's account that do not exceed the *lesser of*:

- $53,000 (for 2015); or

- 100% of the participant's compensation (not exceeding $265,000, for 2015).

As a result, an employee earning $53,000 could conceivably receive a contribution to his account of that same amount. However, it is doubtful that an employer would contribute 100% of an employee's salary to a qualified retirement plan. On the other hand, the contribution for an employee earning $300,000 cannot exceed the annual additions limit of $53,000 (2015), which is only 17.7% of his compensation. Highly compensated employees, therefore, may receive a greater allocation through the use of either integration with Social Security benefits (as discussed in Unit 1) or an age-weighted or cross-tested benefit formula (discussed later in this section).

There are two general types of employer contribution provisions under a profit-sharing plan—discretionary or formula. A *discretionary* provision permits an employer to contribute annually, if the employer so elects, any amount up to the maximum deductible limit. An employer may elect to make no contribution in a particular year, as long as it meets the somewhat vague "recurring and substantial" requirements of the Treasury Regulation. However, if too many plan year contributions are missed, the plan will be treated by the IRS as terminated, causing all nonvested amounts in participants' accounts to become immediately 100% vested.

A *formula* provision requires the employer to legally make a specific contribution to the extent of profits earned. Formula provisions may be drafted to permit the omission of a contribution in certain specified financial hardship situations.

After adopting either a discretionary or formula provision to determine the total amount of employer contributions to a profit-sharing plan, a formula must be in place to determine how to allocate contributions to individual employee accounts. As discussed previously, such allocations must *not* discriminate in favor of highly compensated employees. Typically, such participant allocation formulas use a participant's compensation as a percentage of the compensation of all participants multiplied by the total employer contribution for the year. An equitable method of defining what is meant by compensation is necessary so that the formula does not discriminate in favor of highly compensated employees. As discussed earlier, under qualified plan law, a participant's compensation that may be taken into account in the compensation formula is limited to $265,000 in 2015.

A profit-sharing allocation formula that also factors in a participant's years of service has to meet one of the various safe harbors or use cross-testing (testing defined contribution plans on the basis of benefits, discussed later in this section).

As long as a profit-sharing plan continues to meet the tax qualification requirements discussed in Unit 1, employer contributions are tax deductible as made, up to 25% of the total covered compensation of covered employees. Contributions in excess of this limit are normally subject to a 10% penalty. As discussed previously, only the first $265,000 (in 2015) of each participant's compensation may be taken into account in determining this limit.

Plan participants are not taxed until their account balances are withdrawn. Participants born before 1936 may qualify for special 10-year averaging for lump-sum distributions. Employers establishing a profit-sharing plan may also qualify for a business tax credit of up to $500 for qualified startup costs.

Finally, plan participants may be able to direct the investment of their account balances through a limited number of investment options that, if meeting Department of Labor (DOL) requirements (e.g., minimum of three diversified investment choices), usually relieve the plan trustee of any fiduciary responsibility for account losses resulting from participant-selected investments.

PROFIT-SHARING PLAN VESTING

As a type of defined contribution plan, a new profit-sharing plan must use an accelerated vesting schedule, typically either a two- to six-year graded schedule or a three-year cliff vesting schedule. Nonvested balances left by employees separating from the employer's service (i.e., forfeitures) are typically added to the account balances of remaining participants, but this must be done in a nondiscriminatory manner, typically by allocating forfeitures on the basis of compensation rather than on existing account balances.

PROFIT-SHARING PLAN DISTRIBUTIONS

Typically, a participant in a profit-sharing plan receives either a lump sum or installment payments (subject to the minimum distribution rules) of his account balance, either at termination of his employment or at the normal retirement age specified in the plan.

Profit-sharing plans frequently offer the benefit of in-service distributions (i.e., benefits payable prior to termination of employment). Such distributions may be limited to so-called hardship circumstances, such as medical emergencies, home repair, or educational expenses, with the amount further limited only to a participant's vested account balance. The IRS generally requires employer contributions to be in the plan for at least two years prior to making in-service distributions. Some plans penalize participants for taking in-service distributions by temporarily suspending them from the plan, but such penalties cannot affect a participant's vested benefits under the plan.

As with other qualified plans, there is a 10% early distribution penalty for certain distributions made to participants prior to attainment of age 59½. This penalty may be avoided through the use of a plan loan provision.

AGE-WEIGHTED PROFIT-SHARING PLANS

In many cases, an employer sponsoring a profit-sharing plan would like to allocate a greater percentage of contributions to older owners and other key employees. Using only the normal compensation-based allocation formulas, this may not be possible. An age-weighted profit-sharing plan, however, takes into account the participants' ages in addition to their compensation. Thus, allocations of contributions to *older* employees may be maximized, while allocations to younger employees are minimized. Consider the following example.

EXAMPLE Raybon Company's profit-sharing plan covers the highly compensated, older owner and four nonhighly compensated, younger employees. Contributions to the plan are set at 10% of total compensation per year. The employee profile is as follows.

Name	Age	Compensation	Contribution
DR	50	$150,000	$15,000
A	40	40,000	4,000
B	35	40,000	4,000
C	30	40,000	4,000
D	30	30,000	3,000
Totals		$300,000	$30,000

Under an age-weighted plan, each participant's compensation is weighted by an age factor. A simple method of calculating age-weighted compensation is to discount each participant's compensation from the normal retirement age under the plan to her current age at an allowable interest rate (typically a rate between 7.5% and 8.5%). Using a normal retirement age of 65 and a discount rate of 8.5%, the age-weighted compensation levels and contribution levels in the previous example areas follows.

Name	Age	Compensation	Contribution
DR	50	$44,121	$23,298
A	40	5,204	2,748
B	35	3,461	1,828
C	30	2,302	1,215
D	30	1,726	911
Totals		$56,814	$30,000

The contributions are allocated proportionately but based on the age-weighted compensation levels. In this example, the owner (DR) is allocated nearly 78% of the total allocation under age weighting, compared to 50% under the traditional profit-sharing allocation. While the uniform age-weighted formula in this plan is nondiscriminatory, the allocation rate for the highly compensated owner exceeds the average allocation rate for the nonhighly compensated employees by a considerable amount. In fact, if contributions were to be tested (discussed later in this reading), the plan would not meet the nondiscrimination requirements, but if the contributions were to be converted to equivalent benefits, the plan would meet the cross-testing provisions (discussed later in this reading). Of course, this outcome is the direct result of this particular employee profile (older highly compensated owner and younger nonhighly compensated employees).

When using an age-weighted profit-sharing formula to allocate contributions, it may be necessary to adjust participants' accounts to reflect the various limits applicable to qualified plans. For instance, if any participant's allocation exceeds the annual additions limitation such excess must be reallocated to other employees in a nondiscriminatory manner. As age-weighted profit-sharing plans are used primarily by smaller employers, such plans often run afoul of the top-heavy rules. In fact, the plan in the previous example would be treated as top heavy. While the minimum contribution of 3% of salary was met, the plan would, nevertheless, have to comply with the remaining restrictions of top-heavy plans.

CROSS-TESTED PROFIT-SHARING PLANS

Probably the most popular age-weighted profit-sharing plan is a cross-tested plan, sometimes referred to as a **new comparability plan**. This type of plan makes it easier to satisfy the nondiscrimination requirement applying generally to all types of qualified plans. Cross-testing permits a defined contribution plan to be tested on a benefits basis (known as an equivalent accrual) under the general nondiscrimination test for defined benefit plans. These tests are discussed later in this reading. Age-weighted profit-sharing plans and new comparability plans (also usually profit-sharing plans) are the most common types of plans that rely on cross-testing.

A defined contribution plan is nondiscriminatory with respect to benefits for a plan year if the plan's equivalent accrual rates were substituted for each employee's allocation (contribution) rate and the plan either:

- provides broadly available allocation rates;

- uses certain age-based allocation rates; or

- satisfies a minimum allocation gateway.

A plan is said to provide broadly available allocation rates if each allocation rate under the plan is currently available to a nondiscriminatory group of employees. Plans that use gradual age or service schedules, or provide allocation rates based on a uniform target benefit allocation, also meet the conditions for cross-testing. If the plan does not meet the first two conditions, it must satisfy a minimum allocation gateway. This gateway test requires the allocation rate for each nonhighly compensated employee (NHCE) be at least the lesser of one-third of the allocation rate of the highly compensated employee (HCE) with the highest allocation rate or 5% of the NHCE's compensation.

New comparability plans also have built-in disparities between the allocation rates for HCEs and the allocation rates for NHCEs. In the typical new comparability plan, HCEs (typically older) receive high allocation rates, while NHCEs, regardless of their age or years of service, receive comparatively low allocation rates. For example, HCEs in such a plan might receive allocations of 20% of compensation, while NHCEs receive allocations of 3% of compensation. Therefore, the manner whereby these plans demonstrate compliance with the nondiscrimination rules is by comparing the actuarially projected value of the employer contributions for the younger NHCEs with the actuarial projections of the HCEs. As a result, these plans are generally able to provide higher rates of employer contributions to HCEs, while NHCEs are not allowed to earn the higher allocation rates as they work additional years for the employer or grow older.

TESTING FOR DISCRIMINATION IN DEFINED CONTRIBUTION PLANS

Generally, defined contribution plans demonstrate nondiscrimination with respect to contributions. However, as we discussed in the previous section, any plan may be tested for nondiscrimination on the basis of contributions or benefits without regard to whether it is a defined benefit or a defined contribution plan (i.e., cross-testing).

For defined contribution plans, there are two safe harbor tests that are available in determining whether contributions under a plan are nondiscriminatory. If a plan does not satisfy one of these two safe harbors, it must satisfy a general test for nondiscrimination.

If a plan has a uniform allocation formula, it automatically satisfies the first safe harbor. Such a plan allocates all contributions and forfeitures under a formula that allocates the same percentage of plan year compensation, the same dollar amount, or the same dollar amount for each uniform unit of service (not to exceed one week) performed by a participant during the plan year. A plan that meets the Social Security integration rules does not fail to have a uniform formula because of the differences in employees' allocations attributable to uniform disparities permitted under the integration rules.

The second safe harbor is a uniform points plan under which each employee's allocation for the plan year equals the product determined by multiplying all amounts allocated to all employees in the plan for the plan year by a fraction, the numerator of which is the employee's points for the plan year and the denominator of which is the sum of the points of all employees in the plan for the plan year. An employee's points equal the sum of the employee's points for age, service, and units of compensation for the plan year. Each employee must receive the same number of points for age, service, and unit of compensation. The plan must also grant points for either age or service. A unit of compensation is not required to be used, but if it is, it must be a single dollar amount not in excess of $200. In addition, the average of the allocation rates for HCEs in the plan may not exceed the average of the allocation rates for the NHCEs in the plan.

If neither of these two safe harbor tests is met, contributions will still be considered nondiscriminatory if they satisfy the general test for contributions. This general test is met if each rate group under the plan satisfies the minimum coverage requirements. A rate group exists for each HCE in the plan and consists of that HCE and all other employees in the plan who have an allocation rate greater than or equal to the HCE's allocation rate. Accordingly, an employee is in the rate group for each HCE in the plan who has an allocation rate less than or equal to that employee's allocation rate. The allocation rate of an employee under this test is the sum of the allocations to the employee's account for the plan year, expressed either as a percentage of compensation or as a dollar amount. Amounts taken into consideration for this purpose include employer contributions and forfeitures but exclude income, expenses, gains, and losses attributable to the employee's account. An employer may group employees' allocation rates within a range of no more than 5% above and below a midpoint rate chosen by the employer. If allocation rates are determined as a percentage of compensation, such rates may be grouped within a range of no more than a quarter of a percentage point.

E X A M P L E Employer XYZ has only seven employees, all of whom benefit under Plan S. The HCEs are H1 and H2, and the NHCEs are N1 through N5. For the plan year, H1 and N1 through N3 have allocation rates of 5.0% of plan year compensation. For the same plan year, H2, N4, and N5 have allocation rates of 7.5% of plan year compensation.

Given this employee profile, there are two rate groups in Plan S. Rate group 1 consists of H1 and all those employees who have an allocation rate greater than or equal to H1's allocation rate (5.0%). Thus, rate group 1 consists of H1, H2, and N1 through N5. Rate group 2 consists of H2, and all those employees who have an allocation rate greater than or equal to H2's allocation rate (7.5%). Thus, rate group 2 consists of H2, N4, and N5. Rate group 1 satisfies the ratio percentage test because the ratio percentage of the rate group is 100% (the percentage of all NHCEs who are in the rate group). Rate group 2 also satisfies the ratio percentage test because the ratio percentage of the rate group is 80% [40% (the percentage of all NHCEs who are in the rate group) divided by 50% (the percentage of all HCEs who are in the rate group)].

PROFIT-SHARING PLANS VERSUS OTHER PLANS

Another type of defined contribution plan that is similar to a profit-sharing plan is a money purchase pension plan. While both plans offer a contribution and tax deduction of up to 25% of each participant's covered compensation, a money purchase pension plan involves *compulsory* (rather than flexible) annual plan contributions.

An age-weighted profit-sharing plan has some of the attributes of a defined benefit plan. The age-weighted plan permits the employer to base contribution percentages on the employee's age at the time of plan entry, thereby favoring older owners, HCEs, or key employees. Regular defined benefit plans provide a more secure retirement benefit and allow the employer to make greater contributions for older participants but suffer from increased complexity and cost of design and administration.

While nonqualified deferred compensation plans allow the employer to discriminate in favor of HCEs or key employees, they do not provide a current tax deduction for contributions, as do profit-sharing plans.

Finally, the use of individual retirement savings plans, such as IRAs, is at best only a supplement to an employer plan and permits only very limited, if any, tax deductions for contributions.

STOCK BONUS PLANS

In this section, we will discuss the general attributes of a stock bonus plan. In the next section, we will discuss a specific type of stock bonus plan known as an employee stock ownership plan (or ESOP).

Definition, Purpose, and Pros and Cons

Stock bonus plans are defined contribution qualified plans that are similar to profit-sharing plans. The primary difference between stock bonus plans and profit-sharing plans is that the benefits from a stock bonus plan are payable in the form of the employer's *stock*, rather than in cash. A stock bonus plan is "a plan established and maintained by an employer to provide benefits similar to those of a profit-sharing plan, except that the contributions by the employer are not necessarily dependent upon profits and the benefits are distributable in stock of the employer company. For the purpose of allocating and distributing the stock of the employer which is to be shared among his employees or their beneficiaries, such a plan is subject to the same requirements as a profit-sharing plan."

A stock bonus plan:

■ provides a tax incentive for an employer to make its stock available to employees;

■ creates an additional market for the employer's stock;

■ permits an employer to expand the ownership of its stock (perhaps, for example, to help defend against a hostile takeover);

■ offers an incentive for employees to act in a manner that will increase the value of the employer's stock;

■ allows an employee to defer taxation on the unrealized appreciation of stock held in the plan until the stock is eventually sold (known as the net unrealized appreciation tax rule); and

■ permits an employer tax deduction for either cash or stock contributions to the plan.

Cash contributed by the employer is used by the plan to purchase stock.

However, to achieve these benefits, a stock bonus plan must meet *all* of the qualified plan requirements such as coverage, vesting, funding, reporting, and disclosure, among other requirements. Moreover, an employer must be willing to endure some dilution of its stock value. From the standpoint of the employees, investing a large portion of one's retirement funds in employer stock involves, at best, a large amount of unsystematic investment risk.

Plan Contributions

Annual contributions to a stock bonus plan are normally made in shares of the employer's stock, rather than cash. The ability to make cashless contributions helps a business manage cash flow while operating a qualified plan for its employees.

Most plans allocate plan contributions to participants based on employee compensation in a nondiscriminatory fashion. Only the first $265,000 (2015) of compensation may be taken into account in the plan's allocation formula. Employer contributions are deductible when made, up to 25% of covered employees' covered payroll. Stock bonus plans are subject to the normal defined contribution plan annual additions limit—the lesser of 100% of a participant's compensation or $53,000 (in 2015).

Moreover, as with any qualified plan, participants are not taxed on employer contributions at the time they are made, and certain employers adopting a stock bonus plan may qualify for a business tax credit of up to $500 for qualified startup costs.

Voting Rights

Shares held in plan participants' accounts are subject to specific voting rights. Closely held employer company shares (those not publicly traded on an established securities market) comprising more than 10% of the plan's assets carry with them specific voting rights for the plan participants, including the right to approve or disapprove any proposed corporate merger or consolidation, acquisition, recapitalization, reclassification, liquidation, or dissolution or the sale of substantially all employer assets and other similar transactions as specified in IRS regulations. When the stock is publicly traded, voting rights extend to all issues.

Distributions

A distribution of employer stock or securities is not treated like other qualified plan distributions. If employer stock is distributed as a lump sum, the employee is *not* taxed at the time of the distribution on the appreciation in value of the stock that has occurred since it was contributed to the qualified plan by the employer. Further, this unrealized appreciation on the stock is taxed only as a capital gain when the employee actually sells or exchanges the stock. For example, if an employer contributes employer stock worth $1,000 to a participant's account that grows to $5,000 at the time of the employee's retirement, and if the participant receives the stock in a lump-sum distribution, she will pay tax only on the $1,000 at that time. Taxation of the $4,000 of unrealized appreciation at capital gains rates is *deferred* until the participant sells the stock, unless the participant elects to pay the tax currently. However, if the stock is distributed to the employee in a non-lump-sum (periodic) distribution, only the portion of the unrealized appreciation that is attributable to the portion of the stock that was paid for by the employee may be excluded. All of this is what is referred to as the net unrealized appreciation tax rule.

In addition, a participant has the right to insist that distributions from a stock bonus plan be made in employer stock. If such stock is not publicly traded on an established securities market, a participant may exercise what is known as a put option to require the employer to repurchase the stock at a price determined by an independent appraiser.

EMPLOYEE STOCK OWNERSHIP PLANS (ESOPS)

An ESOP is a special type of stock bonus plan or combined stock bonus and money purchase pension plan qualified under Code Section 401(a) that is designed to invest primarily in qualifying employer securities. Congress has encouraged the growth of ESOPs through favorable legislation designed to broaden ownership of corporate stock, provide a source of funds for capital formation through tax-favored leveraging techniques, and improve the economic performance of sponsoring corporations. Even an S corporation may now sponsor an ESOP, although under somewhat different rules than those applicable to a regular C corporation.

Definition, Purpose, and Pros and Cons

In addition to complying with the general requirements imposed on defined contribution plans, ESOPs must also comply with requirements concerning voting rights, diversification, and account allocation restrictions, discussed later in this reading. An ESOP must meet all the requirements relating to qualified stock bonus plans and, if applicable, money purchase pension plans. These include the participation, vesting, and nondiscrimination rules. The plan document must also formally designate the plan as an ESOP and specifically state that it is designed to invest primarily (or exclusively, if so stated) in qualifying employer securities. While a stock bonus plan generally may be integrated with Social Security benefits, an ESOP created after November 1, 1977, is *not* allowed to integrate with Social Security benefits.

Qualifying employer securities are defined under Code Section 409(1) as common stock issued by the employer (or by a corporation that is a member of the same controlled group of corporations) that is readily tradable on an established securities market. If there is no common stock that meets this definition, then *employer securities* means employer common stock that has a combination of voting power and dividend rights at least equal to those classes of common stock having the greatest voting power and the greatest dividend rights. Employer securities also include noncallable preferred stock convertible at any time into qualifying common stock.

Because an ESOP is a qualified plan under IRC Section 401(a), employees defer recognition of income at least until the stock is actually distributed to them. The employer is able to fund the plan with contributions of stock, thereby avoiding any drain on cash flows. In addition to deducting up to 25% of covered compensation for contributions to the plan, the company may be able to deduct amounts above the normal qualified plan limits if special leveraging techniques are used (*see* Leveraged ESOPs).

Use of ESOPs for Closely Held Buyouts

ESOPs are often used to purchase the stock of a retiring owner in a closely held corporation. IRC Section 1042 permits certain owners to defer recognition of any gain realized upon the sale of company stock to the ESOP. To obtain this special treatment, the retiring owner must use the sale proceeds to purchase replacement securities, meaning stock or securities of another corporation. The tax basis of the company's stock in the hands of the retiring owner carries over to the replacement securities (as does the holding period of the company's stock) with any taxation deferred until the replacement securities are eventually sold, provided the ESOP owns at least 30% of the company's stock after the buyout.

In order for the nonrecognition of gain to apply, however, several rules apply to the employer, the shareholder, the replacement property, and the ESOP. For example, the employer must be a domestic C corporation that has no outstanding stock readily tradable on an established securities market. In addition, the employer must give written consent to be assessed a 10% excise tax if the ESOP disposes of the shares acquired within three years of acquisition.

In the case of the shareholder, she must not have acquired the qualifying employer securities from a qualified plan through the exercise of statutory or nonqualified stock options or from any other plan to which IRC Section 83 (property transferred in connection with the performance of services) applies. The shareholder must also have held the qualifying employer securities for at least three years before selling it to the ESOP. Finally, the shareholder must purchase the qualified replacement property within a 15-month replacement period, which begins three months prior to the sale. To the extent that any sale proceeds are not used to buy qualified replacement property within the requisite period, gain is recognized. The taxpayer or executor must make an election to have IRC Section 1042 apply to the sale of the securities to the ESOP.

The replacement property is any security (including stock, bonds, and so forth) issued by a domestic operating corporation (more than 50% of its assets are used in the active conduct of a trade or business) where the corporation does not have passive investment income in excess of 25% of its gross receipts. Also, the corporation may be privately or publicly held, but it may not be a member of the same controlled group as the one that issued the securities that were sold to the ESOP.

In meeting the 30% ownership requirement immediately after the sale, the ESOP may own 30% of either each class of outstanding stock of the corporation or the total value of all outstanding stock.

Valuation Issues

An extremely important issue is the value that is assigned to qualifying securities of a nonpublicly traded employer. There are several reasons for determining such a value, including the following:

- Determining the amount of a deduction for contributions of securities to the employer's ESOP

- Establishing the sales price for a sale of employer securities to an ESOP (otherwise, if the trustee paid an amount in excess of the fair market value, it is considered to be a prohibited transaction)

- Determining the amount of securities that may be allocated to participants' accounts for purposes of the IRC Section 415 contribution limits

- Establishing values for put options and rights of first refusal

A good-faith estimation of the fair market value (FMV) must be made based on all relevant factors. Such a determination of FMV must be made at least annually and be performed by an independent person who customarily makes such appraisals.

Dividend Deductions

Employers are permitted to *deduct* any cash dividends paid to ESOP participants. However, one of the following conditions must be met:

- the dividends must be paid in cash directly to the participants or their beneficiaries;

- the dividend must be distributed through the ESOP to the participants or their beneficiaries within 90 days after the end of the plan year in which the corporation paid the dividend;

- the dividend must, at the election of the participants or their beneficiaries, be payable as provided in either of the two previous methods, or paid to the plan and reinvested in qualified employer securities; or

- the dividend must be used to make payments on an exempt ESOP loan (for principal or interest), the proceeds of which are used to acquire the employer securities with respect to which the dividends were paid.

The deduction is allowed for the corporation's year in which the dividend is distributed to the participants or used to repay the loan, rather than for the year the corporation paid the dividend. The employer is permitted a deduction, even if participants elect not to receive any dividends. This deduction is in addition to the regular deduction limits allowed for contributions to an ESOP under IRC Section 404 and is not considered to be an annual addition to participants' accounts for purposes of the IRC Section 415 limits.

Dividends distributed to participants are not considered a return of any nondeductible employee contributions but rather are considered to be ordinary income to the recipient. They are not eligible for the reduced tax rates on dividends introduced by Jobs and Growth Tax Relief and Reconciliation Act (JGTRRA) of 2003.

Types of ESOPs

Even though the purpose of an ESOP may not really be to provide for a participant's retirement, the plan, nevertheless, must meet all of the qualification requirements of IRC Section 401(a). An ESOP is a defined contribution plan that must contain a stock bonus plan element. There are basically two types of ESOPs—the nonleveraged ESOP and the leveraged ESOP.

Nonleveraged ESOPs

A nonleveraged ESOP is not designed to borrow money and carries the normal attributes of a stock bonus plan. Inasmuch as an ESOP may invest primarily, or even exclusively, in employer securities, it is exempted from the prudent man or fair return investment requirements. As mentioned previously, the normal deduction limitations (25% of the compensation of participating employees) of stock bonus plans apply to nonleveraged ESOPs.

Leveraged ESOPs (LESOPs)

A leveraged ESOP, or LESOP, is a qualified plan that is specially designed to borrow money under the tax-favored provisions of Regulation 54.4975-7. A LESOP permits the employer to not only provide employee benefits, but also obtain favorable debt financing through the deduction of *both* principal and interest for its contributions to the ESOP to repay the loan.

Generally, the lending and borrowing of money and the guaranteeing of such loans by qualified plans is a prohibited transaction. ESOPs are exempted from this general prohibition by IRC Section 4975. The trust of an ESOP is permitted to secure a loan from a lending institution with the employer guaranteeing to contribute to the ESOP enough money to repay the loan. The ESOP then may use the loan proceeds to purchase newly issued employer stock to provide the employer with working capital or funds for expansion, acquisitions, divestitures of subsidiaries, leveraged buyouts, and for buying out existing owners. The LESOP technique is shown in the following figure.

LESOP

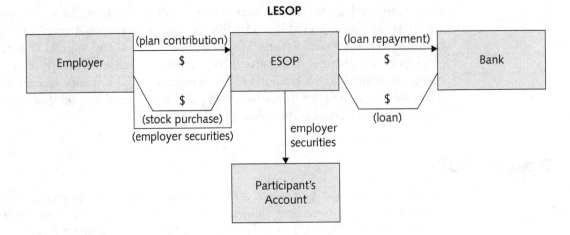

The LESOP must use an exempt loan that meets the requirements set forth in the IRS Regulations. An exempt loan is one that is made to an ESOP by a disqualified person or a loan made to an ESOP guaranteed by a disqualified person. The disqualified person, in this case, is the employer. The loan must be primarily for the benefit of the ESOP participants and their beneficiaries. In addition, the loan must be for a specific term, without recourse against the ESOP, and with only qualifying employer securities, either acquired with the loan proceeds or used as collateral on a prior exempt loan repaid with the proceeds of the current exempt loan, pledged as collateral. Finally, the ESOP's liability for repayment of the loan must be limited to:

- the securities pledged as collateral on the loan;

- any contributions made to the ESOP for loan repayment purposes; and

- any earnings that are attributable to such contributions and collateral.

An ESOP must also use exempt loan proceeds only to:

- acquire qualifying employer securities;

- repay such loan; or

- repay a prior exempt loan.

As the employer makes contributions to the ESOP to repay the loan, the amounts representing interest are fully deductible, with only the amounts representing principal repayment subject to the regular 25% of compensation limitation. Accordingly, the company is able to deduct both principal and interest on the repayment of the loan. These additional deductions for ESOP loan principal and interest are not available for S corporations.

Additional Requirements for ESOPs

As discussed previously, in addition to complying with the general requirements imposed on defined contribution plans, ESOPs must also comply with requirements concerning voting rights, diversification, and account allocation restrictions. IRC Section 401(a)(22) specifies the voting rights applicable to all qualified stock bonus plans, including ESOPs. (See the above Voting Rights section for more information.)

Usually, the fiduciary of a qualified plan is charged with the responsibility of selecting proper investments and properly diversifying the assets of the trust to ensure a reasonable return. Because ESOPs invest primarily in employer securities, they are exempt from these requirements to the extent of their investments in qualifying employer securities. This means that qualifying employer securities held by an ESOP are not required to produce the return that would normally be expected from similar types of qualified plans. Courts have held that fiduciaries may only be liable for failure to diversify the trust investments in a plan that invests *exclusively* in employer stock, if the terms of the plan require a *primary*, but not *exclusive*, investment in employer stock.

An ESOP is required to permit employees who are near retirement age to diversify the investments in their separate accounts. Specifically, an ESOP must give each qualified participant an opportunity to have a portion of his account balance invested in investments other than employer securities each year during his qualified election period. A qualified participant is any employee who is at least age 55 and who has participated in the plan for at least 10 years. The qualified election period is the six-plan-year period beginning with the plan year in which the individual first becomes a qualified participant. During the first 90 days of each of these plan years, a qualified participant must be allowed to elect to diversify up to 25% of his post-1986 stock, reduced by any amounts previously subject to diversification. In the final plan year, 50% of such employer securities are subject to the diversification election.

The diversification requirements may be met in one of three ways under IRC Section 401(a)(28)(B)(ii). First, the ESOP may offer at least three different investment options. Any investment option selected must then be implemented within 90 days after the end of the election period. Second, the ESOP may distribute the amount so elected to the participant within 90 days after the close of the diversification election period, either in cash or in stock (in which case the usual put option rules will apply). This amount is subsequently eligible for a rollover into an IRA or for a transfer to another qualified defined contribution plan that offers at least three investment options. Finally, the plan may permit the participant to direct a transfer of the diversification amount into another qualified plan providing for employee-directed investment and in which the required diversification options are available.

With regard to individual account allocations, the general rules of IRC Section 415(c) for allocating contributions among plan participants apply to ESOPs. Thus, the amount of annual additions to a participant's account is limited to the lesser of $53,000 (in 2015) or 100% of the participant's compensation. As in other qualified plans, annual additions include employer contributions (to all defined contribution plans in which the employee is a participant), forfeitures allocated to the participant's account, and employee contributions. Dividends paid on employer stock to an ESOP that are used to repay an exempt loan are *not* considered annual additions.

Two special provisions apply to ESOPs, both of which can substantially increase the amount of annual additions available to participants. Recall that annual additions include employer contributions, forfeitures allocated to an account, and employee contributions. Under the Tax Code if no more than one-third of the employer contributions for a year are allocated to highly compensated employees (HCEs), then the following items will not be included in annual additions for purposes of applying the general limitations for defined contribution plans under IRC Section 415(c)(1):

- Forfeitures of stock acquired by the ESOP with an exempt loan

- Employer contributions to the ESOP used to pay interest on an exempt loan

Distributions

An ESOP may make distributions either in cash or in stock but must provide participants with the *right* to demand payment in the form of qualifying employer securities. If the employer securities are not readily tradable on an established securities market, the participant must be given the put option, requiring the employer (not the ESOP) to repurchase the securities under a fair valuation formula.

DEFINITION AND PROS AND CONS OF SECTION 401(K) PLANS

A qualified cash or deferred arrangement (CODA) (Section 401(k) plan) is an arrangement within a qualified profit-sharing, stock bonus, pre-ERISA money purchase, rural electric cooperative, Indian tribal government, or tax-exempt organization plan under which a participant may elect either to receive current cash compensation or have the employer contribute an equal amount on a pretax basis to the qualified plan. The arrangement typically contains a salary reduction agreement under which employer contributions are made only if the participant elects to reduce his compensation or not take a pay increase in cash. The agreement may also give the participant the option to receive a portion of the elective amount in cash with the remainder contributed to the qualified plan.

Some of the advantages of such a plan include:

■ employees are empowered to determine how much to save for their retirement;

■ the employer receives an income tax deduction for up to 25% of covered payroll (including elective deferrals or before-tax salary reduction contributions) plus the elective deferrals deposited in the plan;

■ the employer has the option of either relying solely on employee elective deferrals to fund the retirement plan or supplementing this funding by making matching or non-elective contributions; and

■ employees may be able to take in-service so-called hardship withdrawals, discussed later in this reading.

A Section 401(k) plan does carry with it certain disadvantages, such as:

■ the fact that because it is a defined contribution plan, a participant's account balance at retirement will not necessarily provide adequate retirement income;

■ an employee (who may be highly compensated) is limited to a salary reduction of $18,000 (2015), plus another $6,000 (2015) if she is age 50 or older at the end of the plan year;

■ the plan (unless a SIMPLE 401(k) or Safe Harbor 401(k) plan) is subject to the actual deferred percentage (ADP) tests for nondiscrimination (discussed later in this reading), which can be expensive, limiting, and difficult to administer; and

■ the employees bear the investment risk of their account balance.

GENERAL QUALIFICATION REQUIREMENTS

As discussed previously, in order to receive special tax treatment, a Section 401(k) plan must first satisfy the general qualification requirements for profit-sharing and stock bonus plans under IRC Section 401(a). In addition, a Section 401(k) plan must meet special provisions, which relate mainly to nondiscrimination, nonforfeitability, and distribution requirements.

As discussed previously, a Section 401(k) plan must be part of a qualified profit-sharing or stock bonus plan. (Technically, it may also be a part of a rural electric cooperative plan, a plan maintained by Indian tribal governments, a plan maintained by tax-exempt employers, or a pre-ERISA money purchase pension plan.) A Section 401(k) plan cannot be a stand-alone program. Both the Section 401(k) plan and the underlying plan must meet their respective qualification requirements. For example, if the Section 401(k) plan meets the special rules applicable to it but the underlying plan does not qualify under IRC Section 401(a), the entire arrangement is nonqualified for income tax purposes. The underlying plan that contains the Section 401(k) plan may still separately qualify as long as it meets the IRC Section 401(a) requirements, even though the Section 401(k) plan fails to meet the separate requirements. In this latter case, contributions made to the plan on account of elective deferrals are includable in the employee's gross income. However, this may, in turn, cause a qualification problem for the underlying plan due to the restrictions on nondeductible employee contributions (IRC Section 401(m)).

Nondiscrimination Requirements

As with other qualified plans, a Section 401(k) plan must *not* discriminate in favor of highly compensated employees (HCEs) with respect to coverage and benefits or contributions. Specifically, all Section 401(k) plans must satisfy the IRC Section 410(b) general nondiscrimination tests and Section 401(k) plans, other than SIMPLE 401(k) plans or safe harbor plans (discussed later in this reading), also must satisfy the special actual deferred percentage (ADP) tests.

With regard to the coverage or nondiscrimination tests, IRC Section 410(b) requires that a plan must satisfy *one* of the general tests: either a percentage test, a ratio test, or an average benefits test. Because it is likely that a Section 401(k) plan would not satisfy the actual participation requirements due to the lack of contributions by many of the lower-paid employees, a Section 401(k) plan may treat all *eligible* employees, rather than just the *covered* employees, as benefiting under the plan. As a result, the 70% test is met if at least 70% of all employees are *eligible* to participate in the Section 401(k) plan, rather than if they actually do participate.

With regard to the special actual deferral percentage (ADP) tests relating to nondiscrimination as to benefits or contributions, ADPs must be calculated for the group of HCEs and the group of NHCEs. The ADP for each group is computed as the simple average of the employees' deferred percentages. Thus, the first step is to compute, for each employee who is eligible to make elective deferrals under the plan, the actual deferred ratio (ADR) of the amount of elective contributions actually paid over to the trust on his behalf for the plan year to the employee's compensation for the plan year. (Note: any special catch-up contributions and earnings attributable thereto are disregarded when determining ADP ratios for a plan year.) Next, the simple average of these ratios is computed for the group of HCEs and for the group of NHCEs. Any elective deferrals are counted as compensation, except that an employer may elect *not* to include as compensation any amount that is contributed by the employer pursuant to an elective deferral and that is not includable in the gross income of an employee under a cafeteria plan, Section 401(k) plan, tax-sheltered annuity, or SEP. The amount of covered compensation that may be taken into account under any plan is limited to $265,000 (in 2015).

Having performed the calculations called for in the previous paragraph, a Section 401(k) plan must then satisfy, in actual operation, one of two of the following alternative ADP tests:

■ Test 1: The ADP for eligible HCEs for the plan year is not more than the ADP of all other eligible employees *for the preceding plan year* multiplied by 1.25.

■ Test 2: The ADP for eligible HCEs for the plan year does not exceed the ADP for other eligible employees *for the preceding plan year* by more than 2%, *and* the ADP for eligible HCEs for the plan year is not more than the ADP of all other eligible employees *for the preceding plan year* multiplied by two.

Thus, the maximum spreads between the ADPs for the HCEs and the NHCEs are as follows.

EXHIBIT 3.1

Prior Year ADP for the NHCEs	Current Year Maximum ADP for the HCEs
0–2%	2 times that rate
2–8%	2 percentage points more
Above 8%	1.25 times that rate

As just discussed, these tests require a specific comparison of the elective deferrals, expressed as a percentage of compensation, by HCEs and NHCEs. As described in both tests, this comparison is based on *prior* year data in determining the ADP for NHCEs, while *current* year data is used for HCEs. This enables the HCEs to know in advance the overall limit on their combined deferrals. Employers have the option to use current year data for determining the ADP for both HCEs and NHCEs for any plan year, but if an employer decides to change back to the prior-year testing method, such a change is subject to certain restrictions. Also, instead of applying two separate ADP tests, a plan may adopt a single ADP test that compares the ADP of the HCEs with the ADP of the NHCEs who are eligible to participate and who have met the minimum age and service requirements.

Here is an example of the calculation of the ADP for a group of employees.

> **EXAMPLE** Assume an employer maintains a profit-sharing plan with Section 401(k) provisions that permits employees to defer up to 10% of their total compensation, up to a maximum contribution of $18,000 for the 2015 plan year. Information for employees X and Y, who comprise the entire NHCE group, is as follows.
>
> | Employee | Compensation | Deferred Amount | ADR |
> | --- | --- | --- | --- |
> | X | $20,000 | $2,000 | 10% |
> | Y | 10,000 | 0 | 0 |

Thus, the ADP for the group is 5%, the average of 10% and 0%, and not 6.67%, which is the total deferred amount divided by the total compensation.

Once the ADP for each of the two groups of employees has been calculated, a comparison for discrimination is made. The standard method for this comparison is based on the prior-year ADP for NHCEs, while the current year ADP is used for HCEs. In the case of the first plan year, the ADP for the NHCEs is 3%, or at the employer's election, the ADP of the NHCEs for the first plan year.

Following is an example of how to apply these rules.

> **E X A M P L E**   Employees A, B, and C are the eligible employees and earn $30,000, $15,000, and $10,000 a year, respectively. These salary figures are used by the employer in determining contributions up to 10% of compensation to a Section 401(k) plan. Under the arrangement, each eligible employee may elect either to receive, in whole or in part, a direct cash payment of her allocated contribution in the current year or to have the amount contributed by the employer to the plan. For the plan year, A, B, and C make the following elections.
>
> | Employee | Salary | Elected Contribution to Plan | Cash Election | Total Compensation |
> |----------|--------|------------------------------|---------------|--------------------|
> | A | $30,000 | $2,000 | $1,000 | $33,000 |
> | B | 15,000 | 750 | 750 | 16,500 |
> | C | 10,000 | 400 | 600 | 11,000 |

Therefore, the ratios of employer contributions to the trust on behalf of each eligible employee to the employee's compensation for the plan year (calculated separately for each employee) are as follows.

Employee	Ratio of Contribution to Total Compensation	ADR
A	2,000/33,000	6.06%
B	750/16,500	4.55%
C	400/11,000	3.64%

Finally, assume that A owns more than 5% of the employer's stock and is, therefore, an HCE and that B and C are NHCEs. Accordingly, the ADP for the NHCEs group is 4.10% (the average of 4.55% and 3.64%, rounded to the nearest .01%). Thus, in the following plan year, A's maximum deferral is 6.10% of his compensation (i.e., two percentage points more than the ADP of the NHCEs).

"Fail-Safe" Provisions in Regulations

Now that the reader has been exposed to the ADP tests, it is easy to understand why a Section 401(k) plan must be concerned about satisfying these tests year after year in order to maintain its tax qualification. Thus, Section 401(k) plans are subject to the unpredictability of the NHCEs electing to defer a smaller percentage of their compensation in the next year. Although most of this uncertainty has been removed with the change to using the prior year

ADP of the NHCEs in the discrimination test, it still exists for employers who elect to use current-year ADP ratios for the NHCE group. In light of this uncertainty, the regulations provide a "fail-safe" mechanism for employers to be able to exercise more control by making nonelective contributions and/or matching contributions in addition to the employees' elective contributions.

For example, an employer could provide a nonelective contribution on behalf of all employees equal to 5% of salary and an elective contribution of 2% of salary. Thus, even if all of the NHCEs elected to receive the 2% in cash and all of the HCEs elected to have it contributed to the plan, the plan would still meet the ADP tests because it is designed in such a way as to never fail the test. However, the price of being able to combine the employer's nonelective or matching contribution with the employees' elective contribution, for purposes of the ADP test, is that the nonelective or matching portion must comply with the distribution restrictions and full and immediate vesting provisions applicable to elective deferrals.

EXAMPLE Assume that Plan XYZ is a qualified profit-sharing plan that contains a Section 401(k) plan. Plan XYZ elects to compute the ADP for NHCEs based on current year data. Assume that employer contributions on behalf of its nine employees are as follows:

- a qualified nonelective contribution (QNEC) of 2% of each employee's compensation, with such amounts subject to the distribution restrictions of the Tax Code and the full and immediate vesting requirements of Section 401(k) and

- up to 2% of each employee's compensation that an employee may receive in cash or as an elective deferral into the plan.

For the plan year, employees 1 through 9 received compensation and deferred contributions as indicated in the following table.

EXHIBIT 3.2

Employee	Wages	2% Non-Elective Contribution	2% Elective Contribution Deferred	Total Compensation (including non-elective deferrals)	ADR
1	$98,000	$2,000	$2,000	$100,000	2.00%
2	78,400	1,600	1,600	80,000	2.00%
3	58,800	1,200	1,200	60,000	2.00%
4	39,600	800	400	40,400	0.99%
5	27,700	600	300	30,300	0.99%
6	20,000	400	0	20,400	0
7	20,000	400	0	20,400	0
8	10,000	200	0	10,200	0
9	5,000	100	0	5,100	0

Finally, also assume that employees 1 and 2 are the only HCEs. In this case, the 2% elective portion (considered alone) does not satisfy the ADP tests. The ADP for the HCE group is 2.00% (the average ADR for employees 1 and 2), and the ADP for the NHCE group is 0.57%. However, because the 2% QNEC meets the distribution and vesting requirements, it may be considered in computing the ADP for the groups. The ADP for the HCE group, when the nonelective contributions are considered, is 4.00%, and for the NHCE group, the ADP is 2.54%. Although the plan does not meet the 1.25 ADP test, it does meet the second test [that is, 4.00% is less than 5.08% (2.54% × 2) and less than 4.54% (2.54% + 2.0%)].

Other rules in this area are extremely complex and beyond the scope of this text.

TYPES OF SECTION 401(K) PLANS

Salary Reduction-Type Plans

Under the most common type of Section 401(k) plan, the salary reduction type, the employee elects to reduce his normal compensation for the coming year or elects to forgo an increase in his current compensation and have the amount instead contributed to the plan. Salary reductions must be elected by employees *before* the compensation is earned. For example, an employee may elect to have his salary reduced by 4% effective January 1 of the next year. Typically, an employee completes a salary reduction election form before the end of each calendar year effective for the next calendar year. Any amount that an employee elects to have contributed to the plan is not subject to federal income tax for the period in which it was earned (assuming the plan meets the special qualification requirements, described earlier). Consequently, if an employee elects to reduce his compensation by $100 per month, his net pay does not decline by the full $100 because the income tax applicable to this amount is no longer withheld from the employee's pay. These elective deferrals are, however, subject to FICA and FUTA taxes for the period in which they were earned.

Bonus-Type Plans

Under the bonus form of a Section 401(k) plan, an employee may elect to have the employer contribute to the plan all or any portion of an amount in excess of her normal compensation (e.g., a year-end bonus). If the employee does not so elect, the applicable amount may be paid to the employee in cash. For example, a Section 401(k) plan may permit participants to elect to allocate, in any proportion they see fit, 5% of their compensation (in the form of a bonus) between current cash or a contribution to the plan.

A bonus-type plan may not be particularly beneficial to lower-paid employees who may be hard-pressed to defer any portion of their compensation, even in light of the income tax benefits and the possibility of an employer-matching contribution. Other employees may perceive a holiday bonus as an amount intended by the employer to help them pay their holiday bills and, therefore, should be taken as cash compensation.

SIMPLE 401(k)

A savings incentive match plan for employees (SIMPLE) may be either in the form of an IRA arrangement or adopted as part of a Section 401(k) plan. A SIMPLE 401(k) is available *only* to employers that:

- employed 100 or fewer employees who earned $5,000 or more during the preceding year; and

- do not maintain another qualified plan covering the employees who are eligible to participate in the SIMPLE 401(k).

Special rules apply to SIMPLE 401(k)s. First, SIMPLE 401(k)s are *not* subject to the top-heavy rules. Second, eligibility for participation applies to all employees who have received at least $5,000 in compensation from the employer during any two preceding calendar years and who are reasonably expected to receive at least that amount during the current calendar year. Third, the plan does not have to satisfy the special ADP and actual contribution percentage (ACP) tests (for contributory plans) otherwise applicable to plans containing CODAs and matching contributions. Instead, those special tests are deemed met under the following conditions:

- Each eligible employee may elect to make salary reduction contributions for a year of up to $12,500 (in 2015).

- The employer makes a matching contribution equal to the employee's salary reduction contribution, limited to 3% of the employee's compensation for the year, or alternatively, makes a nonelective contribution for all eligible employees equal to 2% of the employee's compensation for the year.

- No other contributions are made under the SIMPLE 401(k) arrangement, nor are any contributions or benefit accruals under any other qualified plan of the employer covering the employees eligible to participate in the SIMPLE 401(k).

- All amounts contributed under the SIMPLE 401(k) provisions are nonforfeitable (i.e., fully vested) at all times.

A SIMPLE 401(k) must use a calendar year as its plan year. Existing Section 401(k)s not currently on a calendar plan year that want to adopt the SIMPLE provisions must convert their plan year to a calendar year.

Finally, a SIMPLE 401(k) must also permit each eligible employee to make or modify an elective deferral during the 60-day period immediately preceding each January 1. The employer must notify each eligible employee of the employee's right to make this election within a reasonable time period before the applicable election period. The plan must also allow a SIMPLE 401(k) participant to terminate an elective deferral at any time during the year.

Traditional Section 401(k) Plans Versus SIMPLE 401(k)s

One of the drawbacks of the SIMPLE 401(k) is that annual employer contributions are *required*, whether the employer matches employee deferrals (up to 3% of compensation) or makes the 2% nonelective contribution (QNEC). As discussed previously, annual employer contributions are discretionary under a traditional Section 401(k) plan, except for years in which the plan is top heavy or years in which one of the safe harbor provisions is used to ensure the ADP test is met.

In addition, SIMPLEs could potentially have broader coverage because each employee who earns more than $5,000 is permitted to make an elective deferral that must be matched by the employer. If the alternative 2% nonelective contribution is made, an employer contribution is required for all eligible employees. Conversely, the traditional Section 401(k) plan requires only 70% coverage for eligibility, not participation.

The annual limit on elective deferrals under a traditional Section 401(k) plan is higher than the SIMPLE 401(k) ($18,000 versus $12,500 in 2015). However, the level of deferral for HCEs under a traditional plan is directly limited by the ADP of the NHCEs. No such limit applies to SIMPLEs.

All employer-matching or nonelective contributions under a SIMPLE are immediately (100%) vested. Employer contributions under a traditional plan are subject to the normal vesting rules, unless the employer contributions are made in accordance with the fail-safe provisions discussed earlier. In either case, employee elective deferrals are nonforfeitable at all times.

Finally, employers adopting a SIMPLE 401(k) cannot make contributions other than those allowed under the SIMPLE provisions. Moreover, the employer cannot maintain any other qualified plan under which additional contributions or benefit accruals may be made. In addition, an employer who adopts a SIMPLE 401(k) must determine in advance of each calendar year whether it will match employee contributions or make the nonelective contribution (due to the 60-day notice requirement).

Safe Harbor Section 401(k) Plans

The Internal Revenue Code provides a safe harbor provision under which a traditional Section 401(k) plan may *automatically* satisfy the nondiscrimination rules. The safe harbor option requires an employer contribution that is either a matching contribution or a nonelective contribution. Similar to the fail-safe provision, employer matching and nonelective contributions used to satisfy the safe harbor rules must be nonforfeitable and subject to the distribution restrictions that apply to employee elective deferrals.

Under the matching contribution safe harbor, the employer matches each NHCE's elective contribution in an amount equal to:

- 100% of the employee's elective contribution, up to 3% of the employee's compensation; and

- 50% of the employee's elective contribution on the next 2% of the employee's compensation.

The match rate for HCEs may not be greater than the match rate for NHCEs at any level of compensation. As an alternative, the matching safe harbor is considered to be met if the employer's match rate does not increase as an employee's elective contribution increases, and the match amount equals at least the amount that would be made under the matching levels listed previously.

Using the nonelective contribution safe harbor, the plan must require the employer to make a contribution, on behalf of each eligible NHCE, of an amount equal to at least 3% of the employee's compensation, without regard to any employee contribution.

Finally, a plan that intends to satisfy the safe harbor requirements for a plan year must, prior to the beginning of the plan year, contain language to that effect and must specify which safe harbor will be used. However, a plan is permitted to be amended, not later than 30 days before plan year-end, to use the safe harbor rules for that plan year. So, if it appears that a plan will not meet the ADP and ACP tests, an employer may adopt the safe harbor 3% employer nonelective contribution for the year as late as December 1 of that year. Moreover, a plan may also be amended during the plan year to forego the matching contribution safe harbor if it otherwise expects to meet the ADP and ACP tests.

Under either safe harbor contribution provision, each eligible employee must be given written or electronic notice of her rights and obligations under the plan within a reasonable period of time before the plan year or, for the year in which an employee becomes eligible, within a reasonable period of time before the employee becomes eligible.

Roth 401(k) Plans

Section 401(k) plans may incorporate a qualified Roth contribution program. Under such a plan, participants may elect to have all or a portion of their elective deferrals treated as Roth contributions. Unlike regular Section 401(k) elective deferrals, Roth contributions are included in the participant's current income; however, qualified distributions from a designated Roth account are *not* included in income.

Under a qualified Roth contribution program, participants are permitted to make designated Roth contributions in lieu of all or part of elective deferrals that they are otherwise allowed to make under the Section 401(k) plan. These Roth elective deferrals are subject to the same immediate vesting requirements and distribution restrictions normally imposed on regular Section 401(k) elective deferrals.

Because qualified distributions are not included in an employee's income, the plan must establish and maintain a separate designated Roth account for designated Roth contributions and attributed earnings for each employee. Failure to maintain this separate account and recordkeeping disqualifies the program.

Because they are part of a participant's eligible Section 401(k) elective deferrals, Roth contributions are subject to the same Section 401(k) contribution limits. Accordingly, Roth contributions are subject to the annual limit on elective deferrals, reduced by the amount of other elective deferrals under the Section 401(k) plan, as well as the ADP limits.

Qualified distributions from a designated Roth account are not included in a participant's income. A qualified distribution from a designated Roth account is equivalent to one made from a Roth IRA account. The distribution must be made after a five-year holding period and:

- made on or after the date on which the participant attains age 59½;

- made to a beneficiary (or to the participant's estate) on or after the death of the participant; or

- attributable to the participant being disabled.

The five-year holding period is the five-year period beginning with the earlier of the first tax year in which the participant makes a designated Roth contribution to any designated Roth account under the employer plan or, if the participant has made a rollover contribution to the designated Roth account from another plan, the first year in which the participant made a designated Roth contribution to that previous plan.

Qualified distributions from a designated Roth account may be rolled over to either another designated Roth account for the participant (if the new plan allows for rollovers) or the participant's Roth IRA. Such rollovers are not taken into account for purposes of the annual limits on elective deferrals.

CONTRIBUTIONS

Two types of contributions may be made to CODAs. Employers may make nonelective contributions that are basically treated the same way for tax purposes as employer contributions to other qualified plans (that is, they are excludable income to the participant). The other type of contribution is elective deferrals that are made under a salary reduction plan. They are also excludable for income tax purposes when contributed but are otherwise subject to FICA and FUTA taxes. The employer may also make matching contributions equal to the amount of or a certain percentage of the employees' elective contributions.

Under the Tax Code, participants in traditional CODAs may make elective deferrals that may be excluded up to $18,000 (2015). In addition, as discussed previously, plan participants who are at least or will become age 50 before the end of the applicable calendar year may make additional catch-up contributions of $6,000 (2015). Hence a catch-up-eligible participant may contribute a total of $24,000 (2015).

Excess Contributions

If the elective deferrals (including the qualified nonelective contributions and the qualified matching contributions) of the HCEs exceed the level permitted by the ADP tests, the plan must distribute the excess contributions (and income) to the HCEs by the end of the following plan year to maintain the qualified status of the plan. This distribution is *not* subject to the 10% tax on early distributions under IRC Section 72(t), but a 10% excise tax may be imposed on the employer for allowing these excess contributions. This excise tax may be avoided by the employer if the excess contributions (plus income) are distributed within 2½ months after the end of the plan year in which the excess was contributed (March 15 for calendar year plans). As a result, if the distribution is made within the 2½-month period, the plan will still be qualified, and no excise tax will be imposed. However, the excess contributions, and the income earned thereon, will still be taxed in the employee's taxable year in which they were made.

If the employer distributes the excess contributions after the 2½-month period, but before the end of the next plan year, the penalty tax will be imposed, but the plan will still be qualified. However, the employee will be taxed on the distribution (the excess contributions plus the income) in the year of the distribution, rather than in the year of the deferral.

Instead of distributing the excess contributions, the plan may permit the employee to recharacterize the excess contributions, and the earnings thereon, as distributions to the employee and then after-tax contributions by the employee to the plan. To be effective, such a recharacterization must take place no later than 2½ months after the close of the plan year. The resulting presumed distribution is not subject to the early distribution penalty. However, because after-tax employee contributions must also meet an ADP test under IRC Section 401(m), such a recharacterization could place the underlying plan in danger of disqualification.

KEOGH PLAN DEFINITION, PURPOSE, AND PROS AND CONS

As indicated previously, a Keogh plan is a qualified or tax-advantaged retirement plan established by an unincorporated business (sole proprietor or partnership) covering one or more self-employed individuals [usually the owner(s)] as well as employees. Except for the contribution limits applicable to self-employed persons (discussed later) versus those applicable to employees, the rules governing a Keogh plan are essentially the same as for any other qualified plan. In the past, the terms *Keogh plan* or *HR-10 plan* were used to distinguish a retirement plan established by a self-employed individual from a plan established by a corporation or other entity. However, self-employed retirement plans are now generally referred to by the name that is used for the particular type of plan (e.g., SEP IRA, SIMPLE 401(k), or self-employed Section 401(k) plan).

Generally, a Keogh plan makes sense for a self-employed businessowner who wants to both provide a benefit for her employees and accumulate funds for her own account on a tax-qualified basis. In some cases, the owner's earned income is substantial, and there is a need to shelter a portion from current taxation. Another situation in which a Keogh plan may be beneficial is when a relatively highly compensated employee also has self-employment income from an outside business, does not need his self-employment income to meet immediate needs, and desires to invest as much as possible of the self-employment income on a tax-deferred basis.

Probably the greatest advantages of a Keogh plan are the tax deductibility of contributions, tax deferral of the income on the plan's investments, and the deferral of taxation to the participant until such time as the funds are distributed. The impact of the deferral of taxation of the income on the plan's investments is cumulatively quite substantial. In fact, after a period of 15 years or more (depending upon the investment rate earned), the cumulative tax-deferred earnings will usually exceed the cumulative contributions to the plan.

Other advantages include the availability of plan loans to owners and employees (if certain specific requirements are met), the availability of 10-year income tax averaging for participants born before January 2, 1936, substantially higher contribution limits than for IRAs, participation by the majority of employees under the qualified plan coverage requirements, and the possible availability of a business tax credit for qualified plan startup costs.

Of course, these advantages are offset by some Keogh plan disadvantages. First, while it can be costly and administratively burdensome to establish and operate a Keogh plan, these effects may be minimized through the use of prototype plans. This cost factor may be compounded by the need to comply with the plan coverage requirements, in the case where the employer has several employees. In addition, there is the potential of the 10% penalty applicable to premature withdrawals of plan funds and the negative impact of the required minimum distribution rules for greater than 5% owners (i.e., required commencement of distributions by April 1 of the year after attainment of age 70½ rather than when the participant retires).

WHO CAN ESTABLISH A KEOGH PLAN

As indicated previously, a Keogh plan sponsor must be an unincorporated business (e.g., sole proprietorship or partnership). Neither an employee nor a partner can establish a Keogh plan. While taxpayers may have more than one Keogh plan, their contributions to all the plans must not exceed the overall limits.

TYPES OF KEOGH PLANS

Self-employed individuals may be covered by any type of qualified or tax-advantaged plan, but Keogh plans generally opt for the defined contribution plan where there is *not* a fixed contribution requirement. One of the distinguishing features of a defined contribution plan is that it includes an individual account to which the employer contributes for each plan participant. While there is no specific promised benefit to each participant in a defined contribution plan, a participant receives contributions to her account as provided in the plan, earnings (or losses) on those contributions, and possible forfeitures of other accounts. In addition, the *participant* (rather than the employer) bears the investment risk of the underlying investments in her account.

A defined contribution plan may be either a profit-sharing plan or a money purchase pension plan. As discussed previously, Keogh plans tend to adopt the profit-sharing form because of the greater flexibility in making annual contributions. While such a plan does not have to provide a definite formula for the sharing of profits, if it fails to do so, it is still required to make recurring and substantial contributions. Moreover, the plan must have a definite formula for allocating contributions among the participants and for eventually distributing the accumulated funds to the participants. Money purchase pension plans, on the other hand, require *fixed* contributions not based on business profits.

A defined benefit pension plan is any plan that is *not* a defined contribution plan. The contributions are those required to provide definitely determinable benefits to plan participants. Actuarial assumptions and computations are required to calculate these contributions. As a result, this type of plan is generally expensive to establish and administer and suffers from the same disadvantage as a money purchase pension plan—required contributions are not based on business profits. For these reasons, Keogh plans generally do *not* adopt the defined benefit option.

ESTABLISHING A KEOGH PLAN

The first action an employer must take in establishing a Keogh plan is to adopt a written plan. This may take the form of an IRS-approved master or prototype plan or an individually designed plan. The plan must then be communicated to employees. A master plan is offered by various plan providers (including banks, trade or professional organizations, insurance companies, mutual funds, federally insured credit unions, and certain savings and loan associations) and involves the creation of a single trust or custodial account that is shared by all employers that adopt the plan. With a prototype plan, a separate trust or custodial account is set up for each employer. An employer electing to establish an individually designed plan typically needs to engage a professional with expertise in this area, pay a fee, if applicable, and seek IRS approval, in the form of a determination letter.

Next, the employer must decide how to invest the plan's funds. This may be accomplished by creating a trust or custodial account, purchasing an annuity contract from an insurance company, or purchasing face-amount certificates (treated like annuity contracts) from an insurance company. Setting up a trust normally involves procuring the services of an attorney, while a custodial account may be created by a bank, savings and loan association, credit union, or other qualified financial institution, with that institution then acting as the plan trustee.

If the employer opts for a money purchase pension plan or defined benefit pension plan, minimum funding standards must be satisfied each year the plan is in existence.

To qualify for an income tax deduction for contributions for a tax year, a Keogh plan must be established (adopted) by the last day of that year (December 31 for calendar year employers).

CONTRIBUTIONS

Depending on the plan, the employer and/or plan participants make contributions. Contributions for a tax year are due by the deadline for filing the tax return (including extensions) for that year.

Employer Contributions

Self-employed owners may make deductible contributions for themselves *only* if they have net earnings (their compensation) from self-employment. Thus, if they have a net loss from self-employment, they cannot make contributions for themselves for the year, even if they contribute for employees based on employee compensation. Compensation for the self-employed is referred to as earned income and consists of the taxpayer's net earnings from self-employment from the trade or business, net of two deductions:

- the self-employment tax deduction (one-half of the self-employment tax) permitted under IRC Section 164(f); and

- the deduction allowed for plan contributions on the individual's own behalf.

Because a self-employed owner's earned income is the amount remaining after taking into account these two deductions, the calculation of her maximum deductible contribution to a Keogh plan becomes mathematically somewhat complex and requires, in effect, an algebraic solution. (See the Deduction Worksheet for Self-Employed later in this reading.)

A defined benefit plan may provide a benefit that does not exceed the lesser of 100% of the participant's average compensation for his highest three consecutive calendar years or $210,000 (2015). A defined contribution plan may make annual contributions and other additions (excluding earnings) to the account of a participant up to the lesser of 100% of the participant's compensation or $53,000 (in 2015). These limits do not include catch-up contributions.

Employee Contributions

In addition to the employer contributions, limited as described in the previous section, nondeductible contributions may also be made by participants. The earnings on participant contributions are tax deferred until distributed. Moreover, these contributions must meet the nondiscrimination test of IRC Section 401(m).

EMPLOYER DEDUCTION

Generally, an employer may deduct, within limits, contributions made to a qualified plan, including those made on behalf of a self-employed owner. The contributions and earnings and gains on the contributions are normally tax deferred until distributed from the plan.

Employer's Deduction Limit for an Employee

In the case of a defined contribution plan (either a profit-sharing plan or money purchase pension plan), which is the most common type of Keogh plan, the deduction is limited to 25% of the covered compensation paid (or accrued) during the year to participating employees. In determining the deduction limit, elective deferrals are *not* subject to the limit, but compensation does include any elective deferrals that are made. The maximum compensation that may be taken into account for each employee is $265,000 (2015).

With regard to a defined benefit plan, the deduction is based on actuarial assumptions and computations and is limited to the plan's unfunded current liability.

Employer's Deduction Limit for a Self-Employed Owner

A self-employed owner is subject to a percentage limit *lower than* 25% for contributions made to his own account. Therefore, to determine the maximum permissible deduction, a special computation is required. A self-employed owner's compensation equals his net earnings from self-employment *after* deducting one-half of his self-employment tax and the deduction for contributions to the plan on his behalf. Because the self-employed owner's net earnings from self-employment and his deduction for his own contributions are dependent upon each other, the self-employed owner must, therefore, reduce the contribution rate specified in the plan document. The IRS provides both a *Rate Table for Self-Employed* and a *Rate Worksheet for Self-Employed* for the purpose of determining the lower contribution rate. After consulting that table, the self-employed owner may then calculate the maximum deduction by using the IRS *Deduction Worksheet for Self-Employed*. These IRS forms are applicable *only* to a self-employed owner who has only one defined contribution plan (usually a profit-sharing plan).

The *Rate Table for Self-Employed* is designed for plans that have a contribution rate that is a whole percentage (e.g., 10% rather than 10½%). The *Rate Worksheet for Self-Employed* is used when the plan contribution rate is not a whole percentage. The *Rate Table for Self-Employed* is as follows.

EXHIBIT 3.3 Rate Table for Self-Employed

Column A If the plan contribution rate is: (shown as %)	Column B Your rate is: (shown as decimal)
1	.009901
2	.019608
3	.029126
4	.038462
5	.047619
6	.056604
7	.065421
8	.074074
9	.082569
10	.090909
11	.099099
12	.107143
13	.115044
14	.122807
15	.130435
16	.137931
17	.145299
18	.152542
19	.159664
20	.166667
21	.173554
22	.180328
23	.186992
24	.193548
25	.200000*

*The deduction for annual employer contributions (other than elective deferrals) to a SEP plan, a profit-sharing plan, or a money purchase pension plan, cannot be more than 20% of the net earnings of the self-employed owner (figured without deducting contributions for the self-employed owner) from the business that has the plan.

Following is an example of how to use this table for illustration purposes only. You most likely will not be required to make a complex calculation on the national examination. The income level will generally require the 20% rate.

EXAMPLE   Assume a sole proprietor does not have any employees. If the retirement plan has a contribution rate of 10% of a participant's compensation, the rate applicable to the self-employed sole proprietor is, therefore, .090909. This rate should be entered in Step 4 of the *Deduction Worksheet for Self-Employed* to calculate the maximum deductible contribution for the sole proprietor.

As discussed previously, if the plan's contribution rate is not a whole percentage, the self-employed owner must use the following *Rate Worksheet for Self-Employed*.

Rate Worksheet for Self-Employed	
1. Plan contribution rate as a decimal (for example, 10½% = 0.105)	_____
2. Rate in line 1 plus 1 (for example, 0.105 + 1 = 1.105)	_____
3. Self-employed rate as a decimal rounded to at least 3 decimal places (line 1 ÷ line 2)	_____

The amount calculated on line 3 should then be entered in Step 4 of the following *Deduction Worksheet for Self-Employed.*

Deduction Worksheet for Self-Employed
Step 1: Enter your net profit from line 31, Schedule C (Form 1040); line 3, Schedule C-EZ (Form 1040); line 36, Schedule F (Form 1040); or box 14, code A*, Schedule K-1 (Form 1065) *General partners should reduce this amount by the same additional expenses subtracted from box 14, code A to determine the amount on line 1 or 2 of Schedule SE
Step 2: Enter your deduction for self-employment tax from line 30, Form 1040
Step 3: Net earnings from self-employment. Subtract Step 2 from Step 1
Step 4: Enter your rate from the *Rate Table for Self-Employed* or *Rate Worksheet for Self-Employed*
Step 5: Multiply Step 3 by Step 4
Step 6: Multiply $265,000 (for 2015) by your plan contribution rate (not the reduced rate)
Step 7: Enter the **smaller** of Step 5 or Step 6
Step 8: Contribution dollar limit $53,000 (2015)
■ If you made any elective deferrals, go to Step 9.   ■ If not, skip steps 9 through 18 and enter the smaller of Step 7 or Step 8 on Step 19.
Step 9: Enter your allowable elective deferrals made during 2015. Do not enter more than $18,000 (for 2015)
Step 10: Subtract Step 9 from Step 8
Step 11: Subtract Step 9 from Step 3
Step 12: Enter one-half of Step 11
Step 13: Enter the **smallest** of steps 7, 10, or 12
Step 14: Subtract Step 13 from Step 3
Step 15: Enter the **smaller** of Step 9 or Step 14
■ If you made catch-up contributions, go to Step 16.   ■ If not, skip steps 16 through 18 and go to Step 19.
Step 16: Subtract Step 15 from Step 14
Step 17: Enter your catch-up contributions, if any. Do not enter more than $6,000 (for 2015)
Step 18: Enter the smaller of Step 16 or Step 17
Step 19: Add steps 13, 15, and 18. This is your **maximum deductible contribution**.
Next: Enter this amount on line 32, Form 1040

USE OF LIFE INSURANCE IN A KEOGH PLAN

If an employer provides life insurance coverage to employee participants in a Keogh plan, the employer deducts those premiums as a plan contribution. The employees are subsequently charged with the value of the pure life insurance element as additional compensation using IRS Table 2001 (replacing the former P.S. 58 table previously used to compute this amount).

However, the pure life insurance element of premiums paid for a self-employed owner is not deductible by the employer. The remaining portion of premiums paid is deductible by the employer as a plan contribution. Unlike the situation with an employee, in which the compensation element is specifically charged to the employee, a self-employed owner is taxed indirectly in that the nondeductible portion of the premium flows through to the owner as additional profit subject to taxation.

At the time of distribution from the plan, an employee is able to offset against her distribution the cumulative amount of Table 2001 costs previously included in income (provided the distribution is made from the same life insurance policy on which the Table 2001 costs were paid). However, in spite of the fact that the self-employed owner indirectly paid tax on the Table 2001 costs applicable to his account, he is *not* able to offset such cumulative costs against distributions made from the plan insurance policy. In effect, an employee has a cost basis in her insurance policy that may be used to reduce the amount of any policy distributions subject to taxation. However, the self-employed owner is *not* considered to have this same cost basis in the plan insurance policy.

OTHER CONSIDERATIONS

In the situation where there is only one self-employed owner and no employees, it may make more sense to adopt a SEP or a SIMPLE IRA because they are probably easier to adopt and may be established as late as the individual's tax return filing date for the previous year, rather than having to be created by the last day of the tax year, as is the case with a Keogh plan.

Some would recommend simply contributing to either a traditional or Roth IRA rather than setting up a Keogh plan. However, there are many limitations on the amount that may be contributed to an IRA, and, generally, the Keogh plan offers the opportunity to contribute a substantially greater amount.

Finally, if a businessowner who has a Keogh plan elects to incorporate his business, the Keogh status of the underlying qualified plan is removed. This offers no overriding advantage inasmuch as corporate plans and Keogh plans receive essentially the same treatment.

REPORTING REQUIREMENTS

The annual reporting requirements applicable to qualified plans are somewhat less onerous for many Keogh plans and other small plans. For instance, if the only persons covered by a plan are the businessowner(s) and spouse(s), the plan may file simplified IRS Form 5500-EZ, instead of the voluminous IRS Form 5500.

Supplemental Reading–Tax-Advantaged Plans and Nonqualified Plans

SAVINGS INCENTIVE MATCH PLAN FOR EMPLOYEES (SIMPLE)

A SIMPLE is a written arrangement that provides an employer and its employees with a simplified way to make contributions for the purpose of funding retirement income. Just like a SARSEP, an employee may elect to make salary reduction contributions (elective deferrals) to the plan rather than receiving these amounts as part of regular compensation. The employer may then make matching or nonelective contributions. SIMPLEs may only be maintained on a calendar year basis and may only be established in either of two ways—using SIMPLE IRAs (SIMPLE IRA plan) or as part of a Section 401(k) plan [SIMPLE 401(k)].

SIMPLE IRA

A SIMPLE IRA is a retirement plan that maintains SIMPLE IRAs for each eligible employee. An employer may establish a SIMPLE IRA if it meets the employee limit and does not maintain another qualified plan, except plans for collective bargaining employees. An employer must have 100 or fewer employees who received $5,000 or more in compensation from the employer for the preceding year. In addition, an employer must take into account all employees employed at any time during the calendar year, regardless of whether they are eligible to participate. This includes self-employed individuals who received earned income from the employer and leased employees. After the plan has been established, the employer must then continue to meet the 100-employee limit each year the plan is maintained. Special rules apply in the case of an employer who maintains the plan for at least one year and then fails to meet the 100-employee limit in a later year and in the case of an acquisition, disposition, or similar transaction.

Another important provision of a SIMPLE IRA is that it must be the *only* retirement plan to which the employer makes contributions, or to which benefits accrue, for service in any year beginning with the year the SIMPLE IRA becomes effective. However, as mentioned earlier, a qualified plan for collective bargaining employees is generally permitted.

Eligible Employee

For purposes of participation in a SIMPLE IRA, an eligible employee is any employee who receives a minimum of $5,000 in compensation during any two years preceding the current calendar year and is reasonably expected to receive at least $5,000 during the current calendar year. The term also includes a self-employed individual who received earned income from the employer. An employer has the option to waive or reduce (but not increase) these compensation requirements but may not add other participation requirements. As with SEPs, union employees and nonresident aliens receiving no U.S. source compensation from the employer may be excluded from participation.

Compensation

Employee compensation that may be considered for purposes of SIMPLE IRA contributions includes their W-2 income plus any salary reduction contributions made under the SIMPLE IRA, compensation deferred under a Section 457 plan, and the employees' elective deferrals under a Section 401(k) plan, a SARSEP, or a Section 403(b) annuity contract. Compensation for a self-employed person is her net earnings from self-employment before subtracting any contributions made to the SIMPLE IRA for her own SIMPLE IRA.

Reasons to Adopt a SIMPLE IRA

Probably the major reason why small employers (say, 100 employees or fewer) would consider adopting a SIMPLE IRA is that, like SEP plans, they are easier and less expensive to both install and administer than a qualified profit-sharing plan. Another significant reason why a small employer would consider adopting a SIMPLE IRA is if the employer wants to fund the plan through salary reductions. Moreover, in the employer's particular situation, the SIMPLE IRA contribution limit may be higher than those permitted under either a Keogh plan or SEP.

Some advantages of SIMPLE IRAs include:

- ease of establishment by using standard IRS forms (5304-SIMPLE or 5305-SIMPLE);

- total portability and 100% employee vesting;

- the transfer of investment risk to the employee; and

- the availability of salary reduction contributions, if IRS requirements are met.

SIMPLE IRAs also have certain *disadvantages*, including:

- no guarantee of an adequate retirement benefit for employees unless they make meaningful and consistent annual salary reduction contributions over many years (older employees entering the plan have a limited number of years to fund their retirement);

- allowable annual contributions may not be as large as would be permitted under a qualified plan (such as a Section 401(k) plan);

- SIMPLE IRA distributions do not receive special income averaging tax treatment as do certain qualified plan distributions; and

- the employer may not also maintain a qualified plan, a SEP, a Section 403(a) annuity, a Section 403(b) tax-sheltered annuity, or a Section 457 plan. A union plan, however, may coexist with a SIMPLE IRA.

Certain lower-income employees making salary deferrals may qualify for the saver's credit (as discussed under SARSEPs), and employers adopting a new SIMPLE IRA may qualify for a business tax credit of up to $500 for the qualified startup costs of the plan (as discussed under SEP plans).

Establishing a SIMPLE IRA

Just as with a SEP plan, an employer may establish a SIMPLE IRA by using a model SIMPLE document found on Forms 5304-SIMPLE or 5305-SIMPLE. If the employer wishes to permit each employee to select the financial institution to receive his contributions, the employer uses Form 5304-SIMPLE. If the employer wants to select the financial institution where all contributions will initially be deposited, the employer uses Form 5305-SIMPLE. When the appropriate form has been fully completed and signed by both the employer and the financial institution, if any, the SIMPLE is considered to be adopted. As with a SEP, using the standard form avoids having to file the paperwork with the IRS. Also, page 3 of this form may be used to satisfy the employer notification requirements to plan participants.

Just as with a SEP plan, the employer may be able to claim a tax credit for part of the startup costs of establishing a SIMPLE IRA.

If an employer establishes a SIMPLE IRA, it must notify each employee of the following four items of information before the beginning of what is known as the election period:

■ The employee's opportunity to make or change a salary reduction choice under a SIMPLE IRA

■ The employer's choice to make either matching contributions or nonelective contributions (discussed later in this reading)

■ A summary description provided by the financial institution

■ Written notice that an employee's balance may be transferred without cost or penalty if the employer uses a designated financial institution

The election period is generally the 60-day period immediately preceding January 1 of a calendar year (November 2 through December 31 of the preceding calendar year). These dates are modified if the SIMPLE IRA is established mid-year or if the 60-day period falls before the first day an employee becomes eligible to participate in the SIMPLE IRA. The plan document may provide a longer period to enter into any salary reduction agreement or to modify a prior agreement.

Contribution Limitations

Contributions to SIMPLE IRAs include both salary reduction contributions (by employees) and employer contributions (either matching or nonelective contributions). No other contributions may be made to a SIMPLE IRA (other than rollover contributions).

An employee may elect to have the employer contribute, on her behalf, to her SIMPLE IRA up to $12,500 (2015). The amount of a salary reduction contribution must be determined as a percentage of the employee's compensation unless the employer permits the employee to contribute a flat amount of money up to the $12,500 limit (in 2015). If an employee participates during the year in any other employer plan and has either salary reductions or deferred compensation under that plan, the salary reduction contributions under the SIMPLE IRA are also considered elective deferrals and accordingly must be included in determining the overall limit ($18,000 in 2015) for exclusion of salary reduction contributions and other elective deferrals.

In addition to the foregoing salary reduction contributions, participants who are age 50 or older at the end of the calendar year may also be permitted by a SIMPLE IRA to make catch-up contributions of up to $3,000 (2015). As with SARSEPs, salary reduction contributions are *not* treated as catch-up contributions until they exceed $12,500 (for 2015). Finally, a participant's compensation must be greater than the total contributions elected.

An employer must also match each employee's salary reduction contributions on a dollar-for-dollar basis up to 3% of the employee's compensation. For example, if an employee's salary is $40,000 and she elects to defer 5% of her salary, the total contribution the employer can make for this employee is $3,200, calculated as follows:

Salary reduction contributions ($40,000 × .05)	$2,000
Employer-matching contribution ($40,000 × .03)	1,200
	$3,200

However, if the employer elects a matching contribution less than 3%, the percentage must be at least 1%. The employees must be notified of the lower match within a reasonable period of time before the 60-day election period (discussed earlier) for the calendar year. The matching contribution requirements just described do *not* apply if the employer instead elects to make nonelective contributions of 2% of compensation on behalf of each eligible employee who has at least $5,000 (or a lower amount selected by the employer) of compensation from the employer for the year. One downside for the employer of choosing nonelective contributions versus matching contributions is that the employer must then make the nonelective contributions each year, even if the employee elects *not* to make salary reduction contributions. No more than $265,000 (2015) of the employee's compensation may be taken into account in calculating this contribution limit.

Salary reduction contributions to a SIMPLE IRA generally must be made within 30 days after the end of the month in which the amounts would otherwise have been payable to the employee in cash. However, matching or nonelective contributions may be made by the due date (including extensions) for filing the employer's federal income tax return for the year.

Deduction Limitations

SIMPLE IRA contributions are deductible in the tax year for which contributions were made ends. Contributions are deductible for a particular tax year if they are made for that tax year by the due date (including extensions) of the employer's income tax return for that year.

A sole proprietor deducts SIMPLE IRA contributions on Schedule C of IRS Form 1040, Profit or Loss From Business, or on Schedule F, if a farmer. Partnerships deduct such contributions on IRS Form 1065, U.S. Return of Partnership Income, and corporations deduct them on IRS Form 1120, U.S. Corporation Income Tax Return, Form 1120-A, or IRS Form 1120S, if an S Corporation. Sole proprietors and partners deduct contributions for themselves on line 32 of IRS Form 1040.

Qualifying contributions made on behalf of employees are deductible by the employer and not taxable to the employees. However, salary reduction contributions are subject to Social Security, Medicare, and FUTA taxes. Matching and nonelective contributions are not subject to these taxes.

Distributions from SIMPLE IRAs

Distributions from SIMPLE IRAs are taxed under the same rates applicable to traditional IRAs. Also, rollovers may be made from one SIMPLE IRA to another, but rollovers from a SIMPLE IRA to a non-SIMPLE IRA may be made tax free only *after* two years of participation in the SIMPLE IRA. Early withdrawals made before fulfilling this two-year participation requirement are subject to a 25% additional tax, rather than the normal 10% tax.

SIMPLE 401(k)

An employer interested in developing a SIMPLE plan also has the option of creating a SIMPLE 401(k) plan instead of a SIMPLE IRA. Of course, doing so involves somewhat more complexity because a SIMPLE 401(k) is a *qualified* retirement plan subject to most of the rules applicable to such plans. The only rules that do not apply to a SIMPLE 401(k) are the general nondiscrimination and top-heavy rules, assuming the plan satisfies the following conditions.

- An employee may elect to have the employer make salary reduction contributions for the year to a trust in an amount expressed as a percentage of the employee's compensation, up to $12,500 (2015) plus up to $3,000 (2015) additional if the employee is age 50 or older.

- The employer must make either

  — matching contributions up to 3% of compensation for the year, or

  — nonelective contributions of 2% of compensation on behalf of each eligible employee who has at least $5,000 of compensation from the employer for the year (as discussed earlier under Contribution Limitations).

- No other contributions are made to the trust.

- No contributions are made, and no benefits accrue, for services during the year under any other employer-qualified retirement plan on behalf of any employee eligible to participate in the SIMPLE 401(k).

- The employee's rights to any contributions are fully vested at all times.

Finally, just as is the case with a SIMPLE IRA, no more than $265,000 (2015) in compensation may be taken into account in figuring salary reduction contributions, matching contributions, and nonelective contributions.

SIMPLIFIED EMPLOYEE PENSION (SEP)

A simplified employee pension (SEP) is a written plan that allows an employer to make contributions toward his own retirement (if he is self-employed) and toward that of his employees' retirement without getting involved in a more complex qualified plan. By adopting a SEP agreement, an employer may make contributions directly to a traditional individual retirement account or a traditional individual retirement annuity (SEP IRA) set up for each eligible employee. A SEP IRA is owned and controlled by the employee, and only the employer makes contributions to the financial institution where the SEP IRA is maintained.

SEP IRAs are established, at a minimum, for each eligible employee and may have to be set up for a leased employee but do not have to be set up for excludable employees (which will be defined later). An eligible employee is an individual who is at least 21 years of age, has worked for the employer in at least three of the past five years, and has received at least $600 in compensation from the employer (2015). The participation requirements established by the employer can be less restrictive than those just described, but they cannot be more restrictive.

Certain employees may be excluded from coverage under a SEP. They include:

- employees covered by a union agreement and whose retirement benefits were bargained for in good faith by the employees' union and the employer; and

- nonresident alien employees who have received no U.S. source wages, salaries, or other personal services compensation from the employer.

Reasons to Adopt a SEP

Probably the major reason why small employers (e.g., 10 employees or fewer) would consider adopting a SEP is that they are easier and less expensive to both install and administer than a qualified profit-sharing plan. Another significant reason why a small employer would consider adopting a SEP is if the employer has had very good financial results for the tax year just ended and wants to shelter some of its high profits from taxation. While qualified plans must be adopted before the end of the year in which they are to be effective, a SEP may be established as late as the due date (including extensions) of the tax return for the year in which the high profits occurred. In effect, this permits the employer to wait until the financial results are available and then decide whether to create a SEP, rather than hurrying to create a qualified plan before the end of the tax year without having final financial results available.

Some advantages of SEPs include:

■   total portability of benefits for employees;

■   employer discretion to make no contribution to the plan in any given year; and

■   transfer of investment risk to the employee.

SEPs also have certain disadvantages, including the following:

■   it will not guarantee an adequate retirement benefit for employees because the employer is not required to make substantial and regular contributions, and older employees entering the plan have a limited number of years to fund their retirement;

■   allowable annual contributions may not be as large as would be permitted under a qualified plan; and

■   SEP distributions do not receive special income averaging tax treatment as do certain qualified plan distributions.

Establishing a SEP

An employer needs to observe three steps in establishing a SEP. First, the employer must execute a formal written agreement to provide benefits to all eligible employees. Second, the employer must give each eligible employee certain information about the SEP. Finally, a SEP IRA must be established by or for each eligible employee.

To satisfy the formal written agreement requirement, an employer may adopt an IRS model SEP using IRS Form 5305-SEP. One main advantage of using this model SEP is that the employer does not need prior IRS approval or an IRS determination letter. An additional advantage is the employer will not have to file annual retirement plan information returns with the IRS and the Department of Labor.

However, an employer is not allowed to use Form 5305-SEP if any of the following applies in a given situation:

■   The employer maintains any other qualified retirement plan. However, if the employer already maintains another SEP, the employer may establish a second one.

■   The employer has eligible employees for whom IRAs have not been established.

■   The employer uses the services of leased employees.

■   The employer is a member of any of the following unless all eligible employees of all the members of these groups, trades, or businesses participate under the SEP

— an affiliated service group described in IRS Section 414(m),

— a controlled group of corporations described in IRS Section 414(b), or

— trades or businesses under common control described in IRS Section 414(c).

Upon establishing a SEP, the employer must give to each eligible employee a copy of Form 5305-SEP, its instructions, and the other information listed in the Form 5305-SEP instructions. An IRS model SEP is *not* considered adopted until the employer gives each employee this information.

A SEP IRA must be established by or for each eligible employee with a bank, insurance company, or other qualified financial institution. A SEP may be established for a particular calendar year as late as the due date (including extensions) of the employer's income tax return for that year. An employer adopting a plan may be eligible for a business tax credit of up to $500 per year for each of the first three years of the plan for the qualified startup costs of creating a SEP.

Contribution Limitations

A limited amount of money may be contributed each year to each employee's SEP IRA. For those employers who are self-employed, the employer may contribute to her own SEP IRA. Contributions must be in the form of money (cash, check, or money order) and not property. However, participants may be able to transfer or roll over certain property from one retirement plan to another.

An employer does *not* have to make contributions every year. However, contributions made must be based on a written allocation formula and must not discriminate in favor of highly compensated employees (defined previously). In a year that contributions are made, the employer must contribute to the SEP IRAs of all participants who actually performed personal services during the year for which the contributions are made, even those employees who die or terminate employment before the contributions are made.

The contributions made under a SEP are treated as if made to a qualified pension, stock bonus, profit-sharing, or annuity plan. As a result, SEP contributions are deductible within limits (discussed later) and are not taxable to the plan participants.

A SEP IRA cannot be designated as a Roth IRA; however, employer contributions to a SEP IRA will not affect the amount an individual can contribute to a Roth IRA.

In order for the employer to obtain a tax deduction, contributions to a SEP must be made by the due date (including extensions) of the employer's tax return for the year.

Contributions made to a common-law employee's SEP IRA cannot exceed the lesser of 25% of the employee's covered compensation or $53,000 (2015). Compensation, however, generally does *not* include the employer's contributions to the SEP. The annual limits on an employer's contributions to a common-law employee's SEP IRA also apply to contributions the employer makes to her own SEP IRA, except that special rules apply when calculating the employer's maximum deductible contribution. This calculation is discussed in the next section on deduction limitations.

In calculating the annual compensation limit, the employer may *not* take into consideration the portion of an employee's compensation that exceeds $265,000 (2015). However, this is somewhat academic because $53,000 (2015) is the maximum contribution for an eligible employee.

If the employer also contributes to a defined contribution plan, annual additions to an account are limited to the lesser of $53,000 (2015) or 100% of the participant's covered compensation. In calculating this limit, the employer must add employer contributions to all defined contribution plans. Because a SEP is considered a defined contribution plan for this limit, the employer's contributions to a SEP must also be added to the employer's contributions to other defined contribution plans.

Employer contributions to an employee's SEP IRA (or to the employer's own SEP IRA) that exceed the contribution limits defined earlier are included in the employee's income for the year and are treated as contributions by the employee to his SEP IRA. Unlike employee elective deferrals, generally, employer contributions to a SEP are *not* subject to Social Security (FICA) or federal unemployment (FUTA) taxes.

Finally, each participating employee is always 100% vested in *all* contributions to his SEP IRA and must receive an annual statement documenting the amount contributed to his account for the year.

Deduction Limitations

Generally, an employer may deduct the contributions the employer makes each year to each employee's SEP IRA and, if the employer is self-employed, the contributions made each year to the employer's own SEP IRA. The maximum deduction for contributions (other than elective deferrals, discussed later) for participants is the *lesser of*:

- the employer's contributions (including any excess contributions carryover); or

- 25% of the covered compensation (limited to $265,000 per participant, in 2015) paid to the participants during the year from the business that maintains the plan, not to exceed $53,000 per participant (2015). Compensation here includes elective deferrals. Elective deferrals to a SARSEP are no longer subject to this deduction limit. However, the combined deduction for a participant's elective deferrals and other SEP contributions cannot exceed $53,000 (2015).

In the case of a self-employed individual who contributes to her own SEP IRA, she must make a special calculation (as mentioned earlier) to figure her maximum deduction for these contributions. The compensation of such an individual is her net earnings from self-employment (defined earlier), which takes into account both the deduction for the employer share of her self-employment tax and the deduction for contributions to her own SEP IRA. As a result of this method of calculation, the deduction for contributions to a self-employed employer's own SEP IRA and her net earnings depend on each other. Consequently, to determine the deduction for contributions to a self-employed employer's own SEP IRA, one must reduce the contribution rate called for in the SEP plan. This requires the use of the IRS Rate Table for Self-Employed or the IRS Rate Worksheet for Self-Employed, whichever is appropriate for the plan's contribution rate. Finally, the maximum deduction is calculated using the IRS Deduction Worksheet for Self-Employed.

As alluded to earlier, when calculating the deduction limitation, treat all of the employer's qualified defined contribution plans as a single plan and all of the employer's defined benefit plans as a single plan. If the employer has both kinds of plans, a SEP is treated as a separate profit-sharing (defined contribution) plan. In addition, if the employer also contributes to a qualified defined contribution plan, the employer must reduce the 25% deduction limit for that plan by the allowable deductions for contributions to the SEP IRAs of those participating in both the SEP plan and the defined contribution plan.

If an employer made SEP contributions that are more than the deduction limit (nondeductible contributions), the employer may carry over and deduct the difference in later years. However, the carryover, when combined with the contribution for the later year, is subject to the deduction limit for that year. Finally, if an employer made nondeductible (excess) contributions to a SEP, the employer may also be subject to a 10% excise tax.

Contributions made for common-law employees are deducted on the employer's tax return. For example, a sole proprietor deducts such contributions on Schedule C of Form 1040, Profit or Loss From Business, or Schedule F of Form 1040, Profit or Loss From Farming. A partnership deducts them on Form 1065, U.S. Return of Partnership Income, and a corporation deducts them on Form 1120, U.S. Corporation Income Tax Return, Form 1120-A, U.S. Corporation Short-Form Income Tax Return, or Form 1120S, U.S. Income Tax Return for an S Corporation. Sole proprietors and partners deduct contributions for themselves on line 32 of Form 1040.

Distributions from SEP Plans

SEP plan contributions and earnings may be withdrawn at any time, but, like traditional IRAs, withdrawals are taxable in the year received and subject to the 10% additional tax if withdrawn before age 59½. SEP plan contributions and earnings may be rolled over tax free to other IRAs and retirement plans and, like traditional IRAs, they are subject to the required minimum distribution rules.

A loan to a SEP plan participant is considered a prohibited transaction (thus, disqualifying the SEP IRA as an IRA), and while in-service withdrawals are permitted, they are includable in income and subject to a 10% additional tax if the participant is under age 59½.

SALARY REDUCTION SIMPLIFIED EMPLOYEE PENSION (SARSEP) PLAN

As discussed in the previous section, only *employer* contributions are permitted to a SEP plan. However, there is a different type of SEP plan, known as a SARSEP plan, which permits *employees* to make what are referred to as elective deferrals to their SEP IRA instead of receiving the amount contributed as cash compensation. SARSEP plans had to have been established prior to 1997 and may no longer be established. However, if a SARSEP plan is grandfathered, the employees elect to have the employer contribute a portion of their compensation to their SARSEP plan rather than receive it in cash. By making this election, employees defer income taxation on a portion of their compensation until it is distributed to them. Nevertheless, such elective deferrals are included in wages for Social Security, Medicare, and federal unemployment (FUTA) tax. A limited nonrefundable tax credit, known as the saver's credit, is available to certain lower-income taxpayers who make elective deferrals to a SARSEP plan.

A SARSEP plan established before 1997 may continue to be maintained by an employer if all of the following conditions are met:

■ At least 50% of the employees eligible to participate choose to make elective deferrals.

■ The employer has 25 or fewer employees who were eligible to participate in the SEP plan at any time during the preceding year.

■ The elective deferrals of the highly compensated employees meet the SARSEP plan ADP test. Under this test, the amount deferred each year by each eligible highly compensated employee as a percentage of pay (the deferral percentage) cannot be more than 125% of the average deferral percentage (ADP) of all non-highly compensated employees eligible to participate. To calculate the deferral percentage for an employee for a year, simply divide the elective employer contributions (excluding certain catch-up contributions) paid to the SEP for the employee for the year by the employee's includable compensation (limited to $265,000 in 2015). In determining the employee's compensation, elective deferrals under the SARSEP (unless elected otherwise by the employer) are included in calculating the employee's deferral percentage, even though they are not included in the employee's income for income tax purposes.

The maximum amount a participant in a SARSEP meeting all of the foregoing conditions can elect to defer is the *lesser of*:

■ 25% of the participant's compensation (limited to $265,000 in 2015); or

■ $18,000 in 2015.

The $18,000 limit in 2015 applies to the total elective deferrals the employee makes for the year to a SEP and is aggregated with a Section 401(k) plan, a Section 403(b) plan, or a SIMPLE IRA (discussed later in this reading).

Another advantage of a SARSEP is that it allows participants who are age 50 or older at the end of the calendar year to also make catch-up contributions. The catch-up contribution limit for 2015 is $6,000. Elective deferrals are not treated as catch-up contributions for 2015 until they exceed:

■ the elective deferral limit (the lesser of 25% of compensation or $18,000, in 2015);

■ the SARSEP ADP test limit discussed earlier; or

■ the plan limit (if any).

Moreover, the maximum permissible catch-up contribution a participant may make for a year cannot exceed the *lesser of* the catch-up contribution limit or the excess of the participant's compensation over the elective deferrals that are not catch-up contributions. Catch-up contributions are not subject to the elective deferral limit (the lesser of 25% of compensation or $18,000 in 2015).

If an employer makes what are referred to as excess SEP plan contributions, the employer must notify its highly compensated employees within 2½ months after the end of the plan year of their excess SEP plan contributions. Excess SEP plan contributions are elective deferrals of highly compensated employees that are more than the amount permitted under the SARSEP plan ADP test, as discussed earlier. Failure to notify the highly compensated employees involved within the 2½-month time limit may result in the employer having to pay a 10% tax on the excess.

Distributions from a SARSEP plan are subject to the same IRA distribution rules.

TAX-SHELTERED ANNUITY PLANS (SECTION 403(B) PLANS)

A tax-sheltered annuity (TSA) plan, authorized by Section 403(b) of the Internal Revenue Code, is a retirement plan designed for certain employees of public schools, employees of certain tax-exempt organizations, and certain ministers. There are three types of individual accounts in a Section 403(b) plan:

■ An annuity contract provided by an insurance company

■ A custodial account invested in mutual funds

■ A retirement income account, invested in either annuities or mutual funds, set up for church employees

To be eligible to participate in a Section 403(b) plan, an individual must be an employee of:

■ a tax-exempt organization established under IRC Section 501(c)(3);

■ a public school system (the employee must be involved in the day-to-day operations of the school);

■ a public school system organized by Indian tribal governments;

■ a cooperative hospital service organization; or

■ the Uniformed Services University of the Health Sciences (USUHS).

Individuals who are ministers may also participate in a Section 403(b) plan if they meet any of the following requirements:

- they are employed by a Section 501(c)(3) organization;

- they are self-employed and perform services for a qualified employer and, accordingly, are treated as employed by a tax-exempt organization that is a qualified employer; or

- they are employed by non-501(c)(3) organizations and function as ministers in their day-to-day professional responsibilities with their employers (including chaplains in a state-run prison and chaplains in the U.S. Armed Forces).

A 501(c)(3) organization is one that is "organized and operated exclusively for religious, charitable, scientific, testing for public safety, literary, or educational purposes, or to foster national or international amateur sport competition . . . or for the prevention of cruelty to children or animals." In addition, the organization must benefit the public, rather than any private owner or individual, and it must not engage in lobbying activities for political purposes or to influence legislation. Prime examples include churches, hospitals, public schools and colleges, and charitable institutions. Educational organizations must have a regular faculty and curriculum and regularly enrolled students in attendance, operated by a state or municipal agency.

Only the qualified employer may establish the Section 403(b) account—not the employee. This is true even for self-employed ministers.

Reasons to Adopt a Section 403(b) Plan

From the standpoint of employees, a Section 403(b) plan permits employees of qualifying organizations to refrain from paying tax on allowable contributions in the year they are made, to defer taxation of earnings and gains on amounts in the Section 403(b) account until withdrawn, and (for lower-income employees) to qualify for a saver's credit for elective deferrals contributed to their 403(b) accounts.

From an employer's standpoint, if the employer has a small budget to provide retirement benefits beyond basic salary and other benefits, a Section 403(b) plan may be funded (except for the installation and administration costs) through the use of employee salary reductions. The employer also has the flexibility of making additional contributions from employer funds. Generally, a TSA plan works best with a young workforce that enjoys the advantage of a substantial amount of time to accumulate retirement funds and is willing to incur some degree of investment risk to accomplish its goals. Moreover, a Section 403(b) plan functions well as a supplement to the employer's existing defined benefit or other qualified plan.

Probably the primary advantage of establishing a TSA plan is the tax deferral achieved, just as in a qualified retirement plan. In addition, employees enjoy the flexibility of deciding how much to contribute to the plan, and the employer does not need to (but has the flexibility to) contribute its own funds to the plan. Finally, TSA plans also offer employee in-service withdrawals.

Some of the downside of establishing a TSA plan is:

- they do not necessarily provide an adequate retirement benefit for employees, especially those who joined the plan when relatively near retirement;

- the annual salary reduction is subject to the elective deferral limit, as described later in this reading;

- ■ the plan is subject to the sometimes onerous nondiscrimination tests, described later in this reading; and

- ■ the investment risk is incurred by the employees (although, oftentimes, they have a choice of investments to minimize this risk).

Contribution Limitations

Generally, except for after-tax contributions described later, only an employer may make contributions to a Section 403(b) account. This includes before-tax elective deferrals made under a salary reduction agreement, employer nonelective contributions (including matching contributions, discretionary contributions, and mandatory contributions) not made under a salary reduction agreement, after-tax contributions (provided from employee funds), and a combination of any of these three types of contributions.

A self-employed minister is considered both an employee and an employer and can contribute to a retirement income account for his own benefit, deducting the contributions on his income tax return.

The limit on the amount that can be contributed to an employee's Section 403(b) account for any year is called the maximum amount contributable (MAC). An employee's MAC consists of the limit on annual additions (discussed later in this reading) and the limit on elective deferrals (also discussed later in this reading). Contributions to an employee's Section 403(b) account are limited to the lesser of the limit on annual additions or the limit on elective deferrals. The type of contributions made to an employee's Section 403(b) account determines whether both, or only one, of these limits apply to that employee. For example, if elective deferrals are the only contributions made, the employee needs to calculate both limits and then select the lesser amount as her MAC. In the case of nonelective contributions, only the limit on annual additions must be calculated to determine the employee's MAC. Where there is a combination of both elective deferrals and nonelective contributions, both limits will then need to be calculated. In order to avoid penalties and additional taxes, an employee should calculate her MAC at the beginning of each tax year by reviewing her actual compensation for the prior year and determining whether the amount contributed for the prior year is within the allowable limits.

Limitation on Annual Additions

The total annual additions that may be made to an employee's Section 403(b) account is the sum of elective deferrals, nonelective contributions, and after-tax contributions. This limit is the *lesser of* $53,000 (2015) or 100% of the employee's includable compensation for the employee's most recent year of service. An employee must combine the contributions made to all of his Section 403(b) accounts (even if with different employers), and if the employee participates in both a Section 403(b) plan and a qualified plan, he must combine contributions made to the Section 403(b) account, the qualified plan, and, if applicable, SEP accounts of all corporations, partnerships, and sole proprietorships in which the employee has more than 50% control.

An employee's includable compensation for his most recent year of service is the total of taxable wages and benefits he received from the employer that maintained a Section 403(b) account for the employee's benefit during his most recent year of service. If the employee's tax year is not the same as the employer's annual work period, the employee's most recent year of service may be a different period of time than that of the employer. Also, compensation of different employers cannot be mixed.

In order to calculate one's most recent year of service, the employee must first determine what constitutes a full year of service for his particular position. An employee who works less than full time or only seasonally may also need to add several previous years of service to arrive at one year of full-time service.

Having identified the most recent year of service, the employee must then determine the includable compensation that corresponds with that most recent year of service. Unfortunately, includable compensation is *not* the same as the income appearing on a W-2 form, which is reported on an income tax return. The term **compensation** refers to the combination of income and benefits received for services provided to the employer. Alternatively, includable compensation means the following:

- Elective deferrals

- Amounts contributed or deferred by the employer under a Section 125 cafeteria plan

- Amounts contributed or deferred, at the employee's election, under an eligible Section 457 nonqualified deferred compensation plan (state or local government or tax-exempt organization plan, discussed later in this reading)

- Wages, salaries, and fees for personal services earned with the employer maintaining the employee's 403(b) account

- Income otherwise excluded under the foreign earned income exclusion

- The value of qualified transportation fringe benefits (including transit passes, certain parking, and transportation in a commuter highway vehicle between the employee's home and work)

Includable compensation does *not* include the following:

- The employer's contributions to the employee's Section 403(b) account

- Compensation earned while the employer was not an eligible employer

- The employer's contributions to a qualified plan that are on the employee's behalf and are excludable from income

- The cost of incidental life insurance as determined by reference to the IRS Table for Uniform One-Year Term Premiums for $1,000 Life Insurance Protection

Limitation on Elective Deferrals

As indicated previously, the second component of MAC is the limit on elective deferrals (the amount that may be contributed to an employee's Section 403(b) account through a salary reduction agreement). Therefore, the limit on elective deferrals applies to amounts contributed to the following:

- Section 401(k) plans, to the extent excluded from income

- Section 501(c)(18) plans, to the extent excluded from income

- SIMPLEs

- Simplified employee pension (SEP) plans

- All Section 403(b) plans

For 2015, the general limit on annual elective deferrals to a Section 403(b) account is $18,000. A special catch-up rule applies to employees of public school systems, hospitals, home health service agencies, health and welfare service agencies, churches, or conventions or associations of churches (or associated organizations) who have at least 15 years of service. An employee qualifying for this 15-year rule may have annual elective deferrals of as much as $21,000 (2015). An employee's years of service are the total number of years she has worked for the employer maintaining her Section 403(b) account as of the end of the year.

EXAMPLE **How the Limitation on Elective Deferrals Works** Assume Frank has already calculated his limit on annual additions to be $53,000 (2015) and now needs to determine his limit on elective deferrals before being able to compute his maximum amount contributable (MAC). Assume Frank has been employed with his current employer for less than 15 years and, as a result, does *not* qualify under the special 15-year rule for an increase in his elective deferrals. Therefore, his limit on elective deferrals for 2015 is $18,000. Further assume that Frank's employer does not make either nonelective contributions or after-tax contributions to Frank's Section 403(b) account. Because elective deferrals are the only contributions made to Frank's account, the maximum amount that may be contributed to a Section 403(b) account on Frank's behalf in 2015 is $18,000, the lesser of the elective deferral or annual additions ($53,000) limit.

Catch-Up Contributions

Employees who will be age 50 or older by the end of the year may make additional catch-up contributions (other than after-tax contributions), as discussed earlier. In order to qualify for these additional catch-up contributions, such employees must have already made the maximum elective deferrals permissible for the plan year. The maximum amount of catch-up contributions is the lesser of $6,000 (2015) or the employee's includable compensation minus his elective deferrals for the year. In determining the maximum allowable catch-up contribution for an employee, the employee must combine all catch-up contributions made by his employer on the employee's behalf to (1) qualified retirement plans, (2) Section 403(b) plans, (3) SEP plans, and (4) SIMPLEs. Catch-up contributions have no effect on an employee's MAC. Therefore, an employee can have contributions made on his behalf equal to his MAC *plus* allowable catch-up contributions.

Excess Contributions

Contributions to a Section 403(b) that are greater than an employee's MAC are considered to be excess contributions. Such contributions may result in income tax, additional taxes, and penalties. In order to avoid these potential taxes and penalties, it is, therefore, important for an employee to monitor her MAC as the year progresses. At the beginning of the subsequent year, an employee should recalculate her MAC based on the actual compensation received during the prior year and the actual contributions made for that year to determine if excess contributions have been made for the prior year. Once it has been determined that excess contributions have indeed been made, it must then be determined whether they are excess annual additions or excess elective deferrals.

In a year in which an employee's contributions are more than her limit on annual additions, the excess amount is included in her income. Any portion of the excess due to elective deferrals may be distributed if the excess contributions were made for any of several reasons, including a reasonable error in determining the amount of elective deferrals that could be made under the limit on annual additions or a reasonable error in projecting the amount of an employee's compensation.

A Section 403(b) account investing in mutual funds that exceeds the limit on annual additions may be subject to a nondeductible 6% excise tax on the excess contributions. These contributions may be corrected by contributing less than the applicable limit in later years or by making permissible distributions. A permissible distribution may be made upon the occurrence of one of the following events:

■ The employee reaches age 59½

■ The employee's employment is severed

■ The employee dies

■ The employee becomes disabled

■ The employee suffers financial hardship because of making salary reduction contributions

If the excess contributions are the result of an excess contribution over the limit on elective deferrals (rather than an excess over the limit on annual additions) the Section 403(b) plan document may permit distribution of such deferrals. A corrective distribution may be made only if the employee or employer designates the distribution as an excess deferral (to the extent there are excess deferrals for the year), and the corrective distribution is made after the date on which the excess deferral was made. Such corrective distributions may be made up to April 15 of the subsequent year and are includable in the employee's income for the year in which the excess deferral was made. Income on the excess deferral distributed is then taxable in the year received.

GOVERNMENTAL AND TAX-EXEMPT EMPLOYER DEFERRED COMPENSATION (SECTION 457) PLANS

Non-qualified plans of deferred compensation described in IRC Section 457 are available for certain state and local governments, governmental agencies or instrumentalities of a state or local government (such as a school district or sewage authority), and non-governmental, non-church controlled entities tax exempt under IRC Section 501. Accordingly, Section 457 plans may be further categorized as an eligible plan under IRC Section 457(b), which permit employees of sponsoring organizations to defer income taxation on retirement savings into future years, and ineligible plans under IRC Section 457(f). An eligible Section 457 plan is one that imposes limits on the amounts deferred, while an ineligible Section 457 plan is one that permits greater deferral, usually targeted at top executives.

Reasons to Adopt a Section 457 Plan

One primary reason to adopt a Section 457 plan is that there are *no* specific coverage requirements. In the case of a *governmental* organization, the plan may be made available to all employees, to a specific group of employees, or even to a single employee. Alternatively, *private non-governmental* tax-exempt organizations are required to comply with ERISA, including its eligibility rules, unless these plans are structured to take advantage of certain specific ERISA exemptions (i.e., unfunded plans covering only top management). Private tax-exempt plans may be financed with insurance or annuities, whereas governmental organization plans are required to be funded by placing plan assets in trusts or custodial accounts.

Because the entities that may establish a Section 457 plan are not subject to income taxation, tax deductibility is not an issue.

Contribution Limitations

The limit on the amount that may be deferred each year by an eligible plan is the *lesser of* 100% of the participant's compensation (i.e., gross compensation before salary reductions) or $18,000 (2015). When calculating the limit, all Section 457 plans in which an employee participates must be included. One of the principal advantages of Section 457 plans is that salary reduction contributions to such plans do *not* affect the amount that can be contributed to other types of salary reduction plans (e.g., Section 403(b) plans or Section 401(k) plans).

Catch-Up Contributions

A complicating factor with regard to Section 457 plans is that participants in a *governmental employer* plan aged 50 or older may be able to make *additional* salary reduction contributions. This is *not* the case with private tax-exempt organization 457 plans. Participants in governmental employer plans age 50 or older may contribute catch-up contributions of $6,000 (2015), provided the amount does not exceed the excess of the participant's compensation over all of his regular elective deferrals. For example, if a participant over age 50 in 2015 has total compensation of $18,000 and makes regular salary reductions of $16,000, he may not contribute more than an additional $2,000 in catch-up contributions.

The IRC Section 415 limitation on annual additions ($53,000 or 100% of compensation) has no effect on the ability of a participant to make 50 or over catch-up contributions. Therefore, if a participant age 50 or older qualifies for $53,000 of regular annual additions (2015) to the employer's defined contribution plans, he may still make a $6,000 catch-up contribution (2015). However, this general catch-up contribution rule does not apply to a participant who qualifies under an earlier three-year catch-up rule. This earlier catch-up rule applies to the three years directly prior to the plan's normal retirement age. During this three-year period, a participant may defer the lesser of:

- double the regular dollar limit; or

- the sum of the regular dollar limit plus the amount by which the limit in prior years exceeded the amount actually deferred by the participant in those years.

This three-year catch-up rule applies to both governmental employer plans and to private tax-exempt organization 457 plans—not just to governmental employer plans.

Distributions from a Section 457 Plan

A participant in a Section 457 plan may not take a distribution before the year in which the participant reaches age 70½, leaves the employer, or has an unforeseen emergency (severe financial hardship resulting from a sudden and unexpected illness or accident of the participant or a dependent, a casualty loss to the participant's property, or other similar extraordinary and unforeseeable circumstances beyond the control of the participant). However, a participant in a tax-exempt nongovernmental organization's plan may take an involuntary distribution up to $5,000 from her account if there has been no deferral by her for the last two years, and no prior distributions have been taken.

Moreover, a participant may defer the start of distributions (if the amounts are otherwise available and before the beginning of distributions) by making a one-time election to do so.

Required minimum distributions must be taken under the same rules applicable to qualified plans.

Participants in governmental Section 457 plans report distributions as income when received. Participants in non-governmental, tax-exempt plans report distributions as income either when received or when they are made available (meaning at the time there is no longer a substantial risk of forfeiture). Just as with Section 403(b) plans, distributions from Section 457 plans do *not* qualify for the favorable lump-sum 10-year averaging treatment available to qualified plans.

Exhibit 4.1 Comparison of Employer-Sponsored Tax-Advantaged Plans

Type of Plan	Who Can Establish	How Established	Eligible Employee	Contribution Limit	Catch-Up Contributions	Deduction Limit	Treatment of Distributions	Rollovers	Advantages	Disadvantages
Simplified employee pension (SEP) plan	Typically small employers, usually 10 employees or less	1. Execute formal written agreement 2. Provide employees with information about plan 3. Must establish a SEP-IRA for each eligible employee	At least age 21; worked for employer three of last five years; at least $600 in compensation from employer	Only employer contributions. Lesser of 25% of employee's compensation or $53,000 (for 2015). Compensation does not include employer's contributions to SEP; maximum compensation of $265,000 in 2015	No	Same as contribution limit; special computation for self-employed participant	Can make withdrawals at any time but subject to income tax and 10% additional penalty if before age 59½; subject to required minimum distribution rules	Contributions and earnings can be rolled over tax-free to other IRAs and retirement plans.	1. Easier and less expensive to install & administer 2. Can create retroactively 3. No required contribution by employer 4. Employee bears investment risk	1. Will not guarantee adequate retirement benefit 2. Annual contributions less than qualified plan 3. No 10-year averaging
Salary Reduction Simplified Employee Pension (SARSEP)	Must have been established prior to 1997.	Employer can continue to maintain plan if: 50% or more of employees make elective deferrals; 25 or fewer employees eligible to participate at any time in prior year; HCEs must meet SARSEP ADP test.	Participants in plans established prior to 1997 can continue to make elective deferrals	Employees can make elective deferrals; lesser of 25% of employee's compensation or $18,000 (in 2015)	Yes. $6,000 for 2015 not subject to elective deferral limit	Same as contribution limit	Same rules as traditional IRAs.	Okay	1. Limits on elective deferrals greater than those for SIMPLE IRAs and SIMPLE 401(k) plans	1. Must meet SARSEP ADP test for HCEs.

Exhibit 4.1 Comparison of Employer-Sponsored Tax-Advantaged Plans (continued)

Plan	Who/Eligibility	Basis	Coverage	Contributions	Catch-up			Distributions	Rollover	Advantages	Disadvantages
Savings incentive match plan for employees (SIMPLE)	100 or fewer employees who received $5,000 or more in compensation from employer in prior 2 years	Calendar-year basis only; IRAs or 401(k) options; must be only retirement plan except union plan.	Must include self-employed and leased employees; can exclude union and nonresident aliens with no U.S. source income from employer	Employees can make elective deferrals; employer can make matching or nonelective contributions; up to $12,500 (in 2015) as percentage of compensation or as flat amount; employer must match up to 3% of compensation unless elects less than 3%—then percentage must be at least 1%; or employer can make nonelective contributions of 2%	Yes. $3,000 for 2015	Same as contribution limit	Same as contribution limit	Okay from one SIMPLE-IRA to another; if from SIMPLE-IRA to non-SIMPLE-IRA, must have two years' participation in SIMPLE-IRA plan to be tax-free; 25% additional tax, rather than 10%, if fail to wait two years	1. Easier and less expensive to install & administer 2. Can fund plan through salary reductions 3. Limits may be higher than Keogh or SEP 4. Employee bears investment risk		1. Will not guarantee adequate retirement benefit 2. Contributions may be smaller than qualified plan 3. No 10-year averaging 4. Cannot also have qualified plan, SEP, 403(a) annuity, 403(b) plan, or 457 plan
Tax-sheltered annuity (403(b)) plan	Public schools; tax-exempt organizations; certain ministers	Only the employer can do so; self-employed minister cannot do so—only the organization with which he or she is associated can do so.	Employee of 501(c)(3) org, public school system; cooperative hospital service org, or USUHS, and ministers employed by 501(c)(3) organization, self-employed and perform services for qualified employer, or employed by non-501(c)(3) organization and functions as minister with employer.	Maximum amount contributable (MAC)-lesser of limit on annual additions or limit on elective deferrals; annual additions limit-lesser of $53,000 (in 2015) or 100% of includible compensation for most recent year of service; elective deferral limit-$18,000 (in 2015) unless have 15 years of service.-$21,000 (in 2015). Alternative limit for ministers and church employees.	Yes. $6,000 for 2015	Same as contribution limit.	No distribution until employee reaches age 59½, leaves employ of employer, dies, becomes disabled, or incurs financial hardship (salary reduction contributions only); generally same rules as other retirement plans	Can make 90-24 transfer to another 403(b) account; trustee-to-trustee transfer to a defined benefit government plan to purchase service credits; can roll to traditional IRA or eligible retirement plan	1. Tax deferral for employees 2. Employer can fund through employee salary reductions 3. Employer can also make contributions, if desired 4. In-service withdrawals as in profit-sharing plans 5. Employee bears investment risk		1. Will not guarantee adequate retirement benefit 2. Salary reductions subject to elective deferral limit 3. Subject to non-discrimination tests 4. Employees have choice of investments 5.No 10-year averaging
Governmental and tax-exempt employer deferred compensation (Section 457) plan	Certain state and local governments, governmental agencies or instrumentalities of a state or local government (such as a school district or sewage authority); also non-governmental, non-church controlled entities tax exempt under IRC Section 501	Employer must adopt plan containing required provisions; forms must be furnished to employees to make salary reduction elections	Employees of eligible organizations.	Lesser of 100% of participant's compensation (gross before salary reductions) or $18,000 (in 2015). All 457 plans in which employee participates must be included.	Participants in government plans may contribute up to $6,000 (in 2015) provided income is adequate; general rule not applicable to participant who qualifies for earlier three-year catch-up rule (three-year rule applies to both government and private tax-exempt organizations)	Employers not subject to income taxation	Cannot take distribution before year in which participant reaches age 70½, leaves employer, or has "unforeseen emergency"; participant in tax-exempt non-government organization plan can take distribution up to $5,000 if no deferral for last two years and no prior distributions taken; may defer start of distributions	Automatic rollover to IRA rule for distribution in excess of $1,000 and less than or equal to $5,000 unless participant elects to have distribution transferred to another eligible retirement plan or to take distribution in cash. Final safe harbor rules not yet issued by DOL.	1. No specific coverage requirements 2. Government entities can make available to any employee or employees 3. Salary reduction contributions do not affect the amount that can be contributed to other types of salary reduction plans (Sections 403(b) or 401(k))	1. May not be funded but may be "financed" with insurance or annuities 2. Government organization plans required to be funded by placing plan assets in trusts or custodial accounts. 3. No 10-year averaging

5

Supplemental Reading–Traditional and Roth IRAs

TYPES OF INDIVIDUAL RETIREMENT ARRANGEMENTS

There are basically four types of individual retirement arrangements. The original IRA, authorized by ERISA in 1974, is referred to as a traditional IRA. Contributions to a traditional IRA may be made *only* by the individual for whom the IRA is maintained or his spouse and not by the individual's employer. Annual contributions to such an IRA are limited in amount and, if they meet other requirements (discussed later in this reading), are deductible from gross income. Generally, a distribution from a traditional IRA is taxable to the extent it exceeds any nondeductible contributions made by the owner.

Another type of IRA enacted in 1978 as part of the Revenue Act of 1978 is the SEP IRA. SEP stands for *simplified employee pension*. The SEP IRA is essentially the same as a traditional IRA, except that only the owner's employer may make contributions to it [unless it is the now defunct salary reduction SEP (SARSEP) that did permit employee salary reduction contributions]. Employer contributions and the related income tax deductions are subject to limitations that are essentially the same as those that apply to qualified profit-sharing plans. On the other hand, owner contributions and tax deductions are subject to the same limitations that apply to traditional IRAs. Again, a distribution from a SEP IRA is taxable to the extent it exceeds the owner's basis (nondeductible contributions).

A third type of IRA, referred to as a SIMPLE IRA, was established by the Small Business Job Protection Act of 1996. SIMPLE is an acronym for *savings incentive match plan for employees*. Only the owner's employer may contribute to a SIMPLE IRA. The owner is not permitted to make either deductible or nondeductible contributions, but the owner may authorize salary reduction contributions, which are treated as contributions of the employer for tax purposes. The employer is required to match such salary reduction contributions. Annual amount limitations apply to salary reduction contributions and to matching contributions. Because the owner can never have a basis in such an account, distributions are taxable in their entirety.

Congress created a fourth type of IRA in the Taxpayer Relief Act of 1997. It is known as the Roth IRA, which prohibits employer contributions and permits limited nondeductible contributions by the owner. Qualified distributions from a Roth IRA are *never* taxable. Nonqualified distributions are taxable to the extent they exceed the owner's nondeductible contributions. Roth IRAs are discussed later in this reading.

Just to further confuse the issue, there are two other types of IRAs. One was formerly known as an education IRA, created by the same act as the Roth IRA—the Taxpayer Relief Act of 1997. These accounts were created to encourage savings for higher education and actually have nothing to do with retirement. They have been renamed Coverdell Education Savings Accounts (CESAs). This type of IRA account is not discussed in this book.

A final type of IRA, initiated in 2003, is known as a deemed IRA. Under the authorizing legislation, a qualified plan, tax-sheltered annuity arrangement, or nonqualified government plan may elect to accept voluntary employee contributions and treat them as contributions to a conventional IRA or Roth IRA, as the employee chooses.

QUALIFICATION REQUIREMENTS

Each method of funding an individual retirement arrangement (i.e., individual retirement account or individual retirement annuity) is subject to specific requirements.

Individual Retirement Accounts

As mentioned earlier, an individual retirement account is a trust or custodial account created and organized under a written instrument for the exclusive benefit of an individual or her beneficiaries. The written document creating the IRA must meet the following requirements:

- The trustee or custodian may be a bank, a federally insured credit union, a savings and loan association, or other entity approved by the IRS to act as trustee or custodian. The IRS has issued a list of approved non-bank trustees. However, the account owner may not serve as trustee or custodian.

- The trustee or custodian generally cannot accept contributions of more than the applicable dollar limit (discussed later in this reading), with these contributions consisting of cash, except for rollover contributions (discussed later in this reading), which are also not subject to the dollar limitation.

- The owner's right to the amount in the account must be fully vested at all times.

- Funds in the account may not be used to purchase a life insurance policy. However, such funds may be used to purchase an endowment policy, under certain conditions.

- The funds in the account cannot be commingled with other property, except in a common trust fund or common investment fund (e.g., as offered by a bank trust department).

- The owner must begin to receive distributions from her account not later than April 1 of the year following the year in which she reaches age 70½. A penalty tax is imposed on excess accumulations after the owner reaches 70½.

Individual Retirement Annuities

An individual retirement annuity is created by purchasing an annuity contract or an endowment contract from a life insurance company. The contract must be issued in the name of the owner and must be for the exclusive benefit of the owner and his surviving beneficiaries. Only the owner or his surviving beneficiaries may receive benefits under the contract. An individual retirement annuity must meet all of the following requirements.

- The contract must be nontransferable, and the owner's interest must be nonforfeitable.

- The contract must provide for premiums that are adjusted for any change in owner compensation.

- The contribution limit (discussed later in this reading) must not exceed that amount also permitted for individual retirement accounts.

- The owner must use any refunded premiums either to pay for future premiums or to purchase additional benefits.

- Distributions must meet the same requirements as those for individual retirement accounts (i.e., they must begin by April 1 of the year following the year in which the owner reaches age 70½).

- Finally, the owner of an individual retirement annuity may not borrow against the annuity, either directly from the issuing insurance company or from third parties using the annuity as security. Violation of this prohibition causes the individual retirement annuity to terminate, resulting in its entire value being included in the owner's income at that time.

CONTRIBUTION AND DEDUCTION LIMITS

Being permitted to make a contribution to a traditional IRA does not necessarily mean that such contribution may be deductible for income tax purposes. And even though a deduction may not be permitted, an individual may still make a nondeductible contribution to an IRA within the contribution limits described in the following. A nondeductible traditional IRA contribution is the excess of the maximum annual contribution amount over the amount deductible (discussed later). Nondeductible contributions are not taxable when they are distributed, but the income earned on those contributions is taxable. Accordingly, amounts withdrawn are partly taxable and partly nontaxable. In the following sections, we will describe the separate limitations for the amounts that may be contributed to an IRA and the amounts contributed that are tax deductible.

Contribution Limits

Only contributions made by or on behalf of the IRA owner or the owner's surviving spouse, who acquired the IRA by reason of the owner's death, qualify for deduction and tax-free buildup. Any other person succeeding to an owner's IRA because of the owner's death (other than the owner's surviving spouse) may *not* make a qualifying contribution to the IRA. A qualifying contribution must be in cash (unless it is a rollover contribution) within the limitations established by law and made in a tax year that ends before the IRA owner has reached age 70½. It does not matter where the contributed funds come from. They may be contributed by a non-owner; however, the contribution and deduction limits are determined with reference to the owner's compensation, adjusted gross income (including that of his or her spouse in the case of a joint return), and status as a qualified retirement plan participant.

In 2015, the contribution limit is the smaller of $5,500 (or $6,500 if the owner is 50 or older) or the owner's taxable compensation. Taxable compensation includes amounts received for providing personal services, such as wages, salaries, tips, professional fees, bonuses, and other similar receipts. It also includes any amounts received that are calculated as a percentage of profits or sales price (commissions), as well as net earnings from self-employment derived from a trade or business (reduced by contributions on behalf of the IRA owner to retirement plans and by the deduction permitted for one-half of the self-employment tax paid). For IRA contribution purposes, compensation also includes taxable alimony and separate maintenance payments received under a decree of divorce or separate maintenance. Rental income, interest income, dividend income, pension or annuity income, deferred compensation payments, income from a limited partnership or where the IRA owner's services are not a material income-producing factor, and foreign earned income and housing costs excluded from income do not constitute taxable compensation for this purpose. The foregoing limitation applies to the total of all IRAs owned by the same individual.

Generally, a person's income tax filing status has *no* effect on the amount of allowable contributions to his traditional IRA. However, a taxpayer who files a joint return with his spouse and has taxable compensation less than that of the spouse is subject to one of the following contribution limits:

- $5,500 ($6,500 if 50 or older) for 2015

- The total compensation includable in the gross income of both the taxpayer and her spouse for the year, reduced by (1) the spouse's IRA contribution for the year to a traditional IRA and (2) any contributions for the year to a Roth IRA on behalf of the spouse

If a taxpayer's contributions to his IRA for a particular year were less than the limits described previously, he cannot make additional contributions after the due date of the tax return for that same tax year. Likewise, if a taxpayer contributes more than the allowable limit for a particular tax year, the excess contributions may only be applied to a later tax year if the contributions for that later year are less than the maximum allowed for that year. However, a penalty or additional tax may then be applicable, as discussed later in this reading.

Also, if a taxpayer has no taxable compensation in a given tax year, he may not make a contribution unless he received alimony or filed a joint return with a spouse who had taxable compensation in that year.

Contributions for a particular year may be made at any time during that year, or even after the year, until the due date for filing the tax return for that year, not including extensions of time to file. When making a contribution between January 1 and April 15, it is important that the IRA owner clearly specifies to the IRA sponsor for which tax year he is making contributions (the current or prior year). Moreover, a taxpayer may file his tax return without having actually made a traditional IRA contribution for that year, as long as the contribution is made by the due date of the return.

Deduction Limits

Generally, the maximum amount that may be deducted from gross income for contributions to IRAs in any tax year is the same as the limit on contributions. However, in the case where the owner is an active participant in an employer-sponsored retirement plan or is a non-active participant filing a joint return with a spouse who is an active participant, the dollar limitation on the deduction may be *reduced*. As mentioned previously, however, even though no deduction may be allowed, an individual may still make a nondeductible contribution to an IRA equal to the IRA contribution limit for the current year.

The deduction rules are as follows:

- In the case of a married couple, if neither spouse was an active participant (defined later) in an employer-maintained retirement plan during any part of a particular year, each spouse may claim a deduction for total contributions to one or more of his traditional IRAs of up to the lesser of:

  — $5,500 or $6,500, if 50 or older, (2015); or

  — 100% of each spouse's compensation.

Where a married couple has unequal compensation and files a joint return, the deduction for contributions to the traditional IRA of the spouse with less compensation is limited to the lesser of:

- $5,500 or $6,500, if 50 or older, (2015); or

- the total compensation includable in the gross income of both spouses for the year reduced by

  — the IRA deduction for the year of the spouse with the greater compensation,

  — any designated nondeductible contribution for the year made on behalf of the spouse with the greater compensation, and

  — any contributions for the year to a Roth IRA on behalf of the spouse with the greater compensation.

If either spouse was covered by an employer-maintained retirement plan, each spouse may be entitled to only a partial (reduced) deduction or no deduction at all, depending on their income and filing status, as discussed later.

Active Participation in an Employer-Maintained Retirement Plan

An active participant is an individual who is an active participant in:

- a qualified pension, profit-sharing, or stock bonus plan (including a Section 401(k) plan or union plan);

- a simplified employee pension (SEP);

- a plan (other than a Section 457 plan, discussed later) established for employees by the United States, a state or political subdivision of a state, or by a federal or state instrumentality; or

- a SIMPLE retirement account.

An individual who is retired and receiving pension annuity payments from any one of the foregoing plans or arrangements is *not* an active participant, nor is an individual who is covered only by Social Security or by a railroad retirement program. The determination of status as an active participant is made without regard to whether an individual's rights under an employer-maintained plan are forfeitable or nonforfeitable. In fact, the U.S. Tax Court has ruled that an employee's active participation in his employer's retirement plans prevented him from taking a deduction on his federal taxes for contributions to an IRA, even though his interest in the funds was forfeited upon his termination of employment.

An individual is considered to be an active participant in a defined contribution plan if amounts are contributed or allocated to his account for the plan year that ends with or within a particular tax year. In the case of a defined benefit pension plan, if an individual is eligible to participate in his employer's defined benefit pension plan for the plan year that ends within his tax year, he is covered by the plan. This is true even if the individual declines to participate in the plan, did not make a required contribution, or did not perform the minimum service required to accrue a benefit for the year. If an individual receives retirement benefits from a previous employer's plan, he is not covered by that plan.

Effect of Active Participation in an Employer-Maintained Retirement Plan

If a married individual is *not* an active participant but his spouse *is* an active participant and the couple files a joint return, the deduction for the nonparticipant is gradually phased out when the couple has modified adjusted gross income (MAGI) of more than $193,000 (2015) and completely eliminated when their MAGI exceeds $193,000 (2015). If a married individual is *not* an active participant but her spouse *is* an active participant and the individual files a separate return, the deduction for the non-participant is phased out between MAGI of zero and $9,999. If MAGI is $10,000 or more, no deduction is permitted.

MAGI is defined as adjusted gross income (AGI) without taking into consideration:

- the IRA deduction;

- the student loan interest deduction;

- the tuition and fees deduction;

- the foreign earned income exclusion;

- the foreign housing exclusion or deduction;

- the qualified savings bond interest exclusion; and

- the employer-provided adoption benefits exclusion.

If a single or head of household filer is an active participant, he may claim a full deduction if his MAGI is $61,000 (2015) or less. If his MAGI is more than $61,000 (2015) but less than $71,000 (2015), he may claim a partial deduction under the phaseout provisions. If his MAGI is $71,000 or more, no deduction is permitted.

If one's filing status is married filing jointly or qualifying widow and she is an active participant, a full deduction may be claimed if MAGI is $98,000 (2015) or less. If MAGI is more than $98,000 but less than $118,000 (2015), she may claim a partial deduction under the phaseout provisions. If MAGI is $118,000 (2015) or more no deduction is permitted.

If one's filing status is married filing separate return and he is an active participant, a partial deduction may be claimed under the phaseout provisions if MAGI is less than $10,000. If MAGI is $10,000 or more, no deduction is permitted.

Special rules apply (not discussed in this text) if the individual received Social Security benefits during the year, received taxable compensation, made contributions to her traditional IRA, and either the individual or spouse was an active participant.

TRANSFER OF RETIREMENT PLAN ASSETS

Money or property residing in retirement programs (including traditional IRAs) may be transferred to a traditional IRA on a tax-free basis without limitation as to amount. There are three types of such transfers:

- A transfer from one trustee to another

- A rollover (as defined in the following)

- A transfer incident to a divorce

If an IRA owner decides to move her IRA funds from an existing traditional IRA to another either existing or new traditional IRA, there are two methods to execute a rollover. The preferable method is to transfer the funds directly from the trustee of the existing IRA to the trustee of the other IRA. Such a transfer is referred to as a direct transfer, and because the IRA owner never has access to the transferred funds, it is *not* taxable to the owner. Also, such a transfer is not subject to 20% withholding tax (discussed later), the 10% additional tax (where the recipient is under age 59½), or the one-year waiting period required between rollovers (discussed later).

A second rollover method is a tax-free distribution to the IRA owner of cash or other assets from one retirement plan that is deposited (called a rollover contribution) in another retirement plan. Rollovers may be made into a traditional IRA from the following sources:

- A traditional IRA

- An employer's qualified retirement plan

- A deferred compensation plan of a state or local government (Section 457 plan)

- A tax-sheltered annuity plan (Section 403(b) plan)

A rollover distribution is not deductible and must be reported on the account owner's tax return for the year distributed.

A rollover may also be made from a traditional IRA into a qualified plan, including the Federal Thrift Savings Fund (for federal employees), Section 457 plans, and Section 403(b) annuity plans. However, qualified plans do not have to accept such transfers from traditional IRAs. A traditional IRA owner may also roll over his interest in one traditional IRA to another traditional IRA.

Generally, a rollover contribution must be made by the 60th day after the day the owner receives a distribution from his traditional IRA or employer's plan. If such distributions are not rolled over within the 60-day period, they do not qualify for tax-free rollover treatment. Instead, they are treated as a taxable distribution. Also, the owner may have to pay a 10% additional tax on early distribution (discussed later) of his interest. However, the 60-day rollover period may be waived by the IRS under specific circumstances.

Normally, if an IRA owner makes a tax-free rollover of any part of a distribution from a traditional IRA, he cannot, within a one-year period, make a tax-free rollover of any later distribution. The one-year period begins on the date the owner receives the IRA distribution, not on the date he rolled it over into an IRA. However, the once-a-year limit on IRA-to-IRA rollovers does not apply to eligible rollover distributions when executed using the direct transfer method.

An eligible rollover distribution from an owner's (or owner's deceased spouse's) qualified pension, profit-sharing, or stock bonus plan; annuity plan; Section 403(b) plan; or Section 457 plan may be rolled over into a traditional IRA. An eligible rollover distribution is any distribution of all or part of the balance to an owner's credit in a qualified retirement plan, with the following eight exceptions:

- A required minimum distribution (explained later in this reading)

- A hardship distribution (explained later in this reading)

- Any of a series of substantially equal periodic distributions paid at least once a year over the owner's life expectancy, the lifetimes or life expectancies of the owner and the owner's beneficiary, or a period of 10 years or more

- Corrective distributions of excess contributions or excess deferrals, and any income allocable to the excess, or of excess annual additions and any allocable gains

- A loan treated as a distribution because it does not satisfy certain requirements either when made or later (such as upon default), unless the participant's accrued benefits are reduced (offset) to repay the loan

- Dividends on employer securities

- The cost of life insurance coverage

- Generally, a distribution to the plan participant's beneficiary

To the extent the distribution is rolled over into a traditional IRA, it is not includable in the owner's income. However, if an eligible rollover distribution is paid directly to the account owner, the payer must withhold 20% of the distribution amount. This is true even if the owner plans to roll over the distribution to a traditional IRA. The key here is whether the check is made out to the account owner or to the custodian of the transferee IRA (on behalf of the owner). The payer does not have to withhold income tax if all distributions from the same plan (or, at the payer's option, from all of the payee's employer's plans) total less than $200 or the distribution consists solely of employer securities, plus cash of $200 or less in lieu of fractional shares.

Conduit IRAs

An individual receiving an eligible rollover distribution from her employer's plan may roll over part or all of it into one or more conduit IRAs. Subsequently, these assets may be rolled over into a new employer's plan. A traditional IRA may be used as a conduit IRA, even if the owner continues to make regular contributions to it or adds funds from sources other than her employer's plan. However, if the owner does so, the qualified plan into which the funds are eventually transferred will not be eligible for any optional tax treatment for which it otherwise might have qualified.

Where an individual receives property (other than cash) in an eligible rollover distribution from a qualified retirement plan, she cannot keep the property and contribute cash to a traditional IRA instead of the property. She must then either roll over the property or sell it and roll over the proceeds. If the individual elects to sell the property and roll over all the proceeds into a traditional IRA, no gain or loss is recognized. One additional limitation is that a life insurance contract distributed from a qualified plan may not be rolled over into a traditional IRA.

The third type of transfer that may be made tax free is a transfer incident to divorce. An interest in a traditional IRA transferred to an individual from his spouse or former spouse pursuant to a divorce or separate maintenance decree or a written document related to such a decree is treated as the transferee's own IRA. Such a tax-free transfer may be accomplished by either changing the name on the IRA or by making a direct transfer of the IRA assets.

A final type of transfer of traditional IRA assets is a conversion of such assets into a Roth IRA. This type of transfer will be discussed later in this reading.

DISTRIBUTIONS OF IRA ASSETS

A traditional IRA owner can withdraw or use his IRA assets at any time. However, if the owner is younger than 59½ years of age at the time of the withdrawal, such a withdrawal is considered to be an early distribution, and he will generally be subject to a 10% additional tax. However, an IRA owner may make a tax-free and penalty-free withdrawal of contributions if he does so *before* the due date for filing his tax return for the year in which the contributions were made (even if the owner is younger than age 59½). The IRA owner must not have taken a deduction for the contribution, and he must withdraw any interest or other income earned on the contribution. The earnings on withdrawn contributions must also be included in gross income for the year in which the contributions were made—not the year in which they were withdrawn. Withdrawals of contributions after the due date (or extended due date) of the owner's return are treated as taxable distributions.

Funds contributed to a traditional IRA must eventually be distributed. If the owner does not take distributions or if the distributions taken are not large enough, the owner may be subject to a 50% excise tax on the amount not distributed as required. The requirements for distributing IRA funds vary, depending on whether the recipient is the IRA owner or the beneficiary of a decedent's IRA.

The amount that must be distributed each year is referred to as the required minimum distribution (RMD). Such amounts are *not* eligible for rollover treatment.

IRA Owner's Required Minimum Distribution

An IRA owner must start receiving distributions from her IRA by April 1 (known as the required beginning date) of the year following the year in which she reaches age 70½. A minimum amount must be distributed each year, starting with the year the owner reaches 70½. If the first minimum distribution is not received in the year in which the owner turns 70½, then it must be made by April 1 of the subsequent year. However, the required minimum distribution for any year after the year the owner turns 70½ must be made by December 31 of that later year. If an owner dies after reaching 70½ but before April 1 of the following year, no minimum distribution is required because her death occurred before the required beginning date.

> **EXAMPLE** John attains age 70½ during calendar year 2015. If John does not take his first required minimum distribution for 2015 on or before December 31, 2015, he has until April 1, 2016, to take that distribution. However, if John does not take the 2015 RMD during 2015, he will have to take both the RMD for 2015 (by April 1, 2016) and the RMD for 2016 by December 31, 2016, resulting in two RMDs in the same tax year.

In the case of an individual retirement account, either the owner or the trustee must calculate the required minimum distribution (RMD) for each year. For individual retirement annuities, special rules apply to figuring the required minimum distribution.

In order to calculate the amount of the RMD for a specific year, one divides the IRA account balance as of the close of business on December 31 of the preceding year by the applicable *distribution period* or *life expectancy*. The IRA account balance as of December 31 of the preceding year must be adjusted for rollovers and recharacterizations of Roth IRA conversions that were not in the account at the end of the preceding year. The distribution period is the maximum number of years over which an IRA owner is permitted to take distributions from her IRA. This period is derived from the IRS Uniform Lifetime Table (Table III), which is for unmarried IRA owners, married owners whose spouses are the sole beneficiaries of their IRAs and are not more than 10 years younger than the IRA owner, and married owners whose spouses are not the sole beneficiaries of their IRAs.

In the situation where the sole beneficiary of an owner's IRA is her spouse who is more than 10 years younger than the owner, the owner must use the IRS Joint Life and Last Survivor Expectancy Tables (Table II) to determine the life expectancy for purposes of the required minimum distribution calculation.

The beneficiary of an IRA who is an individual must use the IRS Single Life Expectancy Table (Table I) to determine the required minimum distribution. If the IRA owner's spouse is the sole designated beneficiary, the life expectancy of the spouse is used from Table I. If the owner died before the year in which he reached age 70½, distributions to the spouse do not need to begin until the year in which the owner would have reached age 70½. Where the beneficiary is someone *other than the owner's spouse*, such beneficiary must use the life expectancy listed in the table next to the beneficiary's age as of his birthday in the year following the year the owner died, reduced by the number of years since the year following the owner's death. For example, if a father died in 2013 and his son is the designated beneficiary of his traditional IRA, the son must use Table I (based on his age in 2014) to determine his life expectancy. If the son is 53 years old in 2014, his life expectancy is 31.4 years. If the IRA was worth $100,000 at the end of 2013, the required minimum distribution for 2014 is

$3,185 ($100,000 ÷ 31.4). If the value of the IRA at the end of 2014 was again $100,000, the required minimum distribution for 2015 would be $3,278 ($100,000 ÷ 30.5).

Where the beneficiary of an IRA is *not* an individual (e.g., the owner's estate) and the owner died on or after the required beginning date, the required minimum distribution is determined from Table I using the owner's age as of her birthday in the year of death, reduced by the number of years since the year of death. If the owner died before the required beginning date, the entire account balance must be distributed by the end of the fifth year following the year of the owner's death. No distribution is required for any year before that fifth year.

In summary, the IRS tables should be used as follows:

- Table I: use for years after the year of the owner's death if the beneficiary is either an individual and a designated beneficiary but not both the owner's surviving spouse and sole designated beneficiary or not an individual and the owner died on or after the required beginning date. If the beneficiary is the owner's surviving spouse and sole designated beneficiary and the owner had not reached age 70½ when he died and the beneficiary does not elect to be treated as the owner of the IRA, the beneficiary does not have to take distributions (using Table I) until the year in which the owner would have reached 70½.

- Table II: use if the IRA owner's spouse is both the sole designated beneficiary and more than 10 years younger than the IRA owner. This table is also used in the year of the owner's death if she died after the required beginning date and would have been used had she not died.

- Table III: use if the IRA owner's spouse is *not* both the sole designated beneficiary and more than 10 years younger than the owner. This table is also used in the year of the owner's death if he died after the required beginning date and would have been used had he not died.

- Do not use *any* of the tables if the designated beneficiary is *not* an individual and the owner died *before* the required beginning date. In this case, the entire account balance must be distributed by the end of the fifth year following the year of the IRA owner's death. In addition, an individual may elect to take the entire account by the end of the fifth year following the year of the owner's death.

Taxation of IRA Distributions

In general, a distribution from a traditional IRA is taxable as ordinary income in the year received, except to the extent that the distribution constitutes a rollover, contributions withdrawn by the due date of the tax return (where a tax deduction was not taken for the contributions), or a return of nondeductible contributions. If the IRA(s) from which the distribution(s) was (were) made contained only deductible contributions, the IRA owner has no tax basis in such accounts and, therefore, the entire amount withdrawn is fully taxable. On the other hand, if the IRA(s) from which the distribution(s) was (were) made included nondeductible contributions, the IRA owner has a tax basis, and she can receive them free of tax as a return of her investment. In this latter case, distributions received will consist partially of nondeductible contributions (tax basis) and partially of deductible contributions, earnings, and gains (if any). Until the entire tax basis is recovered, each distribution is partly nontaxable and partly taxable. The calculation of the portion considered taxable is made on IRS Form 8606 using Worksheet 1-5.

PROHIBITED TRANSACTIONS

Any improper use of a traditional IRA account or annuity by the IRA owner, his beneficiary, or any disqualified person constitutes a **prohibited transaction**. A disqualified person includes the IRA owner's fiduciary (IRA custodian or trustee) and members of the account owner's family (spouse, ancestor, lineal descendant, and any spouse of a lineal descendant). A fiduciary, for these purposes, is anyone who exercises any discretionary authority or discretionary control in managing the IRA or exercises any authority or control in managing or disposing of its assets, provides investment advice to the IRA for a fee or has any authority or responsibility to do so, or has any discretionary authority or discretionary responsibility in administering the IRA. Prohibited transactions with a traditional IRA include:

- the sale, exchange, or lease of any property between an IRA and a disqualified person;

- the lending of money or other extension of credit between an IRA and a disqualified person;

- the furnishing of goods, services, or facilities between an IRA and a disqualified person;

- the transfer to, or use by or for the benefit of, a disqualified person of the income or assets of an IRA;

- an act by a disqualified person who is a fiduciary whereby she deals with the income or assets of an IRA in her own interest or her own account; and

- the receipt of any consideration for her own personal account by a disqualified person who is a fiduciary from any party dealing with the IRA in connection with a transaction involving the income or assets of the plan.

The Code exempts certain transactions that might otherwise be prohibited under the previous rules, but none of these exemptions apply to transactions in which an IRA directly or indirectly lends any part of the corpus or income to, pays any compensation for personal services rendered to the plan to, or acquires for the plan any property from, or sells any property to, the owner or beneficiary of an IRA.

Engaging in a prohibited transaction has very severe consequences. If any of the previously described persons (including the owner or his beneficiary) engages in such a transaction at any time during the year, the account stops being an IRA as of the first day of that year. The result is that the assets in the account are treated as being distributed to the owner at their fair market values on the first day of the year. If the total of these values exceeds the owner's basis, the excess will constitute a taxable gain.

If someone other than the owner or beneficiary of a traditional IRA engages in a prohibited transaction, that person may be liable for certain taxes, including a 15% tax on the amount of the prohibited transaction and a 100% additional tax if the transaction is not corrected. If the owner or beneficiary engages in a prohibited transaction, they are not liable for these excise taxes, but they may be subject to both income tax and the 10% early distribution penalty.

Other Transactions Treated as Distributions

Certain other transactions are not considered disqualifying transactions but are treated as distributions to the owner. These transactions include:

- pledging any portion of an individual retirement account as security for a loan;

- borrowing money against an individual retirement annuity either from the issuing insurance company or from third parties using the contract as security; and

- investing in collectibles (e.g., art works, rugs, antiques, metals, gems, stamps, coins, alcoholic beverages, and certain other tangible personal property specified by the U.S. Treasury Department) by an individual retirement account. Certain types of U.S.-minted (not foreign-minted) gold, silver, and platinum coins; coins issued under the laws of any state; and any gold, silver, platinum, or palladium bullion meeting certain quality requirements are an exception.

Early Distributions

Distributions from a traditional IRA account or annuity are those distributed *before* the IRA owner is age 59½. Such distributions are subject to a 10% tax, which is in addition to the regular income tax payable on such distributions. The 10% tax is applicable to the portion of the distribution that must be included in gross income.

The following are some of the exceptions to the age 59½ rule:

- The owner has unreimbursed medical expenses that exceed a specific adjusted gross income (AGI) threshold.

- The distributions are not more than the cost of the owner's medical insurance. The owner must have lost her job; she must have collected unemployment compensation for 12 consecutive weeks because of losing her job; she must also have received the distributions during either the year the unemployment compensation was received or the following year; and the distributions must have been received no later than 60 days after the owner becomes re-employed.

- The owner is disabled, meaning the owner furnishes proof that she cannot do any substantial gainful activity because of a physical or mental condition. A physician must determine that the owner's condition may be expected to result in death or to be of long, continued, and indefinite duration.

- The recipient of the distribution is the beneficiary of a deceased IRA owner.

- The owner is receiving distributions in the form of an annuity, which are part of a series of substantially equal payments over the owner's life (or life expectancy) or over the lives (or the joint life expectancies) of the owner and her beneficiary [commonly known as 72(t) payments after the Internal Revenue Code Section of the same number].

- The distributions are not more than the qualified higher education expenses of the owner, the owner's spouse, or the children or grandchildren of the owner or of her spouse. Not included in such expenses are those paid with tax-free distributions from a Coverdell Education Savings Account, the tax-free portion of scholarships and fellowships, Pell grants, employer-provided educational assistance, veterans' educational assistance, or any other tax-free payment (other than a gift or inheritance) received as educational assistance.

■ The owner uses the distributions to buy, build, or rebuild a first home if the qualified acquisition costs were paid within 120 days of receiving the distributions, they do not exceed $10,000, and they were paid for the main home of a first-time homebuyer (including the owner, the owner's spouse, the owner's or spouse's child, grandchild, parent, or other ancestor). A first-time homebuyer is someone who did not own a main home during the two-year period ending on the date of acquisition of the home for which the distribution is being used to buy, build, or rebuild. The date of acquisition is either the date the owner entered into a binding contract to buy the main home or the building or rebuilding of the main home begins.

■ The distribution is due to an IRS assessment imposed on the qualified plan.

EXCESS CONTRIBUTIONS

An excess contribution is the amount contributed (whether deductible or nondeductible) to a traditional IRA for the year that is *more than* the amount allowable for that year [usually the smaller of $5,500 (2015) or $6,500 (2015) if 50 or older] or the owner's taxable compensation for the year. As discussed previously in this chapter, if a taxpayer makes contributions to his IRA for a particular year that were less than the limits, he cannot make additional contributions after the due date of the tax return for that same tax year. Likewise, if a taxpayer contributes more than the allowable limit for a particular tax year, the excess contributions may be applied to a later tax year if the contributions for that later year are less than the maximum allowed for that year. However, a penalty or additional tax may be applicable.

Generally, excess contributions not withdrawn by the due date are subject to a 6% penalty tax. If such excess contributions remain in an owner's traditional IRA at the end of the owner's tax year, the owner must continue to pay the 6% tax for each year the excess contributions remain there. The tax is limited to 6% of the year-end value of the IRA.

If the owner withdraws an excess contribution made during a tax year, including any interest or other income earned on the excess contribution, by the due date (including extensions) of the tax return for that year, the 6% tax does not have to be paid. This assumes no deduction was allowed for the excess contribution and the interest or other income earned on the excess contribution was also withdrawn. The interest or other income that was earned on the excess contribution must be included in the owner's gross income for the year in which the excess contribution was made. The withdrawal of interest or other income earned may be subject to the additional 10% tax on early distributions.

If the owner withdraws excess contributions *after* the due date of his tax return for the year in which the excess contributions were made, they need not be included in the owner's gross income if:

■ total contributions (other than rollover contributions) for 2015 to the owner's IRA were not more than $5,500 ($6,500 if 50 or older); and

■ the owner did not take a deduction for the excess contributions being withdrawn.

INHERITED AND SPOUSAL IRAS

When a traditional IRA owner dies and her IRA is acquired by an individual who is not the decedent's surviving spouse, the IRA is referred to as an inherited IRA, and the person acquiring it is called a beneficiary. As a beneficiary, he must include in his gross income any taxable distributions received from the inherited IRA. In fact, the assets of an inherited IRA will not be taxed until they are distributed. If the IRA owner dies before minimum distributions are required to begin, the beneficiary may receive the interest of the deceased owner under one of two methods:

■ the five-year rule, under which the deceased owner's interest in the IRA must be distributed within five years of the owner's death; or

■ the life expectancy rule, under which the deceased owner's interest is distributed, beginning within one year of the owner's death, over the life of the beneficiary or over a period not extending beyond the beneficiary's life expectancy.

Clearly, in most cases, it will be advantageous for the beneficiary to opt for the life expectancy rule to extend the payout period and resulting tax on inherited amounts.

While an inherited IRA may be treated like any other traditional IRA for some purposes, no deduction may be taken for contributions to an inherited IRA. Likewise, no rollover may be made to or from an inherited IRA.

If the individual inherits the traditional IRA from anyone other than his deceased spouse, the inherited IRA may not be treated as his own (discussed later). Accordingly, as mentioned previously, this individual cannot make any contributions to the IRA nor roll over any amounts into or out of the inherited IRA. However, a trustee-to-trustee transfer is permissible as long as the IRA into which amounts are moved is established and maintained in the name of the deceased IRA owner for the benefit of the beneficiary.

The tax basis of an inherited traditional IRA carries over to the beneficiary. Only the surviving spouse of a deceased IRA owner who elects to treat the IRA acquired from her deceased spouse as the surviving spouse's own (discussed later) may combine the carried over tax basis with any basis she has in her own traditional IRA(s).

EXAMPLE Inherited IRA Fred is 70 years old and his son, Jake, is 49 years old and Fred dies before minimum distributions from Fred's IRA are required to begin. Jake may receive Fred's interest in the IRA under one of two methods: the five-year rule, under which Fred's interest in the IRA must be distributed within five years of Fred's death; or the life expectancy rule, under which Fred's interest is distributed, beginning within one year of the employee's death, over the life of the beneficiary (Jake) or over a period not extending beyond Jake's life expectancy. Most likely, Jake will opt for the life expectancy rule to extend the payouts over a longer period and minimize income tax in the long run.

On the other hand, if the individual who acquires an IRA from a decedent is the decedent's surviving spouse, the IRA is *not* an inherited IRA—it is referred to as a spousal IRA. A surviving spouse who inherits a traditional IRA from his spouse has the option to:

■ treat the IRA as his own by designating himself as the account owner;

■ treat the IRA as his own by rolling it over into his traditional IRA, or to the extent it is taxable, into a qualified plan, qualified employee annuity plan (Section 403(a) plan), tax-sheltered annuity plan (Section 403(b) plan), or deferred compensation plan of a state or local government (Section 457 plan); or

■ treat himself as the beneficiary rather than treating the IRA as his own.

> **E X A M P L E   Spousal IRA** Fred is 70 years old and his wife, Alice, is 62 years old. When Fred dies, Alice (as the beneficiary) can treat Fred's IRA as her own and take RMDs based on her life expectancy. Alice can also roll Fred's IRA into her own traditional IRA or roll the taxable portion of Fred's IRA into a qualified plan, Section 403(a), Section 403(b), or Section 457 plan. Alice can also treat herself as the beneficiary of Fred's IRA (rather than the new owner), in which case she will be required to take the minimum distributions that Fred would have had to take after attaining the age of 70½.

If the surviving spouse makes contributions (including rollover contributions) to the IRA acquired as a result of the death of his spouse or fails to take the required minimum distribution for a year as a beneficiary of the IRA, he will be considered to have elected to treat the IRA as his own.

ROTH IRAS

Since the creation of the traditional IRA in 1974, the number of two-income couples, high-income individuals, and active participants in employer-sponsored retirement plans has increased. This trend resulted in a reduction in the number of traditional IRAs established because of the inability of such persons to claim a tax deduction for contributions to this type of IRA. To address this problem, Congress created the Roth IRA in 1997 to permit not only nondeductible contributions (as are permissible with a traditional IRA) but also tax-free distributions from such IRAs (if certain requirements are met) and contributions by active participants in employer-sponsored retirement plans. Like traditional IRAs, Roth IRAs are primarily plans of individual savings and an alternative form of tax-favored individual retirement plan.

An individual may establish a Roth IRA by designating it as such at the time and manner prescribed by the IRS. The document creating the Roth IRA must clearly designate the IRA as a Roth IRA, and such designation is irrevocable. Accordingly, a Roth IRA cannot later be treated as a non-Roth IRA. However, the reverse is permissible; that is, a non-Roth IRA may be converted to a Roth IRA (discussed later in this reading). Moreover, a contribution to a Roth IRA may be recharacterized as a contribution to a non-Roth IRA and vice versa (discussed later in this reading). A deemed IRA (discussed previously and later in this reading) may also be a Roth IRA; however, neither a SIMPLE IRA nor a SEP IRA may be designated as a Roth IRA.

Financial institutions may use any of three model Roth IRA forms (for trusteed accounts, custodial accounts, and annuity contracts) released by the IRS for the purpose of creating a Roth IRA. However, a Roth IRA must be funded using one of these three options.

CONTRIBUTION LIMITS

Except for rollovers (discussed later in this reading), contributions to a Roth IRA must be in cash and are limited in amount. Generally, an individual may contribute to a Roth IRA if she has taxable compensation (as previously defined) and her modified AGI less conversion income, if applicable, is less than:

- $193,000 (2015) for a taxpayer who is married filing jointly or a qualifying widow(er);

- $10,000 for a taxpayer who is married filing separately and lived with his or her spouse at any time during the year; and

- $118,000 for a single, head of household, or married filing separately taxpayer who did not live with his or her spouse at any time during the year.

For a taxpayer who is married filing jointly or a qualifying widow, she may contribute up to $5,500 (2015), if age 50 or older, assuming her taxable compensation is at least that amount, if her modified AGI is less than $183,000 (2015). If such a taxpayer's modified AGI is $183,000 to $193,000 (2015), her contribution is subject to a gradual phaseout.

For a taxpayer who is married filing separately and lived with his spouse at any time during the year, he may contribute up to $5,500 (2015) ($6,500 [2015] if age 50 or older), assuming his taxable compensation is at least that amount, if his AGI is zero. If such a taxpayer's modified AGI is greater than zero but less than $10,000, his contribution is subject to a gradual phaseout.

For a taxpayer who is single, head of household, or married filing separately who did not live with her spouse at any time during the year, she may contribute up to $5,500 (2015) ($6,500, if age 50 or older), assuming her taxable compensation is at least that amount, if her modified AGI is less than $116,000 (2015). If such a taxpayer's modified AGI is $116,000 (2015) to $131,000 (2015), her contribution is subject to a gradual phaseout.

Contributions are limited to $5,500 (2015) [$6,500 (2015) if 50 or older] or 100% of taxable compensation, whichever is *less*. This limit includes contributions made to both traditional IRAs and Roth IRAs. If contributions are made only to Roth IRAs, the contribution limit is generally the lesser of $5,500 (2015) ($6,500 if 50 or older) or the Roth IRA owner's taxable compensation subject, of course, to the modified AGI phaseout ranges. However, if an individual makes contributions to both Roth IRAs and traditional IRAs, the contribution limit for Roth IRAs is generally the same as the limit would be if contributions were made only to Roth IRAs, but this limit is then reduced by all contributions (other than employer contributions under a SEP or SIMPLE IRA plan) for the year to all IRAs other than Roth IRAs. And, of course, the modified AGI phaseout ranges may still apply.

Unlike traditional IRAs, contributions to Roth IRAs may be made *regardless of age* and, therefore, can be made *after* reaching age 70½. Furthermore, eligibility is *not* affected by the individual's (or spouse's) active participation in an employer-sponsored retirement plan. Moreover, as is the case with a traditional IRA, a non-working spouse may also contribute to a Roth IRA, provided the contributions satisfy the spousal IRA limit, the married couple files jointly, and their modified AGI is less than $193,000 (2015).

Modified AGI is as defined previously for IRAs, except for one additional item that must be subtracted. This item is any conversion income resulting from the conversion of a non-Roth IRA to a Roth IRA, discussed later in this reading.

Contributions to a Roth IRA for a specific year may be made any time during that year or by the due date of the tax return for that year (not including extensions of time to file).

As with traditional IRAs, excess contributions (amounts contributed for the tax year to a Roth IRA that are more than the contribution limit for the year plus any excess contributions for the preceding year, reduced by the total of any distributions out of the Roth IRA for the year, plus the contribution limit for the year minus contributions made to all IRAs for the year) are subject to a 6% excise tax. Excess contributions withdrawn on or before the due date (including extensions) for filing the owner's tax return for the year are treated as an amount not contributed, provided any earnings on the contributions are also withdrawn. If contributions to a Roth IRA for a year are more than the applicable limit, the owner may apply the excess contribution in one year to a later year *if* the contributions for that later year are less than the maximum allowed for that year.

CONVERSION OF A NON-ROTH IRA TO A ROTH IRA

Under certain conditions, an IRA owner may be able to convert amounts from either a traditional, SEP, or SIMPLE IRA into a Roth IRA. In addition, contributions made to a particular type of IRA may be recharacterized as having been made directly to a different IRA.

Probably the most common type of conversion is from a traditional IRA to a Roth IRA. Such a conversion may be accomplished in any of the following three ways:

- Rollover—a distribution from a traditional IRA is rolled over (contributed to) a Roth IRA within 60 days of the distribution.

- Trustee-to-trustee transfer—transfer of an amount from the trustee of a traditional IRA to the trustee of a Roth IRA.

- Same trustee transfer—transfer of an amount from a traditional IRA to a Roth IRA when both IRAs are maintained by the same trustee. The trustee may be directed by the IRA owner to redesignate the traditional IRA as a Roth IRA, thus avoiding creation of a new account and the issuance of a new contract.

Recharacterization of IRA Contributions

Sometimes an individual may make a contribution to one type of IRA and then decide later that he should have made it to another type of IRA. Changing the IRA to which a contribution is being made is known as recharacterizing the contribution. In order to accomplish a recharacterization, the funds deposited in the first IRA must be transferred to the second IRA through the use of a trustee-to-trustee transfer by the due date (including extensions) of the tax return for the year during which the contribution was made. The effect of recharacterizing a contribution is, therefore, to treat the contribution as if it had been made originally to the second IRA instead of to the first IRA. In addition, after the transfer has taken place, the election to recharacterize it is irrevocable. A recharacterization is reported on IRS Form 8606 attached to the IRA owner's tax return.

Before a recharacterization may be considered effective, the IRA owner must do all of the following:

- Include in the transfer any net income allocable to the contribution; accordingly, if there was a loss, the net income that must be transferred may be a negative amount

- Report the recharacterization on his tax return for the year during which the contribution was made

- Treat the contribution as having been made to the second IRA on the date it was actually made to the first IRA

The IRA owner is required to notify both the trustee of the first IRA (the one to which the contribution was actually made) and the trustee of the second IRA (the one to which the contribution is being moved) that the owner has elected to treat the contribution as having been made to the second IRA rather than the first. The required notifications must be made by the date of the transfer and must include:

- the type and amount of the contribution to the first IRA that is to be recharacterized;

- the date on which the contribution was made to the first IRA and the year for which it was made;

- an instruction to the trustee of the first IRA as to how to make a trustee-to-trustee transfer of the amount of the contribution and any net income (or loss) allocable to the contribution to the trustee of the second IRA;

- the names of both trustees; and

- any additional information necessary to make the transfer.

In addition, a recharacterized contribution will *not* be treated as having been made to the second IRA to the extent an IRA owner has taken an income tax deduction for the contribution to the first IRA. If an IRA owner receives a distribution from a traditional IRA in one tax year and rolls it over into a Roth IRA in the next tax year but is still within the 60-day rollover period, it is treated as a contribution to the Roth IRA in the year he received the distribution from the traditional IRA. Finally, the recharacterization of a contribution is *not* treated as a rollover for purposes of the one-year waiting period.

Reconversions

It is not permissible to convert one type of IRA to a different type of IRA and then reconvert back to the first type of IRA during the same tax year. However, even if a reconversion takes place in a year subsequent to the original conversion, the reconversion cannot take place during the 30-day period following a recharacterization. If a reconversion takes place during either of these periods of time, it is treated as a failed conversion. For example, if an IRA owner converted an amount from a traditional IRA to a Roth IRA and then transferred that amount back to a traditional IRA in a recharacterization in the same year, the IRA owner could not reconvert that amount from the traditional IRA to a Roth IRA until the tax year *after* the year in which the original conversion took place or, if later, not until waiting at least 30 days after the amount was recharacterized back to a traditional IRA.

ROLLOVERS

The owner of a Roth IRA may withdraw, tax free, all or part of the assets from her Roth IRA if they are contributed within 60 days to another Roth IRA. Most of the rollover rules for traditional IRAs are applicable to Roth rollovers. If the owner receives a rollover from a retirement plan other than a Roth IRA, it is disregarded for purposes of the one-year waiting period between rollovers. Moreover, a rollover from a Roth IRA to an employer retirement plan is *not* permitted.

DISTRIBUTIONS

While it is intuitive to think that all distributions from a Roth IRA are nontaxable, it is only qualified distributions that enjoy this tax treatment. Other nonqualified distributions are treated as a nontaxable return of the owner's contributions to the Roth IRA until those contributions are exhausted, as discussed in the following.

Qualified (Nontaxable) Distributions

Only a distribution that meets *both* of the following requirements is considered a qualified distribution and is, therefore, nontaxable:

- It must be made after the five consecutive tax years beginning with the tax year for which a contribution was first made to any Roth IRA owned by the IRA owner. Such an initial contribution may include an ordinary cash contribution, a rollover contribution from a non-Roth IRA, or a rollover contribution from a designated Roth account.

- It is made

  — on or after the date when the owner reaches age 59½,

  — because the owner is disabled,

  — because the owner has died and the distribution is then made to either a beneficiary or the deceased's estate, or

  — because it meets the requirements of a first-time home buyer distribution ($10,000 lifetime limit), discussed previously.

Because of the five-year requirement, no qualified distribution could have been made by any Roth IRA before a taxable year beginning in 2003 (1998 was the first year a Roth IRA could have been created). In addition, the five-year period does not start over when the owner of a Roth IRA dies. The period during which the Roth IRA is held in the name of a beneficiary, or in the name of a surviving spouse who treats the decedent's Roth IRA as her own, includes the period during which it was held by the decedent.

The five-year period for a Roth IRA held by an individual who is a beneficiary of a deceased Roth IRA owner is determined independently of the five-year period for the beneficiary's own Roth IRA. If a surviving spouse treats her deceased spouse's Roth IRA as her own, the five-year period with respect to any of the surviving spouse's Roth IRAs (including the one that the surviving spouse treats as her own) ends with the termination of the five-year period for the decedent or the termination of the five-year period applicable to the spouse's own Roth IRAs, whichever is earlier.

Nonqualified (Taxable) Roth IRA Distributions

Distributions that do not meet the foregoing requirements as qualified distributions, unless rolled over or constituting a corrective distribution, are first considered to be a nontaxable return of the owner's contributions to the Roth IRA. After the owner's contributions in all of his Roth IRAs have then been recovered, any additional amounts distributed to the owner are taxable to him. Such nonqualified distributions may also be subject to the 10% additional tax on early distributions. For example, if an IRA owner converts an amount from a traditional IRA to a Roth IRA and then takes a distribution from the Roth IRA within the five-year period starting with the first day of the tax year in which the conversion took place, he may have to pay the 10% additional tax on early distributions. This 10% early distribution penalty is payable only on the portion of the amount converted that the owner had to include in income.

One significant difference between distributions from traditional IRAs and Roth IRAs is that the mandatory minimum distribution rules that apply to IRA owners who are at least age 70½ do *not* apply to Roth IRAs. Moreover, in determining the tax consequences of distributions from Roth IRAs, *all* Roth IRAs are to be treated as one contract; *all* distributions from Roth IRAs are to be treated as one distribution; and the value of the contract, income on the contract, and investment in the contract are to be computed as of the close of the tax year.

Ordering Rules for Nonqualified Roth IRA Distributions

As explained earlier, a Roth IRA owner who receives a distribution from her Roth IRA that is not a qualified distribution will be taxed on a portion of the distribution. Such distributions are treated as made in the following order (determined as of the end of the taxable year and exhausting each category before moving to the next category):

■ Regular contributions: conversion contributions, on a first-in-first-out basis (generally, total conversions from the earliest year first); the taxable portion of any conversion contributions are taken into account before any nontaxable portion.

■ Earnings on the Roth IRA contributions: rollover contributions from other Roth IRAs are disregarded for this purpose.

A second set of ordering rules (known as the aggregation, or grouping and adding, rules) are then applied to determine the taxable amounts withdrawn (distributed) as follows:

■ Add together all distributions from all of the owner's Roth IRAs during the year.

■ Add together all regular contributions made for the year (including those made after the close of the year but before the due date of the tax return). This total is then added to the total undistributed regular contributions made in prior years.

■ Add together all conversion contributions made during the year.

Finally, in applying these aggregation rules, add any recharacterized contributions that end up in a Roth IRA to the appropriate contribution group for the year that the original contribution would have been taken into account if it had been made directly to the Roth IRA. In this respect, also disregard any recharacterized contribution that ends up in an IRA other than a Roth IRA. Any amount withdrawn to correct an excess contribution (including the earnings withdrawn) is also disregarded for this purpose.

Minimum Distribution Rules After the Death of the Roth IRA Owner

As discussed previously, the minimum distribution rules do not apply during the lifetime of a Roth IRA owner who reaches age 70½. This means that a Roth IRA owner is not required to take distributions from his Roth IRA at any age. However, when a Roth IRA owner dies, the minimum distribution rules that apply to traditional IRAs (discussed previously) apply to Roth IRAs as though the Roth IRA owner died *before* his required beginning date (RBD).

Ordinarily, the entire interest in the Roth IRA of a deceased Roth IRA owner must be distributed by the end of the fifth calendar year after the year in which the owner died, unless the interest is payable to a designated beneficiary over the life or life expectancy of the designated beneficiary (as an annuity). Where the interest is distributed as an annuity, the entire interest must then be payable over a period not greater than the designated beneficiary's life expectancy, and distributions must begin before the end of the calendar year following the year of death. If the sole beneficiary of the Roth IRA is the decedent's spouse, he may delay distributions until the decedent would have attained age 70½ or he may treat the Roth IRA as his own. If the beneficiary/surviving spouse elects to treat the Roth IRA as his own, that individual's five-year holding period is then used to determine whether a distribution is qualified with no minimum lifetime distributions required to be taken.

If a distribution to a beneficiary is not a qualified distribution, it is generally taxable to the beneficiary in the same manner as it would have been taxable to the owner, had it been distributed to the IRA owner when he was alive.

Treatment of Losses on Roth IRA Investments

When all of the amounts in all of an individual's Roth IRAs have been distributed to the owner and the total of such distributions is less than the owner's unrecovered basis (total cumulative contributions), the owner may claim the loss as a miscellaneous itemized deduction, subject to the 2%-of-AGI limitation.

COMPARISON OF TRADITIONAL AND ROTH IRAS

Whether a traditional or Roth IRA is more beneficial for a particular individual is highly subjective and depends on the person's individual goals, needs, and objectives. By using Exhibit 5.1, the reader may make a side-by-side comparison of the two types of IRAs.

EXHIBIT 5.1 Comparison of Traditional and Roth IRA

	Traditional IRA	Roth IRA
Contributions must be made out of earned income, not investment income	Yes	Yes
Annual dollar limit	Yes (before-tax) (total for sum of Roth and traditional IRA contributions)	Yes (after-tax) (total for sum of Roth and traditional IRA contributions)
Restrictions based on AGI	No, unless active participant in tax-favored employer plan	Yes, contribution limit phased out between $116,000 (2015) and $131,000 (single); $183,000 (2015) and $193,000 (joint)
Restrictions on deduction or contribution if active participant in tax-favored employer plan	Yes, deduction limited based on AGI	No
Tax-free buildup during accumulation period	Yes	Yes
Withdrawals tax-free	No	Yes, after waiting period
10% penalty on early withdrawals	Yes	Yes
Required minimum distributions	Yes, beginning at earlier of age 70½ or death	Yes, beginning at death
Can rollover to (another) regular IRA	Yes (once annually)	No
Can rollover to (another) Roth IRA	Yes, must pay tax	Yes
Can rollover to qualified plan, TDA or Section 457 governmental plan	Yes	No

* *Tools & Techniques of Employee Benefit and Retirement Planning*, 9th ed., Stephan R. Leimberg and John J. McFadden, The National Underwriter Company, 2005. Used with permission.

Supplemental Reading–Plan Distributions–Part 1

DISTRIBUTION OPTIONS AVAILABLE

In the case of a qualified plan, there are three basic options available in selecting the form of distribution:

■ A lump-sum distribution

■ An annuity or other installment form of distribution

■ Roll over to an IRA (including a SEP IRA, but not including a SIMPLE IRA account or Roth IRA) or other eligible qualified plan

Lump-Sum Distributions

A lump-sum distribution may be desirable for retirement planning purposes; however, if the lump sum will be taxed in a high tax bracket, it may not be as desirable. After 1999, a lump-sum distribution (if not rolled over) is taxed as ordinary income unless the employee was born before January 2, 1936; in which case the distribution is eligible for the special tax treatment of 10-year averaging. Employees born before January 2, 1936, are also entitled to a 20% capital gain rate for the capital gain portion of pre-1974 accumulations, if any, and if so elected. However, this grandfather rule no longer benefits such persons in light of the lower capital gain rates enacted in 1997, plus the further rate reductions enacted by JGTRRA of 2003 (i.e., a maximum rate of 15%).

Furthermore, regardless of when an employee was born, if she takes part of her benefits in the form of an annuity and the remainder as a single sum, the single sum is *not* eligible for special tax treatment. Similarly, if the recipient receives a lump-sum distribution and rolls over a portion of that distribution, the retained portion is not eligible for special tax treatment.

In addition, lump-sum distributions may be subject to the early distribution penalty if taken before the recipient has attained age 59½. Moreover, lump-sum distributions generally will be subject to mandatory withholding at 20%.

Definition of a Lump-Sum Distribution

A distribution is a lump-sum distribution if it meets all of the following requirements:

■ It is made by a qualified retirement plan and not an IRA.

■ It represents a participant's entire interest (the balance to the credit of a participant) in the plan.

■ It is distributed within a single tax year of the recipient.

Under the Internal Revenue Code, a lump-sum distribution is not entitled to special tax treatment unless it is made on account of the death of the employee, on account of the employee's separation from service, after the employee has become totally and permanently disabled, or after the employee has attained age 59½.

Employee Contributions

The part of a lump-sum distribution that consists of accumulated deductible employee contributions (DECs) is *not* eligible for special tax treatment. However, the balance of the distribution is eligible if it otherwise qualifies.

Less Than Five Years of Participation

A lump-sum distribution made before the employee has been a participant in the plan for at least five tax years before the tax year in which the distribution is made is *not* eligible for special tax treatment, unless it is made on account of the death of the employee. This rule applies *only* in the case of a distribution made to the employee. Therefore, it does *not* apply to distributions made to a beneficiary of a deceased employee.

Participant's Entire Interest

With regard to determining what constitutes a participant's entire interest in the plan and whether it has been distributed within one tax year, if his employer maintains two or more qualified retirement plans, they may have to be treated as a single plan. Technically, all pension plans must be treated as single plans; all profit-sharing plans must be treated as single plans; and all stock bonus plans must be treated as single plans.

In addition, only amounts that are vested as of the last day of the tax year of the recipient in which the distribution is made are taken into account in determining whether the employee's entire interest has been distributed.

Lump-Sum Distribution to the Employee

If the lump-sum distribution is made to the employee/participant, and she was born before January 2, 1936, she may:

■ apply 10-year averaging to the entire taxable amount;

■ apply 10-year averaging to the post-1973 portion of the taxable amount and pay a flat 20% tax on the pre-1974 portion;

■ pay a flat 20% tax on the pre-1974 portion of the taxable amount and report the post-1973 portion as ordinary income; or

■ report the entire taxable amount as ordinary income.

As discussed previously, if the participant was born after January 2, 1936, a lump-sum distribution is *not* eligible for special tax treatment of any kind.

If the participant is eligible for 10-year averaging, a tax is computed (using a special table set forth in the instructions for IRS Form 4972) on one-tenth of the excess of the portion of the distribution subject to averaging over a minimum distribution allowance. The minimum distribution allowance is the lesser of:

■ $10,000; or

■ one-half of the portion subject to averaging minus 20% of the amount by which the portion subject to averaging exceeds $20,000.

If the amount subject to averaging is $70,000 or more, the minimum distribution allowance is zero.

Net Unrealized Appreciation (NUA) in Employer Securities   If securities of the employer corporation are included in a lump-sum distribution, the net unrealized appreciation (NUA) in those securities is not subject to tax. Accordingly, it is ordinarily excluded from any of the tax calculations that may apply to the lump-sum distribution. However, the distributee may elect to have the NUA appreciation included in gross income for the year of the distribution.

The distributee makes this election simply by including the NUA on his tax return for the year of the distribution. However, the distributee who makes this election is always free to have the entire NUA taxed as ordinary income.

Lump-Sum Distribution to Beneficiaries

If a beneficiary of a plan participant is the recipient of a lump-sum distribution and if the participant was born before January 2, 1936, the options are the same as those of an employee-distributee as discussed earlier, specifically:

■ apply 10-year averaging to the entire taxable amount;

■ apply 10-year averaging to the post-1973 portion of the taxable amount and pay a flat 20% tax on the pre-1974 portion of the taxable amount;

■ pay a flat 20% tax on the pre-1974 portion of the taxable amount and report the post-1973 portion of the taxable amount as ordinary income; or

■ report the entire taxable amount as ordinary income.

Multiple Distributees   If the total balance credited to the account of an employee is distributable to two or more beneficiaries and the share of each beneficiary is received within a single tax year of that beneficiary, the combined distribution is eligible for special tax treatment if all other conditions are satisfied. However, the tax calculation varies depending upon whether any of the distributees are trusts. Such calculations are beyond the scope of this text.

Annuity or Other Installment Form of Distribution

The second basic option in selecting the form of distribution from a qualified retirement plan is the annuity or other installment option. An annuity distribution received from a retirement plan in any tax year of the employee is taxable as ordinary income, to the extent that it exceeds the portion of the employee's basis in the plan allocated to that distribution. For this purpose, basis is determined as of the *later* of the annuity starting date or the date on which an amount is first received as an annuity. If the employee has no basis in the qualified plan (a common occurrence), the full amount of each annuity distribution is taxable as ordinary income.

A participant's cost basis could be composed of any of the following:

■ The total of the participant's after-tax contributions made to a contributory plan

■ Any employer contributions previously taxed to the participant, such as would occur if a nonqualified plan became qualified

■ The amount of any plan loans (discussed later in this reading) included in income as a taxable distribution

■ The total cost of life insurance protection included in a participant's gross income in his income tax return, but only if the plan distribution is received under the same life insurance contract that provides the life insurance protection

In the case of annuities paid by defined contribution plans, the portion of the plan that consists of the participant's nondeductible contributions and earnings and gains attributable thereto may be treated as an entirely separate plan, if the plan so permits. Participants in Section 401(k) plans and salary reduction TSAs may elect to treat all or part of their elective contributions as includable in gross income. If this election is made, a qualified distribution of these designated Roth contributions is excludable from gross income in its entirety. If a distribution of designated Roth contributions is not qualified and takes the form of an annuity distribution, it is not excludable from income in its entirety, but it is taxable under the annuity rules (discussed later).

All pension plans must provide two forms of survivorship benefits for spouses: the **qualified preretirement survivor annuity (QPSA)** and the **qualified joint and survivor annuity (QJSA)**. Stock bonus plans, profit-sharing plans, and ESOPs generally are *not* required to provide these survivorship benefits for the spouse if the participant's vested interest is payable to that spouse as a death benefit.

At the point that a participant's interest in a retirement plan vests, her spouse becomes entitled to a preretirement survivor annuity, payable in the event of the participant's death prior to retirement. In the case of a defined benefit plan, the amount of this annuity is the amount that would have been paid under a qualified joint and survivor annuity if the participant had either retired on the day before his death (where the participant died after attaining the earliest retirement age under the plan) or separated from service at the earlier of the actual time of separation or death and survived to the plan's earliest retirement age, then retired with an immediate joint and survivor annuity. While this explanation is difficult to decipher, the effect is to attempt to put the spouse in the same position she would have been in if the participant had lived, but either retired or otherwise separated from service prior to the normal retirement age.

An unmarried participant typically will receive a straight life annuity under a defined benefit plan—usually monthly payments for the balance of the participant's life, with no continuing payments after his death. Most plans offer, as an option to the joint and survivor or single life annuities, a **period-certain annuity**, which provides payments for a specified period of time (typically 10 to 20 years), even if the participant or the participant and spouse both die before the end of that period. This option guarantees an income stream to the participant's heirs, even if both the participant and his spouse die during the specified period of time. Because of the guarantee involved in the period-certain annuity, the monthly benefit is normally lower than that payable under a life annuity. A participant and spouse in poor health or needing to provide for a survivor should seriously consider a period-certain annuity in lieu of the straight life annuity option.

A defined benefit pension plan may also permit a participant to elect a joint annuity with a beneficiary other than a spouse (such as a son or daughter). However, the benefit available to a much younger beneficiary under such an annuity option is severely limited by Treasury Regulations to prevent an inordinate deferral of benefits beyond the participant's death. This will be addressed later in this reading during the discussion of the required minimum distribution (RMD) rules. Money purchase pension plans, target benefit plans, and TSAs subject to ERISA must also meet the preretirement and joint and survivor annuity rules. Other defined contribution plans do *not* have to meet these rules if there is no annuity option and the plan participant's account balance is payable to the participant's spouse upon the death of the participant.

In the case of a defined contribution plan, the statutory qualified preretirement survivor annuity (QPSA) is an annuity for the life of the surviving spouse that is the actuarial equivalent of at least 50% of the participant's vested account balance, determined as of the date of death.

The surviving spouse does not need to elect a preretirement survivor annuity. If he fails to make any other election, this type of annuity is *automatically* provided by the plan. A participant may not waive the preretirement survivorship benefit without the written, witnessed consent (including an acknowledgment of the effect of the waiver) of the nonparticipant spouse. The nonparticipant spouse should obtain competent legal and/or financial advice prior to agreeing to such a waiver. As a participant approaches the plan's normal retirement age, it may be beneficial to elect out of the preretirement survivorship benefit in order to increase the participant's post-retirement benefit. On the other hand, a participant may want to provide a preretirement survivorship benefit for a nonspousal beneficiary.

The qualified joint and survivor annuity (QJSA) provides a post-retirement death benefit for the plan participant's spouse. This survivor annuity may not be less than 50% or greater than 100% of the annuity payable during the joint lives of the participant and spouse. In addition, annuity payments to the spouse, under such a benefit, must continue even if he remarries. As is the case with the preretirement survivor annuity, a participant may elect to receive another form of benefit, such as a straight life annuity (if the plan so provides), but such a waiver of the joint and survivor annuity benefit requires the written, witnessed consent (again including an acknowledgment of the effect of the waiver) of the nonparticipant spouse. Such an election must be made within 90 days of the annuity starting date (the date when benefit payments to the participant should have begun—not necessarily the date when they were paid). Finally, participants must be provided with a notice of the election period, including an explanation of the effect of the election within a reasonable period prior to the annuity starting date.

What Constitutes Annuity Payments?

To be classified as an annuity, a distribution must satisfy each of the following requirements:

- It must be received on or after the annuity starting date (defined later).

- It must be payable in periodic installments at regular intervals (e.g., annually, semiannually, quarterly, monthly, weekly, or otherwise) over a period of more than one full year from the annuity starting date.

- Except in the case of a variable annuity, the total of the amounts payable must be determinable at the annuity starting date either directly from the terms of the contract or indirectly by the use of mortality tables, compound interest calculations, or both, in conjunction with those terms and in accordance with sound actuarial theory. The total of the amounts payable is not determinable if the payments will only continue or terminate at the discretion of the payor.

The annuity starting date is the *later* of the date when the obligations under the contract become fixed or the first day of the period ending on the date of the first annuity payment. This period may be a year, a half-year, a quarter, a month, or any other period, depending on the interval at which payments are made.

When a participant receives payments under an agreement stating that the retirement plan holds the entire value of the participant's interest in the plan and pays interest thereon, the payments are not taxed as annuity payments, but rather as interest.

Simplified Method of Taxing Annuity Distributions

The simplified method of taxing annuity distributions is now required by law. Under this method, the distributee recovers her basis as of the annuity starting date in level amounts over the number of anticipated monthly payments. Except in the case of payments that are made for a fixed period (rather than over a life expectancy or expectancies), the anticipated payments are determined under IRS Tables I through IV. In cases when the annuity payments are not monthly, an adjustment needs to be made to take into account the period on the basis of which the payments are made.

The amount excluded from each monthly payment remains constant, even though the amount of the annuity payment changes (as when the annuity increases with changes in the cost of living or when the annuity decreases for the survivor after the death of the primary annuitant). If the amount to be excluded is greater than the monthly payment (as may be the case with a survivor annuitant), each payment is completely excluded from gross income until the entire basis is recovered.

Employers and administrators with respect to qualified plans and TSAs must employ the simplified method in reporting the taxable amount of an annuity on IRS Form 1099-R.

> **EXAMPLE** At his retirement, John Farnsworth, age 65, begins receiving retirement benefits in the form of a joint and 50% survivor annuity to be paid for the joint lives of John and his wife, Marcia, age 64. John's annuity starting date is January 1, 2015. John contributed $31,000 to the plan and has received no distributions prior to the annuity starting date. Under plan provisions, John will receive a monthly retirement benefit of $1,000 per month, and Marcia will receive a monthly survivor benefit of $500 upon John's death.
>
> Therefore, John's investment in the contract is $31,000. The expected number of monthly payments is 310 for two distributees whose combined ages are 129 (65 and 64) per IRS Table IV. Accordingly, the tax-free portion of each $1,000 monthly annuity payment to John is $100, determined by dividing John's investment ($31,000) by the expected number of monthly payments (310).
>
> Upon John's death, if the couple has not recovered the full $31,000 investment, Marcia may also exclude $100 per month from each $500 monthly annuity payment. Any annuity payments received after the 310 monthly payments have been made are then fully includable in her gross income. If John and Marcia die before 310 monthly payments have been made, a deduction is allowed on the last income tax return equal to the amount of the unrecovered investment.

If the annuitant is not eligible for, or does not choose to employ, the simplified method of taxing annuity distributions, the following is the basic procedure for determining the taxable and nontaxable portions of annuity payments received in any tax year.

1. Determine the employee's basis in the retirement plan.

2. Determine the expected return from the annuity by multiplying the anticipated number of annual payments by the amount of the annual payment. In the case of annuities with durations measured in whole or in part by one or more lives, it is necessary to turn to actuarial tables to determine the life expectancy (or expectancies) of the annuitant(s). For this purpose, IRS Tables I through VIII are used.

3. Divide the amount determined in Step 1 by the amount determined in Step 2. Round the dividend to three decimal places. This is the exclusion percentage or exclusion ratio.

4. Multiply the first regular annuity payment by the exclusion percentage. The result is the excluded (tax-free) portion of that annuity payment. The tax-free portion of each succeeding payment is the same dollar amount, even though the payments may increase.

5. Multiply the tax-free portion of each payment by the number of full payments received during the year and add the taxable portion of any payment for a fractional period (as may be the case in the first year of the annuity). These computations result in the tax-free portion of the total payments received in the tax year.

6. Subtract the tax-free portion from the total payments received in the tax year. The balance is the taxable portion of the annuity.

Rollover to an IRA or Other Qualified Plan

The third basic option in selecting the form of distribution from a qualified retirement plan is the rollover of the distribution to either an IRA or another qualified plan.

What Constitutes a Rollover?

Technically, a rollover is a direct or indirect transfer from one retirement plan to another of all or part of a taxpayer's accrued benefits, resulting by statute in exclusion of the transferred benefits from the gross income of the owner, employee, or other person entitled to them and disregard of the transferred benefits in determining the limit on contributions to the transferee plan by the employee or owner.[1]

A direct transfer is said to occur when the participant, trustee, or other custodian who holds the assets making up the participant's accrued benefit transfers some or all of those assets to the trustee or custodian of another retirement plan. A direct transfer and direct rollover are synonymous in the tax law. An indirect transfer takes place when the trustee or custodian distributes the assets to the participant who, within a statutory time limit, transfers those assets to another retirement plan. Only one such indirect transfer is allowable in a tax year. This is contrasted to a direct transfer, the allowable number of which is not limited in a tax year.

Originally, the Internal Revenue Code contemplated only indirect transfers; however, in 1992, the IRC was amended to expressly provide for direct trustee-to-trustee transfers from a qualified plan to an IRA or another qualified plan or from a TSA to an IRA or another TSA. Qualified plans (including TSAs and Section 457 plans) must allow an employee to direct the plan to accomplish a planned rollover by means of a direct trustee-to-trustee transfer of assets. If a direct transfer or rollover is not utilized by the employee, 20% of the taxable amount of any distribution that is eligible for rollover is automatically withheld (for income tax purposes), whether or not that amount is subsequently rolled over to another plan.

The foregoing direct transfer or rollover rules do *not* apply to amounts distributable by a traditional IRA (including a SEP IRA), a SIMPLE account, or a Roth IRA. Accordingly, no 20% mandatory withholding applies.

What Constitutes an Eligible Plan?

Rollovers are available for benefits accumulated in the following types of retirement plans:

■ Pension, profit-sharing, and stock bonus plans that are qualified under IRC Section 401(a) (e.g., qualified plans)

■ Traditional IRAs (including SEP IRAs)

---

1   *Retirement Benefits Tax Guide*, 3rd edition, by Thomas F. Rutherford, CCH Incorporated, 2005.

- SIMPLE accounts
- Tax-sheltered annuity arrangements (TSAs)
- Section 457 plans

Rules Applicable to All Rollovers

Important rules applicable to all rollovers include the following:

- Both the transferor and transferee plans must satisfy all statutory requirements for treatment as an eligible retirement plan or IRA, as the case may be.
- Required minimum distributions (discussed later in this reading) may not be rolled over.
- A distribution to an owner or participant from a traditional IRA (including a SEP IRA), a SIMPLE account, Roth IRA, qualified plan, TSA, or a Section 457 plan must generally be transferred to an eligible recipient not later than the 60th day following the date of receipt of the distribution. The 60-day requirement may be waived by the IRS if the failure to waive would be against equity or good conscience, such as casualty, disaster, or other events beyond the reasonable control of the taxpayer.

Rules Applicable to Rollovers from Qualified Plans

A distribution of cash or other property from a qualified retirement plan may be rolled over to any of the following plans or arrangements:

- A traditional IRA (including a SEP IRA)
- Another qualified plan
- A tax-sheltered annuity arrangement (TSA)
- A governmental Section 457 plan, provided it agrees to separately account for amounts rolled into it from a traditional IRA

If the distribution is rolled over no later than the 60th day after the day of receipt by the employee, it is excluded from the employee's gross income to the extent of the rollover. There is no requirement that a distribution represent any minimum percentage of the employee's interest in order to be eligible for rollover. However, a qualified plan does not have a statutory obligation to accept rollovers. It may limit the circumstances under which it will accept them or limit the type of assets it will accept.

As discussed previously, a proposed distribution from a qualified plan that is eligible for rollover treatment is subject to 20% withholding (i.e., 20% of the taxable amount of the distribution), unless it is rolled over by means of a direct trustee-to-trustee transfer of assets. The amount withheld as income tax from an eligible rollover distribution that is not directly transferred is considered to be part of that distribution. Therefore, it is eligible for rollover in the sense that an amount equal to all or any portion of it may be contributed as a rollover to an eligible retirement plan within the 60-day period. This amount is in addition to the net amount of the eligible rollover distribution actually received by the employee. In fact, any amount withheld that is not rolled over is subject to tax under the applicable rules relating to distributions from qualified plans.

> **EXAMPLE** John receives a lump-sum distribution from his former employer's Section 401(k) plan in the gross amount of $100,000, net of 20% withholding tax. Within 60 days of the receipt of the distribution, John decides to roll over the net amount of the distribution ($80,000) into his existing IRA. Accordingly, John endorses the $80,000 check to the trustee of his IRA and mails it to the trustee with the appropriate paperwork for an indirect transfer (or rollover). John may also transfer an amount equal to the 20% withheld as income tax (or $20,000) from the gross distribution because it is considered to be part of the gross distribution of $100,000. In this manner, John will achieve a rollover of the entire gross amount of the distribution of $100,000.

The IRS has ruled that a rollover from a qualified plan to a SIMPLE IRA account is not possible unless it is from another SIMPLE IRA account. However, a SIMPLE 401(k) plan may receive rollovers from qualified plans [including other SIMPLE 401(k)s]. Similarly, a rollover from a qualified plan to a Roth IRA is not permitted.

An employee is not required to roll over the *entire* amount received from a qualified plan; he may roll only a *portion*. To the extent of the amount rolled over, the withdrawal is nontaxable. However, the amount rolled over is not treated as a contribution by the participant to a recipient plan or IRA. As discussed previously, the taxable portion of any amount not rolled over is treated as an ordinary distribution and, therefore, is not eligible for special 10-year averaging tax treatment.

A surviving spouse may roll the distribution to another qualified plan, TSA, traditional IRA, or governmental Section 457 plan on the same terms as if he were the participant.

Distributions Not Eligible for Rollover   As discussed previously, a distribution from a qualified plan may not be rolled over to the extent that it is required by the minimum distribution rules (discussed later in this reading). In addition, a hardship distribution under the terms of the plan may not be rolled over. Moreover, a distribution by a qualified plan may not be rolled over if it is one of a series of substantially equal, at least annual, periodic payments to be made:

■ over the life expectancy of the employee;

■ over the joint lives or joint life expectancies of the employee and her designated beneficiary; or

■ for a specified period of 10 years or more (called a 72(t) distribution after the Internal Revenue Code section permitting such distributions).

The IRS has ruled that deductible dividends paid to participants by an ESOP are not eligible rollover distributions, nor are payments of life insurance premiums by a qualified plan for its participants.

Election of Rollover Treatment   For a contribution of an eligible rollover distribution to an IRA to qualify as a rollover, the distributee must elect, at the time the contribution is made, to treat it as such. This is accomplished by designating to (notifying) the trustee, issuer, or custodian of the IRA that the contribution is, indeed, a rollover. This election is irrevocable. This assures that, once the election is made, any subsequent withdrawal of the contribution from the IRA is taxable under the rules governing distributions from IRAs—not by the rules governing distributions from qualified plans. Accordingly, the withdrawal is also not eligible for the special tax treatment extended to lump-sum distributions from qualified plans or the exclusion from gross income for net unrealized appreciation (NUA) on employer stock distributed by a qualified plan.

Direct Rollovers

A direct rollover may be accomplished by any reasonable method ensuring the transferred assets pass to the transferee plan without coming under the physical control of the participant. Reasonable methods include a wire transfer or the mailing of a check to the recipient plan. If payment is made by check, the check must be negotiable only by the trustee, custodian, or issuer; if by wire transfer, it must be directed only to the trustee, custodian, or issuer. In addition, the transferor plan may provide the distributee with a check and instruct him to deliver it to the transferee trustee, custodian, or issuer, provided the check is made payable to that person. If the name of the distributee does not appear on the name of the plan, the check must indicate that it is for the distributee's benefit (e.g., "for the benefit of" or "FBO Jane Doe").

Rollovers from TSAs

Subject to the same exceptions that apply in the case of distributions from qualified plans, distributions from tax-sheltered annuity arrangements (TSAs) may be rolled over to any of the following plans or arrangements:

- A traditional IRA (including a SEP IRA, but not a Roth IRA or SIMPLE account)

- Another TSA

- A qualified plan

- A governmental Section 457 plan

To qualify for rollover treatment, a distribution from a TSA must satisfy the same rules applicable to a distribution from a qualified plan, as discussed earlier.

Rollovers from Section 457 Plans

Beginning in 2002, a distribution by an eligible governmental Section 457 plan may be rolled over to any of the following plans or arrangements:

- A traditional IRA (including a SEP IRA, but not a Roth IRA or SIMPLE account)

- Another governmental Section 457 plan

- A qualified plan

- A TSA

To qualify for rollover treatment, a distribution from a governmental Section 457 plan must satisfy the same rules applicable to a distribution from a qualified plan, as discussed earlier.

In-Service Distributions

In the previous sections, we discussed annuity, lump-sum, and rollover distributions from retirement plans. In this section, we will discuss distributions that do not fall within any of those three categories. Primarily, these are nonrollover distributions made to a plan participant during the course of her employment, called in-service distributions. Loans to participants by qualified and nonqualified plans are generally treated as in-service distributions.

Generally, in the case of an in-service distribution from a qualified plan or TSA, to calculate the tax-free portion of the distribution, divide the participant's basis in the plan by the value of the *vested portion* of the participant's interest. The resulting percentage is multiplied by the amount of the distribution to determine the amount excludable from the participant's gross income. The same basic rules apply in the case of distributions by IRAs as apply in the case of in-service distributions by plans qualified under IRC Section 401 and TSAs.

An exception to the general rule described in the previous paragraph is the grandfather rule for pre-1987 after-tax contributions to the plan. Contributions made before 1987 may be distributed to participants income tax free until the total amount contributed has been recovered by the participant. Then, excess contributions are taxed in the manner described in the previous paragraph.

Taxable in-service distributions may be subject to the early distribution penalty and are generally subject to mandatory 20% withholding (unless transferred to an eligible retirement plan through a direct rollover, as discussed earlier).

Loans to Participants

Subject to certain exceptions, a loan to a participant by a plan or arrangement that is, was, or was determined to be a qualified plan, a TSA, or a governmental Section 457 plan is treated as an in-service distribution to that participant in the amount of the loan. As such, it is taxed under the rules discussed in the previous section. It is also reported in the same way as other in-service distributions and may be subject to the penalty tax on early distributions.

A loan to a participant by a qualified plan may, under some circumstances, disqualify the plan, with disastrous consequences to both the employer and plan participants. If a plan is to remain qualified, loans to participants must satisfy the following conditions:

- They must be available to all participants or beneficiaries on a reasonably equivalent basis.

- They must *not* be available to highly compensated employees in an amount greater than the amount made available to other employees.

- They must be made in accordance with specific plan provisions regarding such loans.

- They must bear a reasonable rate of interest.

- They must be adequately secured.

These same conditions must be met if a plan loan to a participant who is a disqualified person or party-in-interest is to escape treatment as a prohibited transaction under the IRC or ERISA. If a loan is a prohibited transaction, it is subject, under the IRC and ERISA, to an excise tax of 15% of the amount involved in the transaction.

Under EGTRRA 2001, the previous (prior to 2002) prohibition against retirement plan loans to participants who are owner-employees (sole proprietors of more than 10% partners in an unincorporated business, or an S corporation employee who is a more than 5% owner of the enterprise sponsoring the plan, or participants who are members of their families) was repealed.

If a participant or beneficiary assigns or pledges any part of her interest in a qualified plan, that part will be treated as a loan. Thus, unless an exception applies, it will be regarded as an in-service distribution from a qualified plan and taxed as such.

A loan is *not* treated as an in-service distribution if the loan must be repaid within five years or is used to acquire any dwelling unit that, within a reasonable time, is to be used as the principal residence of the participant. Such a loan is treated as a distribution only to the extent that, when added to the balance of all other loans to the participant (whenever made), it exceeds the *lesser of*:

- $50,000 (which may have to be reduced under a complicated formula); or

- one-half of the present value (but not less than $10,000) of the participant's vested benefits under the plan.

In addition, loan repayments must satisfy certain level amortization requirements (i.e., at least quarterly payments), and the loan must be an enforceable agreement. Interest paid on a plan loan is generally treated as personal interest and, accordingly, *not* deductible unless the loan is secured by a home mortgage.

Death Benefits

Retirement and other deferred compensation plans often pay benefits to the survivors of deceased employees or deceased retirees. If these benefits are payable under a life insurance contract held by the qualified plan, the pure insurance amount of the death benefit is excluded from income taxation. The pure insurance amount is the difference between the policy's face amount and its cash value at the date of death. The taxable amount of the distribution is the face amount of the policy minus the pure insurance amount minus the participant's cost basis in the insurance policy (obtained either by paying a portion of the policy premiums or having paid tax on the insurance benefit provided by the plan). Treasury Regulations Table 2001 rates are generally used in calculating the value of life insurance protection.

If not paid from a life insurance contract held by the qualified plan, the benefits are compensation taxable under the general rules applicable to distributions from retirement and other deferred compensation plans. IRAs, including SIMPLE accounts, may *not* invest in life insurance policies. Therefore, post-death distributions from IRAs and SIMPLE accounts may *not* be excluded from income taxation as constituting the proceeds of life insurance.

A spouse may roll over the death benefit received from a participant to the spouse's IRA or to another eligible retirement plan. This rollover option is *not* available to a nonspousal beneficiary (or any other entity-type beneficiary).

Distributions to Spouse or Former Spouse Pursuant To a QDRO

Normally, a participant's qualified plan benefit may not be assigned or alienated by the participant as his voluntary act or against his will. This rule is designed to protect the participant's benefit from his creditors.

However, when a participant in an employer's retirement plan or the owner of an IRA divorces or separates, the benefits under the plan are a divisible asset—at least to the extent that they have been accumulated during marriage. In virtually every state, this asset is taken into account in one way or another in finalizing a property settlement between divorcing parties. In some cases, all or a portion of the benefits are awarded to the spouse or former spouse. When this happens, a number of special rules govern the tax consequences for participant and spouse when the benefits are distributed. In other cases, the participant or owner is permitted to retain all of the benefits, but the other spouse is compensated by a disproportionately large share of remaining marital or community property. In the latter cases, neither party recognizes gain nor other income from the transaction and subsequent distributions from the plan are taxed entirely to the participant. A plan participant's benefits also may be applied to satisfy her obligations for the support of a spouse, former spouse, or child of the marriage.

A distribution by a qualified retirement plan to an alternate payee who is a spouse or former spouse of the participant is taxable to the *spouse*, rather than the participant, *if* it is made pursuant to a qualified domestic relations order (QDRO). An alternate payee is a person who is recognized by a domestic relations order as having a right to receive all or a portion of the participant's benefits under the plan. A domestic relations order is a judgment, decree, or other order of a court issued under the domestic relations or community property law of a state that relates to alimony payments, child support, or marital property rights. It also includes judicial approval of a property settlement agreement between the spouses.

A domestic relations order is qualified (that is, constitutes a QDRO) if it satisfies all of the following requirements:

- It creates or recognizes the existence of an alternate payee's right to, or assign to an alternate payee, the right to receive all or a portion of the benefits payable to a participant.

- It includes the name and last known mailing address of the participant and the name and mailing address of each alternate payee.

- The amount or percentage of the participant's benefits to be paid to each alternate payee or the manner in which the amount or percentage is to be determined is specified.

- The number of payments or the period to which the order applies is specified.

- Each plan to which the order applies is referenced.

A QDRO may *not* assign a benefit that is already assigned under a previous order *nor* may it assign a benefit that the plan does not provide. Moreover, an alternate payee who is the spouse or former spouse of the participant and who receives a distribution pursuant to a QDRO may roll over the distribution in the same manner as if he were the participant.

MINIMUM DISTRIBUTIONS

A qualified retirement plan must provide that the payment of benefits must begin (unless the participant elects otherwise) not later than the 60th day after the latest of:

- the end of the plan year in which the participant attains the earlier of age 65 or the normal retirement age under the plan;

- the end of the plan year in which there occurs the 10th anniversary of the commencement of participation in the plan; or

- the end of the plan year in which the participant terminates service with the employer.

While a participant may elect to have benefits begin later, Congress never contemplated that taxpayers would be able to make permanent or indefinite the tax deferral available to participants in qualified retirement plans, IRAs, and certain other deferred compensation plans. As a result, Congress enacted provisions requiring plans to make distributions to participants and their beneficiaries and to increase the likelihood that a participant's interest in a plan primarily benefits the participant rather than the participant's beneficiaries.

The minimum distribution rules [including the minimum distribution incidental benefit (MDIB) requirement, discussed later] apply to qualified pension, profit-sharing, and stock bonus plans; IRAs (including SEP IRAs, SIMPLE accounts, and, to a limited extent, Roth IRAs); TSAs; and governmental Section 457 plans. Failure to comply with the minimum distribution and MDIB requirements may result in disqualification for a qualified plan and loss of status as a TSA, IRA, and so forth. In addition to disqualification, the plan may be subject to an excise tax of 50% of the amount by which the required minimum distribution exceeds the actual distribution made for a plan year.

Plans and arrangements may satisfy the minimum distribution requirements by making either annuity or nonannuity distributions. However, a qualified defined contribution plan, IRA (including a SEP IRA, Roth IRA, or SIMPLE IRA account), TSA, or Section 457 plan may satisfy those requirements through annuity payments *only* if the payments are made under an annuity contract purchased from an insurance company. This is in contrast to a defined benefit plan that may either purchase a commercial annuity contract or make annuity payments directly to the distributee.

The Economic Growth and Tax Relief Reconciliation Act of 2001 (EGTRRA) directed the Treasury to issue revised tables to reflect the increased life expectancy of today's population and to replace the life expectancy tables under IRC Section 72. The final regulations, therefore, include three new tables:

- a uniform table for determining the applicable distribution period during a participant's lifetime;

- a single life expectancy table (also known as the single life table); and

- a joint and last survivor life expectancy table for two individuals.

Under the final regulations, there is now a uniform and simplified method for determining a participant's required lifetime minimum distributions. Generally, the required minimum distribution for each calendar year is determined by dividing the participant's account balance as of the last valuation date in the calendar year before the distribution calendar year by an age-based factor from a uniform lifetime table. For lifetime required minimum distributions, the rules provide a uniform distribution period for all employees of the same age. The Uniform Lifetime Table (Uniform Table; *see* Exhibit 6.1) is used for determining the distribution period for lifetime distributions to an employee/plan participant (or IRA owner) *except* when the plan participant's spouse is the sole designated beneficiary and is more than 10 years younger than the employee. (In that case, the joint and last survivor life expectancy table applies.) The Uniform Lifetime Table is also generally used by unmarried individuals.

EXHIBIT 6.1 (Uniform Lifetime Table)* (For Use by Owners)

Age	Distribution Period	Age	Distribution Period
70	27.4	93	9.6
71	26.5	94	9.1
72	25.6	95	8.6
73	24.7	96	8.1
74	23.8	97	7.6
75	22.9	98	7.1
76	22.0	99	6.7
77	21.2	100	6.3
78	20.3	101	5.9
79	19.5	102	5.5
80	18.7	103	5.2
81	17.9	104	4.9
82	17.1	105	4.5
83	16.3	106	4.2
84	15.5	107	3.9
85	14.8	108	3.7
86	14.1	109	3.4
87	13.4	110	3.1
88	12.7	111	2.9
89	12.0	112	2.6
90	11.4	113	2.4
91	10.8	114	2.1
92	10.2	115 and over	1.9

*From Final Regulations 1.401(a)(9)-0 through 1.401(a)(9)-8

> **EXAMPLE** Earl Green is a 71-year-old retiree with an account balance of $200,000. Under the current final regulations and the new Uniform Lifetime Table, Earl may base his distribution on an applicable distribution period of 26.5 years (the factor applicable to account owners who are 71 years of age). Therefore, his first year required distribution is $7,547 ($200,000 ÷ 26.5 = $7,547).

The single life expectancy table, referred to as the Single Life Table, is used for determining the life expectancy of a nonspousal beneficiary at the participant's death.

Distributions Commencing During the Participant's Lifetime

Except in the case of a greater than 5% owner and unless the retirement plan provides otherwise, distribution of the interest of a living participant in a qualified plan (not an IRA) must begin no later than April 1 of the calendar year following the *later of*:

- the calendar year in which the participant attains age 70½; or

- the calendar year in which the participant retires.

The law does not require a plan to defer the commencement of required minimum distributions until the employee retires. A plan may provide for minimum distributions commencing no later than April 1 of the calendar year following the calendar year in which the employee attains age 70½, even though the employee has not retired at that time.

The date when the distribution of benefits must begin is referred to as the required beginning date (or RBD). The first year for which a distribution is required is either the year in which the participant reaches age 70½ or the year of retirement. The distribution for that year, however, need not be made until April 1 of the *following* calendar year. The annual distribution for each subsequent calendar year (including the year of death) must then be made no later than the end of that year. If a participant does not receive a distribution during the first calendar year for which a distribution is required, he must receive distributions for *two* calendar years in the following year as, as illustrated in the following example.

> **EXAMPLE** Fred Winter, a retired participant in a qualified plan, reaches age 70½ on August 1, 2015. Therefore, he must receive the required minimum distribution for 2015 no later than April 1, 2016, and the required minimum distribution for 2016 no later than December 31, 2016. To avoid having to take two distributions in 2016 (and be subject to income tax thereon), Fred should consider taking the 2015 distribution no later than December 31, 2015 (or prior in the year when he must take such distribution).

In the case of a greater than 5% businessowner, the distribution must be completed no later than April 1 of the calendar year following the calendar year in which the greater than 5% owner attained age 70½. The date of retirement exception does not apply to such an individual. A greater than 5% businessowner is any corporate employee who owns (or is considered to own, under the constructive ownership rules of IRC Section 318) more than 5% of the value of the outstanding stock of the corporation or stock possessing more than 5% of the total combined voting power of all the corporation's stock. In the case of an unincorporated business, a 5% owner is any employee who owns more than 5% of the capital or profits interest in the business.

In the case of the owner of an IRA (including a SEP IRA and SIMPLE account, but not a Roth IRA), distributions must be completed or started no later than April 1 of the calendar year following the calendar year in which the owner attained age 70½. A Roth IRA is not required to make any distributions during the lifetime of the owner.

Death of Participant After Benefits Have Begun

When a participant dies *after* plan benefits have begun to be paid, the minimum distribution rules for the post-death distributions (discussed in the following) apply to qualified plans, TSAs, Section 457 plans, traditional IRAs, SEP IRAs, and SIMPLE accounts. However, the IRS has ruled these post-death distribution rules do not apply to Roth IRAs.

If a participant dies after distribution of his interest has begun, the remaining portion of that interest must be distributed at least as rapidly as under the method of distribution being used at date of death. What this means is that if, as of the participant's death, nonannuity distributions have begun that satisfy the minimum distribution requirements, the participant's remaining interest must, unless the plan or arrangement purchases an annuity contract, continue to be distributed so as to satisfy those requirements. In application of this rule, the distribution of a participant's interest is considered to begin on the required beginning date, even though payments have actually begun before that date.

Under the regulations, the at least as rapidly requirement is satisfied if each annual distribution is at least equal to an amount determined by dividing the account balance by the number of years in the applicable distribution period. Accordingly, if a participant dies on or after the date when distribution has begun and has a *designated* beneficiary, the applicable distribution period for calendar years after the date-of-death calendar year is the life expectancy of that beneficiary. If there is *no* designated beneficiary (e.g., the participant's estate), the distribution period is the remaining life expectancy of the participant using the age of the participant as of his birthday in the year of his death.

When the Designated Beneficiary Is Not the Surviving Spouse

If the designated beneficiary is not the participant's spouse, the distribution period is determined by consulting Table I, using the beneficiary's age as of her birthday in the year following the year of the participant's death. The distribution period so determined is used in calculating the minimum distribution for the first year *after* the year of death (that is, no distribution is required in the year of the participant's death). In following years, the distribution period is reduced by one for each year that has elapsed since the year following the year of death. (Note: This is also commonly referred to by financial planning practitioners as the minus one method.)

> **EXAMPLE** Ralph, age 70, dies in 2015 with a vested interest in a qualified retirement plan of $200,000. His son, Frank, age 49, is the beneficiary of his father's interest in the qualified plan. The distribution period, beginning in 2016, is determined by consulting Table I (the Single Life Table) for a beneficiary age 50 (Frank's age in the year after Ralph's death). The applicable factor is 34.2. Therefore, the first distribution in the year 2016 (the year after Ralph's death) is $5,848 ($200,000 ÷ 34.2 = $5,848). No distribution is required in 2015. The distribution is now fixed. The distribution for the year 2017 is determined by subtracting one from the first year's distribution period, resulting in a factor of 33.2 (34.2 − 1 = 33.2).

When the Designated Beneficiary Is the Surviving Spouse

If the sole beneficiary is the participant's surviving spouse, the distribution period for each year during that spouse's lifetime after the year of death is determined by consulting Table I, using the surviving spouse's age as of his birthday in that year. For the first year after the year of the *spouse's* death, the distribution period is determined under Table I, using the spouse's age as of his birthday in the year of his death. In later years, the applicable distribution period is reduced by one for each year that has elapsed since the year after the year of death.

When There Is No Designated Beneficiary

If there is no designated beneficiary (e.g., the participant's estate or a qualified charity), the distribution period for each year is determined by consulting Table I, using the age of the employee as of the employee's birthday in the year of death. The distribution period so determined is used in calculating the minimum distribution for the first year after the year of death. In subsequent years, the distribution period is reduced by one for each year that has elapsed since the year of death.

Surviving Spouse as Successor to an IRA

If the owner of an IRA (including a SEP IRA, SIMPLE IRA account, or Roth IRA) leaves her entire remaining interest in an IRA to her surviving spouse, the surviving spouse may elect to treat the IRA as his own. The surviving spouse may make this election at any time after the required distribution has been made for the calendar year in which death occurred. To make the election, he must be the sole beneficiary of the IRA and have an unlimited right to withdraw from it. This requirement is not satisfied if a trust is named as beneficiary of the IRA, even if the spouse is the sole beneficiary. However, the spouse may make the election by retitling the account in his name as IRA owner (rather than leaving it as the owner's IRA with the surviving spouse as beneficiary).

Distributions Commencing After the Participant's Death

If a participant dies *before* the required beginning date, distribution of her interest in the plan or arrangement must be made under one of two rules:

■ **The five-year rule**   The deceased participant's interest must be distributed not later than December 31 of the calendar year in which the fifth anniversary of the participant's death falls.

■ **The life expectancy rule**   Any portion of a participant's interest payable to (or for the benefit of) a designated beneficiary must be distributed (commencing no later than December 31 of the calendar year immediately following the calendar year of the participant's death) over the life of the beneficiary or over a period not extending beyond the life expectancy of the beneficiary. This is commonly referred to by financial planning practitioners as stretching the distribution. If there is no designated beneficiary, the five-year rule applies.

If a plan or arrangement has no provision regarding which distribution method is preferred and the employee dies before her required beginning date and has a designated beneficiary, the default rule applies. In this situation, the default rule is the life expectancy rule. The Single Life Table is used to calculate the remaining life expectancy of the designated beneficiary under the life expectancy rule, if there is a designated beneficiary. If the employee does *not* have a designated beneficiary, the five-year rule applies.

A plan may provide that the five-year rule applies to distributions after the death of the employee even if the employee has a designated beneficiary, or it may provide that distribution is to be made in accordance with the five-year rule in every case. Further, a plan need not have the same method of distribution for the benefits of all employees. Finally, a plan or arrangement may include a provision under which either the participant or a beneficiary may elect the method that will apply.

The foregoing rules are modified if the designated beneficiary is the participant's surviving spouse who does not, in the case of an IRA, elect to treat the decedent's IRA as his own.

The following table summarizes the current required post-death minimum distribution rules for IRAs and qualified plans.

EXHIBIT 6.2

Beneficiary	Death Before RBD	Death After RBD
Surviving spouse	Life expectancy	Life expectancy
Surviving spouse rollover	Available	Available
Child (or other non-spousal designated beneficiary)	Five-year rule or life expectancy of beneficiary less one each year (with election to switch to Single Life Table under Final Regulations)	Life expectancy of beneficiary less one each year (with election to switch to Single Life Table under Final Regulations)
Nonqualified trust*	Five-year rule	Remaining life expectancy of participant less one each year
Charity	Five-year rule	Remaining life expectancy of participant less one each year
Estate	Five-year rule	Remaining life expectancy of participant less one each year

* If the designated beneficiary is older than the participant, the designated beneficiary may use the participant's remaining life expectancy. Therefore, a limited "stretch" is possible.

Importance of Designating Beneficiaries

We have discussed that the period over which distributions must be made and the amount of those distributions depend on whether or not the plan or participant has designated a beneficiary. A participant may have more than one designated beneficiary, but only one beneficiary (the one with the shortest life expectancy) is taken into account in determining required minimum distributions.

An individual qualifies as a designated beneficiary if he is designated under the plan or arrangement as a person who is entitled to a portion of the participant's benefit, contingent on the participant's death or other specified event. For example, if a distribution is in the form of a joint and survivor annuity over the life of the employee and another individual, it does not satisfy the minimum distribution requirement unless the other individual is a designated beneficiary.

Only *individuals* may be designated beneficiaries. An estate may *not* be a designated beneficiary. Although a trust is not, as such, a designated beneficiary, IRS final regulations do permit certain qualified trusts (e.g., a revocable living trust that becomes irrevocable at the grantor's death) to be treated under the rules applying to a designated beneficiary.

It should be apparent that it is very important to name a beneficiary for purposes of additional tax deferral of plan benefits.

MINIMUM DISTRIBUTION INCIDENTAL BENEFIT RULE

The IRS has long held the position that the principal purpose of a pension plan is to provide retirement benefits for employees and the principal purpose of a profit-sharing or stock bonus plan is to provide deferred compensation for employees. Accordingly, the IRS has developed the principle that post-retirement benefits paid for any other purpose must be incidental to the primary purpose. As a practical matter, the post-retirement benefits that must be incidental are death benefits paid to beneficiaries of the participant. To assure that they are incidental, a special rule is designed to ensure that, from an actuarial point of view, the value of distributions to be made to the participant are indeed greater than the value of the distributions to the beneficiary. This rule applies to qualified plans, TSAs, traditional IRAs, SEP IRAs, SIMPLE accounts, and Section 457 plans.

For purposes of the MDIB rule, distributions from a defined contribution plan that do not take the form of an annuity automatically satisfy the MDIB requirement if they satisfy the basic minimum required distribution rules. If the participant's benefit is payable in the form of a life annuity for the life of the employee and it satisfies the basic annuity distribution rules, the MDIB requirement is considered to be satisfied. When the participant's benefit is paid in the form of a joint and survivor annuity with his spouse as the beneficiary and the basic annuity distribution rules are satisfied, the distributions are considered to satisfy the MDIB requirement. When the participant's benefit is paid in the form of a joint and survivor annuity with a nonspousal beneficiary, the MDIB requirement is satisfied, as of the date distributions commence, if:

■ the amount satisfies the basic annuity distribution rules; and

■ the distribution option provides that annuity payments to the participant, on and after his required beginning date, satisfy the following condition

— the periodic annuity payment payable to the survivor must not, at any time on and after the participant's required beginning date, exceed the applicable percentage of the annuity payment payable to the employee specified in a table provided for that purpose (this condition must be satisfied with respect to any benefit increase after the required beginning date, including increases to reflect increases in the cost of living).

The percentage referred to in the referenced table is based on the excess of the age of the employee over the age of the beneficiary as of their attained ages in a calendar year.

PLANNING FOR DISTRIBUTIONS

While income taxes are not the only factor to be considered in planning a participant's retirement distribution, they are certainly one of the most important considerations, particularly when there is a substantial vested interest involved. Even a long-time middle level employee/participant may accumulate hundreds of thousands of dollars in her account balance at either retirement or termination of employment. As discussed previously, distributions from a qualified plan must take one of three forms:

■ A lump-sum distribution

■ An annuity or other installment form of distribution

■ Rollover to an IRA (including a SEP IRA, but not including a SIMPLE IRA account or Roth IRA) or other eligible qualified plan

To summarize the income tax rules surrounding retirement plan distributions, a lump-sum distribution is taxed as ordinary income unless the employee was born before 1936, in which case the distribution is eligible for special tax treatment (i.e., 10-year averaging). This is *not* the case if the recipient receives a portion of her benefits in the form of an annuity and the remainder as a single sum (i.e., the single sum is not eligible for special tax treatment). Similarly, if the recipient receives a lump-sum distribution and rolls over a portion of that distribution, the retained portion is *not* eligible for special tax treatment. Further, an annuity or other installment distribution is always taxed as ordinary income. A rollover is generally *nontaxable*. In the case of a distribution upon the death of a participant, a rollover is *not* available unless the distributee is the participant's surviving spouse.

In the case of a tax-advantaged plan (including a traditional IRA, SIMPLE IRA account, or employer plan that does not satisfy the requirements of IRC Section 401, but not including a TSA), there are fewer choices than in the case of a qualified plan. A distribution from a tax-advantaged plan may not be rolled over, and a lump-sum distribution is *never* eligible for averaging or other special tax treatment. The best a participant in a tax-advantaged plan (other than a TSA) may do is arrange at the inception of participation to have the benefits paid over a period of years or otherwise deferred.

Distributions from a TSA may be rolled over to a traditional IRA, another TSA, a Section 401(k) plan, or a Section 457 plan, but lump-sum distributions are never eligible for special tax treatment.

Important Factors in Choosing the Form of Distribution from a Qualified Plan

In choosing the form of distribution from a qualified plan, several factors must be taken into consideration:

■ **The manner in which the benefit will be used by the participant**   If, for instance, the participant wants to purchase a retirement home, only a lump-sum distribution will suffice.

■ **Whether the participant has a need for the principal of the retirement benefits or just the income generated by it to support his retirement lifestyle**   Under the rollover or lump-sum options, the participant assumes the risk of superannuation (outliving the assets).

- **The amount of the retirement benefits**   A large amount of benefits receivable tends to favor a rollover to a traditional IRA after the first few years of the IRA's existence, while providing the option of invading principal to maintain a chosen standard of living.

- **The beneficiary designations selected by the participant**   Under a rollover, if the participant selects his estate as beneficiary of the IRA receiving the rollover, minimum required distributions are based on the participant's life expectancy.

- **The expected date of death of both the participant and designated beneficiary**   The amount to which a rollover distribution accumulates (and, therefore, the benefits) is greatly dependent upon the life expectancy of both the participant and designated beneficiary, as well as the order in which they die. Accordingly, the health of both the participant and the beneficiary must be considered.

- **Whether the participant and the participant's spouse (if any) will recalculate life expectancies on an annual basis, under the rollover option**   Beginning in 2003, life expectancies, for the purpose of determining required minimum distributions, must be calculated by using tables provided in final regulations issued in 2002. If the plan or arrangement does not provide otherwise, the life expectancy of the benefit owner as well as that of the owner's spouse must be recalculated each year. If life expectancies are not recalculated, the relevant life expectancy in the first required distribution year is reduced by one for each succeeding distribution year. Over many years, the life expectancies as redetermined are significantly higher than those that have not been redetermined. When the life expectancies are redetermined annually, the effect is to substantially reduce the required annual minimum distributions.

In evaluating distribution choices at retirement, one thing should be clear—there is no such thing as a single best answer for all possible situations.

Retirement Distribution Checklist

In helping clients plan for retirement distributions, the following checklist may prove useful:

- Determine if the client has properly designated a beneficiary for each IRA and/or retirement account. A properly prepared beneficiary form should include a primary beneficiary or beneficiaries and a contingent beneficiary or beneficiaries. If a minor is designated as a beneficiary, the beneficiary form should be prepared in a manner that avoids the jurisdiction of the probate court—either by making the interest of the deceased payable to a custodian under the Uniform Transfer (or Gift) to Minors Act or to a trust for the benefit of the minor.

- If an account owner dies on or after her required beginning date, the required distribution that has not been paid to the account owner prior to the date of death must be paid to the beneficiary of the account owner.

- If an account owner has multiple beneficiaries, the separate share rule should be timely implemented so that each nonspouse beneficiary may be able to use his life expectancy in determining his required minimum distribution from the account of the deceased owner. (Note: This rule means establishing separate IRAs for each designated beneficiary before making required distributions.) Required minimum distributions to nonspouse beneficiaries must start in the year after the year of death of the account owner, regardless of whether the account owner dies before or after her required beginning date. The separate share rule is also useful when multiple beneficiaries cannot agree on how to invest the assets in the decedent's account, when they cannot agree on the speed with which distributions should be taken, when they do not get along with each other, and when they want to designate different successor beneficiaries.

- Determine whether the account owner has a power of attorney that covers the handling of retirement plan distributions.

- Make certain that a nonspouse beneficiary timely commences required minimum distributions from a retirement account. These payments must start one year after the account owner's year of death. Also, make sure the nonspouse beneficiary is aware of the payout period that is applicable.

- Make certain the spouse beneficiary is aware of the spousal rollover rules and timely implements the spousal rollover. Also, make certain the spouse does not roll over a required minimum distribution. Finally, determine that the spousal IRA rollover account has appropriate designated beneficiaries consistent with the spouse's estate plan.

Supplemental Reading–Plan Distributions–Part II

There are no supplemental readings for Unit 7.

8

Supplemental Reading– Social Security

SOCIAL SECURITY

The original Social Security Act, as enacted by Congress in 1935, provided only retirement benefits that first became effective January 1, 1937. In 1939, survivors benefits were added, followed in later years by disability benefits. The Social Security Act has been amended on several occasions and today provides coverage for retirement; survivors; disability; hospital and medical insurance for the aged, disabled, and those with end-stage renal disease; unemployment insurance; black lung benefits; Supplemental Security Income (SSI); and public assistance and welfare services (i.e., aid to needy families with children, medical assistance, maternal and child health services, child support enforcement, family and child welfare services, food stamps, and energy assistance).

The Social Security Administration administers the old age, survivors, and disability benefit programs as well as the Supplemental Security Income (SSI) program. The Centers for Medicare & Medicaid Services is the administrator for hospital and medical insurance for the aged and disabled.

Qualifying for Social Security Retirement Benefits

A person achieves qualification for retirement benefits under Social Security by becoming fully insured. One becomes **fully insured** by meeting one of two tests:

■ having 40 credits of coverage (10 years in covered work); or

■ having at least six credits of coverage and at least as many credits of coverage as there are years elapsing after 1950 (or, if later, *after* the year in which he reaches age 21) and *before* the year in which he dies; becomes disabled; or reaches, or will reach, age 62, whichever occurs first.

A coverage credit (in 2015) is credited to a worker's Social Security record for each $1,220 of earnings (up to four credits of coverage per year). This amount of earnings is automatically increased each year to reflect increases in average wages. The method of calculating a credit of coverage has changed over the years. For years prior to 1978, a worker received credit for a quarter of coverage for each quarter in which wages paid were $50 or more in covered employment. Moreover, each quarter of a year counted as a credit of coverage if the employee's total wages for that calendar year equaled or exceeded the maximum Social Security earnings base for that year.

In addition to meeting the fully insured requirements, a person must also be at least age 62 throughout the first month of entitlement and must have filed an application for retirement benefits in order to qualify for such benefits. A person who is fully insured can elect to start receiving a reduced benefit at any time between age 62 and his normal retirement age (gradually increasing from 65 to 67) or wait until his normal retirement age to receive a full benefit. Normal retirement age will be age 66 for workers reaching age 62 in 2012–2016 and will increase again by two months per year for workers reaching age 62 in 2017–2022. It will reach age 67 for workers attaining age 62 after 2022.

If a person has at least six credits of coverage during the full 13-quarter period ending with the calendar quarter in which he died, most recently became entitled to disability benefits, or became entitled to retirement benefits, he is considered **currently insured**. The six credits of coverage need not be consecutive, but they must be acquired during the 13-quarter period referred to earlier. If a person qualifies as currently insured at his death, child's benefits, mother's or father's benefits, and the lump-sum death payment (discussed later) are available to the deceased's survivor(s). However, benefits for a widow(er) age 60 or older, and benefits for a dependent parent, are payable only if the worker was fully insured at death.

Calculating the Social Security Retirement Benefit

In nearly every case, retirement benefits are based on the insured's Social Security earnings since 1950. In rare cases (i.e., when a person has little or no earnings since 1950), benefits may be computed based on earnings since 1937. Beginning in 1979, a wage indexing formula has been used to calculate benefits. A retired worker whose retirement benefits start on her normal retirement age receives monthly benefits equal to her primary insurance amount (PIA). The PIA is based on indexed earnings over a fixed number of years after 1950. It is calculated by indexing the worker's earnings record for wage inflation, determining the average indexed monthly earnings (AIME), and then applying the PIA formula to the AIME. A person's AIME is based on Social Security earnings for years after 1950, including wages earned as an employee and/or self-employment income, up to the maximum earnings creditable for specific years. Indexing the AIME results in an earnings history for each worker that is in line with national average wage levels at the time of a worker's eligibility. Earnings for each year are indexed up to the indexing year, the second year before the worker reaches age 62. Indexing must be applied to earnings in each year beginning with 1951 up to, but not including, the indexing year. Actual earnings are used for the indexing year and all later years. The indexing year is related to the year of first eligibility and not to the year of entitlement. For example, a person filing for a retirement benefit in 2015 at age 64 is first eligible in 2013 (at age 62), and the earnings record will be indexed based on the indexing year 2011 (two years before first eligibility).

Reduced Benefit for Early Retirement

If a worker elects to begin receiving retirement benefits before his normal retirement age, the resulting benefits are reduced. This is accomplished by reducing the worker's PIA by five-ninths of 1% (1/180) for each of the first 36 months that the worker is younger than normal retirement age when the benefits begin and five-twelfths of 1% (1/240) for each such month in excess of 36 months. Another effect of early retirement is that usually fewer years of higher earnings will be used in computing the worker's AIME.

Increased Benefit for Delayed Retirement

If a worker elects to work past her normal retirement age, her retirement benefit will be *increased* for each year she works between normal retirement age and age 70. Technically, the worker receives a retirement credit which began at 3% for those who attained age 62 in 1979 through 1986 and is scheduled to increase by one-half of 1% every other year until reaching 8% per year in 2009 or later. Another way in which the benefit is increased is that working past normal retirement age may result in a higher AIME. While the year in which the person reaches age 62 and succeeding years are not counted in the number of years used in the AIME calculation, if the earnings in those years are higher than those in the years counted, they may be substituted for earlier years and thereby increase AIME.

Loss of Benefits Due to Excess Earnings

If a person receiving Social Security retirement benefits has not yet attained his normal retirement age for an entire calendar year and earns $15,720 or less (2015), no benefits will be lost for that year. However, if that person were to earn more than $15,720 (2015), he would generally lose $1 of benefits for each $2 of earnings over $15,720 (2015).

If in the year that a person receiving Social Security retirement benefits reaches his normal retirement age he earns no more than $41,880 (2015) in the months before reaching full retirement age (FRA), no benefits will be lost for that year. However, if that person were to earn more than $41,880 (2015) before the month in which the person reaches normal retirement age, he would generally lose $1 for each $3 of earnings over $41,880 (2015).

When a person receiving Social Security retirement benefits is older than his normal retirement age, no benefits are lost because of his earnings.

Excess earnings are offset first against retirement benefits payable on the worker's account for the first month of the year and then are offset in chronological order against subsequent months until all of the excess earnings are exhausted or no benefits remain for the year.

Wages, bonuses, commissions, fees, and earnings from all types of work, whether covered by Social Security or not, are treated as earnings for purposes of the retirement test, as are net earnings from self-employment. Even earnings from family employment and earnings in excess of the Social Security taxable wage base ($118,500 in 2015), while not covered by Social Security, are considered earnings for purposes of the retirement test. There is a long list of income items *not* counted as earnings for purposes of the retirement test. Some of these items include the following:

- Payments received on account of the employee's sickness or accident disability, medical or hospitalization expenses, or death

- Payments from certain trust funds that are exempt from income tax

- Payments from certain annuity plans that are exempt from income tax

- Pensions and retirement pay

- Sick pay if paid more than six months after the month the employee last worked

- Interest and dividends from stocks and bonds (unless received by a dealer in securities in the course of business)

- Gain or loss from the sale of capital assets or sale, exchange, or conversion of other property that is not stock in trade nor includable in inventory

- Workers' compensation and unemployment compensation benefits

- Pay for jury duty

- Prize winnings from contests, unless the person enters contests as a trade or business

- Reimbursements by an employer for travel expenses

- Reimbursements or allowances by an employer for moving expenses, if they are not counted as wages for Social Security purposes

- Payments from IRAs and Keogh Plans

In general terms, a person may receive investment income or passive income *without* loss of benefits.

Qualifying for Social Security Survivor Benefits

Survivors of a deceased insured worker are entitled to various benefits. There are six types of benefits available to such survivors:

■ If the surviving spouse of a fully or currently insured worker is caring for a child of the deceased worker under age 16 or who has become disabled before age 22 and is entitled to a child's benefit on the deceased worker's account, the surviving spouse is eligible for a monthly **caregiver's benefit** regardless of her age. However, the surviving spouse must not be married, must not be entitled to widow's benefits (discussed later), must not be entitled to a retirement benefit based on her own work record that is equal to or larger than the amount of the unadjusted mother's or father's benefit, and must have filed an application for benefits. In addition, the surviving spouse must have been married to the deceased worker for at least nine months before the worker died (unless the death was accidental or occurred in the line of duty while a member of a uniformed service serving on active duty); the surviving spouse must have been the biological mother or father of the *worker's child* or legally adopted the worker's child during marriage and before the child reached age 18; the *surviving spouse's child* was adopted by the worker during their marriage and before the child reached age 18; or the surviving spouse was entitled to or potentially entitled to spouse's, widow(er)'s, father's, mother's, parent's, or childhood disability benefits in the month before the month the surviving spouse married the deceased worker.

■ The surviving child of a fully or currently insured deceased worker may qualify for a **child's benefit** if:

— the child is under age 18, or over age 18 and disabled by a disability that began before age 22, or under age 19 and a full-time elementary or secondary school student;

— the child is not married;

— the child is dependent upon the deceased parent; and

— an application is filed for such benefits.

■ A child may receive benefits based on a deceased parent's Social Security account even though the other parent is still living and supporting the child. The surviving child's benefit is equal to 75% of the deceased parent's primary insurance amount (PIA) unless restricted due to the family maximum limit.

■ A widow(er) of a fully insured deceased worker may be entitled to a **widow(er)'s benefit** based on the deceased spouse's earnings if:

— the widow(er) is age 60 or older, or is at least age 50 but not age 60 and is disabled;

— the worker died fully insured;

— the widow(er) is not entitled to a retirement benefit that is equal to or larger than the worker's PIA;

— the widow(er) has filed an application for widow(er)'s benefits; and

— the widow(er) is not married.

- The remarriage of a widow(er) or surviving divorced spouse after age 60, or the remarriage of a disabled widow(er) or disabled surviving divorced spouse after age 50 and after the date the widow(er) became disabled, will not prevent that individual from becoming entitled to benefits on her prior deceased spouse's Social Security record.

- A disabled widow(er) (or surviving divorced widow[er]) who otherwise qualifies for a widow(er)'s benefit may start receiving a **disabled widow(er)'s benefit** at any time after attaining age 50 and before attaining age 60. The monthly benefit is based on 100% of the deceased spouse's PIA, but it is reduced by 28.5% so the benefit equals 71.5% of the deceased spouse's PIA at age 60. A disabled widow(er) must meet the definition of disability used to determine if a worker is entitled to disability benefits. This means the widow(er) must be unable to engage in *any* substantial, gainful activity by reason of physical or mental impairment. The impairment must be medically determinable and expected to last for at least 12 months or result in death.

- The parent of a deceased insured person is entitled to a **parent's benefit** if:

    — the insured person was fully insured at death;

    — the parent files an application for parent's benefits

    — the parent has reached age 62;

    — the parent is not entitled to a retirement benefit that is equal to or larger than the amount of the unadjusted parent's benefit after any increase to the minimum benefit;

    — the parent was receiving at least one-half support from the insured person;

    — evidence that the support requirement was met has been filed with the Social Security Administration within the appropriate time limit; and

    — the parent has not remarried since the insured person's death.

- The parent must be a natural parent who is eligible under state law to share in the intestate property of the worker as the worker's father or mother; legally adopted the worker before the worker attained age 16; or is a person eligible to claim benefits as the deceased's stepparent by a marriage entered into before the deceased attained age 16. A parent's benefit is equal to 82.5% of the deceased worker's PIA if there is only one eligible parent and 75% for each parent if there are two parents entitled to benefits. A full benefit is payable at age 62, subject to the maximum family limit.

- A **lump-sum death benefit** of $255 is paid upon the death of a fully or currently insured worker, provided he is survived by a spouse who was living in the same household as the deceased at the time of death or is survived by a spouse or dependent child eligible to receive Social Security benefits for the month of death based on his earnings record. If no surviving widow(er) or child (as defined previously) survives, no lump sum is payable.

When multiple family members are receiving Social Security benefits, they may be subject to a **maximum family benefit**. In 2015, the maximum family benefit for retirement and survivors for those reaching age 62 or dying before age 62 (adjusted for inflation annually) is generally 150–180% of PIA.

Qualifying for Social Security Disability Benefits   To qualify for Social Security disability benefits, a worker must:

- be insured for disability benefits (defined later);

- be under age 65;

- have been disabled for 12 months, or be expected to be disabled for at least 12 months, or have a disability that is expected to result in death;

- have filed an application for disability benefits; and

- have completed a five-month waiting period unless exempted from this requirement (discussed later).

Determination of whether a worker is disabled is the responsibility of the Disability Determination Services (DDS) agency of each state. However, DDS determinations of disability may be reviewed and reversed by the Social Security Administration's Office of Program and Integrity Reviews.

In deciding whether a worker is eligible for disability benefits, SSA uses the following five-step process:

1. It determines whether the individual is engaging in substantial, gainful activity. If so, the claim is denied at this point. If not, the process continues to the second step.

2. It determines whether the individual has a severe, medically determinable physical or mental impairment. If not, the claim is denied at this point. If so, the process continues to the third step.

3. It determines whether the individual has an impairment included in its Listing of Impairments. If so, the claim is allowed. If not, the claim continues to the fourth step.

4. It determines whether the impairment prevents the individual from doing relevant work that was performed in the past. If not, the claim is denied at this point. If so, the claim continues to the fifth and final step.

5. It determines whether the impairment prevents the individual from doing any other work. If so, the claim is allowed. If not, the claim is denied.

A person is considered insured for disability benefits if he is fully insured under the Social Security system and has worked under Social Security for at least 5 of the 10 years (20 out of 40 quarters) just before becoming disabled, or if the disability begins before age 31 but after age 24, for at least one-half of the quarters after reaching age 21 and before becoming disabled (but not less than six quarters). If a person becomes disabled before the quarter in which he attains age 24, he must have six credits of coverage in the 12-quarter period ending with the quarter in which the disability began.

A person may receive disability benefits at any age before attaining normal retirement age. If a person is receiving disability benefits when he attains normal retirement age, the disability benefit automatically ends and a retirement benefit begins.

A disabled worker may be exempted from the five-month waiting period if he has had a prior period of disability and if the new disability arises within five years after the previous one ended and is expected to last for at least 12 months or result in death.

As is the case with retirement benefits, the family of a disabled worker may also qualify for a spouse's and/or child's benefit.

Calculating the Social Security Disability Benefit

A disabled worker's benefit is equal to the worker's PIA, determined as if the worker were at normal retirement age and eligible for retirement benefits in the first month of the waiting period. However, the formula for determining a disabled worker's AIME and PIA differs from that used for a retiring worker. There are also different limits on the amount of family benefits that may be paid to a disabled worker and her family. A disabled worker's benefits may also be offset by a workers' compensation benefit or federal, state, or local public law disability benefit.

Moreover, a person's disability benefit has nothing to do with her personal wealth and whether or not the person's spouse is employed. However, a person will lose her disability benefit by refusing, without good cause, to accept vocational rehabilitation services. Finally, an individual will not be considered disabled if alcoholism or drug addiction is a contributing factor material to the SSA's determination that the individual is disabled.

A person's disability benefits end on the earliest of:

■ the second month after the month in which the disability ceases;

■ the month before the month the worker attains normal retirement age (at which point the benefits are automatically converted to retirement benefits); or

■ the month before the month in which the worker dies.

Income Taxation of Social Security Benefits

Social Security retirement, survivor, and disability benefits may be taxable in certain situations. For instance, if the beneficiary's sole income is Social Security benefits, most likely those benefits will *not* be taxable, and a return need not be filed. However, if the beneficiary has income *in addition to* the Social Security benefits, a return will most likely be required even though the Social Security benefits are still not taxable.

In other situations, a portion of a person's Social Security benefits *may* be taxable. Here, the amount that must be included in the beneficiary's gross income is the lesser of one-half of the annual benefits received or one-half of the excess of the beneficiary's provisional income over a specified **base amount** (used for lower provisional income levels). **Provisional income** is the beneficiary's modified adjusted gross income (MAGI) plus one-half of the Social Security or tier 1 railroad retirement benefits. In turn, MAGI is the beneficiary's adjusted gross income plus any tax-exempt interest, including interest earned on savings bonds used to finance higher education, and amounts excluded under an employer's adoption assistance program.

For example, if a beneficiary's provisional income (MAGI plus one-half of his Social Security benefits) is more than a **base amount,** some portion of his benefits will be taxable. The base amount varies with a beneficiary's income tax filing status. Currently, it is $32,000 for a married couple filing jointly, $0 for married couples filing separately and who lived together at any time during the year, and $25,000 for other taxpayers. If a beneficiary's provisional income exceeds the applicable base amount, the lesser of one-half of the beneficiary's Social Security benefits or one-half of the excess of provisional income over the base amount is includable in gross income.

Following is an example to illustrate how the taxable portion of a person's Social Security benefits is determined.

E X A M P L E   Fred and Judy Martin have adjusted gross income of $24,000 for 2015. Fred, who is retired, receives Social Security benefits of $7,200 per year. The couple also receives $6,000 per year from a mutual fund that invests solely in tax-exempt municipal bonds. On their joint return for 2015, the Martins' calculate the portion of Fred's Social Security benefits to be included in their gross income in the following manner:

1.	Adjusted gross income	$24,000
2.	Plus: All tax-exempt interest	+ 6,000
3.	Modified adjusted gross income (MAGI)	$30,000
4.	Plus: One-half of Social Security benefits	+ 3,600
5.	Equals: Provisional income	$33,600
6.	Less: Applicable base amount	(32,000)
7.	Equals: Excess above base amount	$1,600
8.	One-half of excess above base amount	$800
9.	One-half of Social Security benefits	3,600
Amount includable in gross income (lesser of 8 or 9)		$800

To make things more confusing, if a beneficiary's provisional income is more than an **adjusted base amount**, the beneficiary must include in income the lesser of

■ 85% of the beneficiary's Social Security benefits; or

■ 85% of the excess of provisional income over the applicable adjusted base amount, plus the sum of the smaller of

— the amount that would otherwise be includable if the second threshold (adjusted base amount) did not apply, or

— $4,500 ($6,000 for joint filers).

Like the base amount, this adjusted base amount also varies with a beneficiary's income tax filing status. Currently, it is $44,000 for married couples filing jointly, $0 for married couples filing separately and who lived together at any time during the year, and $34,000 for other taxpayers. If a person is married filing separately and lived with his spouse at any time during the year, up to 85% of his benefits is included in gross income.

Using the same facts as in the previous example, except that the Martins' provisional income now is increased from $33,600 to $53,600, the includable amount is determined in the following manner:

1.	Provisional income	$53,600
2.	Applicable adjusted base amount	<u>44,000</u>
3.	Excess of 1 over 2	<u>$9,600</u>
4.	85% of amount in 3	$8,160
5.	Amount otherwise includable (½ of Martins' benefits)	$3,600
6.	Base amount for joint filers	$6,000
7.	Lesser of 5 or 6	$3,600
8.	Sum of amounts in 4 and 7	$11,760
9.	85% of Social Security benefits	6,120
	Amount includable in gross income (lesser of 8 or 9)	**$6,120**

A beneficiary may elect to have federal income tax withheld at 7, 10, 15, or 25% from his Social Security benefits. For tax purposes, the definition of Social Security benefits includes workers' compensation benefits to the extent they cause a reduction in Social Security and railroad retirement tier 1 disability benefits. Because workers' compensation benefits are paid in lieu of Social Security payments in this situation, this assures parallel treatment for tax purposes.

The Commissioner of Social Security files annual returns with the Secretary of the Treasury showing the benefits paid to each beneficiary in each year. Similarly, statements must also be provided to each recipient of benefits by January 31 of the year following the benefit payments.

Social Security Funding

Social Security is funded by a combined payroll tax of 10.4% of covered wages [up to $118,500 (2015)] imposed under the Federal Insurance Contributions Act (FICA), a portion of which is imposed on the employee and the remainder on the employer. The employer may take an income tax deduction for its share of the tax. Self-employed persons are taxed under the Self-Employment Contributions Act at a current rate of 10.4% of their net earnings from self-employment [up to $118,500 (2015)]. These persons are also permitted a tax deduction in arriving at adjusted gross income for the employer share of the Social Security and Medicare (discussed later) self-employment tax paid. While many taxpayers focus on their federal income tax burden, a little recognized fact is that approximately 79% of Americans pay *more* in payroll taxes than they do in income taxes. In additional to the Social Security tax, employees and employers each pay a Medicare tax of 1.45% (2.90% for self-employed). The income on which the Medicare tax is imposed is unlimited.

Beginning in 2013, high-wage earners who exceed certain thresholds are subject to a 0.9% Additional Medicare Tax.

Supplemental Reading–Plan and Investment Considerations for Retirement Plans

INVESTMENT POLICY

In recent years, there has been a growing movement away from defined benefit (DB) plans and toward defined contribution (DC) plans. This has been fueled primarily by the growing complexity of administering a defined benefit plan (including the development and administration of the required formal investment policy statement). Also, it is clear that employer/sponsors generally do not want to assume the investment risks associated with DB plans. Therefore, employers have had to become more creative with encouraging and motivating employees to participate in DC plans and plan for their own retirement. A multiplicity of investment choices has been the result, and it is here that a client/employee's financial planner may provide valuable advice. Among factors contributing to additional investment choices for employee/clients participating in a DC plan has been the growing public awareness of retirement planning and the need to provide for one's own future economic security, as well as the aggressive marketing efforts of leading mutual fund companies in attempting to provide more complete financial planning services to their investors.

In addition to the type of retirement plan that is adopted (i.e., defined benefit versus individual account), there are three broad considerations that must be evaluated in establishing the investment objectives of an employer-sponsored plan. These include:

- the financial characteristics of the sponsor and the industry or profession in which it participates;

- the demographics of the employee workforce; and

- the possibility of plan termination and associated costs.

If an employer is currently experiencing thin profit margins and high labor costs in a highly cyclical industry, it is, in turn, likely to have *less* tolerance for risk than that of an employer in a rapidly growing and dynamic industry. Similarly, demographics are important because a growth company with a young workforce has less concern for cash flow and investment liquidity than does a company with a more mature workforce and the need to provide an immediate or near-term pension to participants. Finally, the possibility of plan termination is an important consideration for companies with some risk of financial decline, merger, or other corporate acquisition because that employer must take into account the possibility of government assumption of plan liabilities to existing participants and the costs associated with the government (specifically, the Pension Benefit Guaranty Corporation) doing so.

There are four primary characteristics of any investment vehicle that need to be considered in assessing its potential suitability as a retirement plan asset. These include the investment's tax advantages, its liquidity, its stability in value, and its ability to preserve purchasing power. Broadly, as with any investment, these factors may be categorized generally as characteristics of risk and expected return considerations. These factors are relevant for each of the following classes of retirement plan assets:

- Common stocks

- Short-term and long-term debt (e.g., certificates of deposit, commercial paper, U.S. Treasury bills, U.S. Treasury bonds, corporate bonds, and other fixed-income assets, including guaranteed investment contracts or GICs)

- Real estate (e.g., real property itself, mortgages secured by real estate, and real estate syndications)

- Equipment leasing (but must avoid UBTI treatment)

■ Mutual funds

■ Collectibles (not for IRAs)

■ Options, commodity futures, and puts and calls

The tax aspects of an asset being considered for a retirement plan is important because of the tax-exempt status of the qualified plan trust that owns the asset. For example, it is not generally a good investment practice to place an already tax-exempt asset (such as a municipal bond) in another tax-exempt vehicle (such as a qualified plan trust). In doing so, several percentage points of potential before-tax rate of return may be sacrificed. Also, the plan adviser needs to know the limitations on the tax-exempt status of qualified plans when selecting appropriate investment assets so a particular investment does not trigger the UBTI, as discussed earlier.

Finally, investors who are accumulating money shortly before retirement need as high of a compounded annual investment return as possible and, therefore, must assume the increased risk of volatility. It has been shown that volatility is a major threat to those already retired. In this regard, studies have shown that, in a retirement portfolio, moderate but consistent returns are much more valuable than high but sporadic returns (see, for example, the website *www.fundadvice.com* for several excellent articles on this phenomenon).

In light of the foregoing considerations, qualified plan investment advisers or investment managers seek to establish certain investment objectives consistent with the interests of plan participants and beneficiaries as well as that of the employer/plan sponsor. These investment objectives usually include high rate of return, safety of principal, and adequate liquidity. Often these objectives are at odds with each other; correspondingly, a balance must be achieved among them in arriving at an overall investment strategy. One must also consider the ERISA and IRC fiduciary requirements discussed earlier. Additionally, ERISA Section 402 requires a "funding policy and method consistent with the objectives of the plan."

LIFE INSURANCE IN A QUALIFIED PLAN

One of the many permissible investments in a qualified plan is life insurance policies on the lives of plan participants. Such policies may be purchased and owned by a qualified plan using deductible employer contributions to the plan to pay the premiums. The pure insurance portion of a qualified plan death benefit (death proceeds less policy cash values at death) is received by a beneficiary income tax free and may be used to pay estate taxes in the estate of the deceased plan participant. The purchase of life insurance policies is most often used in profit sharing or Section 401(k) plans or other defined contribution plans.

Life insurance inside a qualified plan tends to have cost advantages over individual life policies provided by the employer outside the qualified plan or those personally owned by plan participants. Moreover, life insurance policies represent a very safe investment (including the guarantee of an insurance company) and provide highly predictable plan costs. Some experts believe it is possible to structure insured plan death benefits to exclude them from the estate of the plan participant.

The benefit of life insurance policies must be provided to all plan participants under a nondiscriminatory formula related to the retirement benefit or to the plan contribution formula. In addition, such a plan must meet one of the two following incidental benefit tests:

■ A participant's insured death benefit must be no more than 100 times the expected monthly retirement benefit under the plan.

■ The aggregate premiums paid (over the entire life of the plan) for a participant's insured death benefit are at all times less than the following percentages of the plan cost for that participant

— ordinary life insurance   50%

— term life insurance   25%

— universal life insurance   25%

While defined contribution plans typically use the previously listed percentages, defined benefit plans have historically used the "100 ×" limit. However, either type of plan may use either limit. In fact, defined benefit plans are increasingly using the percentage limits.

Life Insurance in Defined Benefit Plans

The cost of life insurance included in a qualified plan may be added to the maximum deductible retirement plan contribution, with the total constituting tax-deductible dollars contributed by the employer. This differs from the treatment in a defined contribution plan where the costs of life insurance must be part of the contributions to each participant's account [that is, those contributions do not increase the Section 415 annual additions limit—lesser of 100% of compensation or $53,000 (in 2015)].

Defined benefit plans typically offer three general types of funding for life insurance policies purchased for plan participants. First is combination plan funding under which the retirement benefit is equal to the combination of policy cash values at death, plus an amount distributed from a side fund or conversion fund. This type of funding offers the advantages of an insured death benefit, the investment security of cash surrender values, and an opportunity to invest more aggressively in the side fund. It tends to be used primarily by small plans due to the administrative costs of carrying life insurance policies on each plan participant. Such plans will also typically use the "100 ×" limit.

The second type of funding is envelope funding, under which the insurance policies are treated as plan assets, just like any other asset. Such funding provides both retirement and death benefits and normally offers a lower initial contribution to the plan than combination plan funding.

The third type of funding is fully insured funding under which the plan funding consists of 100% life insurance policies or annuity contracts; there is no side fund. Such plans, known as IRC Section 412(i) plans after the Internal Revenue Code Section of the same number, are exempt from the minimum funding rules. A fully insured plan is one that:

■ contains exclusively individual or group insurance contracts or annuity contracts;

■ has level premiums extending to retirement age for each plan participant;

■ offers insurance and/or annuity contract benefits guaranteed by a licensed insurance company;

■ pays premiums without lapse;

- has had no rights subject to a security interest during the plan year; and

- has had no policy loans outstanding at any time during the plan year.

Fully insured plans must be nondiscriminatory as to rights, benefits, and features. However, they enjoy more simplified ERISA reporting requirements, are not required to submit an actuarial certification, and are exempt from quarterly pension deposits. Nonetheless, they are still subject to PBGC annual premium requirements. Fully insured plans are characterized by larger initial annual deposits than uninsured plans and are actually the mirror image of traditional trusteed plans in which the initial annual deposits are relatively small and then increase as participants approach retirement.

Life Insurance in Defined Contribution Plans

In a defined contribution plan, part of each participant's account may be used to purchase insurance on the participant's life in one of three general ways:

- Voluntary insurance is purchased by participants, using a directed account or earmarking provisions.

- Insurance is provided automatically as a plan benefit.

- Insurance is provided on a nondiscriminatory basis at the option of the plan administrator.

Of course, the amount of insurance must stay within the incidental benefit limits. As an investment hedge, many such plans maintain whole life insurance premiums at about one-third of plan contributions so as not to run afoul of the incidental benefit limits. Plans that have been in existence for a considerable period of time (e.g., 10 years or more) may make large purchases of life insurance and still avoid the incidental benefit limitation because the tests are computed based on aggregate (or cumulative) plan contributions.

Income Tax Implications of Life Insurance in Qualified Plans

Employer contributions to the plan, including those used to purchase life insurance, are deductible if the amount of life insurance is within the incidental benefit limits. Secondly, the economic value of pure life insurance coverage on a participant's life is taxed annually to the participant based on the lesser of IRS Table 2001 values or actual life insurance company term rates for standard risks. Third, the pure insurance element of an insured plan death benefit, as well as the portion of the death benefit representing Table 2001 costs paid by the participant, are income tax free (assuming they are paid from the same insurance contracts that gave rise to the premium costs). The remainder of the death benefit is taxed as a qualified plan distribution. Finally, life insurance inside a qualified plan receives favorable tax treatment compared to personally owned or employer-provided life insurance (outside a qualified plan), due to the greater deferral of tax with insurance inside a qualified plan. While the death benefits received from qualified plans are generally included in a decedent's estate for federal estate tax purposes, a competent estate planning attorney may assist in structuring a method to eliminate them from the decedent's taxable estate.

Supplemental Reading–Retirement Needs Analysis

There are no supplemental readings for Unit 10.

Supplemental Reading–Appendix: Plan Selection for Businesses

In the previous readings, retirement planning and the broad spectrum of retirement plans extending from tax-advantaged savings vehicles for individuals and government-sponsored programs to employer-sponsored plans for employees were discussed. The discussion has included plans that are qualified for income tax purposes under IRC Section 401(a), as well as plans that share some characteristics of qualified plans yet are not strictly defined as such. Among the latter plans (which are best thought of as tax favored or tax advantaged) are plans for self-employed individuals (Keogh plans) and other individuals planning for their own retirement with use of such vehicles as an IRA, a SEP, or an employer-sponsored SIMPLE plan.

However, the assumption that the implementation of *any* retirement plan by a businessowner will be in the best interests of those involved may *not* be appropriate. A financial planner is often in the position of advising her business client about the adoption of a retirement plan. This appendix explains factors or considerations that should be taken into account before implementing any retirement plan. It is designed to help a financial planner and/or a businessowner make an informed decision about the selection, design, and adoption of a retirement plan that will be the most suitable plan to accomplish the employer/sponsor's business, personal, and employee motivational objectives. In many respects, selecting an appropriate retirement plan is a matching exercise in which the employer/sponsor's objectives are matched with the features offered by a specific retirement plan. This appendix requires readers to apply all of the knowledge they should have acquired from the previous readings to the difficult task of retirement plan selection.

PRELIMINARY CONSIDERATIONS

In many instances, the decision of whether to implement a retirement plan comes down to the threshold question of, can the client afford not to? A primary reason why the implementation of a retirement plan may be so important is because it makes business sense. Retirement plans of any sort have become so popular and are so potentially advantageous for a number of reasons that a business must proceed or risk being left behind.

Nevertheless, the process of arriving at such a conclusion may not be as simple as it appears. First, a businessowner (or an individual planning for his own retirement) should not consider the implementation of a retirement plan until following proper risk management techniques and both personal and business liability insurance policies are in place. In addition, adequate cash reserves, in the event of a business or personal emergency, need to be firmly established. Finally, as with most other financial planning decisions, it should be clear that a business or individual's current cash flow can adequately support such a major investment in one's financial future. Stated very simply, unless adequate discretionary income exists in the first place, the businessowner should *not* proceed with the implementation of an employer-sponsored retirement plan.

In addition to the competitive business reasons, a businessowner may want to implement a retirement plan because of one other primary motivation—to secure personal tax benefits while ensuring his *own* future financial security. This may appear self-serving; however, the fact remains that most businessowners agree to cover the majority of employees *only* because of the tremendous attendant tax and investment advantages they themselves enjoy. Nevertheless, these advantages come at a price—the considerable regulatory and fiduciary responsibility that is attendant to the implementation and administration of a qualified retirement plan.

As discussed previously, a qualified plan is subject to numerous reporting, disclosure, and investment requirements. The financial planner should discuss these requirements with her businessowner/client. Specific annual reports, such as the Form 5500, must be filed with the IRS and/or Department of Labor (DOL) in addition to the sometimes considerable amount of paperwork that must be filed to implement the plan initially. There are also numerous other items that need to be provided to employees, either initially or annually, including the summary plan description (SPD) and summary annual report (SAR). In recent years, the desire to avoid at least some of the regulatory and disclosure requirements has led to the introduction of simplified employer plans (e.g., the SEP and SIMPLE).

Finally, the businessowner, as sponsor of the plan, is in the role of a *fiduciary* and is required to discharge all duties in the interest of plan participants and beneficiaries. As such, this means there is considerable potential liability in carrying out the responsibilities of this role. If the owner is either unwilling or unable to accept this liability, he should reconsider a qualified plan and perhaps install a nonqualified plan only for highly valued employees or encourage employees to save for their retirement on an after-tax basis.

TYPICAL EMPLOYER/SPONSOR RETIREMENT PLAN OBJECTIVES/CONSIDERATIONS

Prior to ascertaining the client's objectives (discussed later), the financial planner first needs to obtain some very essential factual information, including an employee census (i.e., a list of all employees with their compensation levels, ages, and years of service with the employer) and current or previous retirement plans maintained by the employer.

Having obtained the employee census information and data concerning other employer retirement plans (current and past), the financial planner may then turn to the businessowner's objectives. Specific businessowner objectives in establishing a retirement plan usually fall into three general categories: personal, business, and employee motivational. In most cases, the *personal* objectives will be of primary importance. Normally, the business and employee motivational objectives will be secondary, but they will, nevertheless, be important in the plan's selection and design considerations.

In addition to the owner's objectives, other personal factors must be considered in selecting and designing an appropriate retirement plan. These factors include the owner's current age, the size of his retirement savings need, and his attitude toward investment risk. The closer the owner is to his own retirement date, the more he will want to ensure his own financial security. In addition, as the owner gets older, he will generally become more conservative in his approach to investment risk. Accordingly, this factor will tend to push the planner in the direction of a *defined benefit plan*.

Again, the closer the retirement date of the owner, the more immediate the owner's savings need. He will probably wish to get as much money in his retirement account as quickly as possible. Accordingly, because the annual contributions to defined contribution plans are limited, the planner will again be influenced in the direction of a defined benefit plan.

As we discussed earlier, in defined contribution type plans, the employee assumes the investment risk. In defined benefit type plans, the employer is the risk taker. Even though the owner may be older than his employees and would seem to be best suited to the lesser risk of a defined benefit pension plan, he may not wish to assume the risk of investment. Accordingly, the planner may be guided back in the direction of a defined contribution plan.

Finally, the ability of the business to sustain annual plan contributions will be *critical* in choosing between a defined contribution and a defined benefit plan. While all defined contribution plans do not provide flexible employer contributions, all defined benefit plans require *mandatory* annual employer funding. If the current or immediately foreseeable business cash flow will *not* support this mandatory contribution, the planner should orient her client's thinking toward a profit-sharing or Section 401(k) type of *defined contribution plan* and away from a defined benefit plan.

As is the case with most financial planning issues, the planner is advised not to make a plan selection based upon any one of these factors, but to use her judgment in synthesizing all factors into the most appropriate recommendation. This will usually mean the planner must go further and investigate the client's specific objectives.

Businessowner's Personal Objectives

Some of the most common personal objectives of the businessowner include the following:

- To maximize retirement benefits for the owner

- To provide a tax shelter for the owner

- To provide estate liquidity for the owner

- To allow the owner to withdraw funds prior to retirement

Business Objectives

Typical objectives of the business itself are as follows:

- To minimize plan costs by restricting contributions for lower-paid employees

- To place the risk of investing plan assets on the employees

- To provide for predictable annual plan costs

- To maximize annual employer contribution flexibility

- To provide for convenient plan administration

- To create a market for employer stock

- To attract and reward key employees

- To reduce employee turnover

- To maximize the income tax benefits of the plan

Employee Motivational Objectives

Typical employee motivational objectives include the following:

- To maximize retirement benefits for key employees

- To maximize retirement benefits for older employees (typically management)

- To provide a tax shelter for key employees

- To allow employees to withdraw funds prior to retirement

- To share business ownership with employees

- To share business profits with employees

- To increase employee satisfaction

- To minimize employee turnover

- To encourage retirement by providing retirement income for employees

- To encourage employee savings by providing a savings medium that employees perceive as valuable

- To create an incentive for employees to maximize performance

RETIREMENT PLAN SELECTION AND DESIGN

As with any financial planning opportunity, the planner must know the universe of alternatives that is available to satisfy her client's goals. In retirement planning for the businessowner, these are the various types of qualified and tax-advantaged plans, as shown in the previous table. It is fortunate that, in recent years, eligibility for these types of plans has been standardized such that all are generally available to a business entity, no matter what the form. The only notable exceptions to this rule are stock bonus plans and ESOPs, which may not be adopted by *unincorporated* entities such as a sole proprietor or partnership, and the Section 403(b) tax-sheltered annuity (TSA), which is only permissible for certain IRC 501(c)(3) nonprofit organizations and public schools. In addition, as discussed previously, Section 457 plans may be adopted only by nonprofits and state and local governmental entities. With these exceptions, however, all forms of defined contribution and defined benefit plans are permitted for all forms of business entities.

Many of the businessowner's objectives may be met by any well-designed employer-sponsored retirement plan. If the financial planner is in doubt as to which plan to recommend, it is always advisable for the planner to select the *simplest* or least complicated plan that satisfies the client's retirement planning objectives.

In designing an appropriate retirement plan, it cannot be reiterated enough that to help the business, *the financial planner first needs to help the businessowner satisfy his own personal retirement objectives*. In that spirit, here are some suggestions or techniques that may be used to maximize the owner's share of contributions to a qualified retirement plan. All have been discussed previously.

- Impose a minimum age and waiting period for initial plan eligibility. A qualified plan may require a minimum age of 21 and a waiting period of up to one year. However, if all employer contributions are fully vested at that time, this waiting period [except for a Section 401(k) plan] may be up to two years. If the business is one that experiences rapid turnover (such as many retail firms), it may be advisable to delay the eligibility date to two years from the date of an employee's hiring.

- Impose a vesting schedule. A departing employee is only entitled to the vested portion of her plan benefit. The non-vested portion is forfeited and may be used to reduce future employer plan contributions, or it may be reallocated among the remaining plan participants, with the businessowner usually being the major participant.

- Impose a requirement that a participant work at least 1,000 hours during the plan year or be employed on the last day of the plan year to receive an allocation or accrue a benefit.

- Integrate the plan with Social Security benefits using the permitted disparity rules. This results in plan participants whose compensation does not exceed a specified integration level not receiving an additional qualified plan allocation.

- Adopt an age-weighted profit-sharing plan or target benefit pension plan, which favors an older businessowner/employee. Both of these types of plans permit a greater allocation of the employer's contribution to an older employee and, in the case of the age-weighted plan, do not require a mandatory annual employer contribution.

RETIREMENT PLAN INSTALLATION

While a client's financial planner normally will be the client's most trusted advisor with regard to the selection of an appropriate retirement plan, installation of the plan (whether customized or prototyped) is best left to a pension advisory firm, also known as a third-party administrator (TPA). A TPA provides consulting services in the installation of, most particularly, a qualified corporate retirement plan. A TPA will also serve as the administrator of the plan that is implemented, thereby carrying out the duties of communicating regularly with plan participants/employees.

Before we discuss the process of installing a qualified retirement plan, let us first review which of the plans discussed in this text constitute qualified [or IRC Section 401(a)] retirement plans. Qualified plans include the following:

- Section 401(k) plans

- Profit-sharing plans

- Money purchase pension plans

- Savings match or thrift plans

- Stock bonus plans, including ESOP plans

- Cross-tested/age-weighted/target benefit plans

- HR 10 (Keogh) plans

- Traditional defined benefit pension plans

- Cash balance pension plans

Plan Adoption

The first step in installing a qualified retirement plan is plan adoption. While a SEP may be adopted any time through the due date for filing the employer's tax return for the year the employer wants to make the plan effective, a qualified plan must be adopted during the calendar year in which the employer wants the plan to be effective. An employer may elect to make the plan effective on the first day of the year of adoption.

Adoption is effected by a corporation through a resolution of its board of directors. Unincorporated businesses may simply adopt a written resolution in a similar form. It is critical that a valid plan trust be adopted before the end of the year of adoption.

Small employers (no more than 100 employees with compensation in excess of $5,000 for the previous year) may qualify for a business tax credit of up to $500, calculated on 50% of plan startup costs or expenses incurred in educating employees about the plan. However, at least one NHCE must be covered by the plan.

Determination Letter

Some employer/sponsors apply to the IRS for an advance determination letter that the proposed plan satisfies the plan qualification requirements in the Internal Revenue Code. The purpose of doing so is to gain advance assurance that the plan as proposed constitutes a qualified plan in its initial year and all subsequent years. Failure to obtain a determination letter places the employer at risk of a subsequent disqualification upon audit by the IRS. In the event of an IRS audit, not only might the employer's income tax deduction be disallowed, but the plan trust might lose its tax-exempt status, and employee/participants may be taxed on their vested benefits. As retirement plan law is in a constant state of flux, plans must be constantly amended to retain their qualification. Each time a significant amendment is made, the plan administrator/employer should request a new determination letter. However, if a plan is found by the IRS to be discriminatory *in operation*, rather than in its plan provisions, a determination letter will be of no value. Also, the Internal Revenue Code permits retroactive amendments to correct disqualifying plan provisions up to the filing date (including extensions) of the year audited.

Custom/Master or Prototype Plans

Due to the significant costs involved, very few employer/sponsors custom design their qualified plan. Most employer/sponsors use a master or prototype plan offered by various financial institutions, such as insurance companies, banks, mutual fund companies, and various service providers, to encourage the plan sponsor to purchase its investment products in funding the plan. These master or prototype plans use standardized language previously approved by the IRS while they still permit the sponsor to make certain plan choices, such as the plan vesting schedule and contribution or benefit formula. A master plan is one offered by a single financial institution for a number of employers. Adoption of the master plan locks the plan sponsor into using that particular financial institution. On the other hand, a prototype plan provides the sponsor flexibility in selecting a funding institution or medium.

When an employer/sponsor uses either a master or prototype plan, not only is plan installation made easier but so too is the determination letter process because the IRS needs to determine only whether the vesting schedule and contribution or benefit formula are nondiscriminatory.

COMMON CONTROL RULES

Throughout this text, we have made the simplifying assumption that a plan sponsor is a single business entity (incorporated or unincorporated business) and not part of a larger group of businesses owned or controlled in common by the same interests. Under the Tax Code, all employees of all corporations in a controlled group of corporations (defined later in this section) are treated as employed by a single employer for coverage, nondiscrimination, and other plan purposes. In effect, this rule keeps an employer from creating various related business entities and moving employees around to avoid the coverage, nondiscrimination, and other qualified plan rules. For example, in the absence of such rules, an employer could place all the employees it wishes to benefit from a plan in one company while placing other employees in subsidiary or other related companies that offer either lesser plan benefits or no benefits.

There are actually three sets of **common control rules** that are quite complex. The first of these rules requires, among other things, that the participation and coverage tests be applied to the entire controlled group of corporations, rather than to any single corporation in the group. The Tax Code adds partnerships and proprietorships to these rules. The second of the common control rules, under IRC Section 414(m), deals with an **affiliated service group** (defined later in this section) and requires that employees of such a group be treated as employed by a single employer. Primarily, this rule applies to medical doctors who form several clinics and then attempt to cover only select employees. The third common control rule requires that a **leased employee** (defined later in this section) be treated as an employee of the lessor corporation under circumstances specified in Section 414(n).

All employees of members of a controlled group of corporations or controlled group of trades or businesses (whether incorporated or not) that are under common control are treated as employed by a single employer for purposes of most provisions of the qualified plan law. Of main importance are the coverage requirements of IRC Section 410. This means all employees or employers in a controlled group must be taken into account when determining whether a qualified plan maintained by any employer in the controlled group satisfies the percentage participation tests or the discriminatory tests. There are three types of controlled groups:

- **parent-subsidiary controlled groups,**

- **brother-sister controlled groups,** and

- **combined groups.**

A *parent-subsidiary controlled group* is one or more chains of corporations connected through stock ownership with a common parent corporation if at least 80% of the total combined voting power of all classes of stock entitled to vote or at least 80% of the total value of shares of all classes of stock is owned by one or more corporations in the group and the common parent corporation satisfies the same 80% test with at least one other corporation in the group. With regard to unincorporated trades or businesses, the 80% test is applied to an interest in profits or to a capital interest. For example, if Atlantic Corporation owns 80% of the total combined voting power of all classes of stock entitled to vote of Pacific Corporation, and Pacific Corporation, in turn, owns stock that possesses at least 80% of the total value of shares of all classes of stock of Gulf Corporation, then Atlantic is the common parent with the parent-subsidiary controlled group made up of Atlantic, Pacific, and Gulf.

A *brother-sister controlled group* is made up of two or more corporations in which five or fewer individuals, estates, or trusts own stock possessing at least 80% of the total combined voting power or value of all classes of stock (other than nonvoting preferred stock) of each corporation and more than 50% of the total combined voting power or value of all classes of stock (other than nonvoting preferred stock) of each corporation, taking into account the stock ownership of each owner only to the extent that the owner's interest is identical in each corporation. For example, let us assume that Atlantic Corporation, Pacific Corporation, and Gulf Corporation have only one class of stock owned by five unrelated individuals as the following table shows.

Investor	Percentage of Ownership in			Identical Ownership in
	Atlantic Corp.	Pacific Corp.	Gulf Corp.	APG
A	20%	10%	20%	10%
B	20	30	10	10
C	20	20	30	20
D	20	20	20	20
E	20	20	20	20
Total	**100%**	**100%**	**100%**	**80%**

Corporations Atlantic, Pacific, and Gulf constitute a brother-sister controlled group because five or fewer individuals, estates, or trusts own stock possessing at least 80% (100% in this case) of the total combined voting power or value of all classes of stock of each corporation, and more than 50% (80% in this case) of the total combined voting power or value of all classes of stock of each corporation, taking into account the stock ownership of each owner only to the extent that the owner's interest is identical in each corporation.

A *combined group* is three or more corporations, each of which is a member of a parent-subsidiary group or a brother-sister group, and one of which is a common parent of a parent-subsidiary group and is also included in a brother-sister group. For example, assume Keith, an individual, owns 80% of the total combined voting power of all classes of stock of Atlantic Corporation and Pacific Corporation. Also assume Pacific Corporation owns 80% of the total combined voting power of all classes of the Gulf Corporation stock. Atlantic and Pacific are members of a brother-sister controlled group. Pacific and Gulf are members of a parent-subsidiary group. Pacific is the common parent of the parent-subsidiary group and also a member of the brother-sister group. Therefore, Atlantic, Pacific, and Gulf constitute a combined group.

For the purposes of calculating the foregoing percentages, some types of stock are excluded in the controlled group tests. For instance, both nonvoting preferred stock and treasury stock are not taken into account. In addition, there are several other types of stock that are excluded. The primary purpose of these stock exclusions is to keep employers from defeating the controlled group tests by transferring stock to various trusts or other entities.

The Attribution Rules

Even stock owned indirectly (by certain related parties) may be deemed to be owned by an individual in determining the existence of a controlled group. For example, in the case of both parent-subsidiary and brother-sister controlled groups, having an option to acquire stock is treated the same as owning the stock for these purposes. Similarly, stock owned by a partnership is considered owned by any partner having a 5% or more capital or profits interest in the partnership. A beneficiary of an estate or trust (other than a qualified trust) having a present value interest of 5% or more in stock owned directly or indirectly by the estate or trust is treated as being owned by the beneficiary to the extent of his actuarial interest. Stock owned directly or indirectly by or for any portion of a grantor trust is considered to be owned by the grantor. Additional attribution rules (not discussed here) apply only in the case of a brother-sister controlled group.

Affiliated Service Group

Prior to the enactment of IRC Section 414(m), professional corporations or partnerships that did not want to include rank-and-file employees in qualified plans established for the professional owners used creative methods to exclude such employees. For example, if two doctors entered into an equal partnership (or formed two one-person professional corporations, which, in turn, entered into a partnership) and then formed a separate business to provide all support services for the medical practice and have the support business employ all of the support employees, each doctor would own only 50% of the support business. Under the other aggregation rules (other than the affiliated service group rules), each doctor could adopt a qualified plan covering only herself and none of the support employees. However, the affiliated service group rules now prevent this. Basically, the rule provides that the employees of an affiliated service group must be included in any qualified plans that benefit the owners. The affiliated service group is deemed to include both the professional organization and the service organization. The rule treats all employees of an affiliated service group as employees of a single employer.

The applicable proposed regulations apply primarily to service organizations of the type that provide professional services in the field of health, law, engineering, architecture, accounting, actuarial science, performing arts, consulting, or insurance. As an example of the operation of the affiliated service group rules, assume doctors A and B each incorporate and the two corporations form a partnership. Each corporation and the partnership of these two corporations constitutes an affiliated service group because the corporations are service organizations in partnership with each other, and each one is regularly associated with the partnership in performing services for third parties.

Because of the complexity and subjectivity of the affiliated service group rules, it is strongly recommended that an IRS ruling be obtained as to whether a particular organization is a member of an affiliated service group.

Employee Leasing

The rules on employee leasing were designed to reduce the discrimination resulting from employers leasing employees from an independent employee leasing organization, rather than retaining such employees directly on their own payroll. By so doing, employers hoped to be able to exclude such persons from their qualified plans.

A leased employee is considered the employee of the lessee organization for which the services are performed if the employee has performed services on a substantially full-time basis for at least one year, and the services are "performed under the primary direction or control by the recipient."

An exception is if the leasing organization itself maintains a safe harbor plan for the leased employees meeting certain minimum requirements. Because of the one-year requirement discussed in the previous paragraph, the leasing provision does not affect most short-term temporary help.

RETIREMENT PLAN TERMINATION

The purpose of the final section of this text (prior to a sample case illustration) is to explain the plan termination protection afforded by the Pension Benefit Guaranty Corporation (PBGC), the different types of plan terminations, and the possibility of assets reverting to the employer in the event of plan termination.

Unfortunately, there are times when an existing retirement plan must be terminated. This may happen frequently in the merger of two companies or the acquisition of one company by another. However, even though the plan's termination may be viewed as a detriment to a participant's retirement planning goals, the participant is protected when vesting provisions are a part of the plan. In that instance, the participant (no matter in what percentage vested) becomes 100% or fully vested in his (otherwise forfeitable) accrued benefit. In addition, further guarantees are provided for those employees participating in a traditional defined benefit or cash balance pension plan. (For example, monthly benefit amounts in defined benefit types of plans are insured up to the amount of $5,011 in 2015.)

As discussed previously, defined benefit plans promise specific benefits to participants and are required to pay regular premiums to the PBGC to insure these guaranteed benefits. Such benefits include nonforfeitable benefits and any death, survivor, or disability benefits due or in payment status. Plan-specified benefits that are *not* guaranteed by the PBGC include any death and disability benefits not in payment status and any retirement benefits that exceed the PBGC guaranteed monthly amount. For a plan benefit to be guaranteed by the PBGC, it must meet the three following prerequisites:

■ The benefit must be nonforfeitable (vested) and payable other than by reason of acceleration because of plan termination.

■ The benefit must be payable as an annuity or as one or more payments as an annuity.

■ The participant or his beneficiary must be entitled to the benefit according to any one of several legally specified reasons (e.g., the benefit was in pay status on the date of plan termination).

The payment provided for in the PBGC-provided benefit is limited to a specified monthly amount that is periodically indexed for inflation and is a figure payable in level amounts over the participant's lifetime as a single-life annuity commencing at age 65. A lump-sum payment is not available as a PBGC benefit, regardless of plan provisions indicating otherwise. A defined benefit qualified plan, either in the traditional pension form or in the more recent cash balance pension variation, pays for the guarantee of this benefit through the assessment of additional set premiums payable to the PBGC over the active lifetime of the plan.

A qualified plan subject to PBGC coverage may only be terminated voluntarily by the sponsor in the event the plan meets the requirements for either a standard or distress termination. For a standard termination to occur, an employer must generally have sufficient assets to pay *all* plan benefits. However, a plan without sufficient assets to pay these benefits may still qualify for a standard termination if the employer agrees to make up the deficiency in a single payment. If a plan does not have sufficient assets to pay benefits, it may qualify for a voluntary distress termination in any one of the following three circumstances:

■ The employer is being liquidated or reorganized in bankruptcy proceedings.

■ The employer is unable to pay debts as they become due and will not otherwise be able to remain in business.

■ The employer can show that the cost of providing coverage is unreasonably burdensome as a result of a decline in the workforce.

The PBGC may also undertake *involuntary* termination proceedings in a U.S. district court in a jurisdiction where the employer/sponsor of a subject plan does business if the PBGC finds that either the plan does not comply with the required minimum funding standards applicable to a pension plan or that the plan is unable to pay benefits when they will become due.

Finally, what happens if any qualified plan is terminated and there is a reversion of at least some of the residual assets to the employer rather than the plan participants? Residual assets are equal to the plan funds remaining after the satisfaction of all plan liabilities. While Department of Labor regulations provide that an employer/sponsor may *not* recover any surplus plan assets until it has fully vested all participants' benefits and has made any requisite payments, a reversion of assets is quite common in the event of an overfunded pension plan. If a reversion occurs, there is now generally a 50% excise tax penalty on the amount recovered under the reversion. This penalty is reduced to 20% if the employer shares the reversion amount in some stipulated manner with the active participants of the terminated plan.

Notes